I0138919

LATE TO THE FIGHT

CONFLICTING WORLDS

NEW DIMENSIONS OF THE
AMERICAN CIVIL WAR

T. MICHAEL PARRISH,
SERIES EDITOR

LATE
TO THE
FIGHT

UNION SOLDIER COMBAT PERFORMANCE
FROM THE WILDERNESS TO THE
FALL OF PETERSBURG

ALEXANDRE F. CAILLOT

Louisiana State University Press
BATON ROUGE

Published by Louisiana State University Press
lsupress.org

Copyright © 2025 by Louisiana State University Press
All rights reserved. Except in the case of brief quotations used in articles or reviews,
no part of this publication may be produced or transmitted in any format or by
any means without written permission of Louisiana State University Press.

DESIGNER: Kaelin Chappell Broaddus
TYPEFACES: Baskerville 10 Pro, text; Antique Tuscan Condensed,
Bureau Grot Condensed, MPI Gothic, display

COVER ILLUSTRATION: *The Battle of Petersburg, Va., April 2nd 1865,*
by Currier & Ives. Library of Congress.

Portions of chapter 5 first appeared, in somewhat different form, in "'Armies
Are Not Mere Machines': The 17th Vermont and 31st Maine in the Second
Battle of Petersburg," *Army History* 128 (Summer 2023): 6–19, and are
reprinted by permission of the U.S. Army Center of Military History.

Cataloging-in-Publication Data are available from the Library of Congress.

ISBN 978-0-8071-8383-0 (cloth: alk. paper) — ISBN 978-0-8071-
8462-2 (pdf) — ISBN 978-0-8071-8461-5 (epub)

To my parents,

whose support for my study of history made all this possible,

and to my dogs Lukka and Max, who have shared in the challenges and joys

of the historian's quest to better understand the past.

Contents

Illustrations

PHOTOGRAPHS

FOLLOWING PAGE 128

Brig. Gen. Robert B. Potter

Brig. Gen. Simon G. Griffin

17th Vermont state flag

Lt. Col. Charles Cummings

Lyman E. Knapp

Maj. William B. Reynolds

First Lt. Joel H. Lucia

Cpl. Moses Whitehill

31st Maine national flag

Col. Daniel White

First Lt. John P. Sheahan

Sgt. Maj. Leader Otis Merriam

Pvt. Horatio Fox Smith

Company D, 31st Maine

MAPS

Acknowledgments

In some respects, completing a book is not unlike leading an army into combat. Historians and generals alike must act with limited information. Complete understanding of the past always lurks beyond the historian's grasp, just as the fog of war hinders the general's knowledge of the battlefield. Both individuals thus draw upon the help of others to improve their odds of success. My ability to finish this task has depended greatly upon the assistance that mentors, institutions, and friends provided. I am grateful for all of it.

I owe the deepest thanks to Gregory J. W. Urwin. Since I entered the graduate program at Temple University in 2015, he worked tirelessly to provide me with the instruction and guidance to become a professionally trained historian. As Dr. Urwin often reminded me, a work of military history meets the mark when it appeals to nonspecialists, and this is a goal I hope to have achieved with this project. I am also appreciative of Drs. Jay Lockenour, David Orr, and Lorien Foote, who all readily gave of their time to review my work and ensure that it meets a high standard.

The Department of History at Temple University is a welcoming and encouraging environment. I am grateful for the opportunity to have presented my findings at meetings of the Temple Early Atlantic Seminar that Drs. Travis Glasson and Jessica Roney cochaired. I was fortunate to learn from the late Dr. Kenneth Kusmer, who was always supportive of this project. My detailed conversations with him about social history shifted my focus toward the experience of the humble private. Thanks also to administrative coordinator Vangeline Campbell, whose kind assistance on bureaucratic matters made life as a graduate student much easier. I would also like to acknowledge Dr. Andrea Siotto as well as Dr. Paul Cook, who once gave me a timely reminder that effective writing depends on clarity and concision.

Beyond Temple's walls, I have been fortunate to meet others interested in my work and eager to help. They include Drs. Barbara A. Gannon, Earl J. Hess, Brian Matthew Jordan, Thomas Nester, and Peter Porsche. I am also indebted to Dick Dobbins, Mike Evenson, Robert Grandchamp, John J. Hennessy, Bryce Suderow, and Anthony Trusso. I am thankful to have received funding from multiple sources, namely the Society for Military History, the Society of Civil War Historians, Temple University, and the U.S. Army Heritage and Education Center (USAHEC).

A book relies heavily on the availability of archival sources, and I greatly appreciate the aid that the staff at multiple institutions offered. Thanks to the Bowdoin College Library, Historical Society of Cheshire County, Library of Congress, Maine Historical Society, Maine State Archives, Maine State Museum, National Archives and Records Administration, New-York Historical Society, USAHEC, Silver Special Collections Library at the University of Vermont, Vermont Historical Society, Vermont State Archives and Records Administration, and Vermont State Curator's Office. Last but certainly not least, I would like to express my gratitude to the staff at the National Bureau of Economic Research who manage the Early Indicators project.

This study benefits greatly from the inclusion of maps that bring the text to life. I owe much to cartographer Hal Jespersen, whose skillful creations so effectively illuminate the locations and battlefields that are central to this story. I was fortunate to benefit from his long experience designing Civil War maps and his sage advice about the most effective way to communicate ideas to the reader.

Ultimately, this book owes its existence to Louisiana State University Press. Thanks to Rand Dotson, editor in chief, whose interest and help deciphering the mysteries of publishing made this project a reality. I am also grateful to the anonymous reviewer whose insightful suggestions enabled me to further improve the manuscript. I want to recognize managing editor and assistant director Catherine L. Kadair, the rest of the LSU Press staff, and freelance editor Kevin Brock for scrutinizing my manuscript to ensure clarity and overseeing its transformation into a book. Without such support, the scholar's pursuit would be immeasurably more difficult.

LATE ᵀᴼ FIGHT
THE

INTRODUCTION

> The Thirty First Me. Regiment . . . was one of the
> many regiments which were the result of the great and
> supreme effort of the government to raise a force which
> should deliver the final blow to the great rebellion.
> —Sgt. Maj. Leander Otis Merriam, 31st Maine

> How nobly the old Seventeenth did its duty
> and met its terrible disasters in the Wilderness
> campaign and before Petersburgh!
> —Bvt. Lt. Col. Lyman E. Knapp, 17th Vermont

Decades after the Civil War, Americans questioned the value of the contributions made by those men who joined the Union army in time to fight during the second half of the conflict. Such "later arrivals" to military service began donning the uniform after Congress passed the Enrollment Act (the U.S. draft law) in March 1863. This legislation instituted an approach to recruiting that involved the use of high bounties, conscription, and substitution, whereby a draftee paid another man to take his place in the ranks. The characteristics of this system subjected the later arrivals to the charge that they lacked the patriotism of their blue-clad predecessors. And yet one postwar editor challenged this judgmental attitude in the *National Tribune,* the influential Union veterans' publication. Adopting a satiric tone, he demanded, "What . . . joyous picnic was it that these 'eleventh-hour soldiers' had. . . . Did they do nothing but draw their big bounties, feast sumptuously in pleasant camps for a few weeks, and then [go] marching home again?" He then made several observations, beginning

1

with the fact that family commitments had deterred thousands of loyal men from enlisting before 1864. Nevertheless, the later arrivals went on to fight in the Overland Campaign of May–June 1864, which initiated the bloodiest year of the war in the eastern theater. In this journalist's estimation, the promise of bounties as high as $1,000 proved to be a meager reimbursement when the newly raised regiments those soldiers filled suffered up to 70-percent casualties, including those lost due to illness.[1]

Between 1893 and 1903, contributors to the *National Tribune* continued to debate the worthiness of these later arrivals. Back in 1862, Congress had passed a pension law applicable to Federal soldiers and sailors suffering service-related disability, plus those dependent upon such men who were killed or wounded. During the ensuing decades, however, the scope and scale of benefits increased so that almost all Union veterans became eligible. Newspaper coverage attested to the controversial nature of these provisions. One editor allayed concerns by denying that the pension roll was filled with those who had only served for ninety days or joined at the eleventh hour. Most pensioners had actually spent one to three years in uniform, based on a Pension Bureau sample encompassing roughly two-thirds of veterans with benefits in 1893. Conversely, veterans who authored two letters to the editor alleged that the new men had waited at home and were drawn into the ranks for only a brief time, not by patriotism but by the coercion of conscription or a greedy desire for bounties. These naysayers declared that later arrivals should not receive the same pensions as long-serving troops, whose wartime pay had depreciated and whose more advanced age left them in greater need of financial support. In another article, however, an editor rejected such negative claims. He defended the awarding of large bounties late in the conflict as a means for the Union army to compete for recruits who could otherwise secure good pay in civilian jobs. As he pointed out, the U.S. dollar was worth a mere fifty-seven cents in the spring of 1864, so these bonuses were not disproportionately large. Given public awareness by that time about the dangers of military service, volunteers had "required unusual courage and patriotism." This journalist also observed that the "tens of thousands" of youngsters who filled the ranks later in the war had not been old enough to serve in 1861. He cited the example of two Massachusetts regiments that had sustained heavier losses in their single year of service than most three-year regiments. According to him, the fact that some units comprising later arrivals had not suffered such a grievous toll simply reflected the unpredictable nature of war.[2]

These newspaper skirmishes highlighted a postwar struggle over the perception of Billy Yank: to what extent did the severity and duration of a soldier's service determine his worth? Such commentaries attested to the vigorous debate surrounding pensions for aging Union veterans. As political scientist Theda Skocpol explains, this was a "system of national public care . . . for the deserving core of a special generation." The idea that certain combatants were more worthy of benefits than others underlay the contested reputation of the later arrivals. At a time when the vast majority of military personnel served in frontline combat, period critics writing in the *National Tribune* delegitimized the service of the new men. They underscored the belief that a soldier's value rose in accordance with his willingness to risk enemy fire coupled with his length of time in the ranks.[3]

Were the pundits right to dismiss the later arrivals? To determine how well they fought, this book examines the combat performance of the troops who served in the Army of the Potomac during the Overland Campaign and the Petersburg Campaign (June 1864–April 1865). It focuses on a portion of the Ninth Corps, which is ideal for a case study, given its heavy proportion of rookies. Commanded initially by Maj. Gen. Ambrose E. Burnside, this corps commenced the Overland Campaign with about two-thirds of its strength comprising green men. Emphasizing their lack of experience, many of these troops served in new units. Besides the untested Fourth Division, consisting of U.S. Colored Troops (USCT), fourteen of the thirty-five white regiments in the corps only mustered in to service between mid-1863 and spring 1864. Thus, a large share of the outfits had spent little if any time in the field. Moreover, Burnside's soldiers did not undergo the complications suffered by the other infantry corps alongside whom they fought. Maj. Gen. George G. Meade, commander of the Army of the Potomac, broke up and amalgamated the First and Third Corps into the Second, Fifth, and Sixth Corps in March 1864. This process generated consternation among First and Third Corps veterans, who resented losing their unit identities. The editor of the *Vermont Watchman and State Journal* called attention to this problem in April 1864, reporting that while the officers were coming to accept this organizational change, their troops "still manifest[ed] much jealousy." Consolidation led to additional soldier frictions and might have exacerbated veteran grumblings about newcomers. Thus, studying the Ninth Corps draws attention to a fighting force composed largely of novices and avoids the complexities associated with corps reorganization.[4]

This book centers on two regiments, the 17th Vermont and the 31st Maine Volunteer Infantry. Several criteria informed their selection. Infantry is most suitable for this analysis since it constituted the largest and most important combat branch in Civil War armies. The narrative addresses the role of conventional infantry rather than the more specialized units of sharpshooters and heavy artillerymen who also served in the Army of the Potomac at this time. Later arrivals filled the ranks in two ways, by either bolstering depleted outfits or by forming new ones. To be sure, describing the makeup of a regiment in monolithic terms is too simplistic. Historian Carol Reardon explains that the 2nd Vermont Volunteer Infantry Regiment, for example, contained "the initial volunteers of 1861; new recruits in the spring of 1862; additional men from [President Abraham] Lincoln's call for 300,000 more volunteers in the late summer of 1862; drafted men and substitutes of late 1863; and newly arrived recruits for the 1864 campaign." Still, examining untested units comprising primarily greenhorns provides a better means of assessing their fighting ability, as rookies in this case would be less influenced by guidance from or tension with veterans. These units should not be conflated with the "veteran volunteer" regiments, which consisted of troops having previous military experience who reenlisted in large numbers to prevent their unit's dissolution. The outfits under consideration were also distinct from the four regiments that Massachusetts raised during this time consisting solely of seasoned enlistees. Notably, a close look at the 17th and 31st provides insight into the fighting ability of volunteers and substitutes but does not address the role of conscripts. Such men did not serve in these two regiments, which is unsurprising since conscripts equaled only some 6 percent of Federal troops throughout the conflict. It is this parallel record in uniform, not the extent to which the two outfits were demographically representative of later arrivals as a whole, that is most important to this study. Its purpose is to explore how these maligned Federals conducted themselves in battle, a question that calls for a look at units that endured some of the worst combat and shared similar records of service that facilitate comparison. Ultimately, the 17th and 31st are ideal choices for a comparative study of combat performance because of their similar experiences. In April 1864 both regiments reached the front in Virginia to enter the Second Brigade, Second Division, Ninth Corps. They went on to fight in the same eight engagements, beginning with the Battle of the Wilderness (May 5–6, 1864) and ending with the Ninth Union Offensive at Petersburg (April 2, 1865).[5]

This dual unit history analyzes the reasons for victory and defeat at the regimental level. It deals specifically with regiments because they were the building blocks of Civil War armies and the underpinnings of tactical success. The study draws from both the soldier's experience literature so dear to social historians, and the operational narratives of traditional military history. This approach addresses the pitfall that historian John Lynn has identified, namely that "concentrating on the experience of war can lead us away from understanding the nature of the fighting and the conduct of the war." Subjecting small units to this kind of detailed scrutiny produces a narrative that deals with the soldiers' lived experience while highlighting their achievements and missteps in combat. It also limits the research to a practical scope and allows for an examination of combat performance on a case-by-case basis, as soldiers varied widely in their fighting ability. After all, approximately 820,000 later arrivals filled the Union ranks following passage of the Enrollment Act. This figure does not include the roughly 180,000 Black men who also served, nearly all between 1863 and 1865. In a broad commentary on American history, scholar Adrian R. Lewis observes that all men are not equally proficient in combat, despite those convictions to the contrary that emerged during "the formative period of the nation." And yet the Union and Confederate governments perpetuated the assumption that one individual could fight much like another by depending principally on volunteers instead of military professionals. This reflected a citizen-soldier tradition dating back to the raising of militiamen by the thirteen colonies. By attracting all manner of recruits, both the Union and the Confederacy formed armies that defied generalization, hence historian Peter S. Carmichael's argument that "there was no common soldier in the Civil War." Kanisorn Wongsrichanalai likewise finds that efforts to define the average combatant often "reach broad conclusions that do not represent the diversity of [the] individuals who fought." It may seem counterintuitive to use the long-established genre of unit history to produce fresh findings on the later arrivals, but Daniel E. Sutherland suggests that the methodology may enjoy a "revival" after previously enduring the stereotype of being "old-fashioned and restrictive." Indeed, several recent publications offer evidence that this resurgence is underway. This book seeks to justify greater interest in unit history by providing a new perspective on these troops who have been largely understudied by observers and scholars alike. It does not discuss the condition of the graybacks or their actions under fire since the New Englanders faced a wide array of Rebels and such details would unnecessarily hinder the narrative.[6]

The Vermonters and Mainers deserve a reappraisal, for their military service offers insights into the nature of the Army of the Potomac, which crushed the Confederacy in the last two years of the conflict. Lt. Gen. Ulysses S. Grant, general in chief of the Federal armies, achieved victory by using this army to apply unrelenting pressure on the enemy. His soldiers sustained some 55,000 casualties during the Overland Campaign, when seasoned men felt increasingly impotent, given an unprecedented combination of sleep deprivation, poor logistics, continual marching, and relentless combat. Previously, the army had been accustomed to fighting single battles followed by weeks or months of recuperation. This campaign differed, however, as it involved four costly and unsuccessful clashes spaced over roughly six weeks. Grant accelerated the operational tempo to an unheard-of degree against the Confederate Army of Northern Virginia, commanded by Gen. Robert E. Lee. The Union commander advanced on his opponent after each jarring encounter instead of retreating to rest his troops, replace his losses, and consolidate any territorial gains. This grueling pace, combined with the Rebels' formidable fieldworks, pushed the Federals to their physical and psychological limits while winnowing their ranks. They went on to suffer another 42,000 casualties during the Petersburg Campaign, which involved numerous smaller battles over a ten-and-a-half-month period. This extended and largely stalemated warfare directed against an entrenched foe differed markedly from the comparatively fluid and mobile battles typical of the fighting between 1861 and 1863. In response to these trying circumstances, Union soldiers grew more and more resistant to the prospect of throwing themselves against Confederates in fortifications. This was especially true of those men with expiring enlistments who had tired of the endless slaughter.[7]

Reconsidering the combat performance of the new troops helps answer a fundamental question about the path to Union victory: how did the Army of the Potomac, with presumably lackluster rookies and a dwindling number of worn-out veterans, defeat the Army of Northern Virginia? Scholars have long stressed Grant's dogged command style and the Rebel force's deteriorating condition. This leaves some uncertainty about how a Union army, in which only half of its seasoned men reenlisted, overcame an opposing army composed predominantly of veterans who had consistently checked their opponents since the spring of 1862. During the Overland Campaign, Lee marshaled a skillful defense that doomed Grant's attempt to overcome him through maneuver, but ultimately to no avail. Historian Joseph T. Glatthaar explains that "the Army of Northern Virginia did not collapse because of Southern culture, industry, agriculture, slavery, motivations, manpower shortages, discontent at home, or any other solitary factor. . . . Union pressure caused serious fissures in all these areas, collectively bringing down the army and the Confederacy." Indeed, an influx of fresh Federal troops proved critical to sustaining that pressure. These soldiers became the means for a Union commander who recognized the probability of attritional tactics and acknowledged enemy losses at the Battle of Spotsylvania Court House (May 8–21, 1864) by merely noting they were higher than his own. Grant believed the prompt supply of new manpower would "contribute greatly to . . . insuring [sic] a complete victory." His ruthless approach, however, denied the later arrivals the opportunities for acclimation enjoyed by earlier recruits. These new men could only benefit to some extent from the advice of veterans because they faced unparalleled conditions that even the most seasoned old campaigners had never endured before. As scholar Earl J. Hess observes, "Grant . . . left behind scant evidence that he understood how exhausted and dispirited his soldiers had become by mid-June." Meade disagreed with Grant's willingness to order frontal assaults but still echoed this cold, pragmatic calculus. He regarded the large Union population as key to success, writing, "if we can only manage to make the enemy lose more [men] than we do, we will win in the long run." Besides intense combat, seizing the southern capital of Richmond was "a pure question of numbers" dependent on "swelling our armies." In Meade's opinion the destruction of the enemy forces was essential for Union triumph, which in turn relied upon the sacrifice of numerous Federals. The example of the 1st Maine Heavy Artillery Regiment is illustrative. Originally, heavy artillerymen trained both to serve as infantry and to handle large cannon in fortified positions around Washington, DC. Grant repurposed them as infantry to bolster an army depleted by casualties and expiring enlistments. Some of these heavy artillerymen began their service prior to the Enrollment Act, while others joined afterward, but their lack of combat experience made them alike in the eyes of jaded veterans. During the First Union Offensive at Petersburg (June 15–18, 1864), Brig. Gen. Gershom Mott, commanding the Third Division of the Second Corps, ordered the untested 1st Maine to attack the Rebels and thus inspire his reluctant veterans to follow suit. Mott "hope[d] . . . that . . . the First Maine, innocent of the danger it would incur, would lead off with a dash and carry the works with a rush." In fact, a majority of the regiment's men understood they faced a potentially deadly mission. This awareness makes the Mainers' sacrifice all the more striking, for they collapsed after tallying the highest casualty rate of a regiment in a single clash throughout the war.[8]

The 17th Vermont and 31st Maine left behind a legacy of service and sacrifice essential to achieving the destruction of the Confederacy. Scrutinizing the formation of these outfits reveals that most of the recruits made a rational decision to sign up and possessed the potential to develop into hard-fighting veterans. Such troops were geographically diverse and poorly trained, however, which left them without much cohesion at the outset and susceptible to bouts of poor discipline. These New Englanders faced additional challenges on the battlefield. Disease whittled their numbers, unpleasant weather sapped their endurance, and officers at the higher levels of command largely shaped their fate by deciding upon their movements and tactical goals. Over multiple engagements, the Vermonters and Mainers became hesitant to make costly assaults on Rebel earthworks. Regardless, they maintained moderate to high levels of cohesion, showed determination to accomplish battlefield objectives, and sustained heavy casualties in the process. These forgotten boys in blue made their mark by helping maintain a high Federal operational tempo throughout the fast-paced engagements of the Overland Campaign and the siege warfare that characterized the Petersburg Campaign.

Determining the contribution of the later arrivals speaks to the resiliency of the constitutional republic during its greatest crisis. This was not the first time that the American people found their resolve tested in a lengthy conflict. When the War of Independence began, a widespread rebellious zeal, or *rage militaire,* gripped Patriot supporters, but it only lasted through 1776. The northern population experienced this same ardor in response to the Confederate attack on Fort Sumter (April 12–14, 1861).

Men felt compelled to serve, harking back to the revolutionary generation as they strove to preserve the Union. They framed the cause as a defense of liberal democracy with global stakes. And yet this sense of enthusiasm also faded quickly, which put the onus on the later arrivals to sustain the drive toward victory. The ability of Federal leaders to achieve their war aims depended on this fresh manpower initially performing well in combat and continuing to do so over time.[9]

PRIMARY SOURCES

Surveying eyewitness recollections justifies a reevaluation of the later arrivals. If these troops were detrimental to the fighting ability of the Army of the Potomac, one would expect a substantial effort to catalogue their failings. Instead, the authors of a range of published primary sources—diaries, letters, operational histories, and postwar memoirs—offer merely anecdotal evidence concerning the combat record of these soldiers. To provide a more complete survey, this section and the following on secondary sources include references to conscripts and heavy artillerymen, two categories of soldiers not germane to the 17th Vermont and 31st Maine. Ultimately, it is noteworthy that observers devoted little ink to the later arrivals, and in fact, they typically failed to differentiate between the rookies and seasoned men. These commenters offered both positive and negative reviews of the new combatants, an inconsistent perspective indicative of their limited interest in probing the subject. As officers wrote most of the cited material, this inattention is not surprising. Historian Carol Reardon contends that "in most writings on the art of war available to the Civil War generation, soldiers in the ranks existed mostly as nameless ciphers." She faults these period writers for ignoring "the all-important link between a military unit's mission-effectiveness levels and the physical and mental condition of . . . the soldier." Officers focused on securing victory and assumed that a unit's quality depended chiefly on its leadership instead of recognizing the challenges that the rank and file faced. Additionally, Peter Carmichael and Lorien Foote find that veteran officers frequently dismissed the working-class and immigrant men among the later arrivals as lacking the manhood, bravery, restraint, and morality necessary to serve ably in uniform.[10]

Contemporaries of the later arrivals made several claims about their worth as soldiers. First, they argued that the new troops should be assigned to seasoned outfits. Capt. Samuel Fisk of the 14th Connecticut Volunteer Infantry Regiment championed this blending of rookie "ardor" with the "steadiness and experience" of veterans. Col. Charles S. Wainwright, the Fifth Corps chief of artillery, noted that although the Army of the Potomac consisted of one-third new troops on May 1, 1864, it only mustered a small number of unseasoned outfits and so "was never in better condition." Grant addressed the role of draftees, maintaining that a single conscript in an old unit equaled three in a green one. He further stated that the reinforcement of existing regiments avoided the cost of creating more organizations, of which he remarked, "from ignorance of how to cook and provide for themselves, the ranks become depleted one-third before valuable services can be expected." Writing after the war, Bvt. Brig. Gen. Francis A. Walker, who had served as assistant adjutant general of the Second Corps, derided as "suicidal" the typical Union approach of "creating large, raw, and often useless regiments." Such claims should not be accepted wholesale, for these authors did not provide evidence to demonstrate that reinforced older outfits fought better than untested units. They likewise overlooked the potential for animosity between veterans and rookies serving in the same regiments, with only Fisk admitting that "ill feeling" and "collisions" could arise.[11]

Some observers opted not to criticize, or actually lauded, the behavior of the new troops under fire. Later arrivals garnered respectful comments about their efforts at the Battle of Bristoe Station (October 14, 1863) and six engagements spanning the Overland and Petersburg Campaigns. Heavy artillerymen received much of this praise. Several authors claimed that the novices made bold attacks, while their veteran comrades opted to stay in cover. Walker thus alluded to the potential "enthusiasm of a new, fresh, strong regiment, not yet discouraged by repeated failures." Such a courageous assault, in turn, had the potential to boost the confidence of the Federals as a whole. The example of the USCT units serving in the Fourth Division of the Ninth Corps illustrates this point, even though the circumstances of these men's recruitment differed from that of later arrivals and they faced unequal treatment due to their race. These unblooded soldiers may have received some training to attack at the Battle of the Crater (July 30, 1864), part of the Third Union Offensive at Petersburg (July 26–30, 1864). As Col. Henry Goddard Thomas of the 19th USCT contended, "There are times when the ardor, hopefulness, and enthusiasm of new troops, not yet rendered doubtful by reverses or chilled by defeat, more than compensate, in a dash, for training and experience." Burnside selected the Black troops to lead the assault; according to Grant, they would have been successful had Meade not ordered the Ninth Corps commander to begin the attack with his seasoned white troops. These claims about the efficacy of untested soldiers in battle should be regarded with skepticism, as the authors only provided anecdotal evidence instead of assessing how well particular units fought over a series of engagements.[12]

Later arrivals could be worthy additions to the army in the opinion of their officers. Wainwright maintained that a group of American and Canadian greenhorns were "a fine lot generally" and unparalleled in quality "since the first furor of patriotism." He believed such "intelligent," rapid learners were likely too proud to be recalcitrant or desert and described others as being "of a superior class . . . [who] mean to do their best." Col. Robert McAllister, commanding the Second Brigade, Third Division, Second Corps, enthused over some "first rate" recruits and "good men" under his leadership. Similarly, Capt. Elisha Hunt Rhodes of the 2nd Rhode Island Volunteer Infantry Regiment categorized certain recruits as "a fine addition" to his unit. General Walker even contended that particular regiments, especially those of heavy artillerymen, "could not have been surpassed" and that "finer bodies of men, in line of battle . . . would be difficult to find." He explained that novices could serve well when they learned from seasoned men and absorbed the esprit de corps during periods of training and recuperation. This underscored the need for "enough remaining of the old body and the old spirit to take up, assimilate, and vitalize the new material." Other officers longed to train these green soldiers, recognized their responsiveness to instruction, or insisted that the presence of the later arrivals improved the army's morale.[13]

Still, eyewitnesses more typically viewed the new troops with disdain. They frequently depicted them as bounty-obsessed deserters who even switched sides, some to return home or to engage in the purportedly rampant crime of bounty jumping. This referred to the practice of accepting a cash bonus for signing up only to abandon one's unit and repeatedly enlist in others to the same end. Meade castigated "that class who . . . have embraced enlistment with a view to desertion for the purpose of gain." Critics variously claimed that thousands of such men fled before reaching the army, more than 50 percent did so, fewer than one in eight stayed in the ranks, or a scant 20 percent remained in uniform. These divergent statistics suggest that the authors lacked sufficient data to make authoritative claims about the prevalence of desertion. They discussed specific cases, including that of sixty men who abandoned one regiment and another involving the flight of three hundred bounty jumpers from a different outfit, which forced it to withdraw from the lines around Petersburg. Although such examples could be individually persuasive, the observers did not make clear how broadly they applied to the later arrivals. Among these commenters, only Wainwright alluded to another potential cause of desertion. He recounted the case of a corrupt provost marshal who accepted enlistees he had previously turned away as conscripts for being aged and physically unsuitable. This officer then delayed sending the men to the reporting stations, known as depots, so that he could pocket the difference between the monies he received to care for them and the substandard food and housing he provided. Wainwright believed an upstanding fellow would flee instead of enduring such life-threatening conditions among individuals the colonel characterized as "the lowest dregs of society." In any case, the tendency of detractors to rail against deserters outweighed their attention to the fighting ability of the soldiers who continued to serve.[14]

Those critical of the later arrivals described them as greedy, criminal, or unfit for the rigors of campaigning, regardless of whether they deserted. Wainwright castigated the new men as "thousand-dollar patriots," McAllister referred to them as "worthless" troops, and even Lt. Col. Theodore Lyman, Meade's aide-de-camp, wrote that these individuals were "miserable fellows bought with money." In a more extensive commentary, Captain Fisk derided the later arrivals as consisting of "the lowest and vilest classes" as well as "mercenary wretches who care neither for country [n]or reputations." In his assessment, "A man . . . looks on the government as an employer, out of whom he is to squeeze all that he can, and in whose pay he is to do merely a hireling's service." Fisk added that the $300 commutation fee—drafted men paid this to avoid conscription—caused no harm because it did not "run away." Underlying these statements, however, was the jealousy harbored by seasoned combatants who believed the rookies profited at their expense. Besides monthly pay, the enlistees of 1861 could only look forward to a $100 discharge bonus plus the possibility of extra state pay or community financial support for their families. In contrast, the later arrivals enjoyed enlistment bounties that rose to $1,200 to attract substitutes by the summer of 1864. Fisk incorrectly asserted that the novices received such outsized amounts upon their enlistment, thereby inspiring the resentment of veterans. In actuality, these raw soldiers obtained federal bounties in installments during their time in service, although they could generally get local enlistment bonuses as a lump sum up front. Also, the captain wrongly accused these men of receiving higher monthly pay than their grizzled comrades, which he complained was "a present, gratuitous, and constantly repeated insult" to the old-timers.[15]

Contemporaries alleged that the new troops fought poorly, straggled, and pillaged. As Wainwright concluded, "one old three-year soldier is really worth three of them." Such naysayers specified instances of bad conduct in ten battles during the Overland and Petersburg Campaigns. Castigators of the later arrivals often directed their ire at heavy artillerymen or the largely rookie Ninth Corps. Lyman lamented the reliance on raw troops during such heavy fighting by declaring that the Ninth Corps novices would have benefited from "a little more backbone . . . but they started green and that is no way to ripen men." Maj. Gen. Andrew A. Humphreys, Meade's chief of staff, alleged that rookies altered the "character" of famous regiments by filling most of their ranks. Novices could not close the experience gap caused by the loss of veterans, whom Lyman termed the "backbone" of the army during the Petersburg Campaign. Journalist William Swinton was more dismissive, attributing the defeat of the Ninth Corps at the Crater to its paucity of seasoned combatants. In his portrayal the veterans amounted to "a mere nucleus, with which had been agglomerated (not fused) a mass of new, heterogeneous, and inferior material." The green USCT units also suffered critique. According to 1st Lt. William H. Powell, aide-de-camp to Brig. Gen. James H. Ledlie, commander of the First Division of the Ninth Corps, Meade decided these Black soldiers were unsuitable to lead the assault following the mine explosion because "the very best troops" were required to exploit any breach in the Confederate lines. Despite these claims, observers did not closely examine the combat performance of the new troops or the variables that shaped their record under fire.[16]

Eyewitnesses even betrayed ethnic prejudice by complaining that the later arrivals included a disproportionately large number of immigrants. Meade bemoaned the presence of "worthless foreigners," while several others grumbled about these soldiers' unfamiliarity with English, which hindered communication and thereby exacerbated chaos in battle. Colonel McAllister favored native-born conscripts over rookies hailing from "all nations but the Hottentots," whom he mocked as "trash who have no interest in our country and its laws." In like manner Lyman hailed the courage of conscripts born in the United States, contrasting them with immigrant volunteers, who purportedly consisted of "stragglers, pillagers, skulkers, and run-aways." He recognized the courage and fighting ability of Irish soldiers, especially those in well-officered units, but insisted they were "not so good as pure Yanks." But Lyman reserved most of his ire for German troops. This was notable since German Americans living in the North constituted the country's most populous ethnicity during the war. He disparaged such combatants as "imported Dutchmen" and "almost idiotic." In Lyman's estimation a whole brigade of these men was prone to looting, lacked courage, and would flee combat when facing a native-born regiment. He mocked Germans who served as heavy artillerymen, accusing them of being unable to properly operate mortars for fear they would be shot by Confederate marksmen. Anti-immigrant sentiments could endure even after long experience in the field, as Wainwright demonstrated in his recounting of the celebratory two-day Grand Review in Washington, DC, in May 1865. He found that Maj. Gen. William Tecumseh Sherman's command, the Armies of Georgia and the Tennessee, featured a higher proportion of seasoned combatants than the Army of the Potomac. Based on this comparison, the colonel judged Sherman's troops to be physically impressive exemplars of Billy Yank, men who marched better and showed the "great predominance of the American type." Such claims revealed the nativism of these authors, who also neglected to provide the data necessary to prove an unprecedented influx of immigrant soldiers.[17]

Contemporaries advanced an inconsistent portrayal of the later arrivals. Some observers made broad statements about the Federals that omitted discussion of the new men, yet these same authors referred to them at other times. This contrast between general and detailed comments offers reason to doubt the severity of the charges leveled against the rookies. Rhodes, after his promotion to colonel of the 2nd Rhode Island, described his regiment as a seasoned outfit of some four years' experience. In so doing, he left unsaid that it included both long-serving veterans and less experienced soldiers. This begs the question: did Rhodes consider the later arrivals to be worthy of comradeship with his grizzled combatants? Others made sweeping observations about the Army of the Potomac. On the eve of the Overland Campaign, Meade expressed confidence in Union victory by declaring that his troops were "in fine condition . . . and . . . [would] do all that men can do to accomplish the object." This gives the impression that he was unconcerned about the quality of the newcomers. Lieutenant Colonel Lyman wrote similarly of the Federal performance at the Battle of Cold Harbor (May 31–June 12, 1864), boasting, "how admirably they have been handled in this campaign; and how heroically they have worked, marched, and fought." Remarkably, he did not blame this Union defeat on the later arrivals. Reflecting on the Grand Review, Lt. Col. Horace Porter, Grant's aide-de-camp, claimed that the troops marched with a precision that attested to years of drill. He concluded that those hailing from the eastern and western theaters were "both . . . in the highest degree soldierly" in this procession of "a nation's heroes." Porter did not mention whether the greenhorns counted among such vaunted comrades. Most striking was Grant's contradiction of the period consensus on the later arrivals. Focusing on registered voters in uniform, he opined that a majority were not "mercenaries. . . . [but] American citizens, having still their homes and social and political ties binding them to the States and districts from which they come." In Grant's view these men felt individually responsible for the war effort, and their fighting prowess was instrumental to defeating the Confederacy. As he demanded to know retrospectively of the Union rank and file as a whole, "What other Nation can boast of Armies composed of such material?"[18]

Ultimately, the period depiction of later arrivals as unsoldierly does not hold up to scrutiny. The evidence is too uneven and disparate to justify the idea that such troops consisted of deserters, bounty jumpers, lackluster combatants, and supposedly unreliable immigrants. Most contemporaries of the new men likely took the poor conduct of individuals to be representative, as opposed to addressing the subject of later arrivals comprehensively. It is worth pondering how the experiences of these authors informed their views. Perhaps critical eyewitnesses, having seen the horrors of warfare, felt it unwise to depend on uninitiated soldiers in combat and were thus predisposed to look down upon them. Alternatively, wartime traumas could have numbed their emotions, leading them to develop a callous indifference toward the difficulties that the rookies faced in battle. Sociologist Anthony King has similarly noted that seasoned combatants in twentieth-century warfare held a dismissive attitude toward new soldiers, which made it easier to push them into precarious situations. He further observes the tendency of novices to suffer heavy losses by exposing themselves to danger in hopes of earning the affirmation of veterans. In sum, the incomplete nature of such testimony justifies a historiographic review to explore how scholars have assessed the topic.[19]

SECONDARY SOURCES

Since the 1950s, historians have echoed contemporary portrayals of the later arrivals. They have depicted these new men as unpatriotic mercenaries—noting that many were foreigners—generally undeserving of the praise heaped on the altruistic "Boys of '61," who enlisted at the war's start. This interpretation holds that the high bounties, conscription, and substitution resulting from the recruitment system introduced by the Enrollment Act led to self-interested types apt to desert, engage in bounty jumping, or otherwise dodge their duties rather than fight well. Nowhere was this truer than in the Army of the Potomac, which had only half of its veterans reenlist between 1863 and 1864. This stood in contrast to Federal armies operating in the western theater, in which nearly all veterans chose to reenlist. Bell Irvin Wiley, the pioneering figure in the study of the common Civil War soldier, set the tone with his assertion that "the fighting quality of the army . . . seems to have reached its zenith in the early months of 1863 and to have declined thereafter." And yet he later downplayed the number of "shirkers, knaves, rascals, and cowards" in the ranks, arguing that the troops who fought at Cold Harbor were equivalent in quality to those at the Battle of Gettysburg (July 1–3, 1863). Likewise, Allan Nevins referred to a Union soldiery that grew increasingly formidable in skill and number between the summer of 1864 and the spring of 1865, but he subsequently claimed that "the character of the new recruits often left much to be desired." The inconsistency of these early assessments reflects the meager attention afforded this subject in the academic literature, according to which the later arrivals possessed a litany of flaws. This judgmental attitude has occasionally turned to derision, as illustrated by Bruce Catton's description of them as "human refuse" who included disabled, epileptic, or otherwise unsuitable enlistees. Scholars associate these men with rampant disease, the rise of more stringent punishment to curtail unruly behavior, and drunkenness. They also portray the recruits as underage, elderly, unreliable, criminal, and responsible for straining cohesion. In their judgment these troops would have fared better by bolstering existing outfits rather than forming new units. Such accounts give the impression that the rookies were a detriment to the Army of the Potomac's combat performance.[20]

Scholars have not submitted the later arrivals to a comprehensive, book-length examination. They have focused their research on the 1861 enlistees, whose enthusiasm to serve led them to sign up in large numbers. Many but not all of these individuals were ignorant of the conflict's impending human cost. Jason Phillips emphasizes that "short war predictions were louder than warnings of a dire, destructive conflict, but not more prevalent." Work that questions or rejects a negative view of the new men does not fall neatly within one subfield or timespan. Consequently, they continue to be portrayed contemptuously in studies of the soldier's experience, the Overland and Petersburg Campaigns, the draft and community mobilization, and the overall war. This longstanding derogatory depiction highlights a larger trend in Civil War military history, about which Earl J. Hess remarks, "It is astonishing how readily academic historians fall into line behind a salient interpretation on a line of research set by prominent predecessors as if it is inappropriate to reevaluate their work." Illustrative of this trend, scholars repeatedly note the role of money in the enlistment decisions of later arrivals. As proof, they cite anecdotal criticisms from veterans who were bitter because newcomers enjoyed greater pecuniary rewards for their service. The characteristics of the Union recruiting system explained these contemporary complaints. Since the beginning of the war, Victorian Americans had faced tremendous community pressure to join the Union army. According to many academics, they believed that to be drafted into the ranks rather than patriotically volunteer was dishonorable. And yet several other historians find only sparse evidence that this attitude lasted the entire war. J. Matthew Gallman, for example, maintains that "a man who chose not to serve faced little public sanction so long as he weighed his decisions honestly and his behavior did not reveal core hypocrisy." Regardless, civilians seeking to avoid the draft could pay a $300 commutation fee or hire a substitute to serve in their place. Due to inflation and the prospect of a high bounty, substitutes in 1864 could obtain more cash for a one-year term than their predecessors received over a three-year

enlistment. Cash bonuses surged in value in 1864, and Congress's elimi-
nation of commutation that July (save for a few categories of individuals,
including conscientious objectors) likewise caused substitution prices to
rise. This tempting remuneration supposedly motivated enlistees from that
time onward, infecting recruitment with a sordid, mercenary flavor.[21]

Historians disagree about the class makeup of the rank and file. This
hinders a better understanding of the role that bounties played in spurring the enlistment of the later arrivals. Depending on the methodology
and research sample, academics have reached opposing conclusions about
whether this was a "rich man's war, poor man's fight." A few insist that
the impoverished predominated among the new men and that the high
prices of commutation and substitution favored the wealthy. For instance,
Mark A. Snell maintains that later recruits were destitute, young, and "even
less representative of their society than were the soldiers who enlisted in
1861." He finds that the later arrivals were either unable to afford the commutation fee or desired cash in the form of bounties for their service. In
a study of recruiting in Dubuque, Iowa, Russell L. Johnson emphasizes
the neediness of the enlistees, who did not lack the determination to fight
since a disproportionately large number of Federals who signed up again
were laborers. Writing of the draft in 1863, Tyler Anbinder concludes that
"native-born citizens on the bottom rungs of the North's socioeconomic
ladder, especially unskilled workers living in the countryside, were the
only ones driven disproportionately into military service by the conscription law." Many scholars push back against this emphasis on poor recruits. James M. McPherson explains that drafted laborers could draw on
community-based financial aid to pay their way out of service, and other
historians find that a fair number of white-collar men donned the uniform.
Most notably, James W. Geary claims that "the Union army was more representative of the population than many of its counterparts in the twentieth
century." He argues that Civil War conscription was more equitable than its
successors in the 1900s. Almost all Union men could turn to substitution
as well as to commutation, until the congressional legislation of July 1864
largely curtailed this latter option.[22]

Some research demonstrates that the monetary self-interest of the later
arrivals was typical for enlistees rather than a late-war development. Economists Dora L. Costa and Matthew E. Kahn find that a disproportionately
high percentage of working-class and immigrant troops filled the ranks

throughout the conflict. Likewise, historian William Marvel asserts that monetary necessity led many individuals to volunteer during the war. In fact, "a man or boy was twice as likely to serve . . . if he was poor." Anticipating rations, steady pay, and aid for family members, the recruits of 1861 "appear to have been at least as financially desperate as any who later enlisted for exorbitant bounties." The proportion of cash-driven volunteers in 1862 likely equaled that "at the height of the bounty mania in 1864," putting aside the issue of bounty jumping. Although commutation benefited the working class by limiting substitute prices, Marvel regards financial conditions rather than conscription as chiefly responsible for the high proportion of needy troops. Bounties rose to attract recruits of the "next-most-desperate stratum" amid the growing human toll. Inflation outpaced wages, worsened with these cash bonuses, and plateaued in 1864. Despite rising pay, men who would not have been regarded as destitute in 1861 enlisted, and inflated prices diminished only as the spring of 1865 approached. Joseph C. Fitzharris offers a related finding in his study of an early war regiment, the 3rd Minnesota Volunteer Infantry. He partially attributes successful recruitment for this unit to the prospect of steady pay and the federal bonus. By way of further inducement, Fitzharris observes that "some counties, towns, and occasional individuals offered bounties to fill up company ranks, and many communities promised to take care of the soldiers' families—some towns even followed through."[23]

In fact, there may be parallels between the financial need of these new Federals and other American soldiers throughout history. When the colonists' *rage militaire* faded during the War of Independence, they left the burden of defense to soldiers in the Continental Army from America's lower economic echelons. These were typically young, impoverished, and unmarried men. They included whites, ethnic minorities, and African Americans without connections to the communities that recruited them. Amid rising bounties, Continental troops enjoyed a negotiating advantage due to the demand for manpower. A similar situation may even prevail in the twenty-first century, for Marvel insists that the lower classes and unemployed are more likely to enlist in the modern armed forces. Much as with Civil War historiography, however, scholarship on today's U.S. Army remains divided on this socioeconomic question. Beth Bailey maintains that this service branch "is fairly solidly middle class" and that the impoverished are proportionately less represented than those of greater affluence.[24]

It was typical for Civil War combatants to weigh the financial benefits of service. According to J. Matthew Gallman, recruitment throughout the conflict "rarely . . . turn[ed] on the duties of the citizen to his nation." Instead, advertisements emphasized the thrilling prospects of a soldier's life, the quality of officers and equipment, and the availability of bounties. In a related vein Russell Johnson highlights the appeals to class and ethnic interest that dominated the recruiting literature. It is nevertheless unjustified to assume that economic motivations pushed men into uniform. Civilians enjoyed better wages than Civil War troops, and paper-currency inflation outpaced the 23-percent rise in a private's monthly pay between 1861 and 1864. Plus, the U.S. dollar depreciated 60 percent from 1862 to 1864. It is not necessarily the case that recruits even wanted to be soldiers, for Peter Carmichael emphasizes that "joining the army was not a clear matter of individual choice." Substitute brokers, who sought out substitutes to fill the place of draftees for a fee, were to blame for pushing hapless men into uniform. To meet enlistment quotas, they preyed on non-English-speaking foreigners, the impoverished, and the naïve by means of alcohol, drugs, and coercion. Those men who wished to serve were not greedy simply because they desired the highest possible compensation for risking their lives. As Allen C. Guelzo observes, "the volunteer . . . was being asked to stand up to some of the most savage combat ever met by soldiers in the nineteenth century." It bears pondering whether the patriotic fervor of the northern population was sufficient to spur enlistments following the Enrollment Act. Mark Snell contends that such enthusiasm animated few Union troops by the end of 1864, but this may be an overstatement. Looking at the reasons why Continentals signed up for service is illustrative. Founding Father Robert Morris castigated them as "the most mercenary beings" because they enlisted for bounties. And yet historian Charles Royster denies that, for such combatants, "poverty and revolutionary ideals were mutually exclusive." He also finds fault with the idea that the recent immigrants among the American colonists lacked ideological motives and served only for profit. For Royster, the fact that pay, bounties, and land grants drew these men into the army does not mean that they lacked deeper convictions. He concludes that "no materialistic explanation of Continental soldiers' motives can adequately account for the diverse and recurrent instances of self-sacrifice in their conduct."[25]

The later arrivals must be judged on their merits as combatants, not based on the considerations that drew them into the ranks. Regarding the armies of the French Revolutionary Wars (1792–1802), historian John Lynn asserts that "a combination of high motivation plus effective tactics resulted in superior . . . performance." He distinguishes combat motivation from initial and sustaining motivation—the reasons why men enlisted and stayed in the ranks between battles, respectively. Writing of Civil War soldiers, Costa and Kahn observe that "the motives that led men to enlist were not necessarily the same as those that kept them in the army." And yet other scholars have focused much of their attention on initial motivations, namely those of the soldiers who began their service in 1861 and 1862. Historians by the early twenty-first century had come to stress the prewar background of the combatants more than their time under arms. Aaron Sheehan-Dean explains of this interpretation, "factors such as political philosophy and family relations [were]. . . . central to soldiers' conception of the conflict." Thus, a tacit assumption has emerged that if recruits were not eager to serve, they would be poor fighters. As Edwin P. Rutan II rightly argues, however, "from the [Union] Army's perspective, the relevant consideration was not the degree of the men's patriotism, but rather whether they made good soldiers."[26]

Academics share an unduly harsh opinion of the later arrivals' combat performance. They emphasize that these men were unequal to veterans by reporting their lackluster record in six battles across the Overland and Petersburg Campaigns. In a representative comment, Gordon C. Rhea finds it unsurprising that seasoned outfits sustained the majority of Union losses in the Wilderness. This implies that the rookies were not keen to engage the enemy. It is worth underscoring, however, that these later arrivals had not benefited from years of training and campaigning. Just like their predecessors in the Civil War, they underwent a learning period to gain the aplomb of seasoned troops.[27]

Appraising the fighting ability of the new men is essential to a scholarly discourse about the quality of the Union army and its combat record after passage of the Enrollment Act. Academics typically discuss the troops entering the army in the war's latter half in conjunction with a northern home front politically fractured by U.S. conscription and the suspension of habeas corpus. They point to a worsening state of affairs by 1864: Lincoln's imperiled reelection, Democratic dissent, the continued bungling by Union generals such as Benjamin Butler and Franz Sigel, and a population increasingly unwilling to supply replacements for the depleted ranks. This framing supports the idea of interdependent civilian and soldier morale, which has also underpinned academic explanations for Confederate defeat.[28]

The northern political climate did not solely determine the quality of the later arrivals. Notwithstanding Russell F. Weigley's support for the consensus on the new men, he cautions that "the Union and Confederate armies [did not] simply mirror the peoples and the strength of the national organizations behind them." This is notable, as scholars debate whether an uncertain and exhausted populace sent the Union army ineffectual reinforcements. For example, Susannah J. Ural notes the opposition of Irish Americans to the war effort and their participation in the 1863 draft riots. Among the reasons for resistance, these immigrants regarded stories of their abduction into service as evidence that they "were being tricked into fighting a war and serving an administration they did not support." The high casualties of the Overland Campaign also bore heavily on Irish Americans and worsened their antiwar sentiment. Against this backdrop of crumbling enthusiasm for the Union cause, Ural contends that greed mostly drove those men to enlist who immigrated to the United States between 1863 and 1864. As a result, the Army of the Potomac's Irish Brigade largely filled its empty ranks in 1864 with financially driven rookies who lacked the combat prowess of their predecessors. The result, she argues, is that the brigade "would never again be the same fighting force that had made the unit's reputation from Bull Run to Gettysburg." Conversely, Philip Paludan maintains that Irish Americans proved themselves in battle despite their negative outlook on the war effort. He adds that Democrats opposed to the Lincoln administration could fight well, even though they fled the ranks more often than Republicans. Timothy J. Orr points to the large share of Democrats filling two Pennsylvania regiments, noted for their fighting prowess, that served in the Army of the Potomac. Carol Reardon echoes this observation in a study of another Pennsylvania regiment in the same army. Such troops included men whom conscription or a sense of duty spurred to action in 1862, although they opposed abolition, as well as many Democrats who voted for Maj. Gen. George B. McClellan, past commander of the Army of the Potomac, in the 1864 presidential election.

Thus, political views should not be regarded as decisively shaping combat performance.[29]

Immigrants counted heavily among the later arrivals, yet academics have long downplayed the importance of these foreign-born troops. Although some 25 percent of Union soldiers originated from abroad, Don H. Doyle asserts that "a legacy of bias and language barriers" has obscured their role. To explain this inattention, he posits that fellow historians have echoed the prejudiced outlook of astronomer Benjamin A. Gould. In a postwar study this scientist alleged that foreigners joined for cash bonuses, then became bounty jumpers. Doyle adds that nativism and a desire for sectional reconciliation held sway after the Civil War, resulting in an Americentric narrative of the conflict. For example, Bvt. Lt. Col. William W. Swan of the 35th U.S. Infantry Regiment referred negatively to immigrant soldiers by declaring after the war:

> [General] Lee's army was made up of better material than Grant's. They were native-born citizens, and there is a great deal in that. Can we who were of the Army of the Potomac believe that the men we led would have been as patient and enduring of hardship as were the rebels, if, like the rebels, they had been but half fed and half clothed? I like not to speak in disparagement of the many brave men from other nations who fought under our flag, but I do believe in Americans. And I think that any American today must have his heart swell with pride when he remembers that there are native-born citizens in any section of the country who can spurn death as did the Confederates at Gettysburg.[30]

More research is necessary to establish how often later arrivals deserted and why. Eyewitnesses and academics alike have claimed that the new men joined the ranks only to flee after pocketing the bounty. This is a sweeping generalization, given that some 200,000 Federals absconded between summer 1863 and the war's end. Establishing the prevalence of this crime among the rookies requires tabulating the desertion rate in various units. But several historians have contributed to a more nuanced understanding of the misdeed, making it clear that numbers only tell part of the story. They have examined whether certain categories of recruits were especially prone to abandoning their comrades. Randall C. Jimerson, for example, maintains that men from the lower classes were frequently disinterested in fighting for the Union and thus apt to flee. Philip Paludan looks at a different demographic, contending that those newly arrived from abroad rarely deserted. This contrasts with the findings of Judith Lee Hallock in her local study of 1862 recruits. She blames deceitful recruiting agents, focused on their own profit, for encouraging foreigners to immigrate and sign up. As she notes, "such foreign-born soldiers were the most likely to desert." Hallock also calls attention to the characteristics of the home community and a person's relationship to it. In one case she examined, a close-knit town offered financial aid to its soldiers' families and produced few deserters, who were usually new immigrants. A village with widely distributed residents, in contrast, had an above-average number of culprits that included both native-born enlistees and foreign substitutes. And yet James Geary cautions that most later arrivals lacked ties to the communities in which they enlisted, hence it cannot be assumed that this characteristic distinguished steadfast rookies from deserters. Alternatively, Dora Costa and Matthew Kahn argue that the composition of military units influenced their desertion rate. Individuals were more apt to flee if they hailed from urban areas, while outfits proved more susceptible to desertion if they were heterogeneous in terms of age, employment, or place of birth. These two economists cite other variables with differing effects, including marriage, youth, class, and country of birth. Turning to the culprits' mindset, Peter Carmichael urges greater sympathy for these individuals, characterizing them as men who did not believe their interests aligned with those of the United States. He insists that a focus on the combatants' loyalty favors an elite perspective and calls attention to the "differences that class made regarding access to resources, the relationship to the household, treatment by officers, and how a soldier was received by the military justice system." Deserters typically enjoyed deep bonds with comrades, could have strong ideological and political beliefs, and be "governed by a flexible sense of duty and honor." Carmichael asserts that a spirit of pragmatism shaped their decision to flee the ranks.[31]

Some historians look more favorably on the later arrivals. Will Hickox offers the most ringing endorsement of these troops, declaring that "the Union would not have survived without the help of so-called 11th-hour soldiers." In a study of the 179th New York Volunteer Infantry Regiment, Edwin Rutan suggests that bounties alone did not explain why the new men enlisted. As he notes, some of these soldiers were already veterans, while others would have been too young to serve earlier in the conflict. For Rutan, the high casualties of the 179th indicate that the rank and file did not seek to pocket the cash while avoiding danger. Even Carmichael, who embraces the consensus on later arrivals, states that "the Enrollment Act served its purpose in reinforcing Union armies for the final push against the Confederacy." Writing a history of the 15th New York Heavy Artillery Regiment, Edward A. Altemos maintains that desertion was especially frequent among "the recent influx of unwilling conscripts and substitutes." He also echoes the assumption that cash bonuses attracted enlistees. Despite such flaws, Altemos finds that the unit, largely composed of greenhorns and immigrant Germans, left behind a positive legacy. He argues that "by the war's end, many considered the Fifteenth the equal of any infantry regiment in the Army of the Potomac." Other scholars imply that the later arrivals were of good quality and have noted the determination they showed in several clashes. This included two instances in which novices sustained serious losses on the attack as disobedient veterans lay prone or marched away. As William Marvel admits, the green regiments suffered terrible casualties in battle. Such sacrifice was not necessarily in vain, however, for Earl Hess contends that the largely rookie Ninth Corps fought with the same vigor as the Second, Fifth, and Sixth Corps during the Overland Campaign and the First Union Offensive in the Petersburg Campaign. Both he and Marvel point out that Major General Burnside drove his spearheads closer to the Cockade City than the rest of the army. The Ninth Corps thereby suffered a worse human toll than the other Federal commands, save for the Second Corps.[32]

Analyzing the combat performance of the later arrivals underscores the role of the humble private in actualizing the goals of the commanding general. This focus on the soldiers enables a fresh evaluation of the Ninth Corps, whose reputation has suffered from contemporaries who castigated Burnside's reputedly ponderous leadership style. Bvt. Maj. Gen. Orlando B. Willcox, commanding its Third Division, admitted that other Federals held a dim view of the Ninth Corps. Writing after its disastrous showing at the Crater, he opined that Burnside's command "has been considered not an integral part of the old army of the Potomac, & there are not wanting those in the other corps that are glad to get a kick at the brave old dog now he is down." And yet historian Robert Garth Scott argues that "examples of Burnside's inept leadership . . . should not reflect negatively on the abilities of the troops under his command, for under the proper leadership, these men could and . . . did perform their duty admirably." Since citizen-soldiers rather than generals largely shaped the character of Civil War armies, the presence of so many later arrivals in the Ninth Corps likely had a profound effect upon it. Nevertheless, officers tended to downplay the agency of individual combatants, hence Captain Fisk's complaint that Union "generals . . . seemed desirous . . . to make their men mere machines, going into battle without knowing anything . . . save to go forward . . . and fire." Major General Sherman, who was promoted to full general after the war, would illustrate this mindset by asserting that "a 'good captain makes a good company.'" Such thinking ignores the fact that the fighting effectiveness of the rank and file was not merely a question of obedience to orders—it also depended on their ability and desire to carry themselves well under fire. Although military leaders had a greater influence on the results of an engagement, this should not overshadow their subordinates' efforts. A bottom-up approach emphasizes the fact that there is no singular response to combat, for its stresses generate varied chemical reactions in the brain, behavioral patterns, and coping mechanisms. The study of combat performance, therefore, must not drain it of humanity. Academic Stephen G. Fritz aptly cautions against reducing "the actual killing and bloodletting done and suffered by human beings . . . to the sanitized intellectual exercise of evaluating strategy and tactics." Key to understanding how the new men conducted themselves under fire is an adequate framework to conceptualize and study this subject.[33]

METHODOLOGY

To date, Civil War historians have not used a systematic approach to assess the combat performance of the later arrivals. This likely reflects the fact that, as Mark Grimsley once observed, military history is "not nearly theoretical enough." Methodological improvements have lessened the strength of his critique, but Wayne Wei-Siang Hsieh asserts of Civil War scholarship that "military effectiveness . . . remain[s] strangely understudied." Similarly, Earl Hess writes that scholars of the period "have paid far too little attention to the entire topic of military effectiveness in the war. It is not enough to detail the movement of units on the battlefield—one ought to evaluate why and how they achieved their tactical goals on a given day of battle or why they failed to do so. . . . Standalone books that evaluate unit effectiveness on the army, corps, division, brigade, regiment, and company levels would be breaths of fresh air in a genre that tends to be stultifying in its lack of new ideas."[34]

Instead, academics have addressed the related question of combat motivation. Although this literature has yielded many insights, the sheer number and complexity of the relevant factors defies ready use in a case study. For example, Gerald F. Linderman contends that soldiers felt a sociocultural pressure to demonstrate their courage in battle, though "manliness, godliness, honor, and knightliness" were also important. Conversely, Hess cites religion, ideology, comradery, family support, working-class pragmatism, and the likening of combat to prewar experiences. According to James McPherson, "for Civil War soldiers the group cohesion and peer pressure that were powerful factors in combat motivation were not unrelated to the complex mixture of patriotism, ideology, concepts of duty, honor, manhood, and community or peer pressure that prompted them to enlist in the first place." Notably, research on this topic has extended beyond the realm of Civil War scholarship. From the mid-1940s onward, it has been the subject of work in political science, history, psychology, military research, and sociology. Academics have delved into conflicts ranging from the French Revolutionary Wars to the 2003 Iraq War. John Lynn argues that officers across conflicts have driven their troops to fight by using a combination of coercive, remunerative, and normative controls. Ilya Berkovich agrees while pointing to "the broader fabric of values that held armies together." He also calls attention to the "long preparatory process in which training, previous experiences and attitudes . . . come together to prepare the soldier"; the fighting conditions; and the individual's means of coping with battle.[35]

Scholars have focused much attention on the role of cohesion, or the extent to which troops follow orders and fight in a well-coordinated fashion. McPherson contends that these bonds were critical for battlefield success, and Hess similarly maintains that "this was probably the most pervasive and most deeply held source of battlefield morale." Academics have repeatedly cited the influence of cohesion—a key tenet of military policy—because it provides a seemingly logical explanation for soldier behavior and aligns with eyewitness testimony from multiple conflicts. The public likewise accepts the premise that the connections between the individual soldiers enable them to withstand enemy fire, as revealed in films, books, and current military training. Yet even as historians continue to champion the cohesion thesis, it is falling out of favor with social scientists. There is disagreement over the concept's definition, causes, membership, group size, and material effect on combat performance. Finally, the assumption that rookies serving in old outfits fared better than greenhorns composing entirely new units should be subjected to further scrutiny. In a study of the U.S. Army in World War II, for example, Robert E. Humphrey judges the policy of adding individual, fresh enlistees to existing formations wrong-headed since "it overlooked the importance of comradeship in enhancing morale and effectiveness."[36]

This book departs from previous work on why men fight, focusing instead on how well they perform under fire. Using a three-step approach, it assesses the battlefield record of the later arrivals across the eight engagements in two campaigns in which they faced the Confederates. The first concept is *cohesion,* here defined as obedience to commands and the ability to engage the enemy as a unified force. This involves a look at the effects of training, leadership, and discipline on fostering these bonds. It also acknowledges the influence of a shared social identity in helping forge deeper connections between the men. As Dora Costa and Matthew Kahn maintain, the level of cohesion depended upon the soldiers' "diversity in birthplace, social status (as measured by occupation), and age and the percentage of the company of their own ethnicity and occupation." Establishing a regiment's cohesiveness is fundamental to judging its fighting ability, as these infantrymen were expected to engage in battle as tight-knit units that obeyed commands without fear. As Christopher H. Hamner contends, "the effective soldier on the linear battlefield had to be an automaton." Beyond this machinelike quality, cohesion was the sine qua non of combat performance because, as John Keegan puts it, "it is towards the disintegration of human groups that battle is directed." Civil War troops typically fought in linear formations, and Berkovich has observed of such tactics in old-regime Europe that success depended partially on "the psychological breakdown of the opposing infantry line." Cohesion provides a foundational measure of combat performance, without which the soldiers would be unable to contribute meaningfully to the defeat of the enemy.[37]

Combat power offers a second way to analyze the fighting ability of the later arrivals. Adrian R. Lewis defines this concept as that "which achieves battlefield objectives in [a] specific environment." It may be more useful, however, to assess soldiers on a sliding scale rather than on the strict achievement of tactical goals. Troops who fail to drive the enemy off the field as ordered yet exact heavy losses on them must possess at least a modicum of combat power. Coauthors Allan R. Millett, Williamson Murray, and Kenneth H. Watman offer another definition: "the ability to inflict damage upon the enemy while limiting the damage that he can inflict in return." Of course, it is possible to be victorious despite incurring onerous casualties. During the Seven Days' Battles (June 25–July 1, 1862), the newly christened Army of Northern Virginia repulsed the Army of the Potomac's advance on Richmond but sustained higher losses in the process. Alternatively, the U.S. Army currently explains combat power as "the total means of destructive, constructive, and information capabilities that a military unit or formation can apply at a given time. . . . To execute combined arms operations, commanders conceptualize capabilities in terms of combat power. Combat power has eight elements: leadership, information, mission command, movement and maneuver, intelligence, fires, sustainment, and protection." The modern military definition of combat power requires modification to align with the battlefield realities of the Civil War at the regimental level. Such small units did not engage in combined-arms operations, and amid the various elements of combat power listed above, only those of leadership, movement, and maneuver are relevant. In a useful supplement to such definitions, political scientist Stephen Biddle judges effectiveness using three interrelated, though separate, factors: "the ability to destroy hostile forces while preserving one's own; the ability to take and hold ground; and the time required to do so." Ultimately, the concept of combat power and Biddle's formulation can be used to help determine how well the later arrivals fought—namely, their degree of success in completing tactical objectives.[38]

Casualty rates represent a third means of evaluating combat performance. The statistical research of two Union Civil War veterans is illustrative. Lt. Col. William F. Fox of the 107th New York Volunteer Infantry Regiment identified 300 "fighting regiments" that suffered the worst losses in the Union army. Given the wear and tear of long military service, he stated that casualties were the best measure of combat performance, though admitting that regiments could fight well with few losses. Similarly, Bvt. Col. Thomas L. Livermore of the 18th New Hampshire Volunteer Infantry Regiment compared Union and Confederate fighting potential by calculating the number of soldiers wounded and killed per 1,000 men in various battles. Among several observations, he stressed the impossibility of assessing "courage and efficiency" based solely on such figures. A panicked retreat could indicate cowardice, but "the loss suffered in a rout is not a measure of courage." Likewise, an organized withdrawal did not indicate a collapse in morale, for the general who ordered it might be a poor leader or simply decide to fight another day. Troops who recognized their impending victory did not necessarily commit their full energy to vying with the enemy. One side could even fare better due to a tactical edge, the possession of entrenchments, or simply superior numbers. Based on the examples of Fox and Livermore, casualty rates are a useful metric that should be interpreted within the context of a specific battle to avoid oversimplified conclusions. Tellingly, Provost Marshal General James B. Fry, the officer responsible for administering recruitment and conscription at the national level, declared that "the comparative zeal and efficiency of the troops of the different arms and States cannot be inferred from the ratio of casualties in action, without considering in addition the more or less perilous character of the service demanded of each of them."[39]

Thus, this book will pose the following questions regarding the 17th Vermont and 31st Maine. Did these outfits display good cohesion? What were their military objectives, and to what extent did they achieve them? Finally, how many casualties did they suffer? This last question takes into account the proportion of losses among officers as well as that of officers and enlisted Federals with experience serving in other units. The chapters that follow use these lines of inquiry as a methodological framework to analyze the combat performance of the 17th Vermont and the 31st Maine—and by extension many other Union soldiers who arrived late to the fight.

1

RAISING THE REGIMENTS

It [is] a spunky affair that Vermont can't fill this regiment.
—2nd Lt. Charles W. Randall, 17th Vermont

Our President . . . has called for . . . 600,000 first
300 000 next 300,000 next 75,000 3 months men now
100,000 3 months and again 300,000 more and more
than $2,000,000 [spent] per day now if this is not
outrageous waste of life and treasure I dont know.
—1st Lt. John P. Sheahan, 31st Maine

In July 1864 Brig. Gen. Lysander Cutler, who led the Fourth Division of the Fifth Corps in the Army of the Potomac, warned Lincoln that the Federal war effort was in dire straits. His criticism focused on the process of securing men to fill the ranks. As he put it, "for the first time since the war commenced I confess that I am seriously apprehensive for the result . . . because I am almost certain that you will not get the necessary number of men of the right sort, and in season." Cutler decried the current crop of recruits as a waste of public money, for a majority were substitutes made up of "aged paralytics, scorbutics, imbeciles, &c., to be sent to hospitals or discharged." The general recalled that less than two-thirds of the substitutes and conscripts enrolled previously had joined their comrades at the front, and of that proportion, fewer than half had fulfilled their obligations as soldiers. As Cutler saw it, the Union was failing to provide the effective manpower on which its cause depended.[1]

Other northern leaders shared this bleak view about the quality of the later arrivals to the Union army. In the words of Lieutenant General Grant, the new men "nearly all desert[ed]," with only one in five proving to be a good soldier. Among those echoing this pessimistic outlook were Chief of Staff Maj. Gen. Henry W. Halleck, Fry, ten different adjutant and inspector generals, and Major General Meade. Collectively, they lamented the large number of deserters, turncoats, and bounty jumpers entering the ranks. These authorities characterized the troublesome newcomers as substitutes, recruits, foreigners, city dwellers, and rootless men without means. Maj. Gen. John G. Parke, who succeeded Maj. Gen. Ambrose E. Burnside as commander of the Ninth Corps, noted that the later arrivals needed "time for drilling and disciplining." He believed substitutes lacked the "*élan* that displayed itself so gloriously in the patriotic volunteer" and bemoaned "the demoralizing influence of the bounty jumper" on his comrades.[2]

The comments of these contemporary critics provoke a defining question about the Union army: what kind of men donned uniforms in the war's final year? An examination of the 17th Vermont and 31st Maine reveals that the opinions voiced by the later arrivals' detractors were oversimplified. Contrary to the conventional wisdom, the majority of the new troops made a reasoned choice to enlist and had the ability to become dependable veterans. Admittedly, instances of poor discipline that punctuated the history of these outfits highlighted the difficulty of this transformation. The recruitment effort yielded a geographically diverse body of men who would have been strangers to one another and thus lacking cohesion when their service began. As Capt. John L. Yale observed of his 17th Vermont company, "there is but 3 or 4 of the men that I ever saw before." The army's desperate need for manpower meant these troops, predominantly rookies to military service, were committed to combat without undergoing much drill. Additional training would have helped forge tighter bonds and discourage unruly behavior. The later arrivals, therefore, commenced their service unprepared to fight as well-functioning units in the Overland and Petersburg Campaigns, which would witness the most intense combat of the war.[3]

THE RECRUITING SYSTEM,
ITS DETRACTORS, AND ITS SUPPORTERS

Creating the 17th Vermont was an uncertain process. The state adjutant and inspector general, Peter T. Washburn, alluded to previously raised infantry outfits from the Green Mountain State when he asserted that none "met with the difficulties and delays, which . . . baffled this regiment." Governor Frederick Holbrook announced the start of recruiting for this last Vermont infantry unit in August 1863, an effort that continued for another fourteen months. A first lieutenant in the outfit, Joel H. Lucia, maintained that "for many months its growth was so slow and precarious as to raise grave doubts whether it would ever attain the dignity of a regimental organization." This lag persisted despite what Lt. Col. Charles Cummings of the 17th termed the "extraordinary efforts" to obtain recruits between March and April 1864 by the more than 120 officers and men then enrolled. When the outfit departed for the front on April 18, it amounted to a mere battalion of seven companies. Owing to War Department regulations, a colonel could not lead fewer than the ten companies composing a full regiment. The battalion thus started service under the command of Cummings, who remained a lieutenant colonel. Not until October did its tenth company muster in to service. Even then, each of the 17th's companies fielded with less than the typical complement of 100 men, averaging 17 percent below strength. Fortunately, continuing enlistments enabled the state to make up for this shortfall by war's end. Ultimately, 1,106 officers and men served in the 17th Vermont.[4]

In contrast, the 31st Maine formed rapidly. Lincoln called for 200,000 more troops in February 1864, and Governor Samuel Cony promptly began recruiting for this penultimate infantry regiment from the Pine Tree State. The outfit originally had no colonel, for George Varney, previously colonel of the 2nd Maine Volunteer Infantry Regiment, had turned down the position, so the 31st departed for Virginia on April 18 as a battalion of nine companies under the command of Lt. Col. Thomas Hight. Only thirteen days later, the final company mustered in to service. Most of these companies were undersized, and as the regiment's ranks further depleted, the governor allowed two more—originally known as companies of unassigned infantry—to muster in to service in October. An aggregate of 1,163 officers and men thus served in the 31st, not counting 485 personnel from another unit of later arrivals, the 32nd Maine Volunteer Infantry Regiment, that it absorbed in December. This was pursuant to a War Department mandate that the 31st integrate these extra officers and men into its reduced ranks through a process known as consolidation. The additions did not include those officers mustered out because they were unnecessary to meet the leadership needs of the 31st. Col. Simon G. Griffin, who commanded the Second Brigade, Second Division, Ninth Corps in which the 17th and 31st fought, had previously called for this consolidation. In his view the 32nd was "not an effective organization, on account of its reduced numbers, and its scarcity of competent officers."[5]

Observers criticized the individuals filling both the new and existing outfits in Vermont and Maine. Government officials, newspaper editors, officers, and soldiers blamed the availability of large bounties for a decline in Union manpower quality. In line with the period consensus on later arrivals, these naysayers castigated them as criminals, impoverished, the scourings of city slums, foreigners, old men, and boys. Ostensibly, such enlistees were medically unfit to serve, disobedient, drunken, and prone to both desertion and bounty jumping. Washburn cautioned against "procuring, at exorbitant prices, men who have no thought of serving their country, but intend to desert at the first opportunity." His counterpart in Maine, Adj. Gen. John S. Hodsdon, implied that many in the 31st were not "perfectly trustworthy." Brig. Gen. Robert B. Potter, whose Second Division of the Ninth Corps absorbed the two new regiments, echoed these sentiments to some extent. He characterized a small proportion of the fellows in the 17th Vermont and 31st Maine as "a bad lot" who deserted after securing large bonuses. A soldier in the 32nd Maine—it had formed simultaneously in the state capital of Augusta—complained about bounty jumping among those in the last two companies of the 31st. An officer in another Maine unit addressed identical concerns by railing against the practice of "collecting together the 'floating scum of God's creation' with . . . money . . . [an] irresponsible class who . . . skirk[ed] [sic] all the responsibilities and dangers." In the same vein Cummings deplored the inundation of "insane, cripples, fools, jail-birds and bounty-jumpers" in both the 17th and 31st.[6]

Detractors in the two states held an especially dim view of substitutes. According to the acting assistant adjutant general of Maine, Bvt. Lt. Col. Robert McCandless Littler, such individuals were apt to desert in the period between signing their enlistment papers and entering into active service. Washburn focused his ire on those men originating from out of state, the greater proportion of whom had "to be treated and guarded in a manner disgraceful to them as soldiers . . . [but which still proved] insufficient to secure their continuance in the service." A Maine newspaper editor was more expansive, deriding a large share of substitutes as "mere hirelings" composed of Canadians, "the most unreliable men in the community," and those "without . . . reputation." He characterized these individuals as poor youngsters lacking the motivation of "property, a home, a family, [and] a country" for which to keep fighting, hence their tendency to flee upon receiving a sizable bounty.[7]

And yet there were eyewitnesses who praised later arrivals broadly. One veteran viewed a good number of the recruits entering Vermont regiments as "vigorous men who will make good soldiers," while a newspaper editor claimed many of the newcomers were "honest, stalwart fellows . . . anxious to be in at the death of 'Johnny Reb.'" Griffin considered the 17th Vermont to be "composed of the best material." Surgeon Joseph C. Rutherford, who served in the same regiment, enthused, "the men are a crying fair class and I think I shall like them—I do so far." A company in the 17th was even described by one of its officers, Captain Yale, as "composed in the main of first rate boys." He bragged that "most of them . . . look[ed] as if they were not to be scart by bullets & would stand up to the rack whether thier Captain did or not." The 31st Maine also received plaudits, with an observer from Washington, DC, citing its reputation as "one of the finest looking bodies of men" that the Pine Tree State had raised. Leander Otis Merriam, sergeant major of the regiment, wrote that some of his comrades consisted of "the very best material for making soldiers . . . [who] fell into the routine of camp life as though born to it." Referring to both units, a soldier in the 11th New Hampshire Volunteer Infantry Regiment insisted that a fair proportion of the troops were "fired by patriotism," akin to past recruits, and "spoiling for a fight."[8]

Scrutinizing the recruitment process makes it possible to test the validity of these contrasting perspectives on the quality of the later arrivals. In fact, proponents and critics frequently overlooked the difficulty of filling the ranks. An intricate system for raising men partly explained why the 17th Vermont developed more slowly than the 31st Maine. Between October 1863 and April 1865, Lincoln issued five national calls for varying numbers of troops. In response, each town had to meet a quota as part of a larger state total; failing to do so by a specified deadline would result in a draft to make up the difference with conscripts, at which point bounties would decrease. On January 1, 1864, Washburn explained that, according to new congressional legislation, conscripts and substitutes joining the army after the deadline would receive a $100 federal bounty. His counterpart in

Maine, Hodsdon, later announced that individuals donning the uniform in the Pine Tree State would receive an additional $100 state bonus. The Enrollment Act had exempted men from the draft based on mental or physical disability, government employ, family circumstance, or criminal record. In February 1864, however, Congress passed legislation to change the categories of exemption and limit the reasons for which someone could avoid compulsory military service. Those men now ineligible for exemption would be compelled to serve or find a substitute. They could also choose to pay the commutation fee, thereby eluding obligatory service, until Congress rescinded this option in July 1864 (except for several groups of individuals, such as conscientious objectors).[9]

A lack of clarity about the recruiting system hindered progress in Vermont. The public tried to balance two related though distinct objectives: meeting quotas and completing new units. Once a state raised enough men, it no longer faced the pressure of a looming draft to spur continued interest in service. Vermonters contended with ambiguity regarding whether men joining the new outfit counted toward the October 1863 call, something that the War Department did not conclusively confirm until December. Thus, some residents of the Green Mountain State spent months believing that the October call erased their shortfall from the previous draft, even though state officials insisted that the deficiency remained. Turning to the February 1864 call, determining the recruitment obligation produced what one newspaper editor termed "an untold amount of mystification and questioning." Further muddling matters, this particular call turned out to be a recalculation of existing obligations, according to which most Vermont communities could now claim a recruiting surplus. This removed the impetus to raise men, yet the national and state authorities stressed the need to keep doing so lest the tabulation prove incorrect and emphasized that future demands for troops were bound to occur. The governor of neighboring New Hampshire, Joseph A. Gilmore, hardly helped by incorrectly announcing that the Granite State had met its quota. Until the War Department provided clarification, Vermont residents generally drew the same conclusion and stopped funding bounties for the fresh battalion. In addition, newspapers promulgated a lawyer's mistaken claim that communities with recruiting shortfalls would not be subject to the draft so long as Vermont exceeded its quota. One editor subsequently rebutted this false assertion by citing information from the War Department and state officials. As he admitted, however, "so many different statements have been made on this subject that we do not profess to decide which is correct." Another Green Mountain State journalist observed that the various manpower calls had produced "confusion in the public mind."[10]

Uncertainty concerning recruitment details prevailed to a lesser degree in Maine. As a newspaper editor in the state lamented, authorities grappled with "contradictory and conflicting orders and regulations." This could have repercussions at the local level, for another editor explained that officials in the town of Saco at one time stopped funding a community bonus on the premise that everyone signing up counted against the quota. Conversely, those men eligible for the draft urged continued recruiting until a definitive answer emerged. A third editor complained that the residents of Gardiner had to estimate their manpower requirement, only to later learn that the number had changed due to an erroneous calculation by the district provost marshal. More broadly, the same newspaperman mocked the army's efforts at administering the recruiting system. As he asserted, "[Provost Marshal General] Fry's decisions have been the laughing-stock for a year or more, and have been contradicted in the same paper that gave them to the public."[11]

Although the effort to fill the ranks could prove bewildering, the populations of both states still contained men eager to serve with few exceptions. Francis V. Randall, who mustered in as colonel of the 17th Vermont once it attained ten companies in October 1864, subsequently exaggerated the level of "opposition and hostility" he had encountered across his state. The sole recorded incident of resistance occurred in September 1863, when a group of Irish Americans attacked a sergeant and two recruits in the town of Barre after threatening to "lick any one who wore the uniform of a soldier." Lieutenant Colonel Cummings noted little apathy toward military service in the state, remarking that only a small number of Vermonters contributed to the funding of bounties without signing up themselves. Likewise, Maine appears to have experienced but one case of resistance when the residents of Calais protested the efforts of recruiting officers. This was surprising, given the commonsense assumption that war weariness would have cooled popular enthusiasm for the war effort.[12]

The creation of the 17th Vermont and 31st Maine ultimately occurred against the backdrop of a restrictive U.S. policy that favored the replenishment of existing regiments. It reflected the belief that veteran outfits were superior to green ones, hence Secretary of War Edwin M. Stanton's declaration, "the efficiency of the army depends more upon filling up the old regiments than upon any other measure." Fry judged "the system of raising new and disbanding old regiments . . . injurious to military interests" and maintained that "a recruit in an old regiment . . . [was] worth two or three in a new one." Regarding the influx of Vermont and Maine enlistees in the two new units, he concluded that it was "far better . . . to lose the services of these men than to abandon all chances of getting recruits for old regiments."[13]

The governments of Vermont and Maine established these new outfits since it was their prerogative and aligned with their interests. Historian Allen Guelzo observes that a governor could utilize a regiment's formation to advance political patronage. Since the raw unit would need officers, this politician could award his supporters with commissions. Another factor driving the creation of new units was the increased possibility of promotion. According to Washburn, veterans were "usually more willing to go into a new regiment where there is an open chance for promotion, than an old one where the offices will be claimed by those who have served faithfully during the war." Several others, including a Vermont recruiting officer, an unidentified private in an outfit from that state, and a Maine newspaper editor, all noted that service in a green unit offered more opportunities for moving up in rank. Perhaps hinting at this incentive, another editor from the Pine Tree State opined, "Experience has shown that three recruits for a new regiment can be obtained where one can for an old regiment."[14]

Regardless, this approach to recruiting made it more difficult to fill the ranks of the 17th Vermont. Originally, the War Department limited enlistments to veterans in order to attract those men who had fought at Gettysburg in the nine-month regiments comprising the Second Vermont Brigade. Yet few of these seasoned combatants reenlisted, as they were preoccupied with personal affairs and suffering the effects of a widespread and deadly fever—likely diphtheria. Decades later a state health official described this outbreak as "probably the greatest epidemic Vermont had known since the great spotted fever days of 1812–14." As Washburn duly observed of the defunct nine-month units, "in some of them more men . . . died since they returned into the State than died during their entire term of service." The taxing nature of these veterans' stint in uniform, which had left them vulnerable to this disease, thus stifled their interest in resuming a soldier's life. Recuperating from their campaign experience, they regarded donning the uniform again as superfluous, believing that the Union victories at Gettysburg and the Siege of Vicksburg (May 18–July 4, 1863) already foreshadowed the end of the war. Given the tepid pace of recruiting, newly elected Vermont governor J. Gregory Smith successfully lobbied the War Department in September 1863 to allow rookies into the battalion. Whereas veteran volunteers received a $402 bounty for three years in uniform, greenhorns could only look forward to a $102 enlistment bonus. This paled in comparison to the $302 reward available to raw recruits upon joining an established outfit or the high pay that farmers offered to seasonal workers who harvested their crops in a constrained labor market. Only at the end of December did the War Department permit a $300 bonus to rookies entering the 17th for a three-year term. That arrangement ended in April 1864, but the $300 sum became available again in July to anyone who signed up for three years.[15]

In contrast, the Mainers built their new unit more quickly than the Vermonters, with fewer constraints and more funding. A bias toward veterans persisted, owing to the governor's requirement that two-thirds of the officers be seasoned—only one lieutenant could be a rookie—and the implied expectation that the soldiers generally have at least nine months of experience. To the extent possible, seasoned officers were also to lead the unassigned infantry companies. And yet the mustered-out veterans of the nine-month units from that state did not typically reenlist. The 31st benefited from the fact that it was created after the War Department decision to allow rookies the same $300 federal bounty regardless of which outfit they joined. Thanks to the addition of a state bonus, veterans and greenhorns received $700 and $600 respectively for three years of service. In August 1864 this shrank to $400 for enlistees joining the unassigned infantry companies, as they would only serve one-year terms. Additionally, the soldiers availed themselves of a program providing a weekly payment of up to $2.50 for eligible dependents, although communities could provide extra monies to these men. In February 1865, however, the state legislature reduced that form of support, limited those family members who could receive it, and shortened the timeframe for which they would be eligible following the discharge or death of their loved ones in uniform.[16]

Recruitment efforts largely depended on the allure of cash to draw individuals into service. When critics derided the later arrivals as mercenaries,
they overlooked the economic inducements that had served as a standard
recruiting tactic since the war began. In guarded prose Fry said, "without
expressing an approval or disapproval of [the bounty] system . . . as we are
acting upon it, we must get the benefits of it." Other government officials
accepted the use of such enticements, albeit with caveats. Governor Cony
of Maine faulted the reliance on outsized awards but declared his approval
for "a liberal, even a generous provision . . . for those who may be obliged
to enter the army." Similarly, Washburn found hefty sums acceptable so
long as they attracted state residents and not outsiders. He argued that
"high bounties . . . [should] be paid to our own citizens, who we know
will earn them by the best possible service in the field. . . . [keeping] the
money . . . within the State, and . . . merely transferred from one class of
loyal citizens to another." Underscoring the transactional nature of military
service, one seasoned Vermont cavalryman called the later arrivals "men
who seem to have come here to aid in the work, as well as to receive the
pay." This logic surely applied to veterans as well since authorities offered
larger bonuses to secure their reenlistment.[17]

The availability of bounties could lead soldiers to think of their self-
interest, depending on whether these monies were awarded piecemeal or
as lump sums. Those donning the uniform received their federal bonuses
in installments over time in service, which discouraged individuals who
might otherwise pocket the cash and desert. The situation differed for soldiers enlisting in Maine, who benefited from the additional state bounty.
Initially, authorities distributed this cash to each man in two allocations,
then increased the temptation by dispensing the funds all at once. Local
bonuses, available as lump sums, proved particularly captivating to both
Vermonters and Mainers. To meet recruitment goals, communities funded
their own cash rewards to entice enlistees. This practice introduced a com-
petitive element to recruiting, as towns vied for men by seeking to outdo
one another in the dollar amount of their bounties. Helping explain this
mindset, Fry cited the widespread belief "that every [manpower] call was
the last." In Vermont bonuses initially ranged in value between $25 and

$300, then surged to $1,000 by mid-1864. Presumably due to the availability of state monies, however, town bounties appear to have only risen to $400 in Maine. Central to the recruiting drive was the pressure that residents faced to meet their quotas and avoid the shameful connotations of a draft. Newspaper editors argued that conscription damaged community reputations. Some termed the draft a "humiliation" or "disgrace," which explained Washburn's observation that residents exhibited a "zeal to evade" it.[18]

Rising local bounties left a mixed legacy. Some enlistees took advantage by fleeing the ranks after collecting their town bonuses, which inspired efforts at the community and state level to quash such abuses. The selectmen of Rutland, Vermont, stipulated that recruits who were not local residents would only receive the entirety of their $500 bounty six months after the start of their service. Evidently, the town authorities sought to dissuade those men who roved between communities in search of the highest possible bonus with no intention of actually serving. Among Mainers, the practice of granting lump sums changed in February 1865 with the introduction of a policy compelling substitutes to deposit local bonuses with their mustering officer until they arrived at their rendezvous closer to the front. Beyond enticing men who intended to desert or bounty jump, the system of town bounties could also cause potential recruits to bide their time instead of promptly signing up. According to this logic, enlisting at a later date might offer the prospect of an even higher bonus in exchange for a shorter time in uniform. Regardless, local bounties did in fact ensure that military service remained economically attractive, helping draw men in Vermont—and probably in Maine—away from well-paying farm jobs to fight for the Union. Against the backdrop of mounting casualties, this was a significant contribution.[19]

Proponents of military service encouraged the later arrivals to regard enlistment as a way to improve their economic standing. Various parties drove home this message via newspaper advertisements and articles. One of these commenters was a substitute broker, who declared, "the highest price amounting to a small fortune . . . [would] be paid." Likewise, a recruiting officer called attention in his publicity to "the greatest pay ever offered to men." Newspaper editors proclaimed that prospective recruits ought to sign up to "receive the full amount of all the liberal bounties offered," for "the last chance to secure the large bounties . . . [would] soon be gone." These journalistic boosters believed that the combination of available bounty and pay was important, given that "few young men . . . are making as much as this now" and that a bonus would be valuable indeed to those who "may need the amount before leaving" to begin their service. One editor further declared: "The government offers monthly pay and bounties far beyond that of any nation on earth, and the sum is such as to make fighting the most lucrative and best paying business. . . . Even if principle were wanting the pay should be a sufficient inducement."[20]

Cash-focused appeals to service would have been effective in both states, given their largely agrarian economies as of 1860. The average Vermonter's real and personal property value was about $389, compared to roughly $303 for Mainers. These states lagged behind their New England peers, most notably Connecticut, where the average resident's property equaled some $966 in value. Moreover, farmhands and laborers, who made up a large share of the men employed in Vermont and Maine, could only look forward to an average annual wage of approximately $170 and $380, respectively. A robust bounty thus represented a significant boost in income for such residents.[21]

Financial advancement would have garnered plenty of interest among the working-class men who filled the two outfits. Farmers and laborers alone made up at least 70 percent of the 17th Vermont. This figure closely reflected the population of the Green Mountain State, where 61 percent of men were so employed. A sample representing the entire Union army shows that the composition of the 17th was typical for Federal fighting organizations more broadly. Between the war's start and the beginning of recruitment for the Vermont unit, laborers and farmers made up approximately 63 percent of the Union army. At first glance this contrasts sharply with the case of the 31st Maine, in which only about 57 percent of members held such occupations; no other mode of employment represented so large a proportion of residents. By way of explanation, 48 percent of men in the Pine Tree State in the early 1860s worked as farmers and laborers. Thus, contemporary critics oversimplified matters by castigating poor men as an outsized portion of the later arrivals. Such humble folk had always composed a large share of Federal troops. It is therefore unsurprising that they were overrepresented in these two regiments.[22]

The New Englanders exhibited evidence of limited funds and families dependent on their meager incomes. William Kennedy was one such citizen who was destitute, evicted from his hotel residence, and forced to beg to survive. Unable to pass the medical examination for military service, a substitute broker arranged for him to assume an eligible man's identity. His financial woes came to an end when he signed up with the 31st Maine and received a bounty. In another instance an illiterate man named Solomon Anderson sought as much money as he could get for serving with the same unit. These examples help explain why the later arrivals were preoccupied with the bounty and pay levels, as they were able to send home amounts ranging from only a few dollars up to a sizeable $350. As a civilian, Franklin Temple Carter only earned about $85 over seven months in 1863, then learned of a better job as a porter that would earn him $36 for two months' work. Despite such prospects, he still decided to volunteer for the 17th Vermont and make his bounty and much of his pay available to his folks back home. Another case involved Moses Whitehill, who once earned $6 over a five-day period but, after enlisting as a corporal in the Vermont outfit, was able to send $210 to his family. Wagoner Sargent R. Emerson tellingly acknowledged the importance of his income, admitting that he and his wife would have struggled had he chosen to stay home rather than sign up in the 17th. Illustrating the importance of this cash, 1st Lt. John P. Sheahan of the 31st told his father of his pay to reassure him that it was time for the family to stop being renters and purchase a home. Most notably, he and the other members of the 31st were able to mail a total of $50,000 to their loved ones after receiving their back pay in March 1865. It seems likely that many troops—more than those cited here—would have regarded enlistment as a way to support their households. Instances of opportunism should not take away from the stark economic realities facing such working-class men. For example, Pvt. Gustavus Gould of the 17th chose to remain silent when he believed that authorities would overpay him by $80 for his service. Putting aside this kind of dishonest lapse, it does not follow that the later arrivals were greedy if they failed to justify their financial need in writing. Whether jotting down journal entries or addressing relatives and friends in letters, the later arrivals may not have felt compelled to detail such matters.[23]

Both state governments offered incentives that underscored the modest means of the later arrivals. At least 15 percent of the Vermonters who signed up for three-year terms opted to receive their state pay of $7 monthly as a lump sum of $125, a practice known as commuting one's pay. In some cases soldiers who embraced this opportunity may have done so out of fatalism.

Presumably, their desire for the lump sum revealed a belief that there was no point in waiting to secure additional monthly pay if there was little certainty of survival in the struggle ahead. It is possible that these men held such a grim perspective, for Jason Phillips has rightly stressed that Americans anticipated the toll of the conflict before it even began. Moreover, by this point in the war, recruits would have recognized the gruesome realities of combat, as newspapers published casualty lists and soldiers returned home with wounds both physical and psychological. The Maine government did not offer its soldiers a supplement to the U.S. government's monthly pay, so the option to commute was not available to them. Still, its troops could apply for financial aid. Adjutant General Hodsdon believed this program was a boon to the recruitment of units from the Pine Tree State since prospective soldiers who joined outfits from other states were not eligible. This assistance proved important to enlistees, as Pvt. George W. Sargent of the 31st confessed in February 1865 that his "family need[ed] it very bad for . . . [he had] not received a cent of pay from [the] government since . . . [he] left Augusta last spring."[24]

A sense of civic responsibility also helped explain the allure of military service. Newspaper editors lauded enlistees as "noble examples of patriotism," insisted this selfless ideal "should be the main spring of our action," and admonished, "let not our decendents point in shame to us for want of earnestness and patriotism." One described those in uniform as "that noble band of patriots who are engaged in the suppression of this gigantic rebellion." Adjutant and Inspector General Washburn alluded to Vermont's "patriotic soldiers in the field" and exhorted seasoned combatants "to respond to the call of the country" by reenlisting. Military men echoed this view in newsprint, such as an experienced Vermont cavalryman who urged, "as each one would be protected in his rights, so let him fly to the protection of our common rights." A recruiting officer in Maine promoted "the higher Inducements of Patriotism." In like manner Capt. C. H. Ellis of the 31st Maine offered a reminder that "the whole Union must be preserved," while Lt. J. Sumner Rogers declared, "the young man who fails to do his part toward the glorious work will live to regret his lack of patriotism."[25]

This rhetoric found its mark, for some of the later arrivals did in fact articulate patriotic motives. Officers predominated in this group, as enlisted men typically focused on practical matters and their semiliterate prose did not lend itself to discussing more abstract topics. This was unsurprising, given the largely working-class background of these troops. A number of individuals stressed the goal of defeating the Confederacy, such as Pvt. Horatio Fox Smith of the 31st Maine, who declared his intention to serve "till the great desire of all true patriots . . . [was] attained." Similarly, Cpl. Charles A. Manson of the 17th Vermont vowed "to stay and fight for ten years if nessary" and mocked "those delicate fellows who dare[d] not come out here but . . . [were] very patriotic at home." These later arrivals wanted to do their part. Surgeon Rutherford of the 17th derided "bloodthirsty traitors" and affirmed the Union "cause . . . [was] worth . . . making any sacrifice . . . consistant with national honor," while Pvt. George Hodgkins of the 31st stated, "I came away to fight for the cause of my country." Limited evidence points to the fact that some enjoyed family support for their decision to go to war and others did not. Before Manson signed up in the Vermont outfit, his grandmother urged him to stand "ready and willing to do your duty fully as a soldier in maintaining the institutions, and honor of your beloved country." Yale, serving in the same unit, responded to the opposition of his loved ones by arguing that "they should be to happy to say that out of five children they wer happy to send one to defend the liberties of our common country."[26]

The later arrivals expressed a desire to fulfill their duty despite the war's bloody toll. Cummings insisted that no one capable of military service could "lay any claim to patriotism" if he failed to sign up, for this Vermonter felt it better to "die than go home disgraced forever" and was willing to give his life for "this great cause." Sheahan, prior to joining the 31st Maine, lost a brother serving in another unit. Although Sheahan remained in uniform, he sought to dissuade his father from enlistment, arguing that one should not "be tempted by money for what is money to a brothers blood." Nevertheless, he referred to the volunteers of 1861 as "the brave boys [who] left at the first call for men to protect the starry [flag]." Offering a more pragmatic outlook, Sergeant Major Merriam related that his comrades sought to help "deliver the final blow to the great rebellion." Still, they "didn't go to war . . . for the fun of it, but only because 'somebody must.'"[27]

Recruiting promoters warned prospective soldiers that their reputations and financial interests would suffer if they awaited the draft, depicting compulsory military service as a dishonorable fate. Hodsdon acknowledged that a desire to forestall conscription spurred enlistments, while

Washburn noted, "the people have a very natural repugnance to a draft." Members of the 17th Vermont alluded to this popular anxiety. Wagoner Emerson suggested that the residents of one town "must be a good deal frightened . . . about the draft," and Manson predicted "some squirming" among those facing conscription. Various proponents underscored the substantial remuneration for volunteering. These published individuals included the members of a Maine recruiting board, a seasoned Vermont infantryman, and newspaper editors from both states. Illustrative of this rhetoric, a recruiting officer pointed out, "with a draft you can not choose your Company; you cannot choose your Regiment, and you get no Bounty!" Similarly, an editor asked his readers, "had you not better then, take the $400, and have the honor of being a volunteer, than run your risk of going as a conscript?" Another journalist warned against missing the chance for a hefty bonus, a grim prospect since Congress would "see to it that the number of causes for exemption are so reduced as to permit no really able bodied conscript to escape. There will be no boys' play about it." Amid such claims, readers could hardly be blamed for concluding that to serve as a volunteer was the right decision monetarily and would preserve one's good standing in the community.[28]

The promise of money, patriotism, peer pressure, and antidraft sentiment could push men to don the uniform. An unnamed private serving in an unidentified outfit from the Green Mountain State illustrated this point. In a letter home, this only child insisted it was his "duty to be fighting" and spent months seeking his parents' consent while away at school. Several colonels had spoken to the student body, warning of a future draft and asserting that the conflict would drag on at great human cost unless there were sufficient Union troops in the field. As the twenty-year-old remembered, the military men claimed that the soldiers would "curse us with the name of coward forever if we do not turn out." He also noted an offer of a $500 bonus from a man living in Rutland, Vermont, and added, "there never will be another such chance." Remarking that schoolmates "tell me to stay at home," this same young man asked if he should "stay here and always be called a coward (and perhaps be drafted) or go and do my duty to my Country and my God."[29]

Youthful enthusiasm provided another impetus to join the ranks. In the Green Mountain State, a newspaper editor once decried the influx of fifteen-year-olds into the ranks of various units, while in the Pine Tree

State, an entire class of Sunday School students enlisted in assorted regiments. The 17th Vermont and 31st Maine bore witness to boys interested in soldiering. Two adolescents claimed to be eighteen years old so they could enter the Vermont outfit, yet they did not obtain the consent of their parents. In a case of remarkable persistence, a fourteen-year-old named Joseph Granger attempted to enlist up to four times per day over a two-week period before succeeding. The mustering officer, Sgt. Seaver Howard, finally concluded that the young man was telling the truth when he insisted he was eighteen. Granger's eagerness was noteworthy, given that Howard described the lad's parents as "coppery" for their opposition to the war effort, and believed the father guilty of helping three deserters flee to Canada. In another instance an adolescent signed up without his parents' awareness or agreement. As he was a minor, the family got him released but ultimately allowed him to reenlist to the credit of their town quota. Numerous youngsters likewise sought out the 31st, including an eleven-year-old who stole away from his parents to go to war. When this regiment returned home at the end of hostilities—about seven months after its consolidation with the 32nd Maine—a Bangor resident would note its many "boys . . . some of them not over 14 years old when they enlisted." One of the fellows heading off to war was a sixteen-year-old whose parents had "good reason to believe that he enlisted in company with others who were on a spree." This same family had five other sons in uniform. In another example showcasing an enthusiasm for soldiering, a boy of some fifteen years of age followed in the footsteps of his three brothers and father, who were already serving in other units. The lad's mother inexplicably failed in her efforts to have this underage enlistee rejoin his family.[30]

These anecdotes of juvenile exuberance were notable since the later arrivals were younger than their predecessors in the aforementioned Union army sample. Admittedly, minors could misrepresent their ages when signing up, reducing the accuracy of demographic data on the boys in blue. Based on available sources, however, the average age of the Vermonters and Mainers was twenty-four and twenty-five years respectively, in contrast to an average of twenty-six years in the larger sampling. Roughly one-quarter of the New Englanders were eighteen years old or younger upon enlistment, so they would have been too young to join if they had attempted to do so at an earlier time.[31]

Despite the later arrivals' willingness to serve, they initially lacked strong bonds to one another since they hailed from so many different communities. In the 17th Vermont, officers and men signed up in all fourteen counties of the state. A majority came from Windsor, Chittenden, and Franklin, which were three of Vermont's five most populous counties. Still, seven of the ten companies featured no majority from a single county, and as First Lieutenant Lucia maintained, "it would be difficult to name a locality from which any one company originated." Likewise, those officers and men filling up the 31st Maine signed up in all sixteen counties of the state. Most originated from Penobscot, Washington, Kennebec, and Hancock Counties, which were among the seven most populous in Maine. These individuals were probably even less familiar with one another than the Vermonters. Hodsdon alluded broadly to "the migratory character of the people of Maine," while a newspaper editor cited the case of Ellsworth, a town with a prominent lumber industry that drew men from all over the Pine Tree State.[32]

At first glance the attraction of local bounties would seem to be responsible for such geographically fragmented outfits. As Lt. J. Sumner Rogers of the 31st Maine announced, "young men, and aliens not liable to draft, can go on the quotas of those Towns which pay the largest Bounties." Fry hinted at this economic logic when writing to Hodsdon, explaining, "if on account of bounties, or for other cause, a man chooses to go from the North to the South of Maine to enlist and accept bounty, we do not propose to control his movements or question the correctness of the roll which shows him to be credited to the South." Individual examples speak to this behavior. Pvt. Joseph Gilcott Jr. joined the 31st to the credit of China, Maine, even though he lived in Waterville. Likewise, Franklin Carter of the 17th signed up in Kirby, Vermont, because his fellow residents in Concord had not funded a bounty. A contest ensued between communities, which Governor Cony of Maine explained "deprive[d] the poorer towns and plantations . . . of the benefit of enlistment of their own citizens, from their utter inability to enter the lists against larger and more wealthy towns." Reflecting on this dynamic, Hodsdon observed, "the poorer and least populous ones . . . generally have the largest proportion of able-bodied men whose situation and circumstances most readily admit of their entering the service." In contrast, "older and wealthier towns . . . have much money and but few men . . . eligible to enlistment." Historian Tyler Anbinder explains that "newspapers of the era overflowed with advertisements seeking substitutes, and men desiring to hire themselves often traveled great distances to take such work."[33]

And yet the introduction of substantial bonuses was not so transformative since the composition of these outfits was typical of the Federal rank and file. Referring to statistics from the Union army sample reveals that a company included men from an average of three counties. The fact that the Vermonters and Mainers hailed from so many parts of their respective states, therefore, was not unusual. This meant that most of the later arrivals would have been strangers to one another since they did not come from the same home town. Still, a greater degree of state identity may have helped compensate for this grassroots demographic diversity. Only 39 percent of men in that same larger sampling served in a company from the state of their birth. There was no downward trend in this low percentage between 1861 and 1865, so it cannot be explained by a supposed decline in local enthusiasm to fill the ranks over the war years. In contrast, some 52 percent of the officers and men in the 17th Vermont hailed from its home state, and at least 62 percent of those in the 31st Maine were state residents.[34]

Critics rightly described the later arrivals as more diverse than their predecessors yet exposed their own nativism by complaining about the foreign presence in the ranks. Due to the limited information available in the sources, it is not clear whether such new men had immigrated to the United States recently or long ago. Approximately one-third of the officers and men in the 17th Vermont hailed from abroad in contrast to a mere 10 percent of residents in the Green Mountain State, according to the 1860 census. Most of the foreigners in the 17th originated from Canada or Ireland, although others represented Belgium, Cuba, England, Germany, and Scotland. This immigrant presence was proportionately greater than the 23 percent in the Union army up to the start of recruiting for the Vermont outfit. Turning to the 31st Maine, only 13 percent of its members were foreign born, considerably less than that of the Union army sample but still outweighing the 6 percent of residents in the Pine Tree State from other countries. Like the Vermonters, most of the foreign-born Mainers came from Canada and Ireland, while others hailed from Scotland, Wales, and the Philippines. Such statistics reveal that a disproportionately large number of these men served relative to native-born Americans. The later-arrival stereotype suggests that rising bounties attracted immigrants, but the evidence does not bear out this claim. Even though the value of local bounties rose over time, the share of foreign-born soldiers in each company—across both units—did not correspondingly increase. Ethnic pride, however, could drive enlistments. On St. Patrick's Day, seventy men from the 17th Vermont participated in organized festivities in Burlington, Vermont, with speechmaking that stressed the Irish American commitment to the Union cause. Before a crowd of some 2,000 people at the town hall, a representative of the Ladies of St. Mary's Church displayed the Flag of Erin and proclaimed, "with ranks swelled in numbers you will attest your devotion to the land of your nativity, and your gratitude to the land of your adoption." Members of the same unit also took part in a parade to celebrate the arrival of Irish-born Brig. Gen. Thomas Francis Meagher, although he did not make the event. Meagher was the one-time commander of the famed Irish Brigade, which he had led as part of the First Division of the Second Corps.[35]

These outfits benefited to some extent from a core of experienced officers and men. They may have helped their raw comrades adapt to life in uniform, given Merriam's description of his interactions with one veteran, Orderly Sgt. C. B. Cobb. As Merriam put it, "he and I became fast friends, and being pretty green myself, I . . . depended on him for information as to my own duties." Comparing the demographics of experienced and green combatants in these two units reveals that the grizzled Federals were similar to the rookies in age and largely native born. Those railing against the later arrivals overlooked the presence of these seasoned combatants, who made up 21 percent of the Vermonters and 12 percent of the Mainers. The proportion varied significantly by company, despite the common-sense assumption that rising bounties would attract a growing number of rookie fortune-seekers over time. The veteran Vermonters were slightly older than their green comrades, with an average age of twenty-seven years old. Seventy-nine percent of these veterans were born in the United States. Conversely, the seasoned Mainers averaged twenty-five years, matching the average age of the rest of their comrades. More so than the Vermonters, 95 percent of the experienced combatants from the Pine Tree State were native born.[36]

In both regiments the experienced leadership was of mixed quality. More than half the commissioned officers in the 17th Vermont were veterans, with a few lieutenants and a majority of the noncommissioned officers having served in Brig. Gen. George J. Stannard's Second Vermont

Brigade, part of the Third Division of the First Corps, at Gettysburg. Lucia described them as "men of tried bravery and discretion . . . careful of their men, but sparing not when blows were needed." Scattered evidence suggests, however, that Lieutenant Colonel Cummings was not well suited to the task of preparing the Vermonters for field service. In February 1864 he hinted at friction with Randall when he told his wife of his intention "to make the best of it." And yet Wagoner Emerson noted several months later that the colonel "was having considerable trouble with Cummings," who had "no capacity to command." Similarly, the men of the 31st Maine benefited to some extent from seasoned leadership. Most of the officers had previously served in the 2nd Maine, and one had fought in the Mexican-American War (1846–48). Some of these leaders were of questionable merit. For example, Sheahan derided the captain and second lieutenant of his company for failing to instill proper discipline among the troops. Merriam lauded a number of officers in the 31st but confessed of Lieutenant Colonel Hight that his own "recollections . . . [were] in the nature of regret," referring to that regular army officer's fondness for wine. Among other judgments, Merriam regarded Maj. Stephen C. Talbot as a victim of "cannon fever," a term denoting a fear of battle. He considered the regiment's adjutant, 1st Lt. William B. Allyn, to be a capable man prone to putting on airs. Allyn grew inebriated on multiple occasions and gave unreasonable orders, although Merriam noted that the "drunken fool" finally redeemed himself through his conduct in battle. The sergeant major twice alluded to Capt. James Dean's drinking while praising the man's leadership abilities. Finally, Merriam complained of an unnamed captain whom he deemed unable to command his men's respect.[37]

FORGING SOLDIERS OUT OF CIVILIANS

Inadequate training hindered the transformation of the Vermonters into proficient fighting men. Lieutenant Lucia recalled that recruits had "no opportunity for drill and but little for discipline." Sources addressing this matter focused on the experiences of those officers and men readying for the front between February and April 1864. Harsh winter weather hindered their efforts, including snow that had accumulated some fourteen inches on the ground in early January and another snowfall of ten inches in twenty-four hours in March—a seasonal record for Burlington. The troops endured such frigid temperatures that a pair of soldiers even suffered frostbite. Although likely welcome, a midwinter thaw proceeded to cause drainage issues in the camp. Amid these conditions Cummings endured an ongoing head cold from late February to early March that must have impaired his performance. Yet for some time he labored night and day to distribute clothing and equipment, complete paperwork, recruit, and train the men. Boasting of his efforts, the lieutenant colonel related in March that "camp order . . . [was] gradually evolving from chaos." The greenhorns tried to spend four hours daily on drill in mid-March until the arrival of spring made regular practice possible, though the Vermonters only managed to train for about eighteen days between February and April. As Cummings grumbled, they required "ten days to do four days work in," a state of affairs partly attributable to the outfit's sluggish recruitment. Not only did the unit lack a full complement of officers but also many of them as well as detachments of soldiers were off recruiting and hence unavailable for drill. The lieutenant colonel admitted he struggled "to control all this motley crew," for he had "no major, no surgeon here, no quartermaster, nor no adjutant nor no nothing."[38]

The Mainers faced a comparable plight. As Merriam complained, "there was but little time for drilling the men." The weather impeded the training of the 31st. For example, an April blizzard lasted up to three days and piled snow nearly knee high. The soggy conditions of springtime added further to the men's discomfort. A private in the 32nd Maine, which readied for the front at the same time as the 31st in Augusta, wrote that his own comrades "were almost wholly ignorant of the proper execution of company and battalion movements, and knew only imperfectly even the manual of arms." Fortunately, the men in the 31st could benefit from instruction by the likes of Captain Dean. Citing the support of Adjutant General Hodsdon, Bangor resident Charles W. Roberts insisted that Dean was "unequalled as a drill officer." Available sources offer minimal insight into the readying of the last three companies except for the praise offered by a newspaper correspondent from the outfit. The soldiers filling one of the unassigned infantry companies, which entered service in late 1864, enjoyed what this participant termed "many encomiums from the brigade and regimental officers for . . . fine appearance . . . and their proficiency in drill."[39]

Disciplinary issues tarnished the reputation of the later arrivals, and chief among them was a tendency to desert. A total of 195 men fled the 17th Vermont, an 18 percent desertion rate. This slightly exceeded the 15 percent rate in the Union army between the commencement of the war and the start of recruitment for the regiment. In comparison, 114 men left the 31st Maine, or 10 percent of the whole. Thus, desertion was less widespread among these Mainers than the previous Federal norm. Both units suffered more extensively from this crime than was typical in a sample of 205 hard-fighting Federal regiments from 1861 to 1865, which only averaged an 8-percent desertion rate. Still, the detractors exaggerated their case when they castigated the later arrivals for an overwhelming willingness to flee. Both regiments' desertion ratios pale in comparison to the example of the antebellum U.S. Army, in which over 40 percent of troops fled the ranks between 1851 and 1861.[40]

Deserters from the 17th and 31st were predominantly rookies, immigrants, and substitutes. A desire to bolt after securing bounties probably drove many of these men to commit this crime. About three-fifths of the Vermont deserters left in July and August 1864, when town bonuses surged in value. Just over half of the men who deserted the 31st did so in October and November 1864 as the regiment's last two companies filled their ranks. By way of explanation, these most recent soldiers may have possessed even worse cohesion than those filling the first ten companies of the 31st. The connotations of service in an unassigned infantry company, which lacked the sense of identity shared by multiple companies in a single regiment, were hardly conducive to strong bonds between the men. Across both units, it appears that men from abroad, perhaps lacking substantial local ties, felt less compunction about escaping service after pocketing the bounty. Immigrants composed 82 percent of deserters from the 17th Vermont, far outweighing the roughly one-third of foreign-born men in the unit. This high ratio also equaled two and a half times that in the Union army sample. In a related trend, substitutes proved desertion prone and represented the bulk of culprits from the 17th. Just over three-fourths of substitutes ran away, and as a group composed 61 percent of the Vermont deserters. These statistics are unsurprising since men hailing from other countries made up 91 percent of the substitutes in the 17th, in contrast to about one-fourth of its volunteer members. To put this in context, a mere 14 percent of the Vermonters served as substitutes. The prevalence of foreign-born substitutes was not unusual, for Tyler Anbinder observes that "the North's substitutes . . . were disproportionately immigrants." The enlistment contracts available for the Mainers do not indicate which ones were substitutes, but it is notable that 42 percent of the 31st's deserters were foreign born. Although a less significant problem than among the Vermonters, this was still a disproportionately high desertion rate given the more modest 13 percent of the ranks comprising immigrants.[41]

Some of the men who absconded did so to bounty jump. For example, Pvt. John Andrew of the 17th ran away, shaved his whiskers, assumed a false name, and signed up in the 2nd Maryland Veteran Volunteer Infantry Regiment. Other wrongdoers from the Vermont unit included Pvt. Henry Cherry, who had previously fled the 16th Connecticut Volunteer Infantry Regiment, and Pvt. Peter A. Morgan, who subsequently joined the 1st Vermont Heavy Artillery Regiment. In the 31st Maine three privates escaped, only for the authorities to capture them in civilian attire. As a newspaper editor explained, these circumstances pointed to bounty jumping, for this kind of deserter wore "citizens clothing . . . under the army blue. . . . in order . . . to lose his government suit and, using the other as a substitute forget that he was a soldier."[42]

Many later arrivals may have left the ranks because they only wanted the cash for enlisting. Desertion of this type differed from bounty jumping because it was a one-time offense rather than a serial crime. Private Kennedy of the 17th Vermont was one such example, bolting shortly after enlisting, which suggests he joined solely for the money. Among the deserters from this regiment, more than half left before mustering in to service, and another 7 percent did so within a month of joining the unit. Just over three-fifths of the deserters from the 31st Maine did so in thirty days or less of their enlistments. Still, later arrivals keen to secure money in exchange for their service did not necessarily go on to desert. Among those Vermonters who commuted their state pay to receive the $125 lump sum, only 7 percent took off, which was much lower than the desertion rate across the 17th. Perhaps the fatalism that could have driven some of these men to commute their pay also left them resigned to staying in the ranks.[43]

Personal factors could also push men to flee. Pvt. Emory E. Young of the 31st Maine headed home before securing his bonus, while Pvt. Frank Wiser of the 17th Vermont ran away after signing up while drunk. Private Granger of the same unit—the fourteen-year-old who lied about his age— deserted after a couple weeks in the ranks. Despite the boy's desire to serve, his parents opposed the war effort and likely urged him to return home. They had tried to secure his release, for they had not approved or even been aware of his enlistment. And yet they were unsuccessful in seeking his discharge when he originally joined, perhaps because the mustering officer, Sergeant Howard, and several citizens encouraged Adjutant and Inspector General Washburn to keep the youngster in uniform.[44]

Even a veteran could desert, albeit by accident. When the 17th traveled through New York City on its way to the front in April 1864, Pvt. Joseph Coty received his captain's permission to explore the area. After several hours the Vermont soldier realized that the battalion had left, and he tried to catch up by taking a train to Baltimore. Injuring his ankle in a fall en route, he returned to his home in the state of New York with the intention of rejoining the outfit once his leg had healed. The experience of this veteran, who had been honorably discharged at the end of his previous enlistment, hardly aligned with the cliché of the unreliable greenhorn.[45]

Soldiers might choose to desert as a form of protest. When Pvt. Francis Nailor of the 17th suffered arrest for a charge of assault and battery predating his service, enlistments dried up and desertions surged in his unit. Once Nailor was freed, the opposite occurred. As Capt. Stephen F. Brown explained, "he was temperate and law-abiding, a fine type of American Manhood, a soldier who commanded the affectionate respect of his officers and comrades." According to Brown, Nailor's fellows lamented "that one who was patriotic and guiltless should be imprisoned by 'stay-at-homes,' who cared nothing for their country and less for its defenders."[46]

Even an injured sense of unit identity could push men to leave, for the consolidation of the 31st and 32nd Maine proved controversial. The newspaper correspondent for the 31st believed this process would "create some little jealousies and heartburnings, which will be speedily obliterated." Yet a private in the 32nd indicated that many of his fellow soldiers deserted because they felt "an extreme dissatisfaction with the new conditions, and a lack of identification with, and soldierly pride in, the new organization."[47]

For many who fled the ranks, however, the strain of life in uniform had proven too much to bear. After several months in the Vermont unit, Cummings argued, "a majority of both officers and men would like to . . . go home." He attributed this desire to the fact that loved ones with "well-meant anxiety" exhorted them "to get out of the service." Desperate to escape their military obligation, a total of four soldiers from the 17th Vermont and 31st Maine fired their weapons to wound themselves in the hopes of being discharged. The experience of Pvt. William Goldthwait of the 31st highlights the relationship between wartime trauma and desertion. This soldier straggled during a trek, owing to what he called "a ruptured side," and fell prisoner to the Confederates, whereupon he languished at the infamous prisoner-of-war camp at Andersonville until he was paroled. After going home on a thirty-day furlough, when it expired he remained there instead of returning to his outfit. Based on this case, some who abandoned their units may just have been unwilling to repeatedly face the risk of injury, death, or capture in the field. It would have surely taken Goldthwait more than a month's time to recuperate from the traumatic experience of Andersonville, especially given the likelihood that he contracted an illness while a prisoner there. Merriam shed more light on the motivations of deserters while reflecting on the Overland Campaign. He felt that intense combat and marching had whittled down the Mainers' number of "weak brethren and those troubled with 'cold feet' or 'cannon fever.'" Such a mindset could have informed the actions of the thirty-two Vermonters and sixteen Mainers who fled after spending time in hospitals. Manson of the 17th became a malingerer, bragging that "a man gets as much pay and praise to be loafing around the hospital as he does to be down at Petersberg." He confessed to his mother that he had acted as a man in misery to gain the surgeon's sympathy. Ashamed of his actions, he warned her against "let[ting] this letter be read out of the family as you know what a talk it would make." Manson implied that Cpl. Newton J. Howard of the 17th was of a similar ilk, explaining the latter was "sick enough of the war." Howard was originally "keen to have the boys enlist," but his enthusiasm faded after learning "how they used soldiers." Despite such gripes, few Vermont and no Maine deserters fled the ranks to join the enemy. Twelve percent of deserting Vermonters and 18 percent of deserting Mainers redeemed themselves by returning to their outfits. Such individual examples restore the humanity of the later arrivals, who fall victim all too often to dismissive stereotyping.[48]

Apart from desertion, these men committed other, less severe infractions. Major General Burnside's military secretary, Capt. Daniel Larned, the assistant adjutant general of the Ninth Corps, derided most of the new troops in the corps as "a crowd of roughs." Historian Lorien Foote defines such individuals as "those from the very bottom of the economic ladder whose manly identities seemed to be centered on violence and drink." And yet only a small number of officers and men in the 17th Vermont and 31st Maine were found guilty of intoxication. This was notable, given the practice of periodically distributing a whiskey ration during the Petersburg Campaign. As Merriam recollected, "whiskey was furnished to the men in the trenches by the pailful." Those inebriated included less than a dozen noncommissioned officers and soldiers in the 17th and one noncommissioned officer in the 31st. Given the lack of information on this subject in the roster and regimental books, it appears as though such behavior was far less prevalent among the Mainers, although anecdotal comments provide evidence to the contrary. Private Smith castigated the men of his company as "a graceless lot of drunkards with no ambition or self respect." In a comment with xenophobic undertones, Sergeant Major Merriam described the Irish-born fellows in his outfit as being "ready at all times for a drink of whiskey." Turning to more specific cases, Corporal Manson wrote of a man who had returned in an intoxicated state, which was unfortunate since he was "a good soldier where he cant get Whiskey," while Pvt. Henry W. Lancaster of the 31st once reported himself among a handful of drunk soldiers. Outbursts of fighting were also uncommon, with only four known episodes among the Vermonters. One of these clashes involved a private who verbally abused a soldier in the 31st and, with an officer's spurring, fought him. Conversely, little evidence indicates that the Mainers were extraordinarily pugnacious, despite Merriam's prejudicial insistence that the Irish Americans in his company were "always suffering for a fight and apparently indifferent as to whether it was among themselves or with the 'Johnnies.'"[49]

Egregious misconduct culminated in the tragic case of Vermont private James Sweeny. In mid-April 1864 Sweeny spent three days in the guardhouse as punishment for drinking and fighting with a comrade. During this time, he made several escape attempts in defiance of the sentry on duty, Pvt. Henry A. Luce. During the last breakout, Sweeny grabbed Luce's rifle musket, hit the guard in the head, and began to flee. The escapee ignored multiple commands to return, so with help from a nearby private, Luce managed to stab the fellow nine times with his bayonet, fatally wounding him. In Private Carter's succinct retelling, "the guards killed Sweeny tonight." By way of justification, Luce cited his orders to bayonet transgressors, while Capt. Andrew J. Davis, officer of the day, reiterated his own instructions "to keep those prisoners in there if they had to kill every devil of them." The captain judged "Sweeny . . . one of his worst men, quarrelsome, and in general giving much trouble," while Wagoner Emerson revealed his anti-immigrant bias by describing the fellow as "a dreadful mean quarrelsome Irishman."[50]

Instances of criminal behavior marred the reputation of the 17th Vermont. Nearly all these incidents occurred in the Green Mountain State. A few recruits, imprisoned in the guardhouse located in the original unit encampment at Burlington, set this structure ablaze. Two new enlisted men destroyed a window in the building that served as the officers' quarters there. Beyond the encampment, a pair of soldiers even confronted a deputy provost marshal in search of a deserter. As that officer reported, the assailants attacked him "in a brutal manner by knocking him down and then pounding him to their satisfaction." Securing reinforcements, he finally apprehended the two men following a second fight. Thievery of wide-ranging severity appears to have been another issue in the regiment, although there is little information available on that offense. Carter once blamed guards for swiping three towels in the Burlington camp. At Petersburg Colonel Randall reduced a sergeant to the ranks in hopes that this punishment would "prove sufficient . . . throughout the Regiment to correct a practice of petty theft." He then lectured his troops that they were "not expected to abandon their manhood, but . . . inspired by a calling so noble and chivalrous [were] . . . to cultivate . . . feelings of honor and propriety."[51]

Sheer exhaustion also led some Vermonters to disobey orders. On February 17, 1865, Pvt. Delinus L. Melvin relinquished his guard post to rest in a hospital. He defended his actions by saying that "his Army shoes were old and his feet were wet and cold, and he went to the stove to warm them." The soldier was worn out from having spent several nights sitting with his ill wife. That same month some half-dozen Vermonters failed to line up one morning, and Randall punished the culprits by assigning them to fatigue duty. One of the offenders, Pvt. William Moore, responded to this order with incendiary language and thus spent time in the guardhouse. To justify his conduct, the fellow decried a difficult schedule of fatigue duty one morning, then picket duty from that evening to the next, and fatigue duty again the following morning.[52]

Disorderly behavior among the Mainers could reflect the reluctance of civilians-turned-soldiers to accept authority. Before heading into the field, Merriam had to temporarily lead Company F in camp without the aid of any officers. As he admitted, the troops were "a pretty tough lot" who looked down upon him "as the only 'Country Jake' among the non-coms, and a schoolmaster." One evening an inebriated Irish-born soldier went to bed and started yelling. Since this was disruptive to the camp, Merriam ordered him to be silent, but the private declared that "he was not to be ordered around by any 'd——d schoolmaster.'" Merriam then commanded the recalcitrant fellow to leave his bed to no avail, leading him to seize the man by the collar and drag him to the guardhouse. This devolved into an argument and scuffle until 1st Lt. Byron C. Gilmore arrived and announced he would summon the guards, a warning that caused the difficult soldier to return to bed. Underscoring the transitory nature of this dispute, Merriam soon became friends with the Irish lads in the company.[53]

All told, only a small proportion of the New Englanders spent time absent without leave. Those guilty averaged a mere 5 percent out of the total manpower in both units between April 1864 and April 1865. Some individuals offered no explanation for their actions, yet the eclectic experiences of other transgressors justify a reappraisal of the assumption that the later arrivals lacked the will to serve. Other reasons included falling out of the line of march due to fatigue, overstaying furlough, visiting family members, recovering from ill health or a wound, or avoiding service after suffering as a Confederate prisoner of war.[54]

Few of the later arrivals received punishment for bad conduct. Over the year following April 1864, approximately 1 percent of Vermonters and Mainers suffered arrest. Reasons for their confinement included absence without leave and desertion. In an indication of lower-level leadership issues, twenty-eight Vermont and thirty-one Maine noncommissioned officers were reduced in rank due to problems that included drunkenness, disorderly conduct, desertion, absence without leave, and in one case abandoning one's post without leave. These figures amounted to 17 and 23 percent of the noncommissioned officers who served in the two regiments respectively.[55]

Behavior of this type, however, did not characterize most of the officers and men in these two units. Cummings noted that the Vermonters exhibited commendable discipline in their treatment of the Confederate population. On one occasion he railed against those Federals who laid waste to the possessions of southern civilians, insisting the bluecoats displayed "a fiendishness that would delight savages." Yet he absolved the Vermonters, writing to his wife that if he witnessed anything of this sort, "I would shoot them down as I would so many dogs." Echoing this supportive view of the 17th, a relieved Captain Yale observed of his company that merely "a half dozen or so . . . [were] fit subjects for the strictest military discipline." Sheahan differed by highlighting a transformation in the comportment of his troops in the 31st Maine, who originally disregarded his commands. This officer did not relent, explaining that he was "strict with [the troops] . . . and when I tell a man to do a thing it is done and no words back." By the time the whole regiment returned home, a state resident observed that its members were reasonably well behaved.[56]

Exploring the formation of the 17th Vermont and 31st Maine offers a reminder regarding the interpretative dangers of relying on the persuasively worded anecdote. It is all too easy for the historian to quote from the likes of Lieutenant General Grant or Provost Marshal General Fry to make the point that the later arrivals were substandard to the celebrated "Boys of '61." And yet a closer inspection of long-neglected units reveals that the period consensus concerning these new troops teemed with kneejerk generalizations and oversimplification. Creating fresh regiments in a timely manner proved difficult from mid-1863 onward, given the confusing nature of the Union recruiting system and the fixation on meeting local manpower quotas rather than filling regiments.

A comprehensive look at recruitment justifies rethinking the role of pecuniary motivation. When critics derided the later arrivals as self-interested, they ignored that prospective soldiers faced a figurative bombardment of newspaper advertisements and articles highlighting the remunerative aspects of service. It was unsurprising that working-class men, concerned about their income, chose to sign up in large numbers. Admittedly, early war soldiers looked more selfless than the later arrivals who received such large bonuses. Speaking in 1868, Washburn pointed out that the Green Mountain State enlistees of 1862 had "volunteered their services . . . with a very slight bounty in a few cases—a very large proportion with none." Two years later the Maine Commissioners in Equalization of War Debts referred to those men who had enlisted in 1861 and early 1862 as "brave and patriotic men who rallied unselfishly at the first call of the country for defenders, without bounty." This is surely an exaggeration, for William Marvel observes that "the recruiting frenzy of 1861 drained off those who were desperate enough to enlist for nothing more than monthly pay and family subsidies, and by the summer of 1862, bounties had to be paid in advance to coax enough recruits." In any event, the prospect of cash that attracted greedy and unreliable recruits also secured the large number of working-class men whose service made it possible to field the 17th Vermont and 31st Maine.[57]

Contrary to the period consensus, economically driven later arrivals could exhibit ideological impulses, too. The promoters of life in uniform insisted that signing up was a civic responsibility, and the writings of the officers and men who responded to such pleas offer evidence of their commitment to the war effort. In an 1877 Memorial Day speech, former brevet lieutenant colonel Knapp of the 17th declared that its soldiers had enlisted "as a matter of duty and patriotism" to protect "their homes and their loved ones." He movingly asserted

> that the man of sound mind who went forward cooly to sign the enlistment papers "for three years or during the war," . . . was consciously signing his own death warrant. Let no man insult us by intimating the possibility of a mercenary motive. . . . The proverbial recklessness of the soldier in the expenditure of his money to the last cent, is in itself conclusive evidence that it was no mercenary motive which prompted him. . . . Many did not enlist cooly, or soberly. Some may have been mercenary. But as a rule there must have been a higher and stronger motive than either of these.[58]

A sense of duty steeled the resolve of these New Englanders, for cash alone was not enough to keep them in uniform amid the rigors of campaigning and the dangers of the battlefield. About a year after war's end, former brevet major general Joshua L. Chamberlain, who had commanded the First Brigade, First Division, Fifth Corps, gave a speech during the dedication of a monument to the fallen in Gorham, Maine. Among those names etched on this Italian marble obelisk was that of Horatio Smith, a member of the 31st. As Chamberlain reminded his audience, "there are harder things to bear than battles," and he went on to list other challenges with which the rank and file had contended. These included "the wear and tear of a campaign; picket duty in [the] cold and wet . . . the hard march, in extremes of weather . . . the roadside bivouac . . . hunger and thirst . . . and . . . his heroic devotion and effective service unrewarded." As the general opined, "these are the things that try the soul." They were among the trials faced by those serving in the 17th and 31st Regiments.[59]

Finally, the later arrivals were better disciplined than their naysayers suggested. Examples of poor conduct indicated the men's difficulty in adapting to a soldier's life, but only desertion occurred in sufficient numbers to blemish their units' image. Still, a variety of reasons besides monetary inducements caused such men to sign up and then flee. Instead of focusing on these malefactors, perhaps it is more revelatory to center attention on the vastly greater number who stayed in the ranks amid the staggering losses of the Overland and Petersburg Campaigns. To sustain Grant's drive on the Confederate capital of Richmond, the Union needed to supply enough men who showed up to fight and carried themselves well. Reflecting on the recruitment of the later arrivals, the fact that so many of the Vermonters and Mainers met the mark was the real achievement.

2

THE BATTLES OF THE WILDERNESS AND
SPOTSYLVANIA COURT HOUSE

The Wilderness was a decisive battle only to the poor
fellows who died there or who went back to their homes
with crippled bodies to burden their future lives.

—Sgt. Maj. Leander Otis Merriam, 31st Maine

The battle of Spottsylvania was more
terrible than that of the Wilderness.

—Sgt. Amasa O. Gates, Sgt. Albert C. Raymond,
and Pvt. Daniel Watts, 17th Vermont

In the October 1884 issue of the widely read *Century Magazine,* Union Civil War veteran George F. Williams, brevet major of the 146th New York Volunteer Infantry Regiment, asserted, "all men are naturally afraid of death, but the trained and experienced soldier learns to keep down that fear, and nonchalantly do whatever is required of him." This begs the question: did the large proportion of greenhorns filling the ranks of the 17th Vermont and 31st Maine quickly develop into proficient combatants? Such rookies needed physical and mental stamina to endure the rigors of soldiering during the Overland Campaign, which involved multiple engagements in rapid succession. Major General Meade highlighted this challenge by admitting that it was "hardly natural to expect men to maintain without limit the exhaustion of such a protracted struggle." The later arrivals could only contribute to Federal victory during this stage of the war by proving their steadiness under fire and ability to fight well over four battles in roughly six weeks. The combat performance of the officers and men of these two New England outfits in the Battles of the Wilderness

(May 5–6) and Spotsylvania Court House (May 8–21), the first two clashes of the Overland Campaign in the spring of 1864, provided the initial indications of whether they would meet the mark.[1]

But any small-unit analysis should not be conflated with an assessment of the entire Ninth Corps. Major General Burnside commanded this force, which on May 5, 1864, numbered forty infantry regiments, four cavalry regiments, one dismounted cavalry regiment, two heavy artillery regiments, and fourteen artillery batteries. Marshaling these troops to achieve success on the battlefield was the responsibility of Burnside and his subordinate commanders at both the division and brigade levels. Addressing the contrast between the realm of leadership and that of the common soldier, Sergeant Major Merriam distinguished between "two battles of the wilderness." Besides "the great historical battle" that the high command managed, he also referred to the "little part of the great fight that I myself saw," that is, the experience of the rank and file at the regimental level.[2]

Scrutinizing the operational history of the 17th Vermont and the 31st Maine makes it possible to assess their combat performance by taking a close look at their cohesion, achievement of military objectives, and casualty rates. Examining battles from the bottom up reveals many silences in the historical record since there is not always a clear explanation for why soldiers behaved a certain way or even what they did during a particular stage of the fighting. The swift pace of engagements during the campaign afforded the participants little time to record their thoughts on what transpired, requiring the historian to occasionally make reasoned inferences to compensate for the scattered nature of the evidence.[3]

Telling the story of the later arrivals underscores the role of contingency in combat. There was no way for these men to know whether they were capable of defeating veteran graybacks, or even what their experience under fire would be like. Merriam observed that the new troops plunged into battle unaware of where they were headed, quipping that they "might as well be blindfolded." In a similar vein, an unnamed member of the 17th Vermont, believed to be Lieutenant Colonel Cummings, spoke to the limited purview of those lower-ranking officers and men who made up the Union army. He wrote: "[They] are not presumed to know anything beyond orders, tactics and regulations. . . . It is not our business to know, nor is it our privilege under military etiquette, to even inquire. It is our duty to obey." Such comments underscore that the soldiers moved, sought cover, and braved enemy fire without the benefit of hindsight. A hope for success in combat, not certainty about the outcome, propelled them to risk life and limb on one battlefield after another. The fact that so many rookies made the ultimate sacrifice underscores the tragic cost of Union victory.[4]

The New Englanders ultimately fought well enough to help maintain a high Federal operational tempo during the first half of the campaign. Initially, these combatants left home to spend a short time in camp, then endured a grueling, two-week stint of marches, headlong assaults, firefights, and trench warfare. Twice the officers and men in both battalions demonstrated their cohesion by staying in the fight longer than the veteran regiments in their brigade, which chose to fall back. This was notable since minimal field preparation left these new soldiers at a disadvantage to seasoned troops in terms of their physical fitness, mental conditioning, and tactical mastery. Evaluating the Union and Confederate forces before the Overland Campaign, Merriam insisted that a large proportion of Rebel "companies [were] more than a match for the best green regiment" clad in Union blue. This interpretation validates commonsense assumptions about the superiority of tried combatants to novices. Closer analysis is necessary, however, to determine how these raw troops carried themselves under fire overall. Fortunately for the Union cause, the Vermonters and Mainers emerged from their first combat experiences with a generally favorable record.[5]

GREENHORNS ON THE WAY

APRIL 18–MAY 5, 1864

The later arrivals endured an intense introduction to field service. On April 18, 1864, Lieutenant Colonels Cummings and Hight led the 17th Vermont and 31st Maine respectively on four-day journeys from their home states by foot, train, and steamboat to reach Alexandria, Virginia. Despite stretches of free time to eat meals and relax, this trip was lengthy, which meant the men did not enjoy a full night's sleep until they arrived at their destination. Attesting to the hectic preparation of the troops for battle, their training was limited to short periods over the next few days. Cummings fittingly lamented the hours he spent "supplying spare parts of arms, organizing our quartermaster and commissary departments . . . getting necessary blanks . . . [and] turning over all surplus baggage."[6]

For these Union soldiers, the leadership structure of the Ninth Corps was a double-edged sword. While in Alexandria, the New Englanders joined the Second Brigade, Second Division. This gave them the benefit of seasoned officers in the form of Colonel Griffin, leading their brigade, and Brigadier General Potter, in command of their division. Auguring well for the fighting ahead, Griffin was on good terms with both Potter and Burnside. And yet the Army of the Potomac had an awkward command arrangement with the Ninth Corps, which in Burnside's estimation "acted as a separate army." He was senior to Meade thanks to his commission date and thus took orders directly from Grant instead. Since Meade could not directly command Burnside, the Army of the Potomac commander was unable to easily coordinate the movements of the Ninth Corps with those of his own three infantry corps. This promised to slow the rapid communications necessary for success on the battlefield.[7]

The trip to Alexandria likely fatigued the rank and file, whose mood combined anxiety with optimism. Merriam noted the sight of "invalid soldiers from the hospitals with which the city was crowded, just able to walk with the help of cane or crutch, [and] soldiers with empty sleeves or single legs horribly suggestive to the new recruits." Second Lt. Charles W. Randall of the 17th Vermont differed in outlook by insisting on the confidence of the troops, especially among the rookies who planned on "killing rebels by the dozen." The later arrivals also held varying opinions about those in charge. The Vermonters, and especially those veteran officers and men who had served under Colonel Randall in the 13th Vermont Volunteer Infantry Regiment, wished for his leadership rather than that of Cummings. Conversely, one visitor to the battalion's camp judged that the lieutenant colonel possessed true martial bearing and would win the approval of his fellow Vermonters once they witnessed his conduct in the field. Private Lancaster may have reflected the views of at least some Mainers when he similarly lauded the noncommissioned officers best known to him.[8]

The later arrivals were right to be concerned because Grant had an aggressive campaign vision that would demand heavy sacrifices from the Federal rank and file. He expected the Army of the Potomac to traverse the Rapidan River, flank left around the Army of Northern Virginia through the dense forest known as the Wilderness, and engage it in battle between Culpeper and the Rebel capital. This was to avoid confronting the graybacks while they enjoyed the protection of fieldworks and the defensive

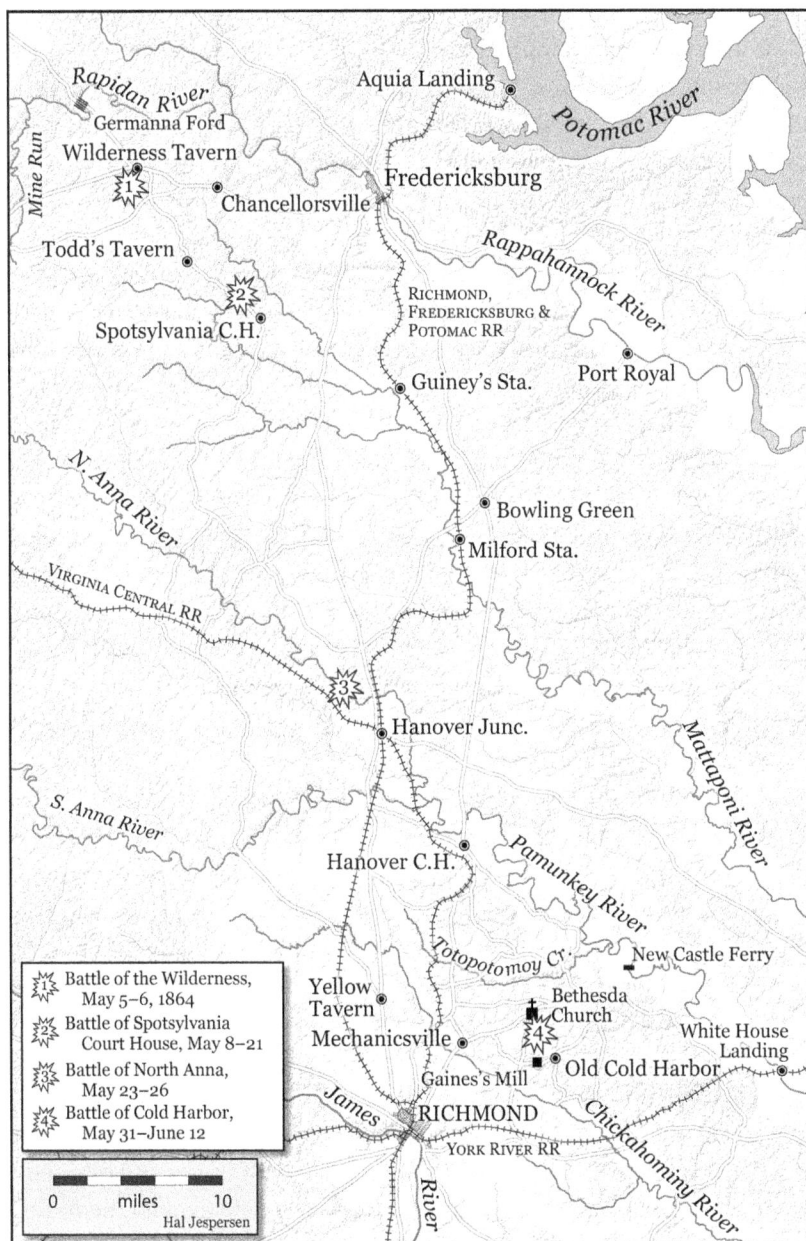

Rapidan River

Germanna Ford

Wilderness Tavern

Mine Run

1

Todd's Tavern

Chancellorsville

2

Spotsylvania C.H.

Aquia Landing

Fredericksburg

Potomac River

Rappahannock River

RICHMOND,
FREDERICKSBURG &
POTOMAC RR

Guiney's Sta.

Port Royal

Bowling Green

Milford Sta.

N. Anna River

VIRGINIA CENTRAL RR

3

Hanover Junc.

S. Anna River

Hanover C.H.

Pamunkey River

Mattaponi River

Totopotomoy Cr.

New Castle Ferry

Yellow
Tavern

Mechanicsville

Bethesda
Church

4

White House
Landing

Gaines's Mill

Old Cold Harbor

James

RICHMOND

YORK RIVER RR

Chickahominy River

River

Battle of the Wilderness,
1   May 5–6, 1864

Battle of Spotsylvania
2   Court House, May 8–21

Battle of North Anna,
3   May 23–26

Battle of Cold Harbor,
4   May 31–June 12

0   miles   10

Hal Jespersen

Battles of the Overland Campaign involving the
17th Vermont and 31st Maine, May–June 1864.

advantages of the locality, including the Wilderness itself, the Blue Ridge Mountains, the hilly terrain around Gordonsville, and the waters of the Rapidan and Mine Run. The goal was to either force the Confederates into retreat or greatly reduce their numbers in battle so that Lee could not divide his force, leaving some to defend Richmond while others pushed north. Grant only planned on seizing the heavily fortified capital city once he had inflicted a total defeat on Lee's army.[9]

On April 27 the Vermonters and Mainers began the first of two strenuous treks. Leaving Alexandria, they made a forced march of some forty-two miles to reach Bristow Station, a stop on the Orange and Alexandria Railroad, by the following day. In an encouraging sign for the campaign, a soldier in the 11th New Hampshire believed the enthusiasm of the Ninth Corps was at a peak, with the rank and file convinced of victory. Although the rookies pushed onward for the sake of their home states' reputations, Cummings rightly observed in a published letter that this "was a long march for new troops under a warm sun and in dusty roads." With inconsistent rations and infrequent breaks, these soldiers unsurprisingly grew critical of their officers as knapsack straps dug into flesh and shoulders grew sore from carrying burdens. The men nearly dropped their weapons when their limbs began to fail them, which led to straggling among those who developed foot blisters and others who were unable to maintain the pace. The worn-out New Englanders reached their destination in the middle of the night. Despite being only a private, Smith related that he had "to drive the tired boys back into the ranks when they fell out from exhaustion," while Corporal Whitehill complained that his brethren were "as tird a set of men as [there] ever was."[10]

The movement revealed tensions between the greenhorns and the seasoned men in Griffin's command. Given a lack of conditioning, the raw outfits had difficulty keeping up with the experienced ones. The veterans intentionally hurried forward in hopes that the rookies would lag behind to be mocked by their grizzled comrades upon arrival in camp at night. One brigade member further harped on the ignorance of tactics and discipline among the green soldiers. This unawareness may help explain the hazing by the old-timers. According to a soldier in the 32nd Maine, "the veterans questioned somewhat indignantly whether these new troops . . . deserved to stand side by side with them."[11]

From April 29 to May 3, the later arrivals had an opportunity to recuperate. The Ninth Corps assumed position to defend a section of the Orange and Alexandria Railroad stretching between Bull Run and the Rappahannock River. They relieved troops from the Army of the Potomac that Grant then assigned to secure a ford across the Rapidan, at which point Burnside's men would march toward the Wilderness. The Vermonters and Mainers contributed to the protection of this railway at Bristow Station, where danger lurked beyond the confines of their camp. Confederate cavalry and guerrillas roamed the countryside, the latter not keen to take prisoners. The New Englanders made the most of this generally stationary assignment by training, which included honing their marksmanship. Private Carter found the instruction tiresome, however, writing on April 29 of being "ordered to attention and then to rest then to attention again and so on all day."[12]

Straggling and disease had taken a toll on the later arrivals. Twenty-three percent of the 584 officers and men in the 17th Vermont were either absent without leave or sick as of April 30. Due to a lack of morning reports, there is no equivalent data available for the 31st Maine. But soldiers in Federal regiments created in 1864 were less susceptible to fatal illnesses than their predecessors. Still, newspaper coverage of other units from the Pine Tree State highlighted the prevalence of malady among the rookies. After all, they had just embarked on life in the field, and most had previously led a bucolic existence in small Vermont and Maine towns with average populations of about 1,300 and 1,500, respectively. Historian Joseph T. Glatthaar points out that inexperienced men from relatively unpopulated states would have had immune systems unprepared for marching and camping alongside thousands of comrades. Sickness was apt to spread among such individuals and would remain a long-term issue. Across the Union army throughout the war, most victims of illness succumbed between their third and sixth month of service. The related mortality rate decreased only slowly afterward.[13]

On May 4 the New Englanders began a trek of some forty-two miles to reach the Wilderness. They awakened at 4:00 a.m. and stepped off later that morning, finally bivouacking near Spotswood House after nearly thirty-four hours on the road. Pursuant to Grant's order, this involved a forced march. The effort exhausted the men, who endured dusty roads, high temperatures, inadequate water and food, and the threat of bushwhackers, who captured or killed stragglers. As a precaution Burnside ordered that the soldiers not leave their formations without the permission of their commanding officers. Roughly one-quarter of the Vermonters nevertheless collapsed en route, and Merriam acknowledged that the marching since April 27 "had broken down quite a number of . . . green men" in the 31st Maine. He cited the difficulty of maintaining "that steady, monotonous tramp, hour after hour . . . for the boys in the ranks, who carried the rifle and ammunition." Easing the strain somewhat during this second leg, the troops enjoyed periodic five-minute pauses and longer breaks of two to three hours each day. They remained keen to fight during their advance on May 5, when the Army of the Potomac unexpectedly engaged the enemy in the Wilderness. Explaining this turn of events, Grant and Meade decided to halt the rest of the army while the Ninth Corps caught up. They wrongly assumed Lee would contest the Federals along Mine Run, yet he actually opted to confront them in the forest. The emanating roar of artillery and rifle musket fire told the later arrivals that heavy combat was underway. So motivated, they completed a one-hour stretch late that same day at nearly the double-quick, roughly 165 paces per minute. One 11th New Hampshire soldier believed this to be the most difficult movement that the brigade conducted during the entire war. In fact, Grant termed the effort "a remarkable march," particularly since the corps included so many rookies unused to wearing military equipment or such strenuous travel.[14]

The journey from home state to battlefield left the later arrivals depleted for the test awaiting them at daybreak on May 6. Straggling on the two forced marches was not a matter of disobedience, but rather one of soldiers whose bodies could not bear such trying conditions. For example, Pvt. George Hill of the 17th Vermont had outpaced his fellows during the trek to Bristow Station. He took a break for coffee and waited until the battalion passed by, then sought to catch up. Hill proceeded to rest for an hour due to sheer fatigue, a sojourn that left him unable to join his comrades for several days. This scenario speaks to the way that exhaustion could reduce the manpower of these two New England units even before they faced the enemy for the first time. When the troops fell asleep near the Rappahannock around 10:30 p.m. on May 5, they had only a few hours to regain their strength before heading into the fray. During that night, fighting continued elsewhere on the battlefield, which caused the later arrivals to doze lightly and with their weapons at their sides. The possibility of additional movement orders or a Confederate attack occupied the thoughts of these Federals, who were already suffering from weakening morale. They had seen wounded bluecoats along their route to the Wilderness, and now the cries of fallen Union combatants mingled with the crack of rifle muskets overnight. Some of the veterans were understandably fatalistic, moving one corporal in the 9th New Hampshire to describe a shared conviction that this was "in all probability . . . [their] last night" alive.[15]

BAPTISM BY FIRE

MAY 6, 1864

Fighting at the Wilderness on May 6 would test the Vermonters and Mainers. They had an important role to play, for Union victory depended substantially on the prompt and sustained involvement of the Ninth Corps. This influx of unbloodied Federals was a boon to Grant as he prepared for the second day of the battle against Lee's Army of Northern Virginia. According to his orders, Burnside's men were to fill the gap between the Second and Fifth Corps, situated on the Orange Turnpike and Orange Plank Road respectively. The Ninth Corps would then take part in an offensive movement in concert with the Army of the Potomac. The lieutenant general's plan stipulated that Burnside's troops push through an opening in the Rebel center to hold the attention of the graybacks. This would reduce the manpower that Lee could direct against the Second Corps. The objective of the Ninth Corps was to capture the enemy defenses atop the uneven high ground of the Chewning Farm, then to attack the rear and left flank of the Confederate right wing at Parker's Store. Such an undertaking was especially arduous for the novice later arrivals since they would not benefit from fighting alongside the entire Ninth Corps. Burnside only commanded his Second and Third Divisions on the field that day, the rest of his soldiers temporarily serving in other corps or holding terrain near the Rapidan.[16]

Unfortunately, the Union leadership doubted the promptitude of the Ninth Corps. Grant originally instructed Burnside to commence his advance at 4:30 a.m., but the other corps commanders and Maj. James C. Duane, chief engineer of the Army of the Potomac, predicted that Burnside would not even awaken until that time. Meade proposed that Grant delay the offensive until 6:00 a.m., and the latter compromised by selecting a start time of 5:00 a.m., lest the Rebels attack first. Subsequent events would bear out the reasoning behind Meade's suggestion. Rather than informing Grant of Burnside's expected tardiness, the army commander drew attention to the difficulty of leading exhausted soldiers in the dark through the undergrowth.[17]

Indeed, problematic terrain and adverse weather promised to impede the progress of the later arrivals. They would have to navigate meandering, narrow, and dusty roads that cut across a heavy forest. As a 32nd Maine soldier described, this was "a thick growth of stunted pines, dwarf oaks and underbrush, so dense as to be in many places almost impenetrable." A mere handful of small clearings broke up the wooded landscape, which was filled with marshy areas, hills, ravines, and rocks. Only limited numbers of troops could traverse this ground at a time, hence the postwar observation of Bvt. Brig. Gen. Adam Badeau, who had served as Grant's military secretary in 1864–65, that a "superiority in numbers was an impediment rather than an advantage." Vegetation blocked out the little sunlight available from an overcast sky, reducing visibility to between fifteen and three hundred feet. Officers would struggle to see and ultimately lead their units, while high temperatures and humidity would further tax the soldiers' endurance.[18]

The New Englanders appeared unlikely to perform well that day, owing to the uncertain quality of their leadership, lack of training, and depleted manpower. While Cummings had yet to establish his reputation under fire with his troops, recently promoted Colonel Hight had served as a regular-army officer. And yet this Mainer's predilection for drink had the potential to adversely affect his conduct. The 17th Vermont was not well prepared for the field, as some of its members testified, something probably true also of the 31st Maine given how little time had passed since the creation of both units. Cummings insisted that his soldiers needed six weeks of drill to be effective in combat, an unnamed member of the unit expressed similar concerns, and First Lieutenant Lucia noted that the companies only conducted battalion drill for the third time after reaching the Wilderness. The sources make no mention of Mainers completing such training. Determining the exact number of officers and men in each New England battalion is impossible due to the lack of consolidated morning reports for the days leading up to and including the battle. Nevertheless, it appears that the later arrivals did not enter their first fight with the entirety of their companies. Among the Vermonters, 444 officers and men were present for duty

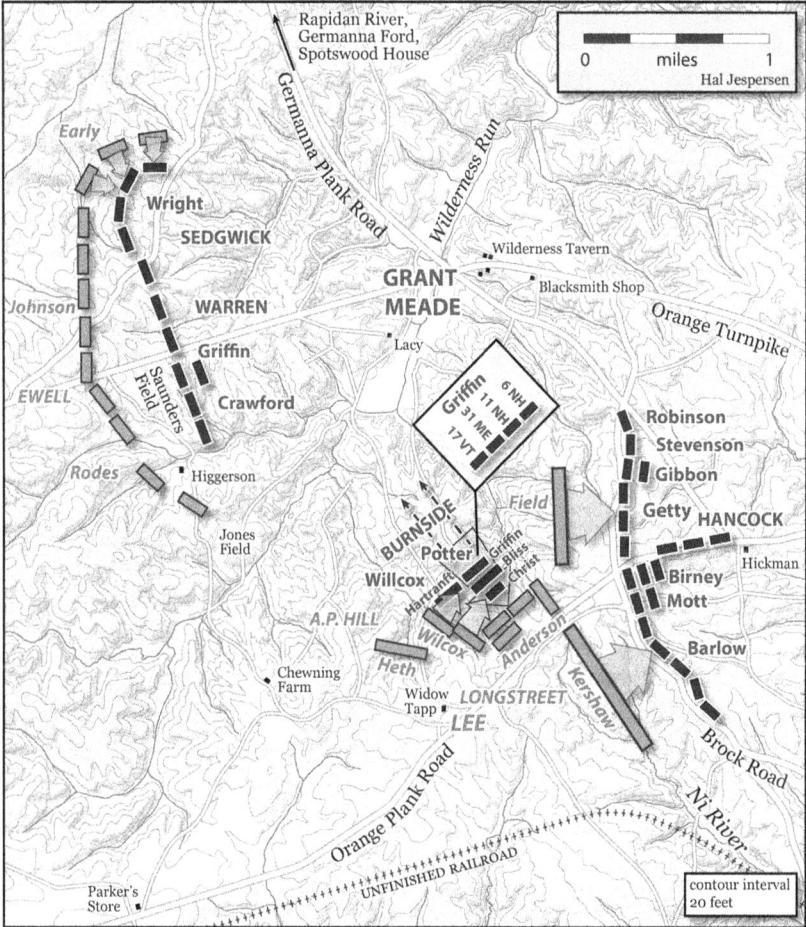

Battle of the Wilderness, May 6, 1864.

on April 30, although Davis provided a smaller headcount of 313 on May 6. Roughly one-quarter of the total were thus absent without leave or sick, reflecting the men's depleted condition from their previous travels as well as the spread of diseases such as mumps and measles. As for the Mainers, the morning reports available for three out of the nine companies reveal an average present-for-duty figure of 68 percent, with sickness accounting for the bulk of those unable to fight. Applying this ratio to the total of 939 Mainers suggests a present-for-duty strength of approximately 638 troops. This may be a conservative estimate, given that a sergeant in the 31st Maine wrote vaguely of 884 officers and men "at the opening of the campaign." Such manpower reductions were not unique to the 17th and 31st, for the proportion of Burnside's entire command present for duty likewise shrank by at least 25 percent after the forced march of May 4–5. Telling was the postwar observation of Capt. of Ordnance Morris Schaff, an acting aide-de-camp to Fifth Corps commander Maj. Gen. Gouverneur K. Warren. Schaff recalled that Burnside's troops "were nearly marched to death . . . and . . . altogether too fagged out" to fight on the sixth.[19]

May 6 did not begin auspiciously for the later arrivals, who failed to reach their destination on time. Awakening shortly after 12:00 a.m., they started moving roughly two hours later per Grant's instructions. The exhausted officers and men were hardly in shape for a brisk trek, having slept for a mere hour and a half, with only a few having a chance to drink their morning coffee. Along with the rest of Griffin's men, they formed the vanguard of the Second Division, which in turn led the advance of the Ninth Corps onto the battlefield. Leaving Spotswood House near the Rapidan River, they headed south on the Germanna Plank Road to reach Wilderness Tavern and from there took the road leading to Parker's Store. The brigade formed a line of battle around 5:00 a.m. just south of the Orange Turnpike–Parker's Store Road intersection. The Vermonters held the right flank of the front line, with the Mainers to their left. But the New Englanders had yet to arrive at the jump-off point for their attack, an area less than three-quarters of a mile to the south between the Germanna Plank Road and the Parker's Store Road.[20]

Even under these circumstances, the New Englanders moved with commendable speed. They achieved a pace of 2 miles per hour, compared with their rate of 2.24 miles per hour during the most recent forced march. Both efforts were impressive, given the example that Maj. Gen. Thomas "Stonewall" Jackson set with his Confederate infantry, famous for their rapid movements. Jackson had expected a marching speed of about two miles per hour from his "foot cavalry" in the Valley District in the Department of Northern Virginia. Nevertheless, several factors explain why these Union soldiers did not promptly arrive at their attack position or advance sufficiently to confront the Rebels at the Chewning Farm until 9:00 a.m. Grant had not ordered the Ninth Corps advance to start before that of the Army of the Potomac, an oversight on his part, given that Griffin's men faced a twelve-mile journey to the front line. In contrast, the army had engaged the enemy on the day prior and thus did not have far to travel. Straggling was also likely an issue for these exhausted greenhorns, who lacked the physical endurance of seasoned troops. Although the brigade had instructions to march quietly in close order, suggesting a disciplined movement, some Vermonters and Mainers probably counted among the many worn-out Ninth Corps rookies lingering in the Union rear. Exacerbating the delay, an 11th New Hampshire soldier bemoaned that the men stumbled over "loose stones, broken planks . . . wash-outs and gullies" without the aid of moonlight. They further delayed their progress by stopping for breakfast, then wended their way through artillery and infantry from the Sixth and Ninth Corps on the Germanna Plank Road. The blue-clad lines became tangled upon reaching the wooded area near the Parker's Store Road, hence Captain Schaff's description of the terrain as "very difficult to form on speedily." These soldiers may have even slowed as they approached the fighting. The roar of combat, plus the sight of ambulances and wounded Federals, justified Sergeant Major Merriam's assertion that the New Englanders knew themselves to be "marching straight to the death of some . . . and to the mangling of many more."[21]

The later arrivals exhibited soldierly determination in their first encounter with the enemy. During the advance of the brigade, the graybacks repulsed its skirmishers. This may have shaken the confidence of the New Englanders, who subsequently received a bombardment of Confederate case, solid shot, and shell. Merriam hinted at the frightening nature of this experience for the raw men, likening the explosion of an overhead shell to "a keg of nails flying through the air" and noting his own apprehension about dying from the fire of an unseen enemy. The Federals entered Jones Field to the right of the Parker's Store Road, then pushed south to the forested edge of the Chewning Farm and arrayed themselves into a line of battle. Just under four hundred yards away, a large body of Rebel skirmishers and a battery stood atop the tree-dotted high ground of the property. Withstanding the enemy rifle musket fire, the later arrivals pushed through the nigh-impenetrable thicket of trees and brush, which reduced their visibility to a few feet. The Vermonters crawled on their hands and knees for some fifty yards, then expelled a group of Confederates from behind a rail fence bordering the clearing. Meanwhile the Mainers, who nearly broke formation while negotiating this foliage, took up a position alongside their comrades.[22]

Command decisions now drove this assault to a standstill. Lieutenant General Grant ordered Maj. Gen. Winfield Scott Hancock, in charge of the Second Corps, and Burnside to attack along their respective fronts. And yet the Ninth Corps commander decided that his men should not attempt the capture of the Chewning Farm. He made this determination after mulling over the subject with Major General Parke, his chief of staff; Lt. Col. Cyrus B. Comstock, Grant's aide-de-camp; and Maj. Washington A. Roebling, Fifth Corps commander Warren's aide-de-camp, all of whom concurred with him, given the impracticality of assaulting the graybacks defending this high terrain. In the pithy words of journalist William Swinton, "an attack on this position was not thought advisable."[23]

The stalemate was psychologically trying for the rank and file. For several hours, the men braved artillery and sharpshooter fire from Confederates who presented few targets amid the thick foliage hindering the Federals' visibility. In response, the later arrivals could only shoot in a scattered and ineffectual manner, which inspired Merriam's complaint, "one of the hardest places to put a soldier in, and especially a raw soldier . . . [was] to keep him in waiting and doing nothing under fire." Likewise, Private Smith wrote that there was "no opportunity to defend ourselves—forced to lie on our faces and be shot at." In the opinion of Sgt. Amasa O. Gates, Sgt. Albert C. Raymond, and Pvt. Daniel Watts of the 17th, they "could accomplish but little." Still, the Vermonters enjoyed the protection of the captured rail fence, while the 31st drew shelter from the surrounding trees. The men of both units lay prone at the base of the hill, shielding them from most of the Rebel missiles, which sailed overhead. Ultimately, the 17th sustained fewer than two dozen officers and men killed or wounded, while the Mainers tallied only a few casualties. The later arrivals had successfully used the environment to their advantage, as in the manner of veterans. An anecdote suggests how quickly their grasp of tactics improved, for Merriam abandoned his reluctance to be the first Mainer seeking cover behind a tree once he witnessed several other officers doing so. For the Vermonters, however, fighting in this area put them under greater strain when the brigade began leaving the area around midday. Now isolated, these troops defeated enemy assaults on each flank, despite the wounding of one of their leaders, Captain Brown.[24]

Owing to Burnside's decision to hold ground at the Chewning Farm for hours, the New Englanders would be slow to reach their next position. At

11:45 a.m. Brig. Gen. John A. Rawlins, Grant's chief of staff, exhorted Burnside to "push in with all vigor," adding, "Hancock has been expecting you for the last three hours, and has been making his attack and dispositions with a view to your assistance." The Ninth Corps commander had to shift Griffin's men leftward a mile toward the right flank of the Second Corps, close to the Orange Plank Road, to push the graybacks away from Hancock's frontage. The later arrivals did not get to this location until 1:00 p.m., so they were not present to aid the Second Corps in repelling a noontime Rebel onslaught. Burnside defended his lack of progress at the Chewning Farm that morning by claiming that he received Grant's relocation order "just as preparations were being made to charge the enemy and drive them from the woods." Potter concurred with his superior, adding that "the action had become quite brisk." And yet there was no indication of an impending Federal assault at the Chewning position during the morning hours.[25]

The 17th Vermont and 31st Maine negotiated a challenging environment on the way to their destination. Traveling about one mile per hour, the soldiers achieved a laudable pace, given Burnside's complaint that the "dense and almost impenetrable undergrowth caused considerable confusion, irregularity, and delay." Potter led his men by compass through an area without roads, having received orders to assault any nearby graybacks. As the Second Division commander admitted, the heat and humidity caused his troops to grow "exhausted and disorganized." A forest fire exacerbated these conditions, probably caused by burning gunpowder coming into contact with dry vegetation. The onrushing flames obliged the Federals to keep shifting leftward. Not only did the wildfire's smoke make it difficult to see and breathe, but a captain in the 11th New Hampshire recalled that "the air was sickening with the effluvia arising from the burning of dead bodies." Merriam added that passing through charred areas exposed these novice soldiers to "the cries and groans of wounded men who could not be saved." Burnside seemingly downplayed the urgency of moving his troops by leisurely dining en route, but the misery of the rank and file was more responsible for slowing their rate of advance.[26]

Soon after arriving on site, the later arrivals confronted a spectacle of terror and confusion. They briefly rested under the shade of trees, then formed a line of battle along the north side of the Orange Plank Road. A more heavily forested area lay ahead, blocking from view the Confederate infantry and artillery holding entrenchments across a marshy ravine. For the first time, the rookie New Englanders bore witness to the bloodshed of close-range fighting. A large number of Federals stood before them, engaging the Rebels in a contest of increasing intensity. Casualties dotted the ground, with wounded men attempting to drag themselves beyond the reach of enemy rifle muskets and Union troops using stretchers to extract—and occasionally drop—the injured. Although Griffin's men avoided incoming rounds by lying prone, such an agonizing spectacle was not apt to embolden the greenhorns. During the early afternoon, they watched as the Federals ahead suddenly retreated in chaos toward them, which inspired Merriam to recall, "it seemed almost as if the earth and sky were coming together." Some of the Mainers, plus soldiers from the 6th New Hampshire and likely a number of Vermonters, began falling back as well until stopped by their officers and more disciplined comrades.[27]

The new men soon demonstrated their courage by launching an assault. First, Confederate infantry rushed out of the tree line in front of them, supported by Rebel artillery shell and shot. In response, Griffin's troops commenced an attack with a yell. Their commander proudly related that the troops were "well aligned in order of battle, advancing with a steady step and colors flying." He credited the later arrivals with contributing to his brigade's "imposing appearance . . . being fresh from their states, with well filled ranks and bright new uniforms and colors." The Vermonters held the right flank, with the Mainers probably in reserve behind the front line. An enemy volley caused the Vermonters to briefly hesitate before working their way through the prone troops of Potter's First Brigade, Second Division and the First Brigade, Third Division. Griffin's men then unleashed a point-blank volley upon the Confederates, engaged in a short firefight, and drove them back. These Federals continued to shoot while pushing toward the Rebels. As an 11th New Hampshire soldier explained, this left them vulnerable to "bullets raining upon the men like hailstones." Yet they pressed on, crossing the ravine to capture the enemy entrenchments and 199 prisoners around 2:00 p.m. For their part, the Vermonters sustained the wounding of Capt. Frank Kenfield but managed to lay claim to a rifle pit and a large proportion of the enemy prisoners. Some of the brigade continued onward to capture part of the second Rebel line, although the later arrivals do not appear to have advanced that far. Witnessing this successful attack, the troops of both Ninth Corps brigades in the rear became inspired to bolt forward, cheering wildly as they joined the advance.[28]

This drive, however, would grind to a halt after roughly a half mile. The smoke of the ongoing wildfire wafted among the dense trees, forcing the combatants to rely on their hearing to determine how the struggle was evolving along their flanks. Colonel Griffin could not effectively lead his men in such conditions, as it proved impossible to maintain command and control over the onrushing Union troops. The 31st Maine now pushed into the front line between the 11th New Hampshire to its left and the 17th Vermont to its right. In Brigadier General Potter's words the soldiers "advanced without sufficient concert of action." His own First Brigade and the First Brigade of the Third Division exacerbated this chaos by intermingling with the Second Brigade of his division in their front. The forward progress of the Federals stopped as they engaged the graybacks in a brief and increasingly bitter exchange of rifle musket fire. Few officers were visible, although the presence of the experienced ones appeared to have steeled the resolve of some greenhorns. As Merriam recalled, Maj. Daniel White of the 31st, a veteran, led a handful of soldiers with the colors while seeking "to rally the line around him as cooly as [if] on parade." Potter and Griffin subsequently praised the major for this display of leadership.[29]

Due to the actions of seasoned troops, the Union attack devolved into a rout that marked the beginning of the end of this battle for the later arrivals. A little before 2:25 p.m., the graybacks counterattacked the brigade, whose members found themselves within an angle of the Confederate position. Drawing on reserves, the Rebels struck the formation head on and along its exposed left flank while also swarming around the right flank and rear. The officers of the 6th New Hampshire, which held the left end of the line, found their unit separated from the rest of the Union troops. Judging the position untenable due to the mounting enemy response, they withdrew the regiment. The 11th New Hampshire, which was also isolated from the other Federals, did the same. After the cheering graybacks fired a volley at the Mainers, White sounded the retreat, and the Vermonters followed suit. Complicating Griffin's struggle to command, enemy artillery projectiles struck down his horse and those of acting aides-de-camp who served as his messengers. A Third Division officer captured the situation's severity by writing of soldiers who "broke and fled to the rear in disorder," while Merriam alluded to "a promiscuous crowd of fugitives . . . running as fast as their legs could carry them." One soldier in the 11th New Hampshire regarded the flight as a necessity, however, for otherwise "hardly a man could have escaped." Most of the later arrivals who became prisoners that day were captured at this time. When the Vermonters pulled back, Cummings fell wounded and Maj. William B. Reynolds, a veteran, assumed command, ordering the battalion's survivors into partial cover. The 17th unfortunately endured the wounding of two other officers during the fighting. Potter attempted to halt the streaming of Griffin's men to the rear, but by roughly 2:45 p.m., they had withdrawn to the Union starting position. As the Vermonters and Mainers were not directly engaged any further that afternoon, they went on to support other elements of the Second and Third Divisions in a fierce but indecisive exchange until 6:00 p.m. Finally, the later arrivals entrenched and slept that evening among the trees, with their weapons at hand in case of an attack. During the night, two Rebel assaults occurred elsewhere on the field, leading a 32nd Maine soldier to recall that their "rest was somewhat broken and feverish, and . . . [their] dreams disturbed by visions of charging columns sweeping down . . . with irresistible force." This fitful repose left the troops ill prepared for the next, and more demanding, portion of the campaign.[30]

BLOODSHED MISUNDERSTOOD

EXAMINING THE SIGNIFICANCE
OF THE WILDERNESS

By the end of May 6, the later arrivals had passed the first test of their combat performance. A comparison of the casualty totals for the two battalions reveals, however, that they did not share the same proportion of casualties. Seventy Vermont officers and men were killed, wounded, missing, or captured, whereas the Mainers tallied twenty-two casualties. Based on the more conservative estimates of their present-for-duty strength that day, their numbers had declined by 22 and 3 percent respectively. This difference can be explained by the Vermonters having spent more time closely engaged with the enemy. Near midday they fended off Confederate flanking attempts on their own, then formed part of the brigade's front line in the afternoon assault. Conversely, the Mainers had not fought as an isolated unit that morning. And moreover, during the combat along the Orange Plank Road, they started in the second line of the brigade and only pushed forward once the contest was underway. Regardless, the leadership of both outfits suffered similarly, making up 6 percent of the 17th Vermont's total and 9 percent of the 31st Maine's casualties. These proved to be roughly typical rates, given that officers composed 6 percent of the brigade's losses for the period of May 5–7. Such figures in the 17th and 31st offer evidence that the rank and file performed reliably in combat on the morning of May 6. It would otherwise be reasonable to expect higher casualties among the officers, who might have felt compelled to steel the resolve of their men by engaging in reckless displays of bravery. But the officers would have stood behind their troops that afternoon when they halted retreating Mainers and probably Vermonters as well. Such positioning would have reduced their exposure to incoming missiles, helping explain their modest loss figures. Scrutinizing the casualty statistics makes clear that the rookies did their part and could even have suffered more heavily than their seasoned comrades. In the 17th Vermont 24 percent of the losses were veterans, which closely matched the proportion of such grizzled combatants who helped fill the battalion throughout its history. In contrast, only 5 percent of casualties in the 31st Maine were experienced officers and men, markedly less than the 12-percent ratio of veterans in this unit during its time in service.[31]

The grim results of the Wilderness testified to the sacrifice of the later arrivals. Such bloodshed is easily overlooked since the Ninth Corps played a modest role in the battle. For example, Capt. Louis C. Duncan of the U.S. Army Medical Corps distinguished between Burnside's command and "the three corps that really did the work." Using losses sustained as a measure of involvement in the fighting, the Ninth Corps tallied a mere 1,640 casualties over the three-day period, or 9 percent of the Union total. Such a low share was to be expected, as the Ninth Corps was substantially smaller than any of the infantry corps in the Army of the Potomac. In terms of present-for-duty strength, Burnside's troops only equaled 60 percent of the Second Corps, 66 percent of the Fifth Corps, and 75 percent of the Sixth Corps. The smaller size of the Ninth Corps and its delayed participation in the fighting were responsible for its limited portion of the army's casualty total.[32]

Contemporaries generalized about the performance of the Ninth Corps at the Wilderness. According to Union officers, early historians, and at least one journalist, Burnside's men contributed little to the cause of Federal arms there. Several of these commenters insisted, without evidence, that the greenhorns of that command were unreliable. Reflecting on the afternoon assault, others more generously conceded that these troops diverted the graybacks' attention away from the Second Corps or provided all the bluecoats involved in this engagement an advantage. They even cited inadequate Federal manpower to explain the repulse at the Orange Plank Road or insisted that these new soldiers received excessive blame for failing to take control of their area. Unsurprisingly, those most inclined to sympathize with the experiences of the Ninth Corps offered the most praise. Burnside lauded his men for maneuvering "most creditably under" Confederate fire in the morning and extolled their bravery throughout the day. The likes of Adjutant and Inspector General Washburn, Colonel Griffin, Lieutenant Colonel Cummings, his subordinates, and Green Mountain State newspaper editors celebrated the New Englanders, some even crediting them with matching the prowess of veterans.[33]

Ultimately, the 17th Vermont and the 31st Maine proved themselves in combat in the Wilderness. Several factors explain their failure to engage the Rebels on time. A combination of heavy marching, sleep deprivation, and sickness had exhausted these men and likely caused them to straggle. Higher-level command decisions and the obstacles that the soldiers encountered on the way to the front further slowed progress. Reconstructing the operational history of the later arrivals at the Wilderness, therefore, offers evidence that contradicts period stereotypes about these troops. Contemporary critics went too far when they sweepingly decried the inexperienced combatants as unsoldierly or lacking the aggression of their predecessors. Most importantly, these barely trained and physically drained novices fought well. During the morning hours, they demonstrated good tactical instincts by lying prone to avoid enemy fire at the Chewning Farm. These soldiers thus held the position without suffering undue casualties, whereas rookies might be expected to have unwittingly offered the graybacks a clear target by standing upright out in the open. During the afternoon, the later arrivals courageously helped seize Confederate entrenchments. They maintained their cohesion and achieved their military objectives, falling back only after their veteran comrades in other units did so. Underscoring the significance of this feat, these largely untested soldiers persevered despite losses that, in the case of the Vermonters, were proportional to those of the Army of the Potomac at Gettysburg. As a result, the experienced Federals serving in other regiments in Griffin's brigade came to think of their greener comrades differently after the Wilderness. According to a 32nd Maine soldier, these experienced men realized that the newcomers now "deserved their respect and confidence . . . and [regarded the greenhorns] as worthy of membership with them."[34]

A TIRESOME INTERLUDE

MAY 6–11, 1864

The later arrivals would soon commence a short journey to what would become the battlefield of Spotsylvania Court House. During the evening of May 6, Grant realized the futility of another assault upon the Army of Northern Virginia in the Wilderness. He thus ordered the Army of the Potomac and the Ninth Corps to flank left around the Confederate position in a 12.5-mile march, with the goal of placing themselves between the Rebels and the enemy capital of Richmond. Grant anticipated that Lee would respond by attempting to block the Federals' progress toward the city. In this case he might be able to confront Lee "in a more open country, and outside of his breastworks." For Griffin's men, this trek would begin on the night of May 7 and finish in the afternoon two days later, when they reached the Alsop Farm 2.5 miles northeast of the courthouse. The Federals needed to move quickly lest the graybacks reach the area first. In this eventuality the blue-clad troops would have to go on the attack in another costly engagement.[35]

The Vermonters and Mainers had little time to relax after their first battle. These combatants were likely tired on May 7, for after a late night, they awakened early and worked on entrenchments. Nevertheless, they could have drawn solace from the knowledge that the Confederates had fallen back and no longer posed a direct threat. The men were finally able to enjoy coffee and wash themselves. That night Griffin's men neared Wilderness Tavern, then waited for the Sixth Corps to march by on the road. After two hours had passed, the later arrivals fell into slumber, arising at 5:00 a.m. to find the roadway clear. Unfortunately for these soldiers, the Ninth Corps brought up the Union rear via a longer route than some of the other commands. They marched under heavy loads amid dust, high temperatures and humidity, and the thick smoke from portions of the Wilderness that still burned. Such oppressive conditions caused hundreds of men from the Sixth and Ninth Corps to collapse on the way, although most tried to resume their places in the ranks after stopping for a bit. Finally acknowledging the widespread fatigue among the Union troops, Grant canceled any movement on May 8. Still, Griffin's men had to skirmish and even entrench in anticipation of a Rebel attack that did not transpire. They had two opportunities for rest, one of which lasted for nearly four hours and did them little good. A soldier in the 11th New Hampshire dismissed that pause as "lying in the broiling sun upon a sandy plain."[36]

From May 9 to May 11, the later arrivals performed a range of tiring duties that left them in a weakened condition. The graybacks reached Spotsylvania Court House in time to obstruct the Federals, so Burnside committed his troops to finding a vulnerable stretch in the Confederate defenses. The men of the 17th Vermont and 31st Maine suffered through continuing heat and dust to travel short distances that totaled about eighteen miles, including a forced march and a movement at the double-quick. At one point the New Englanders were less than one-fourth of a mile from the courthouse. These men also skirmished periodically, supported the First and Third Divisions, and readied for a possible change in location. Such activities exposed the later arrivals to enemy artillery and rifle musket fire, obliging them to dig in whenever they changed position. This defensive tactic was effective, as the danger from the missiles turned out to be low when taking such precautions, for just one Vermonter and one Mainer were wounded. The experience of these several days still proved fatiguing, however, for the New Englanders enjoyed but a few hours of sleep per night. In this stressful environment they had to doze lightly with weapons close by, even as Union and Rebel picket fire disturbed their repose. It was only at 10:00 p.m. on May 11 that they learned of their role in a plan to attack the enemy the following morning. Since they lacked tents or blankets to shield themselves from the weather, retiring for the night offered no promise of slumber before this assault. A downpour had started that afternoon and continued into the next day, which moved a member of the 32nd Maine to complain that "the whole situation was a dismal and dreary one." As the soldiers' anxiety mounted about the upcoming fight, they bid farewell to one another in advance. A 6th New Hampshire captain recalled fearing "the morrow would be a day of blood," while an 11th New Hampshire soldier remembered questioning their ability "to survive the terrible carnage."[37]

THE STRUGGLE FOR THE SALIENT

MAY 12, 1864

On May 12 the later arrivals would be among those to attack the formidable Confederate defenses around Spotsylvania Court House. Grant ordered the Army of the Potomac and the Ninth Corps to move against different parts of the Rebel line, with Burnside targeting the right flank of a salient known as the Mule Shoe. The Ninth Corps would advance at 4:00 a.m. and seek to hold the enemy's attention along its front. In so doing, these Federals would hinder General Lee from redirecting his manpower to counter the assault of Hancock's Second Corps on the apex of the salient. The task promised to be difficult, for the Federals had to negotiate abatis and slashings to reach the graybacks atop the fortified crest. Moreover, the Confederate artillery holding this position could unleash an enfilading fire on the attackers. In Sergeant Major Merriam's view, such entrenchments "seemed impregnable to any assault," while a lieutenant in the 9th New Hampshire afterward declared, "the wonder [was] . . . that any man . . . escaped alive."[38]

Reminiscent of the Wilderness, Burnside again suffered the stereotype of lacking initiative. Grant blamed him for having failed to commit his troops more fully to the fighting of May 10 and dispatched Comstock to help the Ninth Corps commander the next day. Tellingly, Grant insisted that Comstock would "not lose a chance to push the enemy," implying that his aide-de-camp was leading the troops rather than Burnside. Suggesting some truth to this assertion, Burnside responded to the lieutenant colonel's suggestions on May 11 by snapping that "he would command his own divisions." A critical undertone also surfaced in Grant's May 12 orders, which exhorted the Ninth Corps commander to attack simultaneously with Hancock, "promptly and with all possible vigor." Looking ahead to the fighting, evidence emerges to justify a focus on Burnside's supposedly flawed leadership. Grant held a low opinion of his subordinate, for as Brevet Brigadier General Badeau later recalled, the general in chief was "disappointed with the result of Burnside's operations." During that morning's combat, Grant would urge the major general to lead his men forward with greater assertiveness, even pointing out that the Fifth and Sixth Corps had "been attacking vigorously all day."[39]

In fact, the outcome of the May 12 contest depended on the efforts of the rank and file at least as much as on Burnside's command decisions. Hancock's onslaught was more likely to succeed if the Vermonters, Mainers, and the rest of the Ninth Corps pushed ahead on time in a convincing display of aggression. Several factors promised to hamper the movement of these troops, however, no matter how energetically their commander behaved that day. To reach the Confederate line, they needed to traverse a marsh dotted with trees, thickets, and two creek-filled ravines, hence Brigadier General Potter's complaint that this "ground [was] very bad." The Rebels' disposition obliged his men to travel a greater distance to engage in combat than the Second Corps, and the inclement weather made this transit more challenging. Besides a dense fog, Potter's brigades would have to fight amid a persistent downpour that would mix with the blood of casualties puddling on the ground. The combatants would thus plunge up to their calves into what early Ninth Corps historian Augustus B. Woodbury termed "a mass of gory mud."[40]

The 17th Vermont and the 31st Maine, along with their Ninth Corps comrades, appeared unlikely to keep the enemy occupied along their front. A combination of fatigue, illness, and casualties had reduced the strength of the Vermonters. Two days earlier the 17th had only tallied 342 officers and men present for duty, with about one-third of its members sick or absent without leave. From May 10 to May 12, the unit's numbers appear to have dropped to as little as 250 officers and men present for duty. Under these circumstances, the 17th was fortunate to serve again under Major Reynolds's proven leadership while Cummings recovered from his earlier wound. The men also had an opportunity to conduct battalion drill again before the fighting began on May 12. In contrast, Merriam estimated between 600 and 700 Mainers present for duty that day. This larger total can be explained by the fact that the 31st had started the campaign with a sizable complement of men (though still not a full regiment) and had sustained fewer casualties at the Wilderness. Although the battalion does not appear to have continued training, it benefited from the leadership of Major White, who had shown courage at the Wilderness. As a result, the Vermonters were more practiced as they approached their second battle, while the Mainers possessed the advantage of sheer mass.[41]

Despite all that these New Englanders had endured, their morning advance started favorably. Griffin's men composed the vanguard of the

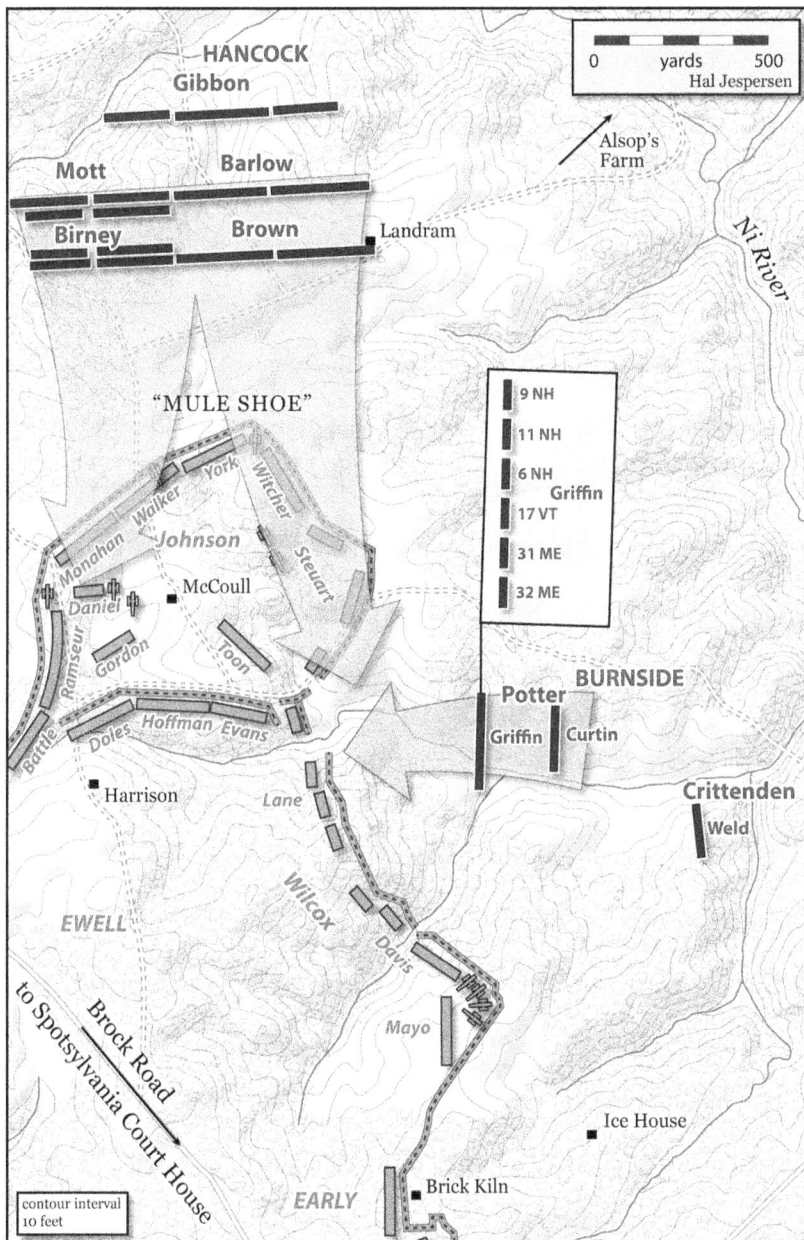

HANCOCK
Gibbon

Alsop's
Farm

Ni River

Mott
Barlow

Birney
Brown
Landram

"MULE SHOE"

9 NH
11 NH
6 NH
Griffin
17 VT
31 ME
32 ME

York
Witcher
Monahan
Walker
Johnson
Steuart
Daniel
McCoull
Ramseur
Gordon
Toon
Battle
Doles
Hoffman
Evans

BURNSIDE
Potter
Griffin
Curtin

Harrison
Lane

Crittenden
Weld

Wilcox

EWELL
Davis

to Spotsylvania Court House
Brock Road
Mayo

Ice House

contour interval
10 feet

EARLY
Brick Kiln

0   yards   500
Hal Jespersen

Battle of Spotsylvania Court House, May 12, 1864.

Second Division, which in turn led the assault of the Ninth Corps. The 17th took position to the right of the 31st, with both units on the left side of the brigade line. At 4:00 a.m., these Federals lurched forward cheering and in skirmish order, as Griffin ordered them to advance "obliquely to the right and front." They quickly covered about a mile and a half at the double-quick. The enthusiasm and timeliness of this movement countered Grant's concerns about Burnside. The Ninth Corps's display of vigor outshone Hancock's conduct, since he decided to delay his own attack until 4:35 a.m., while awaiting sunrise and for the fog to lift.[42]

The progress of this attack briefly stalled. After a half hour of marching, the Vermonters and Mainers encountered Confederate skirmishers, who fired at them from two rows of rifle pits hidden within a body of trees. The Federals halted in the open, probably to dress their line, and as casualties mounted some Mainers attempted to flee. Exemplifying brave leadership, Capt. A. K. P. Wallace of the 31st stood before his troops and tried to steel their resolve when a Rebel bullet struck him down. Merriam underscored the trying nature of this experience. Echoing his comments about the Wilderness, he described the plight of withstanding fire in an exposed position without shooting back as "the hardest place in which men can be put." Finally, Griffin's brigade succeeded in driving the graybacks from this position and took some of them prisoner.[43]

The 17th Vermont and 31st Maine hurried onward to engage in an intense firefight. They traversed a mile of ground in only a few minutes, which a soldier in the 32nd Maine termed a feat of "almost breathless struggling." By 5:00 a.m., the troops had passed through a line of abatis to arrive within fifty feet of the main Confederate position and to stand along the rear face of a hill. The Rebels proceeded to open a small arms barrage that this same brigade member claimed went "sweeping over and through . . . the line like a blast of death," one that Private Smith stated "blew us right off our feet." In response the later arrivals dropped to a prone position under the crest. This ground sloped down into a creek-filled ravine, then rose toward the salient. The Federals exchanged fire with only those graybacks who exited their fieldworks to stand along the ravine banks. Still, the Union soldiers struggled to shoot accurately, for the black-powder smoke from their rifle muskets worsened the hazy conditions and obliged them to find their targets by spotting gunfire flashes. In addition, trees concealed the main line of enemy entrenchments and their occupants as they shot at the oncoming Federals. The Rebels' familiarity with this terrain gave them the advantage of knowing where they could aim to strike their blue-clad assailants.[44]

This slugfest lasted for two hours, proving the later arrivals' fortitude. A body of Confederates stood before the Vermonters and along the near bank of the ravine. The Federals fired upon them, driving the graybacks into the limited cover of the underbrush dotting the ravine about 500 feet away. Unfortunately for the Rebels, they could neither repulse the Union troops nor risk leaving this sheltered position to return to their main works. Poor visibility for shooting and the difficulty of using rain-soaked weapons arguably helped explain the length of this fight, which ended at 7:00 a.m. By then, the Vermonters had depleted their individual allotments of forty rounds as well as the ammunition they scrounged from those wounded or killed. They withdrew to await resupply as the 48th Pennsylvania Volunteer Infantry Regiment took position. At this point some fifty Confederates surrendered while the rest fled. The Mainers had spent the past two hours exchanging fire with the enemy standing on the far bank. As Merriam observed, this "place was getting to hot for comfort." Since the officers and men of the 31st were close to the Rebel line, it was likely around this time that they captured an unspecified but large number of graybacks. Whereas the Vermonters enjoyed a break from combat for the next few hours, it is unknown whether the Mainers also shifted out of the front line. If not, they would have helped defeat the enemy counterattack that started at 9:00 a.m.[45]

The later arrivals did not have another opportunity to press the assault until late morning. At 11:00 a.m. the 17th Vermont pushed forward in support of the 48th Pennsylvania, which was driving toward the Confederate line. The troops from the Green Mountain State traversed a clearing some 150 yards in length, braving Rebel missiles to reach cover atop forested high ground several yards from the graybacks. When the Pennsylvanians withdrew, however, Reynolds led his men in retreat to the crest that overlooked the ravine. The Vermonters had sustained few casualties during this brief effort. Over the remaining hours of combat, they would face an enemy battery some 400 yards away, which sought to repel the Federals by bombarding them with canister, case, and shell. Before midday the Mainers launched a headlong assault on the Confederate defenses and suffered grievous casualties from artillery fire. Given the Rebel guns' proximity to the Vermonters, the same battery was probably responsible for inflicting these losses. Persevering, the 17th finally managed to shoot down its gun crews. Potter acknowledged this effort by subsequently recommending Sgt. Franklin Hoyt of the 17th for a Medal of Honor. He explained that the fellow had "bravely maintained a position in advance of his regiment, and as is believed was of material and extraordinary service in silencing and keeping silenced a piece of Artillery whose fire had been very destructive in his Brigade." Despite such praise, Hoyt did not receive the decoration.[46]

Indecisive fighting continued for the rest of the day. During the earlier advance of the later arrivals, at 11:00 a.m., the rest of Griffin's men slowed their shooting out of fatigue and in hopes that the Confederates would follow suit. After a half hour or so, this de facto ceasefire took effect, and the Federals began to entrench. When the smoke and fog cleared around noon, however, the graybacks discovered the work in progress and their sharpshooters opened fire. Casualties mounted in the brigade, which advanced a skirmish line and split the rest of its manpower between entrenching and shooting at enemy soldiers who left cover. Griffin's troops withstood Rebel artillery fire, defeated up to three counterattacks, and made a half-dozen advances of their own to finally get within a few yards of the Confederates. Combat ended for the New Englanders at dusk, when they trekked a short distance, fortified their position, and retired for the night. Sleep must have been elusive, for the men made do without tents amid a continued downpour. Their weapons remained close by as the sound of combat elsewhere on the battlefield lasted until roughly midnight. These soldiers also had orders that kept them on edge, for they had to be ready to support the Second Corps and to fend off an anticipated 3:30 a.m. Rebel attack; neither eventuality transpired.[47]

A TRIAL IN THE TRENCHES

MAY 13–17, 1864

At the end of the hostilities on May 12, Colonel Griffin characterized the men of his Second Brigade as "exhausted tigers" who were "pretty well crippled." Nevertheless, they could bask in the glory of their commander, who received a promotion to brigadier general with the support of Grant and Burnside. This was to recognize Griffin's leadership during the fighting that day, when the right end of the brigade temporarily foiled an enemy counterattack on the Second Corps. Since the 17th Vermont and 31st Maine both stood on the opposite end of the line, they were not involved in this action. These depleted later arrivals now spent the period of May 13–17 engaged in trench warfare. Given the need to watch for Confederate assaults, they could not rest much during the day and only fitfully for a few nighttime hours, with their weapons nearby. The experience of Private Carter is illustrative, for he counted the evening of May 14 as his first chance for repose in five days. Nevertheless, these Union troops needed to remain alert and perform a variety of tasks that drained their energy, both late at night and in the early morning. Besides the likelihood of dealing with Rebel movements or responding to new orders, the New Englanders found themselves changing position, scouting, skirmishing, and interring fallen comrades. With the graybacks only some 800 feet distant, it was fortuitous that the later arrivals had grown proficient by this time in the rapid construction of earthworks. As Sergeant Major Merriam remarked, "if picks and shovels were not at hand, then bayonets and dippers and tin plates were brought into use." They subsequently reinforced the field fortifications in anticipation of an unrealized Confederate assault.[48]

The Vermonters and Mainers were responsible for part of the front line. They attempted to pick off Rebels, who responded with rifle musket and artillery fire that underscored the importance of the protection that the defenses provided their Federal occupants. Such danger inspired Burnside's military secretary, Captain Larned, the assistant adjutant general of the Ninth Corps, to decry living "under a constant shower of shot & shell listening every moment for a bullet or round shot sometimes dodging your head every two minutes as they come whizzing past you—and being shelled out of camp two or three times in one day—or as you sit at breakfast to see wounded men carried past on stretchers." Corporal Whitehill simply observed, "balls ar flin over our heads all the time now." Despite such dramatic pronouncements, the entrenchments appear to have done their job of keeping the men safe from Confederate missiles, for Merriam and a 32nd Maine soldier agreed that Rebel fire inflicted minimal casualties. Likewise, Sgt. Henry O. Perry of the 31st wrote dismissively that the enemy "gave us a few shell but done no damage."[49]

Unpleasant living conditions defined this confrontation between the entrenched opposing forces. Meals were unsatisfying, as the soldiers made do with an inconsistent supply of hardtack, coffee, and uncooked pork. The Vermonters and Mainers also faced the prospect of very early repasts, for they had breakfast at 3:00 a.m. on at least one occasion. To avoid attracting the attention of the Confederates, these Federals did not light candles or campfires along their frontage, so food preparation had to occur behind a wood line hundreds of yards to the rear. This obliged the men to leave cover to retrieve food that grew cold in transit. Such moving to and fro also exposed the Union soldiers to the fire of Rebel sharpshooters, who often perched in the trees dotting the no-man's-land between the lines. Intermittent downpours further tried the New Englanders until the wee hours of May 17, when they finally gained the protection of tents. Comstock blamed the precipitation for the "roads [becoming] horrid," and Perry grumbled that he and his comrades were "having a very hard time wet tired and cold." Over these several days, heat and sunlight combined with the rainfall to accelerate the effects of exposure on the corpses of graybacks and horses dotting the ground. As a soldier in the 11th New Hampshire griped, "the air soon became sickening."[50]

This first taste of trench warfare was a psychological trial for the later arrivals. In contrast to the stand-up fights on May 6 and May 12, they now endured the unnerving reality of spending days below ground level and within range of Confederate weapons. The Federals were probably not keen for another clash of arms, as a moment's carelessness could expose them to the fire of watchful Rebels. This stands in contrast to the testimony of certain eyewitnesses, including Burnside, Ninth Corps assistant adjutant general Captain Larned, Cummings, and 31st Maine adjutant and First Lieutenant Allyn, who all insisted the troops were in good condition and intent on victory. Despite such optimism, the final phase of this battle would end in disappointment.[51]

THE LAST HURRAH AT SPOTSYLVANIA

MAY 18, 1864

For the later arrivals, an ill-fated Federal assault on May 18 marked the end of the fighting at Spotsylvania. Grant opted to try to break through the Confederate army's last line of defense, which stretched across the bottom of the Mule Shoe Salient. This attack was to involve two divisions each from the Second and Ninth Corps, plus the whole of the Sixth Corps. Burnside's men held the left flank of this formation, with Brigadier General Griffin's troops supporting one division of the Second Corps. The Vermonters and Mainers would have to traverse broken terrain through the fog and woods to target the Rebel position. For a captain in the 6th New Hampshire, this plan did not inspire confidence. He remembered believing that to approach such impressive entrenchments was "almost sure death." Lieutenant Colonel Lyman, Major General Meade's aide-de-camp, explained: "The high parapet was . . . traversed as often as every ten or twelve feet . . . [and] inclosed in the rear, so that the line was . . . divided into a series of square pens, with banks of earth heavily riveted with oak logs. From space to space was . . . an elevated post for sharpshooters, with a loophole in front." Even more difficult, the soldiers would be advancing in the heat against an enemy forewarned of the onslaught. When the Federals had moved forward on the previous night to reach their point of attack, some of them had clashed with the graybacks patrolling in front of their defenses. This confrontation worked to the advantage of the Confederates, who realized an offensive was forthcoming. The blue-clad soldiers remained unaware, however, that many of the enemy were already well entrenched. The Vermonters, at least, had the consolation of going through battalion drill to ready them before this fight, whereas there is no evidence that the Mainers did so.[52]

The start of this assault tested the resolve of the 17th and 31st. At 3:00 a.m. they began filling their portion of the brigade's front line. Then, around 4:30 a.m., the Vermonters and Mainers pushed forward with the rest of Griffin's command under a brightening sky and with a fervor and speed reminiscent of their morning attack on May 12. Passing through the trees disordered the formation, so they paused and dressed their line in the field between the opposing forces. This halt out in the open left the men vulnerable to Confederate fire, which struck the Union troops head on and along their left flank as a storm of rifle musket rounds and artillery shell, solid shot, case, and canister. Making the experience more daunting, these Federals had to hurry across the field due to the gruesome scene that lay before them. A 6th New Hampshire captain recalled that "it was impossible to breathe" amid the unburied corpses "lying thick in all directions . . . loathsomely swollen and disfigured." The explosion of Rebel artillery rounds among the bodies launched rancid pieces into the air, which contributed to this ghastly spectacle.[53]

And yet the Vermonters and Mainers displayed their courage by helping sustain the already faltering offensive. First they entered a ravine on the far side of the field, sitting or lying prone in support of the Second Corps troops who led the attack. Few Confederate missiles struck amid Griffin's men, given their use of the ground for cover and the fact that the graybacks focused their fire on the other, more closely engaged Federals to the New Englanders' right. Disaster suddenly loomed, however, with the flight of these Second Corps troops, who poured through the brigade from its right flank. A soldier in the 11th New Hampshire described the scene as "thousands of troops running back and away from the deadly fire like so many cowards." The later arrivals and the rest of the brigade momentarily retreated, then continued forward. The Vermonters and Mainers may have drawn encouragement from the fact that the Second Corps men who withdrew subsequently returned to the fighting as well. Griffin's command now exited the ravine, climbed over the opposite bank, and seized a tree-dotted crest. This subjected them to a Rebel fire of growing intensity. A 6th New Hampshire captain recalled that "the shot and shell came nearly as thick and fast as the Minie balls," while a soldier in the 32nd Maine alluded to the missiles "scattering death and wounds on every side." An enemy counterattack repulsed other Federals posted to the left of the Second Brigade, and the defeated troops fell back in chaos through its ranks. Although the Vermonters held their position, two other units began to temporarily retreat.[54]

The later arrivals made limited gains during this attack, which soon petered out. Only four outfits in the brigade, including the 17th Vermont but not the 31st Maine, continued forward to reach within roughly 50 feet of the first Confederate line. This position consisted of two rows of rifle pits on higher ground that skirmishers controlled. The Mainers held back, likely to protect the left flank of the brigade, hence Merriam's recollection that they fought "mostly on the defensive." Perry similarly recounted that the Mainers "moved a little and lay under the works all day." In contrast the Vermonters met the enemy at close range and, along with the other attacking units, poured in a volley that caused the grayback skirmishers to withdraw to their main line by 6:30 a.m. This advanced portion of Griffin's command seized the rifle pits, with the Vermonters laying claim to two of them. Driving forward and realigning, the Federals confronted the abatis and slashings in front of the principal Rebel line some 130 feet away. To gain protection from the blizzard of enemy minié balls, case, and canister, a 6th

New Hampshire captain remembered that they promptly entrenched "like beavers, rolling up old logs, cutting down small trees, adding brush and earth, and in less than an hour had breastworks three feet high." The Union and Confederate soldiers then began firing on each other whenever anyone broke cover. Griffin's men, however, accomplished little more for the rest of the day. After three futile attempts to advance, their effort devolved into a stalemate by late morning. The brigade fell back to defend the captured rifle pits, stopped Confederate attempts to outflank them, and skirmished until just before sunset. Subsequently, the Federals withdrew to their starting position amid Rebel fire and went to sleep around midnight.[55]

CRUMBLING UNDER FIRE

THE IMPLICATIONS OF
SPOTSYLVANIA COURT HOUSE

The 17th Vermont and 31st Maine emerged from their second battle showing signs of hesitancy to attack entrenched Confederates. Union casualty figures provide evidence of this gradual decline in their eagerness for such fighting. These statistics point to a heavy toll when compared against the more conservative estimates of the present-for-duty strength of the New Englanders. On May 12 a total of sixty-three Vermont officers and men were killed, wounded, or captured, which equaled 25 percent of the battalion's present-for-duty strength. Likewise, the Mainers tallied ninety casualties, representing 15 percent of those present for duty. It appears that the later arrivals fought without depending on brash displays of bravery by their leaders. A mere 5 percent of the Vermont and 1 percent of the Maine casualties were officers. Such ratios are comparable to the 3-percent loss rate among officers throughout the Second Brigade over the longer period of May 8–21. And yet veterans bore an outsized share of the casualties, which suggests that the newer men grew less keen to attack at some point during May 12. Forty-one percent of the Vermont casualties were seasoned officers and men, which was disproportionately high since only 21 percent of those in the 17th Vermont throughout its time in service were experienced combatants. This trend was less pronounced in the 31st Maine. Sixteen percent of its casualties were veterans, slightly exceeding the percentage of grizzled Federals who served in this unit during the war. Conversely, the trench warfare of May 13–17 was not especially hazardous to the troops. Only one Vermonter and one Mainer were wounded, the former due to friendly fire from a 6th New Hampshire soldier who believed him to be a Rebel. The experience of living near the enemy was still mentally taxing, however, which could explain the tentative nature of the May 18 assault. The 17th may have either enjoyed greater protection than the sources indicated or not advanced as near as described, for it emerged unscathed from this stage of the battle. Perhaps the later arrivals, after the bloody clash of May 12, drew from their trench warfare experience of May 13–17 the lesson that it was unwise to charge a strong defensive position. By means of comparison, the 31st reported a modest five men wounded, which was unsurprising given its limited role that day. These two units were not alone in holding back, for Griffin's entire brigade sustained only some fifty casualties—a mere 8 percent of its total losses from May 8 to May 21.[56]

Contemporaries differed in their assessment of the Ninth Corps's performance at Spotsylvania. These included early historians, a journalist, and Union officers. Some lamented the troops' inability to seize ground on May 12, arguably an unfair criticism. After all, Grant had only expected Burnside's troops to capture the attention of the Confederates along their front. Various commenters did note the success of the corps in doing this, with a few even highlighting the courage of its combatants. Assistant Secretary of War Charles Dana celebrated the "determination" of the "good soldiers" filling the Second Division, and Brigadier General Potter insisted they "never fought as well before." Turning to the 17th Vermont and the 31st Maine, Lieutenant Colonel Cummings proudly related that the Vermonters had "not faltered, nor did they lose their colors," while 2nd Lt. Voranus L. Coffin of the 31st maintained, "our boys fought like heroes, even excelling old veteran regiments." Nevertheless, observers gave the Ninth Corps a mixed review for the assault of May 18. They believed that the attack put the enemy's main line at risk, though some more bluntly judged it to be a failure. Several individuals offered praise, specifically for the Vermonters' conduct throughout this engagement. Besides a newspaper editor's positive account, Major Reynolds credited his troops with having "evinced a courage and an endurance worthy of veterans." Likewise, Lieutenant Lucia wrote of the unit that its "soldierly conduct increased the admiration of its officers and the confidence of its associates."[57]

At Spotsylvania the two outfits ultimately turned in a mixed record. On May 12 they had the objective of helping keep the Confederates busy along their front to facilitate the Second Corps's onslaught against the Mule Shoe Salient. The New Englanders achieved this goal, engaging the Rebels in a close-range firefight, making headlong assaults, and sharpshooting from the protection of their entrenchments. These Federals demonstrated their ability to withstand enemy fire by taking heavy losses and still managed to capture a large number of graybacks. Conversely, the increasing role of veterans in sustaining this effort indicates that the later arrivals' cohesion was waning. Between May 13 and May 17, they adapted to a reliance on fieldworks, which would come to define the campaign. The half-hearted attack against the strong Confederate defenses on May 18 offered proof that their fighting ability was in decline.

The combat performance of the 17th Vermont and 31st Maine runs counter to commonplace assumptions about their conduct under fire. Before joining the 17th, Surgeon Rutherford, a veteran, highlighted the need for "experience to make a good soldier, one that will stand in the face of leaden showers and the cannons blast." He concluded that "raw recruits even with vetrians to back them cannot be depended upon in a sharp fight." Claims of this sort were inaccurate, for the later arrivals did not collapse at either the Wilderness or Spotsylvania Court House.[58]

Physical and mental exhaustion, not an unwillingness to fight, explains the diminishing combat performance of the two outfits. The period of May 6–18 was surely the most difficult introduction to military service that Civil War soldiers ever faced. The Wilderness was a brutal baptism in the realities of combat, but Spotsylvania proved even more arduous. The New Englanders could not hope to endure marching, inclement weather, inadequate food, close-range combat, and trench warfare without a corresponding reduction in their effectiveness under fire. The medical director of the Army of the Potomac, Dr. Thomas A. McParlin, noted the increasing "shock and depression of vital power . . . in the wounded" at Spotsylvania. Consistent with this view, Lieutenant Colonel Comstock and Brigadier General Potter agreed on the intensity of the Second Division's fight on

May 12. The general described it as "the severest I ever was in" up to that point. Such strenuous duty depleted the later arrivals, helping explain their lack of aggression on May 18.[59]

The plight of the Vermonters and Mainers speaks to the callous assumptions that underlay Grant's plan for the Overland Campaign. Reflecting on Spotsylvania, Potter noted the mounting Confederate casualties and declared of the opposing forces, "which[ever] has the most reinforcements will live the longest and come out [the] victor." This laid bare the expectation that the troops should continue to throw themselves against entrenched Rebels, regardless of the losses. With hindsight, Grant's approach may have been necessary if the Union was to prevail. But the later arrivals could not fully appreciate this vantage point, for as Cummings and Merriam noted, the lower-ranking officers and soldiers making up the army had only a limited understanding of the military machine of which they formed a small part. A bottom-up perspective of the fighting, however, underscores the reality that they faced a struggle for survival. From the burning woods of the Wilderness to the rain-soaked fields and trenches of Spotsylvania, the 17th Vermont and 31st Maine fought as well as could be expected of units with so many men new to soldiering.[60]

3

THE BATTLES OF NORTH ANNA
AND COLD HARBOR

The crossing of the North Anna by the 31st . . . was one
of the intensely exciting moments of my army life.
—Sgt. Maj. Leander Otis Merriam, 31st Maine

If we have achieved no brilliant exploits, I feel safe in saying
that we have endeavored to do our duty [at Cold Harbor].
—Lt. Col. Charles Cummings, 17th Vermont

On May 23, 1864, *New York Herald* reporter Sylvanus Cadwallader rosily depicted the progress of Union arms in the Civil War. Reflecting on the Overland Campaign, he praised the "transcendant genius" of Grant and Meade. This journalist proclaimed that the two generals had "triumphed over all obstacles" and "other glorious victories await[ed] our grasp." Cadwallader made it appear as though the Union effort to crush the Confederacy depended solely on effective leadership and thus overlooked the contributions of the rank and file at the Wilderness and Spotsylvania Court House. Yet he anticipated "hard fighting" should the opposing Army of Northern Virginia assume a defensive position along the North Anna River on the road to Richmond. Such a concession highlights an important question for this stage of the campaign: to what extent did the later arrivals overcome the stresses of their first two battles and continue to fight well as newly minted veterans? Contemporary historian John C. Ropes differed from Cadwallader by offering a bleaker assessment of Meade's Army of the Potomac. Summing up the nature of this campaign, he noted that sacrifices were demanded every day . . . which had hitherto been required only occasionally, and then only from those selected for some special post of honor and danger. To lie in a new-dug rifle-pit a hundred yards from the enemy for several days under constant fire is much like the experience of the engineer troops in a siege. To rush from this rifle-pit upon the enemy's works is the act of a forlorn hope, whose gallant performance is the admiration of a storming column, itself selected for a special and dangerous service. But it is not every day that the sap is pushed forward or the breach assaulted. Yet the soldiers in the Army of the Potomac had to make these exceptional feats their daily duties.[1]

The experiences of the 17th Vermont and 31st Maine provide insight into the ability of small units to withstand the rigors of multiple battles in rapid succession. To contribute meaningfully to Federal victory, these troops needed to demonstrate enough physical and mental endurance to outlast the Confederates in the attritional struggle of the campaign. Burnside now led the Ninth Corps through two engagements that tested their resolve against an entrenched enemy: the Battles of North Anna (May 23–26, 1864) and Cold Harbor (May 31–June 12, 1864).

The later arrivals would turn in a good combat performance. Their efforts helped sustain the Union drive on Richmond. Now battle hardened, they exhibited cohesion, accomplished their objectives, and sustained casualties indicative of their willingness to endure enemy fire. This record offers evidence to rebut the assumption—made by period observers and modern historians alike—that the influx of later arrivals as a group into the Army of the Potomac dulled its fighting edge. Admittedly, these New Englanders played only a modest role at North Anna, but they were more involved at Cold Harbor. These Vermonters and Mainers would not enjoy an unblemished record over this period. They engaged in unruly behavior on one of their lengthy marches and showed a reduced willingness to fight as the trying nature of the Overland Campaign took its toll. Yet such lapses did not prove the later arrivals were deficient in the qualities required of good soldiers. These missteps should actually be understood as the predictable response of depleted troops enduring a campaign unprecedented in the American experience. It is remarkable that these bluecoats, already worn down by prior service, persevered during more than three weeks on the move, under fire, and within entrenchments. In the words of contemporary Ninth Corps historian Augustus Woodbury: "Armies are not mere machines. They are composed of ordinary flesh and blood."[2]

ONWARD TO THE NEXT CONTEST

MAY 19–23, 1864

Between May 19 and May 23, the later arrivals conducted a slow march of about fifty miles to the North Anna River. The relaxed pace enabled them to recover somewhat from their previous combat experiences. Since the Federals had been unable to break through the Confederate lines at Spotsylvania, Grant continued his offensive by ordering the Army of the Potomac to outflank the Army of Northern Virginia to the east. In so doing, he hoped to catch the Rebels in the open before they could build fieldworks again. The Union soldiers were doubtless thankful to begin this trek without having to endure enemy fire, for the graybacks opposite them were in the process of falling back. The men of the 17th Vermont and the 31st Maine made little progress, though, owing to a Confederate attack upon other bluecoats that delayed the army's movement until approximately 4:00 p.m. on May 21. Burnside also had orders to keep his men on the Spotsylvania battlefield to convince the Rebels that he was preparing to attack while awaiting potential combat if these graybacks exited their defenses. This ploy would occupy the enemy while two other Union corps sought to gain a head start and place themselves between the enemy capital and its protectors. The New Englanders on the battlefield had to remain on edge because, as Lieutenant Colonel Cummings observed, "if a man raises his head above the works on either side pop goes a musket and duck goes the head at the sight of smoke." Although tiresome, he admitted the troops suffered few casualties in this way. Over the following days, the 17th and 31st only managed a leisurely advance. This belied the claim of a soldier in the 32nd Maine who described the effort as "a race between the two armies . . . with Richmond as the prize." Illustrative of the uneven tempo, a soldier in the 11th New Hampshire wrote of one day's activities by confirming that they "made a slow march, as usual, in the forenoon . . . and a quickstep in the afternoon." The Federals traversed 30 miles in one twenty-three-hour period, or 1.3 miles per hour, and 4–5 miles each on two other days. Such efforts paled in comparison to the brisk rate of 2.24 miles per hour they had achieved during their previous trek to the Wilderness. As a result, when the Federals reached the North Anna, they encountered an enemy dug in on the battlefield, for the Rebels had already completed their shorter journey to the river. This Union sluggishness begs explanation, as the soldiers traveled along passable roadways in an area unravaged by war. According to Assistant Secretary of War Dana, this portion of Virginia was "fine, clear country, good to move and fight in."[3]

Navigational challenges and frequent interruptions slowed the advance. Burnside's men sought a quicker route than that which several different Union corps used. And yet his troops soon confronted fortified Confederate skirmishers and a battery at the ford near Stanard's Mill on the Po River. Such Rebel opposition caused the Federals to reverse course and use the same, meandering route utilized by other bluecoats. Subsequent developments impeded the progress of the later arrivals, including the outbreak of cavalry skirmishes ahead of the column and an encounter with Union horsemen who fired upon members of the brigade after mistaking them for the enemy. The New Englanders enjoyed numerous opportunities for recuperation, which reduced their time on the move. These included a night of unbroken sleep and periods of daytime rest lasting up to eighteen hours, allowing them time to wash and change clothes.[4]

Tiring duties, unpleasant weather, and combat also hindered the advance of the Vermonters and Mainers. Before even departing for the North Anna, they likely emulated their comrades in the 6th New Hampshire by searching for and burying any weapons and materiel they found scattered across the Spotsylvania landscape. Lacking the transportation necessary to haul this cargo, they sought to deprive the graybacks of its use. These Federals went on to face early morning starts and long stretches on the move. Such treks included a thirteen-hour stint without a break and night marches, one of which stretched fifteen miles. To add to the New Englanders' toil, they carried on amid conditions ranging from dust and high temperatures to rain and a thunderstorm. Nevertheless, Cummings believed his men were "in good spirits." Various duties further taxed the soldiers' endurance during their pauses. Besides late-night fatigue duty, they performed combat-related activities that underscored the perils of the march. The troops scouted and stood ready to support other bluecoats should the need arise. They also made preparations for combat that only ended once the Confederates fell back, and twice they arrayed for battle in anticipation of unrealized Rebel attacks. Finally, the men braved enemy projectiles while skirmishing, endured artillery fire, and repelled an onslaught upon their own pickets. Captain Larned fittingly complained, "we are never certain of the next five minutes."[5]

The Vermonters, and probably the Mainers as well, counted among those Federals who took advantage of this sluggish advance to lag behind and pillage nearby areas. Lieutenant Colonel Lyman lamented that the men of the Ninth Corps were unruly and that many of their number, including rookies, were guilty of "straggling badly—whole companies fell out and deliberately halted to rest." Deprivation appears to explain the bad conduct of these soldiers, who only received a two-thirds ration without whiskey and occasionally had but a single hardtack for a meal. The men likely restocked their supplies by seizing water and food from the farms and firewood from the fences that dotted and lined the unspoiled landscape along their route. According to Private Carter, "some of the boys got a lot of tobacco hens Pigs etc." A 9th New Hampshire sergeant wholly blamed his comrades for a broader range of misdeeds, including "houses ransacked, destroying things . . . even to the women's scanty clothing and the bedding and furniture. . . . Every bit of corn, every hen and pig and cow has been killed and eaten, every mule has been taken along, and in the wake of our army everything has been desolated. We have dug up their corn-fields building breastworks, also their wheat-fields. The wheat was well headed out, and our huge droves of beeves have trodden it all down." This type of behavior inspired Meade's complaint about "the gross outrages perpetrated by stragglers . . . upon the helpless inhabitants." The severity of this issue spurred efforts to improve discipline at both the corps and division levels. Brigadier General Rawlins, Grant's chief of staff, instructed Burnside to assign a regiment the role of acting "as rear guard . . . to summarily punish all men . . . straggling from their ranks, and especially those . . . going to farm-houses for the purpose of pillaging." Capt. Samuel Wright, the assistant adjutant general of the Second Division of the Ninth Corps, announced that "the disgraceful laxity of all officers of the division in the matter of straggling . . . [had] called forth the severest animadversions at the headquarters of the army." He ordered officers leading brigades and regiments to appoint rear guards to stop laggards, using their bayonets on the culprits and firing upon them if required. Wright further called for the prompt punishment of thieves and threatened to recommend the dismissal of officers absent from their commands without authority. Regardless of these actions, the provost marshal general of the Army of the Potomac, Brig. Gen. Marsena Patrick, still found fault with the discipline of the corps. It remained to be seen whether the later arrivals would exhibit the same kind of unsoldierly conduct on the battlefield.[6]

A TEST OF SKILL

MAY 24–26, 1864

The 17th Vermont and 31st Maine appeared to be in poor shape to fight yet differed in their preparedness for the Battle of North Anna. Dana claimed these troops suffered from "great fatigue." Several factors distinguished the Vermonters from the Mainers, starting with tested but uneven leadership. The officers and men of the 17th served under Lieutenant Colonel Cummings, who resumed his duties after largely recovering from the head wound he had suffered at the Wilderness. The service of Colonel Hight, who again commanded the Mainers, was likely marred by his fondness for alcohol. Training represented an additional variable for the two units. The Vermonters conducted another round of battalion drill, which should have boosted their confidence, although it is unclear whether the Mainers did the same. Manpower offered another contrast between both outfits. The number of officers and men present for duty in the 17th plummeted from 251 on May 20 to 120 on May 24. Straggling was partly to blame, but the drop was more attributable to diseases such as measles. This was despite the fact that the daily sick ratio in the Army of the Potomac and Ninth Corps was lower in May than during the time spent encamped in April. Due to a lack of morning reports, there is no equivalent information on the present-for-duty strength of the 31st. As recently as May 12, the Mainers on hand had outnumbered their Vermont brethren. On May 25 they would receive an infusion of officers and men with the arrival of newly formed Company K from the Pine Tree State. With the addition of this tenth company, the 31st officially changed in status from a battalion to a regiment.[7]

These men needed to overcome significant challenges to succeed at North Anna. For the first time, the New Englanders would attempt a river crossing under enemy fire. Fighting at the Wilderness and Spotsylvania had left them not only seasoned but also wise to the danger of attacking entrenched graybacks. Consequently, it was not yet evident whether these Federals would be willing to traverse this body of water—the North Anna River promised to slow their rate of advance while affording them not the slightest cover—to overrun fortified Rebels. Increasing the difficulty of this task, the Union soldiers would again fight for several days amid conditions ranging from high temperatures and humidity to thunderstorms and rain. Sergeant Major Merriam would tellingly describe "the night of the 24th . . . as one of the stormiest nights in my experience." Only some soldiers enjoyed the shelter of gum blankets or tents during periods of rest.[8]

May 24 inaugurated the fighting at North Anna for the Vermonters and Mainers, who would face formidable Confederate defenses. The later arrivals awakened early that day to the sound of skirmish fire to find themselves facing Ox Ford, the central of three crossings over the river. They spent the morning on its north bank, confronting the salient of the V-shaped Rebel line. To explain why the Ninth Corps delayed its expected attack, Burnside stated that his troops had reached their destination during the evening of May 23. Ignorant of the terrain, they could not be expected to launch an assault at dawn the next day. The general stressed the forbidding nature of the enemy position, which featured a battery and numerous rifle pits in an area thick with trees against a backdrop of higher ground. Hardly inspiring confidence, Burnside mused, "the prospects of success are not at all flattering, but I think the attempt can be made without any very disastrous results, and we may possibly succeed." He explained that the Third Division seized "an island near the ford," from which the troops confirmed that "the enemy were in strong force on the opposite bank of the river, and well intrenched."[9]

Changing position, the Vermonters and Mainers went on to confront another set of imposing fieldworks under adverse circumstances. They did so under an ad hoc arrangement when Burnside temporarily detached the Second Division to serve under Major General Hancock, commander of the Second Corps. This decision was in accordance with Grant's orders that on May 24 Burnside would keep his soldiers "as a reserve to re-enforce the Second Corps . . . or to effect a crossing at Ox Ford, as may be deemed most advisable." Griffin's men headed east around midday with the rest of the division to support their Second Corps comrades. They traveled some four miles along the north bank to reach the Chesterfield Bridge, the east-

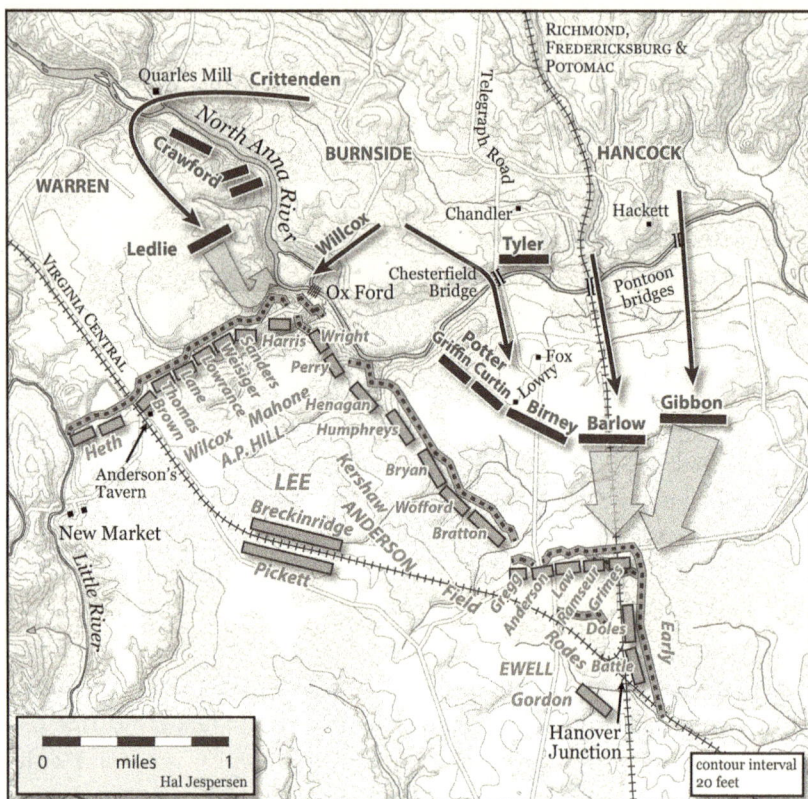

Battle of North Anna, May 24, 1864.

ernmost of the existing three river crossings in the area. Hancock doubted the feasibility of traversing the North Anna at this location, even though the enemy there had fallen back from the front line of entrenchments on the south bank. Fifteen Confederate redoubts with cannon still dotted the high ground on the far side of the river, presenting an attacker with the threat of artillery fire on both flanks. Cummings also called attention to a line of "formidable rifle pits" along this frontage. The Rebels holding these defenses had a commanding view of the bridge. If the Federals traversed the river, however, they could drive westward along the south bank to expel the enemy from their defenses near Ox Ford. The New Englanders set out to accomplish this goal under conditions that suggested their fighting ability would suffer. When Burnside divided his command, it portended ill for the cohesion of the later arrivals, for according to Larned, the detachment of Ninth Corps manpower to other commanders was damaging to corps identity. A soldier in the 32nd Maine likewise complained that doing this denied the men the full acclaim they and the Ninth should receive by fighting as a unified force.[10]

Although delayed, the later arrivals defied the odds by bravely forcing their way across the North Anna. They transited the river just past noon, after the Second Corps did so via nearby pontoons and the bridge. Hancock's troops outflanked the Confederate batteries on their right, which impeded enemy crews from training the guns on Griffin's men when they crossed. Cummings estimated that Hancock's move "saved us thousands of lives." With the Mainers in the vanguard, Griffin's brigade began to advance ahead of Potter's First Brigade. The frightening noise of incoming Rebel artillery rounds from either flank inspired these soldiers to march at the double-quick before the aim of the graybacks improved. The Federals therefore completed this movement in just a couple of minutes, demonstrating what Merriam described as the speed of "men . . . who know they are running for their lives." He recalled that "the roar of the guns, the crack of the musketry firing in the front, the howl of the solid shot, [and] the explosion of the shells all around . . . made a pandemonium hard to imagine." In a similar vein a soldier in the 11th New Hampshire regarded this cacophonous bombardment as "one of the most severe experiences of the campaign." Most of the missiles sailed overhead, however, which explains why Cummings referred dismissively to this fire as "a moderate discharge of shells."[11]

Now the Vermonters and Mainers engaged the graybacks at close range. Along with the rest of the Second Division, they formed along the right flank of the Second Corps on the far bank. The 17th and 31st then climbed the hill to reach the Rebel defenses. Enemy skirmishers in front briefly opposed the bluecoats' advance, but once Griffin's men surmounted the ridge, they caught sight of dug-in Rebels who opened with a deadly volley. As a result, the Federals fell back to the cover of the crest to dig in. When the graybacks cheered and launched a counterattack, Merriam summed up the brigade's response as "a volley that sprinkled the crest of the hill with their dead and wounded." Forced to withdraw to their entrenchments, the enemy survivors kept up an intermittent fire deep into the night. Meanwhile, the later arrivals filled part of the Union front line and constructed more fieldworks, finally throwing themselves down to rest at 2:30 a.m. with their weapons at hand. Far removed from the soldiers' minds, their regiments underwent an organizational change that evening when Burnside and Major General Parke, his chief of staff, formally waived their seniority to Meade. This enabled Grant to assign the Ninth Corps to serve as part of the Army of the Potomac.[12]

Throughout May 25 and May 26, the New Englanders faced nearby Confederates but did not receive orders to engage them in a full-on fight. Grant's decision not to proceed with a large-scale assault can be explained by his observation that the Rebel line was more impressive than those faced earlier in this campaign. Instead, these Union soldiers entrenched, skirmished with the graybacks, and monitored the enemy defenses. Increasing the physical demands of this two-day stretch, the 17th Vermont and 31st Maine negotiated what Second Corps veteran Bvt. Maj. William P. Shreve remembered as "almost impassable marshes" on a battlefield reminiscent of the Wilderness. On May 26 Griffin's brigade launched an attack to distract the Confederates from a Second Corps effort to break up the Richmond, Fredericksburg, and Potomac Railroad leading to Milford Station. During this assault, the men drove the Rebels back from the fieldworks along their frontage and took up to 700 prisoners. The fighting only lasted an hour, as these Federals stopped after reaching a more formidable enemy line. This short-lived clash, which Merriam called "an ugly job," enabled the bluecoats to secure what the 9th New Hampshire regimental history editor later termed "a highly favorable position."[13]

Such arduous service would have reduced the morale of the later arrivals. Not only did they lack the comfort of campfires, presumably to avoid detection by the graybacks, but they also had to continue to make do with a two-thirds ration of hardtack, coffee, sugar, and beef. A soldier in the 32nd Maine described his own comrades as "worn and haggard" after withstanding Confederate fire for nearly three of the preceding five weeks. He added that the need to endure night marches and long stretches of combat without adequate rest or nourishment left his brethren "thin and pale." According to this veteran, "torn and ragged" uniforms and a flag "in tatters" bore testimony to the trials of their short yet difficult campaign.[14]

In particular, the nature of the North Anna battle further tempered the offensive spirit of the Vermonters and Mainers. One combatant serving in the 32nd Maine detailed how the Federals spent their time from the afternoon of May 24 until midday on the twenty-fifth, writing that the "line advanced cautiously, feeling the enemy, and when he appeared disposed to make a stand, we halted and built a line of breastworks, to hold the ground over which we had come." Merriam hinted at a reluctance to assault the Rebel position, explaining that he "managed to keep . . . pretty well protected keeping a little in the rear of our line when not wanted, as that brought me so far below the crest of the ridge that no Johnny could see me without exposing himself." Likewise, a soldier in the 11th New Hampshire wrote that during May 25, he "lay all day under fire, and until the night of the 26th." Confederate sharpshooters posted in trees had a commanding view of the hillside that allowed them to spot the sheltered Federals. By the end of this fight, less than 170 feet separated the opposing forces at select points along the line. The entrenchments provided the only source of protection on which the bluecoats could rely. According to Merriam, the two armies "were so near together that no man could raise his head on either side without great risk of having it broken."[15]

A SUCCESSFUL STALEMATE

EVALUATING THE RESULTS
OF NORTH ANNA

The 17th Vermont and 31st Maine suffered a modest toll in this battle, which is unsurprising as it was the Federals' least costly action of the campaign, tallying two and four soldiers wounded respectively. These loss figures are too low to draw meaningful conclusions about the degree to which officers as a whole or the officers and men who entered these units as veterans sacrificed in comparison to the preponderance of individuals who joined them as rookies. Such low numbers of casualties were typical for the Second Brigade, which only suffered seventy-two officers and men killed, wounded, missing, or captured over the longer period of May 22–June 1.[16]

Contemporaries offered a mixed review of the Ninth Corps's performance at North Anna. Brevet Brigadier General Badeau, Grant's military secretary, later wrote that the Second Division "met with no success." Conversely, historian Woodbury insisted that the Second Division "came near gaining a decisive advantage . . . and [secured] a highly favorable position." Burnside merely affirmed that his officers and men "behaved with the utmost gallantry and efficiency." Although the 31st Maine did not receive special mention, a newspaper editor wrote that the 17th Vermont accrued "an honorable, often bloody share" during the engagements of the Overland Campaign, including North Anna.[17]

Ultimately, the later arrivals did well in this battle. They exhibited resilient cohesion and completed their objective of crossing the river and establishing a lodgment on the opposite bank. These New Englanders gained little more ground, however, despite their attempt to exert pressure against the Confederates and drive toward Ox Ford. They sustained few casualties, which speaks more to the limited scope of the fighting than to the willingness of the later arrivals to engage in combat. After all, Grant concluded that "to make a direct attack from either wing would cause a slaughter of our men that even success would not justify."[18]

UPON PERILOUS ROADS

MAY 26–JUNE 2, 1864

The Vermonters and Mainers commenced their final march of the Overland Campaign on May 26. To resolve the impasse at the North Anna River, Grant again ordered the Army of the Potomac to flank left around the Army of Northern Virginia. His aim was to keep the enemy sufficiently westward that the Federals could get to the James River. Thus, the later arrivals trekked forty-four miles in four days, stopping northeast of Richmond at Cold Harbor, where the opposing forces confronted each other once again. Grant put this movement in context when he subsequently outlined his approach to the entire campaign. He sought "to beat Lee's army, if possible, north of Richmond, then, after destroying his lines of communication north of the James . . . to transfer the army to the south side and besiege Lee in Richmond, or follow him south if he should retreat." Fortunately, Cold Harbor proved to be a strategically significant location from which the bluecoats could protect their supply lines extending back to the depot at White House Landing and defend the routes leading to the Pamunkey River.[19]

The trip was demanding for the later arrivals. They started to move during the evening hours, hurriedly rejoining the Ninth Corps on the march after their recent stint under Hancock's command. The New Englanders went on to achieve an inconsistent rate of advance ranging between three and twenty-three miles a day. Cummings tellingly admitted that they "commenced marching in a round about way." Despite Grant's intention that they push forward "as rapidly as possible," he noted that "the country . . . was a difficult one to move troops over." Reducing their pace, the soldiers had to rely on bridges and roads to cross deep streams as well as swamps dotted with undergrowth and trees. Their responsibility for guarding the rear of the army, and briefly its sluggish wagon train, further slowed progress. Other Federal troops and artillery impeded the transit of the 17th Vermont and 31st Maine by crowding the way ahead. In addition, these comrades of the later arrivals churned the rain-soaked routes into mud, causing some Vermonters and Mainers to lose their footing and fall deep into the muck. The need to repair these roadways delayed the bluecoats even more. During one portion of this trek, the New Englanders found themselves having to drive through dust clouds amid high humidity and heat. The officers and men had some opportunities to rest, although early starts in the mornings and night marches kept them on the move for long periods of time, most notably a grueling twenty-hour stint. Along the way they entrenched, filled the front line of earthworks, supported their comrades in combat, skirmished, served as pickets, and awaited the command to change position. Fittingly, a soldier in the 32nd Maine described this journey as "one of the most tedious and fatiguing marches we ever knew."[20]

Such travel left the Vermonters and Mainers increasingly depleted. On May 29 Burnside complained that his "men . . . [were already] very weary, being almost constantly on the road for two days and nights." This was unsurprising, for Major General Humphreys, chief of staff for the Army of the Potomac, emphasized "the well-known exhausting effect of a night march upon troops in hot weather, on dusty roads." More anxiously, Lyman questioned how the Federals survived since they "no longer [had] the bodily strength they had a month before." Regaining energy would have been a time-consuming struggle. Admittedly, the troops enjoyed scattered breaks, a night of undisturbed slumber, and a rare opportunity to bathe. Nevertheless, they slept at least once with weapons at hand and persisted in their duties despite meager nourishment. These Federals had to slake their thirst with inadequate and sometimes undrinkable water. They also occasionally made do with only a two-thirds ration. To supplement this diminished fare, the later arrivals foraged on the properties of Rebel civilians. This activity seems to have been more restrained than the pillaging that had occurred on the march to the North Anna. In any case, Assistant Secretary Dana blamed the food shortage on "the commanding officers [of the Ninth Corps], who take no measures to prevent their men from wasting their rations, or throwing them away." He also chastised Burnside for previously distributing additional food after the Wilderness instead of encouraging the troops to realize the importance of treating their allotments with care. Without proper rest and nourishment during this challenging movement, Ninth Corps soldiers dropped out of the ranks by the thousands, while those who pushed forward fell asleep whenever they halted. Some exhausted combatants fainted or even died from sunstroke, whereas others carried on woozily enduring dizziness, sore muscles, blisters, and parched throats. By the time his men reached Cold Harbor, Cummings declared them "fatigued . . . with marching and fighting and entrenching."[21]

Between May 31 and June 2, the later arrivals maneuvered into position on what became the Cold Harbor battlefield. For most of this period, they stayed in the environs of Totopotomoy Creek, which Dana described as "thickly wooded with pines, with few good openings." They did march some six miles, however, most of it at a slowed pace on June 2, to reach the area of Bethesda Church. This move proved less trying for the Federals than their previous effort of May 26–30, for they were now taking opportunities to rest and address personal hygiene. Still, these troops suffered through more early reveilles as well as weather that ranged from hot and dusty to rainy. The soldiers also continued to entrench—once doing so overnight—in a testament to the ongoing danger of enemy missiles. Over these three days, the bluecoats endured Confederate artillery fire, engaged in small-scale skirmishing, watched for Rebel advances, and even repelled a probing attack around midnight.[22]

Most importantly, large skirmishes tested the resolve of the New Englanders. The first bout of fighting occurred on May 31 at 3:00 p.m., when Brigadier General Griffin's command drove back the enemy roughly a mile over terrain that Brigadier General Potter judged "the worst ground . . . [he] ever knew." They worked through the trees to reach a creek bed in an eighty-foot-deep ravine. Climbing up the far side required the troops, according to a 9th New Hampshire sergeant, to hoist themselves "up by the bushes about two thirds of the way." Once the men got across, they paused briefly to recover from the exertion and re-form their line. They were now looking upon a clearing dotted with entrenched graybacks. Surging forward with a shout, the 17th Vermont and 31st Maine helped their brigade capture multiple lines of rifle pits and some 600 Rebels. Yet stiffening resistance from the enemy's main line on the ridge across the field brought this Union onslaught to an end. The defenders poured in a rifle musket fire while their cannon blasted the bluecoats with canister, shell, and case. During this push, the Vermonters outpaced their comrades. As Cummings explained, "the [enemy's] fire was too hot," causing him to order his men to fall back and take cover below the top of the ravine. They lay prone and entrenched to withstand this Rebel response that was so intense that it moved a 32nd Maine soldier to avow he had "never heard such firing before." The opposing sides kept up a sporadic exchange up to nightfall, but even then the later arrivals could not rest easily, as half of the brigade had to remain on watch overnight.[23]

The New Englanders proved themselves in another intense clash on June 2. They shifted position to Bethesda Church, where fighting began around 3:00 p.m. The Rebels launched an assault upon the rear and right flank of the Ninth Corps by engaging the brigade's pickets, who probably included both Vermonters and Mainers, all serving under Captain Knapp of the 17th Vermont. The enemy pushed forward, taking numerous prisoners from among these Federals as they withdrew from their works and across a marsh. Knapp's men still managed to defeat what early historian and Civil War veteran George G. Benedict, who had served as a second lieutenant in the 12th Vermont Volunteer Infantry Regiment, termed "three vigorous advances" by Confederate skirmishers over a few hours. The pickets did not realize they fought alone, for the rest of Griffin's command had continued onward instead of remaining behind to provide support. Still, this small band of bluecoats held their position until the graybacks attacked with greater numbers. This aggression compelled the troops under Knapp to fall back and catch up with their brigade. That evening the New Englanders sheltered within entrenchments under a downpour that lasted overnight, inspiring Private Carter to remark, "it commenced to rain . . . like fury." The Union soldiers hunkered down in their tents, then proceeded to change position around 3:00 a.m. to labor on fieldworks for four hours. Wanting to supplement their limited rations with additional food in the rear, they dug an entrenched route, known as a covered way, to protect themselves in transit from the front. Others stood on picket duty, while those who could actually rest did so uneasily. They kept their weapons nearby, awaiting the prospect of either opposing a Rebel onslaught or commencing their own attack early the next morning.[24]

A FORLORN HOPE

JUNE 3, 1864

On June 3 the later arrivals would charge fieldworks for the last time in this campaign. Grant decided that the Army of the Potomac should launch an assault after determining that the Army of Northern Virginia was too close to Richmond to be outflanked again. He sought to defeat the Confederates while they remained northeast of their capital, forcing Lee's men to withdraw into the city's fortifications. But the Federals needed to defy significant odds to emerge victorious. Amid torrential rain, the 17th Vermont and 31st Maine would have to descend into an area of varied terrain, from marshy meadows to what Merriam described as a "barren sandy plain with here and there patches of scrub pine and an occasional roll of ground covered with a heavier growth of wood." Then they would ascend a crest some 900 feet in height to assault three lines of Rebel defenses consisting of abatis, slashed timber, and rifle pits situated along the edge of a woods. The graybacks had spent the past thirty-six hours fortifying this area, and their artillery held a commanding view of the frontage. Brevet Brigadier General Badeau recalled that "the [enemy] position was quite as formidable as any assumed by the rebels during the entire campaign," while Cummings emphasized the challenge of breaching this position.[25]

The Ninth Corps played a secondary role in this fight. Burnside's men composed the right flank of the Federal line near Bethesda Church and were expected to assault the Confederates before them while Grant's major thrust transpired along the Union left. These instructions also applied to Major General Warren's Fifth Corps, which lay to Burnside's left. As Grant explained, these two corps were to press the attack if Lee shifted troops away from their front "or if a favorable opportunity should present itself." Assuming the push along the Union left progressed well, Burnside and Warren should direct their efforts toward the Rebel center. Relative to the rest of the Federals, Badeau encapsulated the involvement of the Fifth and Ninth Corps as "dependent upon the other operations."[26]

And yet the bluecoats' widespread reluctance to attack entrenchments augured poorly for the later arrivals' own willingness to do so. Lieutenant Colonel Lyman wrote expansively of the Army of the Potomac's condition on the eve of the climactic assault at Cold Harbor, arguing that

> man for man, it was in no wise equal to its former self. A series of severe battles usually unsuccessful, or only half successes, closely connected by fierce skirmishes, and accompanied by weary marches and the heavy labor of building intrenchments, had enfeebled the muscles and unstrung the nerves of these hardy soldiers. Then the flower of the force was *hors du combat;* for the best officers and men are liable by their greater gallantry to be first disabled, and of those that are left even the toughest become demoralized by failure and the loss of good leaders; so that, after a time, the men will no longer charge intrenchments, and will only go forward when driven by their officers.[27]

Brevet Major Shreve adopted a more nuanced perspective, asserting that the troops in the army were leery of fieldworks because they recognized the futility of attacking them. He observed that the failure of previous Union assaults had damaged their morale, yet Grant was able to restore their courage by outflanking the Confederates instead of ordering a retreat. In Shreve's opinion, "never were the men more hopeful or in better spirits, more willing for marching, more ready to fight, than at this time." It appears that both the Vermonters and Mainers were cautious, leading Cummings to observe that his troops "move[d] about in a meek and lowly manner" within their defenses. He likely encouraged this behavior since he condemned another brigade officer as "brave to a fault" for leaving cover and falling victim to enemy fire. In the days leading up to the assault, Merriam offered comments of a similar nature. Thanks to the entrenchments, he explained that the troops "could stretch . . . out . . . paying no attention to the frequent zip of the minnies flying over us." This Mainer also doubted the graybacks would "live to get across the open ground" separating the opposing forces and insisted that to make the attempt "would have been playing into our hands." The sergeant major even admitted a desire "to hustle down behind the breastworks," yet he chose not to bolt for cover so hurriedly lest he be judged a coward by more seasoned peers. His example illustrated how quickly a rookie could adapt to the realities of life within entrenchments and points to a risk-averse mindset among the later arrivals. As they undoubtedly understood, whoever held an entrenched position had an advantage over the attacker—an unpleasant prospect for the New Englanders when they found themselves taking the offensive on June 3. Burnside thus showed excessive optimism when he judged the soldiers to be in fine shape for combat without acknowledging their anxieties about assaulting dug-in Rebels.[28]

The worn-out state of the 17th Vermont and 31st Maine suggested they would not fight well on June 3. After their long march and bouts of skirmishing, these units would lack the vigor to complete a headlong attack. They further suffered from reduced numbers, which limited the threat they could pose to Confederates defending earthworks. Owing mostly to sickness, only 236 Vermont officers and men were present for duty on May 31, or 44 percent of the whole. An absence of morning reports impedes an accounting of the Mainers, but they probably suffered a similar reduction since the daily sick ratio in the Army of the Potomac during June nearly matched the previous high of April. The unhealthy environment of the Chickahominy River facilitated the spread of disease, Lyman writing that the sluggish, "sickly-looking water" represented "the incarnation of malaria and swamp-fever."[29]

Still, experienced leadership and continued training offered some hope of success for the later arrivals. Cummings remained in command of the Vermonters, while Major White, whom Merriam described as "a splendid officer and one of the coolest men in action that I ever saw," led the Mainers. White had behaved courageously at the Wilderness, and his selection to command the 31st was fortuitous, considering the regiment's leadership woes. The other officers in this unit had already informed Griffin on May 31 that Colonel Hight was "not . . . in shape to command the regiment that day . . . to the best advantage." The general subsequently removed Hight from command due to his "want of courage in battle." Conversely, Cummings decried as "miserable" an unnamed field officer who believed that serving under White freed him "of much responsibility." In terms of training, the situation was reminiscent of previous battles. Another round of battalion drill likely boosted the morale of the Vermont rank and file, although no source indicates whether the 31st did such exercises.[30]

Grim determination must have stiffened the backbone of the later arrivals for this contest. Rain-soaked and tired from the last few days, they could not be expected to match the enthusiasm of new troops unversed in the bloody realities of combat. Regardless, Cummings had reason to believe the Vermonters steeled their resolve by reflecting upon their own fine record in the field. As he opined, the men knew their superiors "appreciated" their efforts and that Griffin was "satisfied" with them. Asserting the Federals could seize Richmond in a month, Cummings subsequently admitted that the graybacks might choose "to fight every inch with skirmishers and sharpshooters, digging line after line of entrenchments." Merriam wrote simply that the Mainers "were ready for the work which was to begin at daylight," although they had little advance warning of their role in the coming clash. Prior to midnight on June 2, Meade's orders had stipulated that the Ninth Corps would function as a reserve. After conversing with Grant, however, the army commander instructed Burnside to commit his forces to the June 3 assault. This late-night change in plans doubtless deprived the later arrivals of any opportunity to ready themselves physically and psychologically for the coming offensive.[31]

Several factors contributed to the slow participation of the New Englanders in this Federal onslaught. Grant ordered the Army of the Potomac to attack at 4:30 a.m., yet the Second Brigade did not engage the enemy for several hours. Meade permitted Burnside to decide how he would commit his troops, which helps explain this delay. The brigade held Burnside's right flank and thus the far end of the entire Union line, fronting on Matadequin Creek. Further slowing progress over the coming hours, Griffin's command started the morning in a refused formation relative to the rest of the Federal line. His troops thus pivoted back and to the right, facing northeast, obliging the bluecoats to cover a longer distance than the remainder of the Ninth Corps to reach the Confederates to the west. At roughly 7:00 a.m. the later arrivals and their comrades supported the First Brigade of the Second Division by participating in its advance on the enemy's main line. Griffin's soldiers pushed forward with skirmishers in front, causing the graybacks to withdraw before them. This was not an expeditious movement. These Federals often stopped along the way,

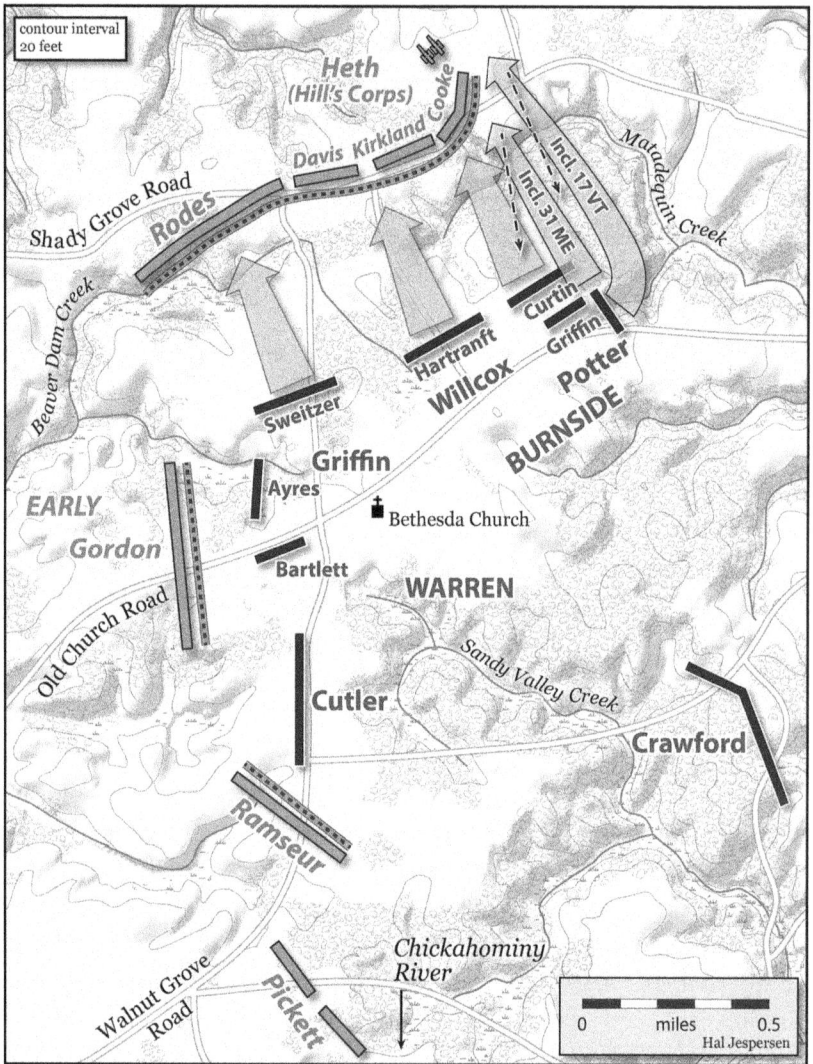

Battle of Cold Harbor, June 3, 1864.

probably to re-form their lines as they negotiated a forested area amid mounting casualties from enemy rifle musket and artillery fire. Although they progressed in a disciplined manner, it was at a sluggish rate, the first sign of their reluctance to approach the Rebel position.[32]

The New Englanders faced another delay at noon. Although they reached the enemy line, they did not attack until just after 1:00 p.m., largely because Burnside wanted them to wait until all of the Second and Third Divisions could attack in tandem. One soldier in the 32nd Maine recalled that everyone in the brigade also "paused to gather [a] breath," hesitating at the sight of the Confederate fortifications atop the crest from fifty to eighty-three yards away. Finally, the Union soldiers formed a line of battle along the forested edge of a clearing at the base of the ridge. According to Merriam, these troops ascended the slope "at the usual route step" and "slowly formed up in front of the line of rebel works." Consequently, they endured a storm of buckshot and rifle musket balls from the defenders that he likened to "a great bunch of fire crackers." The 31st Maine and two other regiments in the brigade advanced straight toward this Rebel position, which included six cannon and sharpshooters. These Federals halted once they were roughly 250 feet away. Cummings explained that the 17th Vermont and the rest of Griffin's command, composing the Second Division's right end, "swung around at many a right angle with the line of battle and against and at right angles with the enemy's left." In response, the graybacks poured in a fire from straight ahead and in enfilade on these troops. The Mainers stood firm despite suffering increasing losses from the barrage of enemy projectiles, and inspiring leadership likely bolstered their courage. Merriam picked up a rifle musket to shoot at the Confederates, and it was probably during this time that Second Lieutenant Coffin displayed the bravery that would subsequently garner him a promotion to first lieutenant.[33]

Although holding their ground, the later arrivals made little progress against the graybacks. A cloud of black powder smoke obscured targets, reducing the effectiveness of Union fire by compelling the men to aim at the discharges from Rebel weapons. To counter the enfilading fire from enemy troops on the other side of Shady Grove Road, Cummings detached two companies to join the skirmishers to their right, who promptly suppressed some of this Confederate resistance. Both units waited in vain for additional support along that side, although it is unclear which units they expected to arrive. Griffin then ordered the capture of a hidden enemy battery that his sharpshooters had momentarily silenced. But Cummings decided that the 17th and two other nearby Federal units should not proceed with the headlong assault. This action seemingly disregarded the chain of command. By way of justification, Cummings noted he was the most senior officer leading a regiment or battalion among the three

Union outfits engaged in that location. This suggests that Griffin had delegated responsibility to the Vermonter to deal with the battery since the lieutenant colonel never faced court-martial for disobedience. In lieu of a close-range attack, Cummings instructed the troops to unleash a "smart and well-directed fire" upon the battery. He opted for this more cautious approach, given the Rebels' strong defensive position, which included a large rifle pit and sharpshooters along the right flank of the Vermonters.[34]

The New Englanders now conducted an orderly withdrawal. At 12:30 p.m. Grant ordered the assault to cease, and Meade relayed this command an hour later. The Federal left had not made much headway despite hours of combat. Burnside, on the right, was alone among the Union corps commanders who looked optimistically upon the prospect of more fighting. Thus, the attack came to an end. The 17th Vermont and those units fighting alongside it now aligned themselves with the rest of the brigade, including the 31st Maine. Griffin's troops fell back, and despite a lack of information on the Mainers' experience, the retreat of the Vermonters proved dangerous. The Confederates holding the large rifle pit poured lead into their ranks while the battery unleashed canister and case upon them. Still, the soldiers of the 17th maintained a high rate of fire as they retreated. They managed to gain some protection en route by entering the sunken Shady Grove Road, which now acted as a makeshift trench with a split-rail fence along its length. Ultimately, the two outfits returned to the forested base of the hill.[35]

Sporadic combat filled the remaining daylight hours for the later arrivals. Around 3:00 p.m. they pushed forward to reenter the sunken road. In response the graybacks, positioned less than 500 feet away, loosed what a captain in the 6th New Hampshire termed "an incessant and furious fire, to which our boys were not slow in replying." These Union soldiers went on to help defeat a counterattack, to engage with sharpshooters, and to use their own accurate fire to stymie a Confederate withdrawal of cannon. At 4:00 p.m. Meade ordered another assault on the Rebel line. He instructed his corps commanders to move their troops forward at will rather than coordinating their movements with one another. But ultimately Meade called it off after learning that his subordinates neither believed it could be successful nor commanded their troops to resume the attack. The army commander would not have been surprised at this turn of events, as he later acknowledged the futility of assaulting a dug-in enemy. For the 17th Vermont and

31st Maine, it was now time to return to their original position and assume the defensive. While bluecoats across the Union line kept up a skirmish fire until dusk, these two units constructed fieldworks until 12:00 a.m.[36]

MISERY DEEPLY ENTRENCHED

JUNE 4–12, 1864

The disappointing results of the June 3 clash lowered the later arrivals' morale as they began another period of trench warfare. After the day's fighting subsided, a soldier in the 32nd Maine noted "sadness and gloom in the hearts of the survivors," who would spend more than a week under the scrutiny of the Confederates in nearby fortifications. Since it was impossible to outflank the Army of Northern Virginia so close to Richmond, Grant decided to hold a line facing the Rebels, keen to "any favorable circumstance," and gradually shift left toward the Chickahominy River. The New Englanders likely recognized that defeating the enemy depended on their ability to outlast these graybacks in an attritional contest. Cummings alluded "to . . . the settled understanding of our brigade officers that we shall advance to Richmond only by slow approaches and by entrenching ourselves as fast as we advance." This bleak outlook could not have been encouraging to Federals already worn down by weeks of service against a persistent enemy.[37]

Confederate cannon, mortar, and rifle musket fire posed a continual threat to the Vermonters and Mainers. The lethality of Rebel marksmen inspired the most commentary. Griffin asserted that "if a head was raised above our parapet it was very liable to have a bullet put through it." Likewise, a 32nd Maine soldier complained that "the merciless and unerring rifles of the enemy's sharpshooters were continually claiming new victims." He judged this eight-day stalemate more trying than the impasse in the trenches of Spotsylvania. He went on to quote a Sixth Corps surgeon's assertion that the Federals had "never before . . . been in a position where there was such constant danger." Impeding rest, the men even exchanged fire with Confederates periodically at night.[38]

The New Englanders embraced whatever protection field fortifications could provide. Suggesting the scale of this construction effort, Colonel Wainwright, the Fifth Corps chief of artillery, claimed that the men of the

Ninth Corps exceeded "all others . . . in the height and number of their breastworks." Merriam fittingly recalled that "this neighborhood had the appearance of a great prairie dog town, excavated everywhere, and with mounds of earth thrown up everywhere." The ever-present threat of Rebel fire made this task more difficult. The troops were obliged to turn the soil at night, lest they present obvious targets to the graybacks, and to divide their manpower between laborers and sentries prepared to return fire. Likewise, they could only withdraw from the front line in the dark. To avoid becoming casualties, the men had to traverse the trenches on hands and knees, even while heading rearward to refill canteens. This period in earthworks proved an unpleasant ordeal, which a sergeant in the 9th New Hampshire summed up as "lying in rifle-pits, digging, or crawling . . . or lying flat on the plowed ground."[39]

The later arrivals endured changing weather and uncomfortable living conditions in the trenches. Besides high heat and humidity, Captain Larned bemoaned that the soldiers "eat dust—sleep in dust + are a perfect mass of dust." Although lacking sufficient water of good quality, the men could at least cool themselves down by turning to nearby Confederate stockpiles of ice. They used tents or blankets as protection against high winds, cold temperatures, and rain. Once the troops even endured a downpour without being allowed to warm themselves with campfires. Sodden roads hampered the soldiers from easily changing position. Making this service drearier, the bluecoats were forced to consume a repetitive and nutritionally inferior diet. Their standard rations included meat from malnourished cattle supplemented by ham and salt, although they regained access to vegetables after more than a month. Since the men were largely stationary, they took the opportunity to improve camp maintenance, which had grown lax during the preceding weeks of movement and combat. This was timely because the rank and file were suffering from poor hygiene and resulting sickness. A sergeant in the 9th New Hampshire recalled that lice feasted on the "wasting bodies" of surviving Union troops, who also endured malaria, dysentery, and fevers. Their environs were not conducive to good health. Excrement, along with the bodies of mules and horses, pockmarked the landscape, while the corpses of combatants offered mute testimony to the dangers of crossing no-man's-land.[40]

Few opportunities existed for the Vermonters and Mainers to gather their strength for combat. They spent much of the period between June

4 and June 12 in the front line but also supported other Union soldiers, notably in the successful multiday struggle with the Rebels to control a hill near the Tucker House. These later arrivals skirmished, sometimes chancing Confederate artillery and rifle musket fire by leaving their rifle pits to approach the graybacks. Attesting to limited rest, the Federals had at least one early morning when they drew near the enemy's fortifications at sunrise and once spent the hours of 12:00 a.m. to 3:00 a.m. moving to and fro to obtain rations. Every night half of each unit stayed on guard while the remainder rested with their weapons beside them. Men on picket duty typically spent cold nighttime hours in rifle pits 55–110 yards from the Confederates. With this taxing schedule, the bluecoats could only avail themselves of a single two-day stint in the rear, where they were still exposed to enemy artillery fire. The New Englanders may have counted among the pickets who negotiated a ceasefire with the nearby Rebels to trade coffee for Confederate tobacco, even though Meade forbade such fraternization. Regarding this, historian Lauren K. Thompson argues that Civil War soldiers, "surrounded by privation, disease, and death," drew upon "prewar traditions of fraternity and resistance," concluding that "fraternization demonstrates how men managed their duty by restoring the independence military life indisputably suppressed. Those who fraternized were not cowards, deserters, or bounty jumpers, but loyal soldiers." Sharpshooters on both sides, however, continued to ply their deadly trade regardless of such ad hoc agreements. Surviving in this environment would surely have sapped any remaining physical endurance of the already wrung-out soldiers.[41]

Holding trenches at Cold Harbor must have contributed to the weakened resolve of the later arrivals. Bvt. Maj. Gen. Martin T. McMahon, chief of staff and assistant adjutant general of the Sixth Corps, wrote postwar of the period June 1–12, "in none of its marches by day or night did" the Army of the Potomac "suffer more than during those twelve days." An ordnance sergeant in the 11th New Hampshire alluded to "the body . . . cramped, the clothes soiled, the water scarce, the food scanty or half cooked." Even Lyman admitted that "the sufferings of those in the advanced lines were wellnigh intolerable." Furthermore, soldiers' spirits would have plummeted amid visual reminders of the grisly fighting that included the nearby graves of their fallen brethren. The Vermonters and Mainers also spent days listening to the cries of wounded comrades who lay in no-man's-land. According to Doctor McParlin, the army's medical director, "the greater number . . . died of their wounds and exposure, hunger and thirst." Other unfortunates expired after being caught in the ongoing crossfire, although the later arrivals may have helped rescue some of the wounded during the nighttime. It was not until June 7 that Grant and Lee agreed to a truce, which enabled the opposing sides to bury the dead and rescue any survivors. Doing so remained dangerous, for the Confederates continued to shoot at Federals who left their earthworks. Under such trying circumstances, perhaps the Vermonters drew courage from the example of Lieutenant Colonel Cummings, who declared himself "willing to work and to suffer deprivations . . . [to] enjoy the proud satisfaction of leading the 17th Regiment into the Rebel capital." The arrival of fresh manpower on June 8 in the form of Company H may also have boosted their spirits. Still, the later arrivals could not be regarded as keen for battle after such fatiguing and traumatic days in the field. A 9th New Hampshire sergeant probably captured the broader sentiment of the rank and file when he opined that all were "disgusted with anything that looks like war, and weary and worn from long watching and exposure."[42]

TWO WEEKS OF HARDSHIP

INTERPRETING THE OUTCOME
OF COLD HARBOR

The 17th Vermont and 31st Maine suffered a toll at Cold Harbor that attested to their steadfastness under fire. During the skirmishes of May 31–June 2, they braved Confederate fire, as demonstrated by the total of seven Vermont soldiers killed or wounded, with seven Maine soldiers killed or wounded as well as one officer wounded. And yet the disparity in casualties during the main assault of June 3 suggests a difference in the volume of fire that the two outfits faced. Attacking the Rebel flank, the Vermonters sustained only one officer and nine soldiers killed or wounded, a 4-percent reduction in their present-for-duty strength. Since the Mainers advanced toward the enemy head-on, their losses were more substantial, numbering forty soldiers killed, wounded, or captured. A lack of morning reports during this period makes it impossible to determine the exact drop in the 31st's present-for-duty strength. Merriam later estimated the unit's manpower just prior to June 3 as 400 officers and men. He deemed this figure accurate as of May 19 and argued that the addition of Company K and return of those wounded or sick offset the losses that the regiment sustained up to the main clash at Cold Harbor. The Mainers' casualties may have therefore represented a 10-percent drop in their present-for-duty strength. Scrutinizing the casualty totals is revelatory. Only a single Vermont officer fell wounded, suggesting that the leaders in both units did not feel obligated to expose themselves to motivate their troops. Referring to statistics for the rest of the brigade offers evidence to conclude that the later arrivals were more dependable than their peers. Officers constituted 10 percent of the losses in Griffin's command over the longer stretch of June 2–15, even though most of his units were more experienced than the 17th and 31st. Also, data indicates that those entering these two outfits as veterans continued to take greater risks under fire than their less experienced comrades. Among the Vermonters, seasoned troops and the aforementioned officer represented 30 percent of the losses. This outweighed the proportion of veterans who ever served in the 17th. The case was much the same with the Mainers. Sixteen percent of their casualties were veterans, slightly exceeding the proportion of such combatants who ever served in the 31st. Between June 4 and 12, deadly trench warfare likely reinforced the later arrivals' hesitation to assault fieldworks, which they had already shown on June 3. Whereas the Vermonters sustained one officer and seven soldiers killed or wounded, the Mainers tallied eighteen officers and men killed, wounded, missing, or captured.[43]

Most contemporaries believed that Burnside's command had not performed well. Regarding the midafternoon skirmish on June 2, Grant complained that the Ninth Corps defeated the Confederate attacks without having "followed [them] up as they should have been." Badeau echoed this perspective, while Wainwright simply judged, "the Ninth Corps do not seem to have covered themselves with glory." Commenters generally focused their criticism on the June 3 assault. Two Civil War veterans and early historians, Pvt. Theodore Gerrish of the 20th Maine Volunteer Infantry Regiment and Pvt. John S. Hutchinson of the 10th Virginia Volunteer Infantry Regiment, insisted these Federals "did not meet with any success that would throw a gleam of sunshine upon the results of that disastrous day." Several others admitted that the later arrivals had faced poor odds of success. Although Badeau chided Burnside for tardiness, he explained the failure of the Union assault by declaring, "behind entrenchments, Lee's gallant soldiers were almost invincible." Sharing this dismal view, Cummings insisted, "the whole movement was an error." Merriam likewise decried this "desperate attempt" to pit the Federals against seasoned graybacks in "a very strong position" whom only "overwhelming force could have driven . . . out."[44]

Despite these admonishments, not all coverage of the June 3 fighting was negative. Grant lauded the Ninth Corps for securing ground, as did Badeau, who maintained that these troops "had really made more progress than any other portion of the army." Historian Woodbury celebrated their courage and exaggerated by insisting they "were on the point of winning a decisive advantage." Burnside declared that his "command never fought more bravely," and those serving under him reiterated such rhetoric. According to Brigadier General Potter, the Second Division imperiled the Confederate line and "handsomely repulsed" advancing Rebels, causing them to fall back overnight. Most notably, the later arrivals received praise. Cummings quoted Potter as saying that the 17th was "a G–d-D–n good fighting Regiment," and Brigadier General Griffin announced that "the Thirty-first . . . [had] won . . . imperishable renown." The 17th Vermont and 31st Maine received plaudits from their respective commanders and the press, with the Vermonters earning additional accolades from a lieutenant in the 11th New Hampshire. But observers paid little attention to the trench warfare that ended this battle, save for Cummings, who bragged on June 6 that his "pickets are the only ones in the Division that have not yet been driven in."[45]

Overall, the later arrivals did perform well at Cold Harbor. Between May 31 and June 2, these troops showed their mettle in skirmishes with the enemy, capturing fieldworks and numerous prisoners. Despite a lack of clear objectives, they exhibited cohesion during this unexpected fighting as they drove back the Confederates. Although the Vermont and Maine pickets broke before the graybacks during the midafternoon skirmish of June 2, they collected themselves to conduct an effective delaying action over several hours. Thus, Grant overstated matters by decrying a lack of aggression on the part of the Ninth Corps that day. The New Englanders accrued significant casualties, which was indicative of their continued determination to fight after several grueling weeks in the field. During the main clash of June 3, they accomplished their task of holding the enemy's attention. These later arrivals showed reluctance to attack the Rebel works, which was not surprising for soldiers taxed to their limit by intense combat. Inspecting the frontage afterward, Cummings remarked that "the trees and ground gave evidence of them having suffered severely shot and shell had scarred every tree so much that as high as I could reach . . . I could not cover a round spot with my hat." In the last stage of the engagement, however, spanning June 4–12, the later arrivals further demonstrated their ability to quickly build and defend entrenchments. Regardless, this tiring and stressful experience reduced the soldiers' ability to participate effectively in their next trial, the Petersburg Campaign.[46]

The 17th Vermont and 31st Maine emerged from the Overland Campaign as battle-hardened outfits. Despite the brutal contests at the Wilderness and Spotsylvania, these troops persevered to fight well at North Anna and Cold Harbor. This was impressive, for Woodbury declared that "no campaign during the progress of the war was at all so severe in its demands upon human endurance and human courage." From May 6 to June 12, the Vermonters and Mainers sustained a high operational tempo of marching and combat that epitomized Grant's strategy to defeat the Confederacy. Each engagement saw the Federals strive in vain to achieve a decisive breakthrough of the Rebel position on a given battlefield. In response, Grant ordered the Army of the Potomac to repeatedly flank left on treks that would endanger the Army of Northern Virginia's lines of communication. Such movements compelled Lee's troops to leave their defenses and assume new positions on subsequent fields of battle. The unrelenting pace strained the New Englanders physically and mentally, yet they emerged from this period capable of further soldiering.[47]

Assessing the combat performance of the later arrivals at North Anna and Cold Harbor reveals a dilemma in Grant's drive for Union victory. The cautious approach that enabled the Vermonters and Mainers to survive this campaign ran counter to the offensive mindset that the lieutenant general's strategy required. As a result, his inability to crush the Army of Northern Virginia can be partially blamed on his insatiable need for a supply of green soldiers willing to take risks their seasoned comrades would refuse. Grant does not appear to have recognized this problem, given his baseless assertion on June 5 that the "army is . . . confident of protecting itself without intrenchments." Studying the experiences of the 17th Vermont and 31st Maine does not yield evidence to support this optimistic perspective. Conversely, the general in chief hinted at the Federals' reluctance to charge the Rebel works by declaring they could "drive the enemy whenever and wherever he can be found without this protection." Instead of adapting to this mental shift among the troops, he measured progress in terms of casualties imposed and sustained. Grant conceded that the Union offensives at the Wilderness, Spotsylvania, and North Anna were not all successful but had still "inflicted upon the enemy severe losses, which tended in the end to the complete overthrow of the rebellion." The June 3 onslaught at Cold Harbor alone inspired regret, for he confessed that "it was the only general attack made from the Rapidan to the James which did not inflict upon the enemy losses to compensate for our own." The lieutenant general was not alone in his failure to appreciate the plight of the rank and file, for Meade inexplicably wrote on that same June 5 that his troops "as yet . . . show no evidences of" tiredness. Nevertheless, he cited the poor record of Union assaults on fortified Confederates during this campaign to underscore his conviction that such efforts were generally bound to fall short. Doubtless, the Vermonters and Mainers would have agreed.[48]

Reappraising the contributions of the New Englanders in the second half of the Overland Campaign reveals the value of studying combat performance on the small-unit level. A top-down perspective on Civil War battles, which emphasizes the influence of command decisions on their outcome, can oversimplify the struggles and achievements of the troops. In this vein Wainwright sweepingly declared of Burnside's command that "from the start the corps has done nothing; it has been put in very little, and when sent forward always stuck at the first impediment." In fact, focusing attention on the 17th Vermont and 31st Maine reveals their determination to advance the cause of Union victory despite the human cost. Since these units first marched onto a battlefield at the Wilderness, they had suffered a heavy toll. Based on present-for-duty numbers back on May 6, the Vermonters went on to sustain a 51-percent casualty rate in the bloody fighting that spanned the next thirty-seven days. For their part, the Mainers withstood a lower yet still sizable 29-percent casualty rate. As Badeau observed, such "losses were the price at which only the country could be saved."[49]

Brig. Gen. Robert B. Potter
(LIBRARY OF CONGRESS)

Brig. Gen.
Simon G. Griffin
(NATIONAL ARCHIVES)

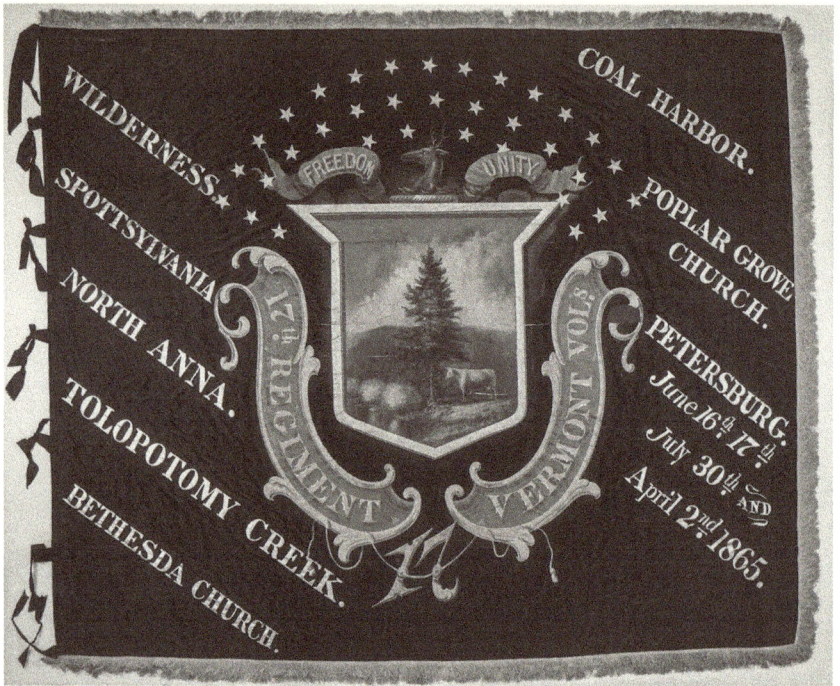

17th Vermont state flag
(VERMONT STATE CURATOR'S OFFICE)

Lt. Col. Charles Cummings
(LIBRARY OF CONGRESS)

Lyman E. Knapp as either major or
brevet lieutenant colonel, rank unclear in photo
(VERMONT HISTORICAL SOCIETY)

Maj. William B. Reynolds

(VERMONT HISTORICAL SOCIETY)

First Lt. Joel H. Lucia
(VERMONT HISTORICAL SOCIETY)

Cpl. Moses Whitehill

(VERMONT HISTORICAL SOCIETY)

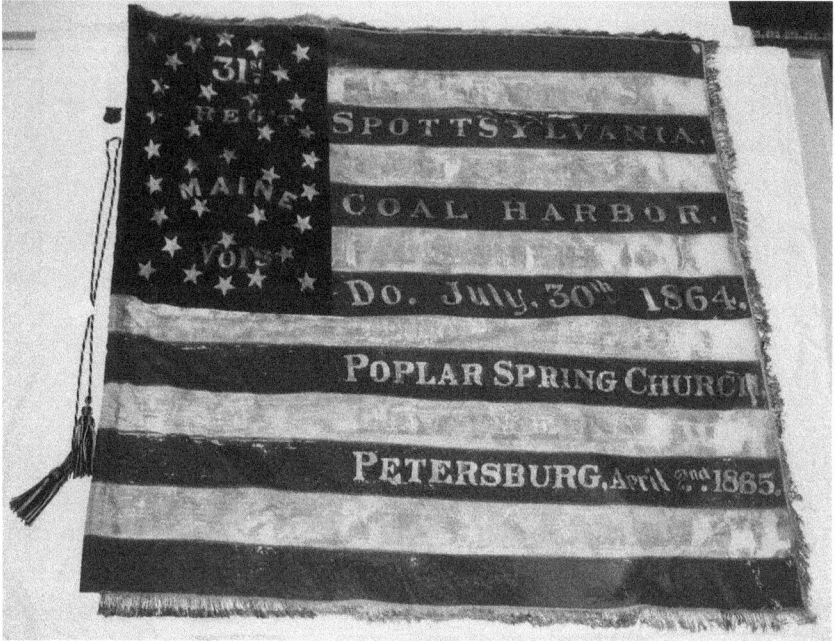

31st Maine national flag
(MAINE STATE MUSEUM)

Col. Daniel White
(DIGITAL MAINE)

First Lt. John P. Sheahan

(DIGITAL MAINE)

Sgt. Maj. Leander
Otis Merriam
(DIGITAL MAINE)

Pvt. Horatio Fox Smith
(DIGITAL MAINE)

Company D, 31st Maine

(U.S. ARMY HERITAGE AND EDUCATION CENTER)

4

THE FIRST UNION OFFENSIVE
AT PETERSBURG AND THE
BATTLE OF THE CRATER

It is just three years since the first Bull Run battle was
fought, and even Virginia is not conquered, Richmond is
not taken, nor the "back of the rebellion" so badly broken
as to produce much of a paralysis of its lower extremities.

—Lt. Col. Charles Cummings, 17th Vermont

If you could see what I have seen in these last battles
you would say, O Victory dearly bought! never
do I wish to look upon such sights again.

—1st Lt. John P. Sheahan, 31st Maine

In an 1866 report on the Civil War, Provost Marshal General Fry asserted,
"generally, a battle is but the culmination of preceding physical exertions
and hardships." Fry's words prompt a defining question about the combat
performance of later arrivals in the Union army as they gained in experience: to what extent did their past service influence their fighting ability in
subsequent engagements? The example of the 17th Vermont and 31st Maine
is informative, for these raw outfits emerged from the Overland Campaign
as seasoned units after participating in four battles in just six weeks. This
trial justified a newspaper correspondent from the 17th who claimed his unit
was "old at least as a fighting regiment," a judgment equally true of the 31st.
The Vermonters and Mainers would next participate in the Petersburg Campaign. They could steel themselves with the knowledge that the bloodshed
they had endured from the Wilderness to Cold Harbor was advancing the
cause of Union victory. As First Lieutenant Sheahan admitted, a grueling
period of "many months" lay ahead, but at least "the Rebels have been

pushed back, the [Army of the Potomac's] days of disorderly retreat are over." To keep up this high operational tempo, the later arrivals would have to persevere against a foe whose defensive skill had exacted a heavy toll in past engagements. During the first and most arduous stage of the coming campaign, when the New Englanders fought in the First Union Offensive at Petersburg and the Battle of the Crater, they experienced their greatest triumph and worst defeat, respectively, on the tactical level.[1]

The Vermonters and Mainers performed solidly in combat, given the difficulties they faced. They did their part in the First Union Offensive and at the Crater, although the Federals were twice unsuccessful in their attempt to capture Petersburg. Still, the rank and file could not be held responsible for such dismal outcomes. The command decisions of Union generals had a greater effect on the course of these actions, especially the high command's insistence on driving the worn-out army forward as it approached the limits of what could be accomplished without a break from active campaigning. The New Englanders still maintained their cohesion, partially achieved their objectives, and unflinchingly absorbed casualties that reduced their outfits to shadows of their former selves. Contemporaries and scholars who derided the fighting ability of later arrivals did not consider how these soldiers performed as they matured into more seasoned troops. Contrary to dismissive stereotyping, such bluecoats demonstrated their worth under fire at this stage. Providing evidence of this fact, a majority of officers in the 17th and 31st did not judge it necessary to risk enemy fire unduly in order to drive their men forward. Conversely, veterans suffered disproportionate losses at the Crater, which suggests their less seasoned comrades held back during this particularly trying clash of arms. Perhaps such diminishing resolve was unsurprising, for the later arrivals' greatest achievement was their ability to endure such an exhausting period of marching, entrenching, and fighting. That staying power, so essential to success in the attritional struggle they faced, would represent an important contribution to the northern cause.

ON TO PETERSBURG

JUNE 12–16, 1864

The later arrivals began this period with the greatest endurance trial of their time in uniform. Grant launched the campaign to attack Petersburg, a railroad center south of Richmond, and thereby cripple the logistics of the Army of Northern Virginia. According to Badeau, by taking this city, "Lee could not remain one week in Richmond, or on the northern side" of the James River. This was overstating matters somewhat, given that the Rebel capital could receive supplies from two railroads independent of Petersburg. Still, imposing a high level of strain on the Rebels would advance Grant's objective of crushing the enemy host. To approach Petersburg, he ordered the Army of the Potomac to depart the Cold Harbor battlefield and execute a longer left-flanking movement to get around the opposing force. The soldiers would have to cross over the James to its south bank and march miles to the city. Subsequent fighting there would inaugurate the First Union Offensive. Maj. Gen. William Farrar Smith, commanding the Eighteenth Corps in the Army of the James, was to strike the first blow against the enemy on June 15. Over the following days, Meade would commit his men to a large-scale assault to take the city before Lee could sufficiently bolster the Rebel defenders to condemn the Federals to a lengthy siege. After capturing Petersburg, the next Union goal would be to drive toward Richmond, at which point the outflanked graybacks would have to exit the Rebel capital and head for either Danville or Lynchburg.[2]

Leaving Cold Harbor on the evening of June 12, the Vermonters and Mainers undertook a grueling 68-mile, four-day trek to reach positions near Petersburg. Meade expected the Ninth Corps to "move promptly and quickly," which proved impossible, given the challenges of the journey. To begin with, Burnside's men had the greatest distance to cover of all the Union corps. They made do with limited food as they suffered through high temperatures and humidity, dust, biting insects, and sandy roads more akin to rude footpaths. They pushed on through long hours on the move and night marches, including a two-day stretch with no more than four hours of sleep. Still, the 17th and 31st only managed to travel 35 miles in twenty-six hours, including a one-hour stop. This equaled a mere 1.3 miles per hour, much slower than the rate of advance they had maintained on their trip to the Wilderness. Several delays along the way help explain this sluggish pace. The soldiers once paused to entrench, had to coordinate their movements with wagons and other bluecoats on the road, and awaited the completion of a bridge to cross the James. Despite these obstacles, the New Englanders did not have much opportunity to recuperate until June 15. They halted for most of that day to await the construction

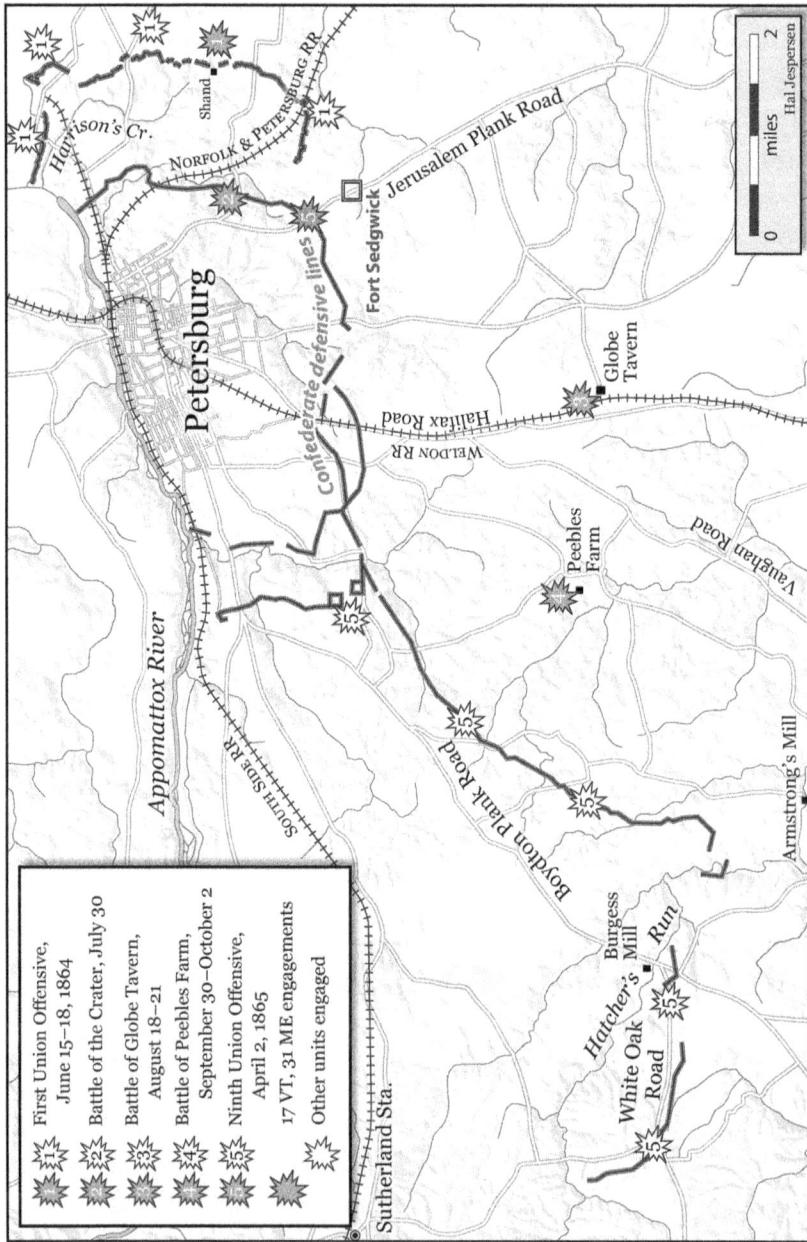

Union Offensives and Battles of the Petersburg Campaign involving the 17th Vermont and 31st Maine, June 1864–April 1865.

First Union Offensive, June 15–18, 1864

Battle of the Crater, July 30

Battle of Globe Tavern, August 18–21

Battle of Peebles Farm, September 30–October 2

Ninth Union Offensive, April 2, 1865

17 VT, 31 ME engagements

Other units engaged

of another bridge and the arrival of wagons carrying rations. The men took this opportunity to wash themselves and to try to relax in surroundings that Lieutenant Colonel Cummings described as "a delightful plantation."[3]

The New Englanders began the twenty-two-mile forced march that constituted the last leg of their trek on the evening of June 15. Typically, the men stopped for five minutes per hour of travel, whereupon they would fall asleep and struggle to awaken in order to resume the march. These troops finally enjoyed a break of some two hours overnight when Burnside paused the corps to determine the way forward and allow for the movement of wagons. Nevertheless, straggling and heat exhaustion were pervasive, as revealed during a roughly two-hour stop for breakfast the next day, when a mere four to eight Vermonters per company were present for duty. Alternatively, Capt. Eldin J. Hartshorn offered a larger headcount of approximately seventy-five soldiers for the 17th, which exceeded the present-for-duty strength of any other unit in Griffin's command. Not including officers, this nevertheless represented only about one-fourth of the Vermonters' manpower available for combat back on June 10. Along the route of the Ninth Corps, ambulances and the rear guard collected worn-out and sick soldiers who had collapsed. Falling behind could be risky, however, as the Rebels demonstrated by capturing a Vermont private. Straggling was not necessarily a sign of poor cohesion, for historian Kathryn Shively observes that this type of behavior "enabled . . . self-care, such as foraging or locating clean water."[4]

The tired soldiers finally reached the outskirts of Petersburg on June 16. Lieutenant Colonel Lyman, an aide-de-camp to Meade, claimed they were suffering "without water, broken by a severe march, scorched by the sun, and covered with a suffocating dust." The men had also contended with smoke-filled air from other troops setting fire to homes along their route. Indeed, the Vermonters were in poor shape, for Cummings complained that his "ranks . . . [were] rapidly depleted from hard marching on very short rations." First Lieutenant Lucia, reflecting on the history of the 17th, judged this to be "the most severe march of its entire service." The Mainers were also in a lamentable state, having already consumed their half-rations before the trek ended. Private Smith decried it as "very fatiguing" and a "fearfully hard march" in which "men dropped dead in their tracks." Even a lieutenant in the much older 11th New Hampshire judged this to be "the hardest night's march we ever made." Griffin's men were fortunate to enjoy a break long enough to brew coffee and recover to a degree, with further opportunities to rest once they arrayed themselves on the Union left in front of the city. This change in position reflected Grant's orders to be ready "as soon as possible either for attack or defense." Despite the urgent command, Burnside's slowed rate of march delayed a Federal assault during the First Union Offensive. After arriving, Brigadier General Potter ordered Griffin's brigade to temporarily serve under Brig. Gen. Francis C. Barlow, commanding the First Division of the Second Corps. Not until 6:00 p.m. did the Vermonters and Mainers support the attack by the Second Corps on Confederate entrenchments two and a half miles east of Petersburg. When this offensive failed, Brigadier General Griffin's troops shifted their position to the Union right. Rushing through a mile of undergrowth on uneven ground, they braved enemy rifle musket and artillery fire to occupy terrain that other bluecoats had already captured. Although the fighting sputtered out around 9:00 p.m., skirmishing continued until midnight as the Rebels tried to retake the lost ground. The later arrivals had no time to recover, for they went on to entrench and serve as pickets less than 165 feet away from their foe.[5]

GLORY AT THE POINT OF THE BAYONET

JUNE 17–18, 1864

On the morning of June 17, the Vermonters and Mainers would face a test of their willingness to storm entrenchments. After making several costly assaults during the Overland Campaign, it remained to be seen whether they had the fortitude to do so again. Potter had orders to capture the Confederate works facing his Second Division. He gave Griffin the responsibility for organizing the attack, but the troops had little warning of their role, receiving word of it only at midnight. They concentrated before the Shand House, which stood upon the tip of Hickory Hill, a piece of land jutting out about a half mile from the Rebel lines. Two ravines with brooks running through them bordered the area. Griffin's troops, composing the right flank of the division, would attack the northern face of this salient, while Potter's First Brigade focused on its eastern face. Passing through one of the ravines, the later arrivals were to climb its roughly twenty-foot bank to confront what a sergeant in the 9th New Hampshire described as "extensive, well built, and complete" enemy fortifications. These works included rifle pits, a redoubt with six guns that could fire along the brigade's left flank, and an elevated two-gun redan. A four-gun battery lay behind the house and nearby outbuildings. Still, Union forces were favorably situated to attack the salient, as the undulating terrain liable to slow the soldiers' progress would also serve to cover their approach.[6]

Auguring poorly for the fight ahead, the 17th Vermont and 31st Maine were reduced in numerical strength. Past experience stressed the importance of ample troops to compensate for the heavy losses incurred while attacking enemy defenses. But Cummings counted only 135 Vermonters present for duty—22 percent of the whole unit as of June 10. In a letter, Smith later noted roughly 150 Maine soldiers present for duty, although it is not possible to determine what percentage of the total this represented due to a lack of morning reports. Neither tabulation accounted for the number of officers. Disease was chiefly responsible for whittling the ranks of the New Englanders, as they were more vulnerable to maladies than long-serving soldiers. As most of the later arrivals had not spent time in older units, their immune systems were still adapting to the unhygienic realities of life in uniform. This was especially true for Company H of the 17th, which had only joined the battalion nine days earlier. According to Meade, "the heat, hard service, bad water, and swampy regions" negatively affected the well-being of all his troops. Other contributing factors included a lack of food, sleep, and shelter; intense marching; and gunshot wounds that had left their weakened victims more likely to suffer a future ailment.[7]

The later arrivals consequently approached their next clash with dogged determination. Five thousand Federals were necessary to make this assault according to an army estimate, but the unsuccessful bid to capture the ground the night before had involved only two thousand troops. Exhausted and few in number, the New Englanders were still expected to help seize a well-fortified enemy position. Although contemporary historian John C. Ropes claimed the men "were in good condition," the circumstances justified the pessimism of a Second Corps brigade commander who likened the attack on the Shand House to the ill-fated Charge of the Light Brigade during the Crimean War (1853–56). Cummings echoed this bleak outlook, for he did not believe he would personally survive the encounter. Reflecting on the inadvisability of the pending assault, the lieutenant colonel railed that "it was Burnside's order, Made as too often such orders are upon information furnished by some incompetent popinjay on the staff who comes into some safe place and looks a minute when all is quiet." Even Private Smith alluded to a widespread belief "that the corps placed in advance in an attack on such fearfully strong works . . . must suffer terribly." Still, as Sergeant Major Merriam explained, delaying the offensive would allow the Confederates time to improve their defenses so that "twenty four more hours could see us confronted by another Cold Harbor." That prospect surely encouraged the rank and file to persevere lest they experience a repeat of the infamous Union defeat.[8]

Good leadership may have helped further steel the resolve of the Vermonters and Mainers. Smith would subsequently describe Griffin as "our old hero," which suggests that his presence had instilled confidence in the members of the Second Brigade. Likewise, the officers and men of the 31st Maine had expressed high regard for their regimental commander, Major White, near the end of the fighting at Cold Harbor and urged Griffin to request his rise in rank to colonel. Griffin concurred and declared White to be "a brave, able & efficient commander," leading to the Mainer's rank change in early July. In the 17th Cummings advocated for the promotion of Orderly Sgt. Henry D. Jordan to second lieutenant. He not only praised the man's general performance but also specified that "his character is excellent and his influence good."[9]

Strict discipline remained necessary to maintain the element of surprise in this attack. After midnight Griffin's men stealthily traversed thickets and fallen trees to enter the ravine along the northern face of the salient less than 200 yards from the Confederate defenses. The brigadier general deployed his brigade into two lines. He regarded the 17th Vermont as his most dependable outfit and placed it along the right flank in front, where he anticipated encountering the most intense combat. Meanwhile, Griffin positioned the 31st Maine toward the right end of the second line. The troops were careful to whisper since Rebel pickets lay nearby. In further preparation the bluecoats proceeded to stow dinnerware in haversacks to stifle rattling, remove firing caps from rifle muskets to prevent accidental discharges, fix bayonets, and then collapse into slumber after 1:00 a.m.[10]

Griffin caught the enemy off guard with an early morning charge. At 3:00 a.m. the later arrivals arose and climbed the ravine bank, traversing the area crowded by some troops of an entrenched Second Corps brigade. The New Englanders and the rest of their own brigade then re-formed their

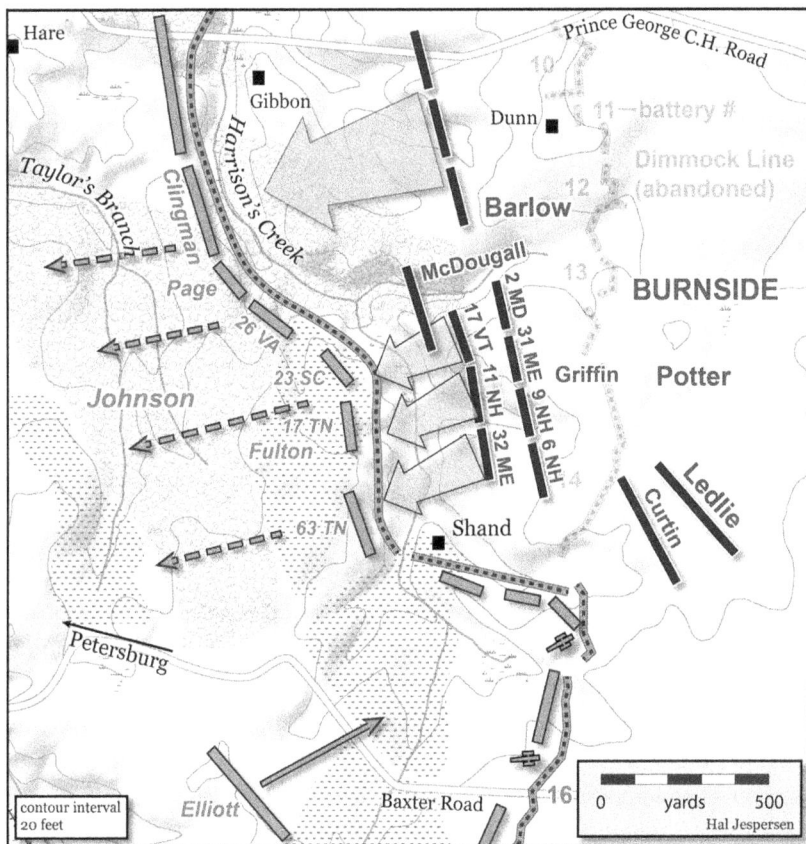

First Union Offensive at Petersburg, June 17, 1864.

lines. Following Meade's attack order of 3:45 a.m., these troops advanced at the double-quick with what early Ninth Corps historian Augustus B. Woodbury called "the fury of a tornado." Sunrise illuminated the attackers, but most of the Confederates were still asleep. Once the oncoming bluecoats neared the high ground, however, some of the dozing graybacks awakened and grabbed their weapons. The Rebels unleashed a scattered picket fire, followed by a haphazard infantry volley from their line and what Smith described as "a perfect tempest of . . . canister" from several cannon. According to Merriam, those enemy projectiles "finished many a poor fellow," including 1st Lt. Guy H. Guyer of the 17th Vermont, who suffered a fatal gunshot wound while leading his men onward. Although this fire struck down Federals in the front, the graybacks had poor aim, leading them to shoot over the heads of the men in the second line. The 31st Maine still tallied nine casualties, however, among those who outpaced their comrades to enter the first line during the advance. Such enemy opposition caused the nearest Union soldiers to hesitate, so their comrades in the rear rushed forward in support. With this surge, the Vermonters and Mainers used their bayonets to help drive out the Rebel occupants from the fieldworks in just fifteen minutes. They impaled those who resisted the onslaught. As Captain Knapp of the 17th remarked, "It is said that bayonet wounds are seldom known; but I can vouch for many that were made that early morning." First Lt. George Hicks of the 17th inspired his comrades by seizing a Confederate regiment's flag, a feat that justified his subsequent rise to brevet captain. First Sgt. Samuel Busley and Sgt. H. G. Smith, both of the 31st, also offered courageous examples that partially underpinned their nominations for promotion.[11]

The assault now petered out. For a short while, the New Englanders chased and shot at the Confederates, whom Cummings observed "broke and run like sheep" across a field. The Federals halted when they encountered what Burnside termed "a . . . very strong position." Bvt. Maj. Gen. Andrew A. Humphreys, Meade's chief of staff, later recalled that this line was situated "on the west slope of Harrison's Creek." From the safety of these entrenchments, the enemy opened fire with rifle muskets and masked batteries. As Merriam recalled, "solid shot, shells . . . cannister and minnies came in lively shape." Pressing forward would have obligated Griffin's men to brave this deadly storm of projectiles while crossing that same open ground. Instead, the bluecoats withdrew and dug in to gain protection from the enemy fire. A majority of the Mainers were nonplussed about the cannon barrage, an attitude that the Vermonters likely shared. Once the graybacks realized this Union attack had ended, they slowed their shooting, and the later arrivals performed less demanding tasks for the rest of the day. Some Vermonters and Mainers skirmished with the Rebels. The rest of the 17th, plus the 31st, stood downhill roughly 200 yards from these enemy troops, whose guns fired too high to cause injury. After having constructed earthworks, the New Englanders then changed position that afternoon when Potter relieved the Second Brigade from the front line. The two outfits then worked again on field fortifications, with the 31st benefiting from an example of motivational leadership. Sheahan took part in the entrenching effort that day, which inspired his men to yell their appreciation. The later arrivals also profited from time spent recuperating, prepared to support Burnside's First and Third Divisions if called upon, and skirmished more that night.[12]

June 18 marked the last day of the offensive and involved little fighting for the Vermonters and Mainers. At 4:00 a.m. the depleted men moved ahead a half mile in high humidity and under Confederate artillery fire to support the Third Division's advance. Some later arrivals temporarily served as pickets under Capt. J. N. Jones of the 6th New Hampshire, who led a force of roughly 100 men drawn from Griffin's command. These select Federals pushed forward around 7:00 a.m. and halted just under 1,000 feet away from the Rebel rifle pits, enduring sharp fire along the way. Jones drove his pickets farther ahead than originally planned, then directed them to shoot at the enemy from the protection of a fence. Cpl. Almeron C. Inman of the 17th showed courage during this exchange, helping justify his subsequent recommendation for the Medal of Honor, although he did not ultimately receive it. Pursuant to orders, Jones instructed the bluecoats to retreat at 10:00 a.m. The rest of the 17th Vermont and the 31st Maine spent the day along a wood line protecting a Union battery, later joined by the pickets upon their return to the brigade. They were fortunate to have less demanding duties on June 18, for Burnside emphasized his troops were in such bad shape that "it [was] necessary to move carefully and to keep the men well in hand." Once this offensive finally ended, the Second Division advanced that night to assume control over most of the corps frontage, with some Vermonters and Mainers serving as pickets. After four days of combat, the Federals had failed to capture Petersburg, leaving the survivors to ponder the meaning of their sacrifice.[13]

SUCCESS IN THE SHADOW OF FAILURE

THE COST OF THE
FIRST UNION OFFENSIVE

The First Union Offensive, and the June 17 assault in particular, proved damaging for the later arrivals. Meade downplayed the bloody toll that his army had sustained, arguing that these casualties simply reflected the scale of the combat. Despite this explanation to Grant, he wrote candidly to his wife, "[the] loss is severe, and shows how hard the fighting was." Potter adopted an optimistic tack, asserting that the price paid was modest in exchange for what his men had won. And yet the present-for-duty strength in both New England units dropped by about one-fifth, a high cost given that they were so undermanned. The 17th Vermont tallied twenty-nine officers and men killed or wounded, while the 31st Maine suffered thirty-two commissioned and enlisted casualties. Notably, officers made up a proportionate share of these losses. Their casualty rates in the 17th and 31st closely matched that of the entire Second Brigade between June 16 and 17, in which 7 percent of those killed, wounded, or missing were officers. This could suggest that many officers did not feel their men needed to be led from the front, where heroic displays of leadership would have placed them at greater risk from enemy fire. It is also possible that they had to remain behind their lines to drive hesitant men onward, although there is no record of such coercion required that day. Moreover, combatants who had previously served in other outfits did not amount to a disproportionately large number of the casualties, which indicates that officers and men for the first time in uniform persevered instead of shirking their duty. The more seasoned Vermonters accounted for 28 percent of losses in the 17th, just slightly higher than the ratio of such experienced combatants who ever served in this unit. Likewise, 13 percent of the Maine casualties consisted of individuals with previous stints in uniform, about equaling their proportion in the Maine outfit during the war.[14]

The New Englanders secured a large portion of the Union gains, which partially explains the bloodshed they suffered. Griffin's men, along with the First Brigade of the Second Division, seized about a mile of the Confederate fieldworks, approximately 600 Rebels, 1,500 stands of small arms, ammunition, four guns with twenty-four horses, an unspecified number of caissons, and the colors of five enemy units. Of this total, the Vermonters laid claim to 71 graybacks, a set of colors, one cannon, a caisson, and six horses. The Mainers took a caisson, one limber, seven horses, and at least 52 Confederates. The results of this attack proved to be the highlight of Federal efforts during the First Union Offensive.[15]

Officers and the press celebrated the performance of the bluecoats at the Shand House. Grant issued an order lauding their courage, while Meade enthused that "their persistence and success is highly creditable." A similar tone prevailed within the Ninth Corps. Burnside commended his troops, citing "the high appreciation in which their services . . . are held at the headquarters of the army." Potter and Griffin also praised the Vermonters and Mainers. More expansive was Captain Larned, who stated that "the noble fellows only waited to be told what was required, and they went at it with a courage that accomplished more than was designed." Even officers in the 17th and 31st reflected proudly on the charge. Cummings noted the fortitude of his battalion and insisted he could have secured any objective if he had had his full complement of 800 men at hand. Colonel White celebrated "the bravery, gallantry and good conduct of both officers and men," whereas three fellow Mainers, Adjutant and First Lieutenant Allyn, Captain Dean, and Capt. George A. Bolton, focused on the impressive comportment of the soldiers.[16]

According to the three measures of combat performance, the later arrivals fought well. Admittedly, Confederate fire caused the Vermonters to waver, but this was to be expected of fatigued men well versed in the danger of frontal attacks. Yet during this brief pause, the Mainers displayed cohesion by forging onward with the rest of the second line to help the front line continue the assault. The two outfits went on to achieve their objective of seizing the Rebel position at the Shand House. This served to bring the Second Division closer to Petersburg than the rest of the army except for parts of the First and Third Divisions, which pushed ahead later on June 17. Such forward progress imperiled the enemy's position and put the Ninth Corps artillery within range of the city. Helping explain this achievement, the 17th and 31st proved capable of withstanding intense fire. The heavy casualties they sustained did not deter them from making sizable gains during this battle.[17]

CAUGHT BETWEEN TRENCHES
AND A HARD PLACE

JUNE 19–JULY 29, 1864

The exhausted New Englanders spent the next forty days engaged in trench warfare. This heralded a change in Grant's approach, as he decided against making further assaults upon the Confederate fortifications surrounding Petersburg. Now the Army of the Potomac would seek to wear down the enemy by digging in around the city. This involved pushing toward the various railroads and roadways entering Petersburg in a gradual leftward shift around the enemy flank. Grant cited the depleted state of the Federals to justify this recourse to siege methods, as he opted "to rest the men and use the spade for their protection." And yet this would still prove to be an endurance contest with the enemy for which the bluecoats were ill suited. As Meade declared, "the army . . . requires rest to prevent its morale being impaired." Spending so many days moving, entrenching, and fighting across Virginia had left the men haggard, something that little changed even after the turn to more sedentary duties near Petersburg. Grant and Meade repeatedly complained of weary troops, and in late July Army of the Potomac medical director Doctor McParlin felt that the rank and file needed further recuperation. The condition of the Second Brigade justified this dismal perspective, for as the editor of the 9th New Hampshire regimental history observed, "mortal men could endure no more." Cummings deplored the period spent in earthworks, which he claimed was unparalleled in the eyes of the most seasoned combatants, and First Lieutenant Lucia of the 17th insisted it "was the most severe and trying time of its service." The Mainers espoused a similar viewpoint. Surgeon J. B. Mitchell regarded this "campaign . . . [as] probably the hardest since the commencement of the war." Reflecting on the days after Cold Harbor, First Lieutenant Sheahan grumbled that he could "still feel the effects of our night marching and sleeping in the damp air." More simply, Private Smith described himself as "a ragged powder-burnt veteran."[18]

The difficult environment exacerbated the soldiers' misery. Excessive heat inspired Cummings to declare, "the heavens are as brass and the earth as molten iron." In a similar vein, Wagoner William H. King lamented, "the heat is to mutch fore our boys." Captain Hartshorn was more optimistic, asserting this "weather [was] almost intolerable but the boys bear it bravely." The temperature reached a high of 110°F under shade at the beginning of July, with 98°F being the norm around midday. Conversely, the men faced cool, damp nights. The movement of animals, troops, artillery, and wagons transformed the dry soil into dust up to a foot deep that filled the nearby roadways and clouded the air. As Wagoner Sargent R. Emerson of the 17th Vermont complained, this powder "would blow into the tents like snow when the wind blew hard." Merriam summed up this plight by bluntly declaring, "we roasted in the trenches, we breathed dust, ate dust and smelt dust." On some occasions these Federals sweltered in high humidity. With rarely a chance to wash, Cummings unsurprisingly described his battalion as "a dirty, lousy set of men." A second lieutenant in the 32nd Maine wrote that his soldiers' "clothes were tattered and torn. Some had no coats and some no blankets; some wore one boot and one shoe, while others had none. Officers, by their dress, could hardly be distinguished from their men, save by the sword they carried in place of a musket." To protect against the scorching sun, these Federals gathered bushes and tree branches to cover the entrenched areas wherein they rested. The bluecoats quenched their thirst by digging wells and awaiting periodic provisions of ice. Such efforts were necessary, given the scarcity of nearby water, as the closest spring and brook to the two New England outfits lay a mile behind the front line. Otherwise, as noted by Major General Humphreys, the Army of the Potomac chief of staff, "there was no surface-water; the springs, the marshes, the ponds, and even streams of some magnitude were dry." In late July the skies finally loosed two heavy rains, but unfortunately this did not provide much relief. Cummings observed that the one rain spasm had little effect on the water supply, while the other failed to cool the air. Still, this second rainfall was heavy enough to fill the earthworks, which suffered from varying degrees of poor drainage. Emerson rightly anticipated from his hospital bed, "the poor fellows . . . will have a hard time laying in the rifle pits." Despite such hardship, the generally arid conditions spared soldiers the toil of digging through mud to entrench.[19]

Service in the fortifications confronting Petersburg was physically demanding for the New Englanders. Holding a salient approximately two miles from the city, they occupied the section of the Union line that proved the closest to the Confederate defenses that any bluecoats would reach throughout the campaign. A few days into the stint of June 19 to July 29, the later arrivals and the rest of the Second Division shifted from controlling most of the Ninth Corps frontage to defending only a portion of the line while the First and Third Divisions held their share. This left the Vermonters and Mainers vulnerable to Rebel fire, as they were less than 100 yards from the graybacks. Sheahan claimed that his comrades could actually "throw stones into their works." In fact, the opposing forces had friendly conversations owing to their proximity. The later arrivals proceeded to entrench over this period to safeguard against the danger posed by such a nearby enemy, for Griffin observed that "no picket could live in the narrow space" between the lines without this protection. Although the

Federals dreaded the task of building fortifications more than Confederate artillery fire, they doubtless agreed with Sheahan's understanding that "the enemy can be dislodged from his position only by the spade." The 17th and 31st were important to this entrenching effort given that Burnside observed, "the length of our line renders the work very hard with the small number of men in the three divisions."[20]

The Vermonters and Mainers endured an unhealthy environment in the defenses. Crawling on hands and knees to avoid enemy fire, the New Englanders struggled to keep their earthworks clean and in good repair. They made do with a handful of subpar toilets, a newly-dug example filling with a couple inches of maggots within twenty-four hours. Burnside thus lectured his command about "the importance during the hot season of proper attention to cleanliness." The men had to stay low while finding spots within the works to relieve themselves. According to the Ninth Corps assistant inspector general Lt. Col. Charles G. Loring, "the long confinement of the men in the trenches . . . in a situation where attention to personal cleanliness is almost impossible, is causing the appearance of vermin and some minor indications of impaired health." Subsequently, he warned in mid-July that the ground could "soon become pestilential." The combination of high temperatures, dusty air, insufficient rest, and inadequate potable water contributed to the soldiers' declining health. Surgeon Edward B. Dalton, chief medical officer of the Depot Field Hospital at City Point, Virginia, largely attributed the spread of malaria "to the prolonged exposure and hard service to which the men have been subjected in the trenches." Brigadier General Potter found that building field fortifications left many of his men sick and lethargic.[21]

During this period, the 17th Vermont and 31st Maine suffered exceptionally from poor health. Diarrhea and dysentery proliferated, while less common maladies included typhoid, pneumonia, and other respiratory afflictions. Malaria affected the bluecoats only somewhat, as the usually dry conditions in which they served tended to eliminate the stagnant pools of surface water needed to sustain disease-bearing mosquitoes. Between June 20 and July 20, the number of sick Vermont officers and soldiers rose from 48 to 51 percent of aggregate strength. A lack of morning reports impedes a full accounting of the 31st, but the disease rate in Company C surged from 49 to 57 percent between July 1 and July 29. Thus, illness was more widespread in both outfits than in the Army of the Potomac as a whole, even though it saw a rise from 15 to 27 percent from June to July. Such increases are consistent with the fact that deadly disease throughout the Union army would reach its second-highest peak that August.[22]

Sickness hindered officers from effectively commanding the later arrivals. Lieutenant Colonel Cummings exercised little supervision over the 17th, for besides the demands of court-martial duty, he suffered from illness. As this Vermonter explained, he experienced fever, diarrhea that included "23 bloody discharges" in one day, and a poor appetite. Consequently, his "health . . . [was] such for some weeks as to incapacitate me from field duty," causing him to spend at least eight days in a hospital. Major Reynolds of the 17th was also sick for about eight days during this period. Perhaps most severe was the case of Hartshorn, who claimed to be afflicted by what he likened to "Gastric fever" for well over a month. Nevertheless, he had to serve as a witness in a court-martial and thrice attempted to fulfill his duties only to relinquish the post due to illness. Struggling to eat and suffering bouts of vomiting, the captain summed up the widespread misery by writing on June 22, "I am about Sick tonight and So are nearly all the boys." While recovering, Sgt. Albert C. Raymond of the same outfit hinted at the lack of available personnel, lamenting that he would have to "go on duty . . . I think as there is no one [else]." The 31st also had its share of rampant disease, for Sheahan repeatedly carped that he largely had to lead his company on his lonesome. Unfortunately, the morning reports for the Mainers are insufficient to determine what proportion of officers struggled with maladies during this time. Based on the available sources for the 17th, however, the percentage of ill officers dropped from 38 to 20 percent between June 20 and July 20. It is unclear why this happened, especially since the average throughout the Army of the Potomac rose from 13 to 17 percent in the same period.[23]

The increasing quality and quantity of rations as supplies caught up with the army helped abate disease among the New Englanders. Early on at Petersburg, Wagoner King of the 17th Vermont mentioned a ration of thirteen pieces of hardtack over four days and claimed "the beoys are as thin [as] the last run of Shad." More complete rations remained nutritionally limited, as the men made do with fresh beef, coffee, and hardtack, which led to scurvy for the first four weeks in front of Petersburg. Alleviating this condition, they came to enjoy what Sergeant Major Merriam called "an abundance of good wholesome food" that included bean soup, salted meat, sauerkraut, and the periodic fresh vegetable or fruit. A regular distribution of whiskey invigorated the rank and file, and in early July they even savored bread for only the second time since the start of the Overland Campaign. Pvt. William Elmore Howard of the 17th wrote excitedly about "a sutler . . . [who] keeps butter & cheese and pie and a good many things that are good for a fellow." Putting aside such improved nourishment, conditions remained unpleasant. Cummings complained of "flies . . . as numerous as the frogs and lice of Egypt," whose larvae doubtless soured appetites by blanketing fresh beef.[24]

To regain energy, the Federals tried to sleep at night even as the opposing forces kept up their fire. As a 9th New Hampshire sergeant remembered, "It is certainly strange how a man can become accustomed to shells falling around, big guns booming, and musketry at his side; but I can sleep as soundly in the midst of it as you can in your comfortable bed." Even the newest additions to the two outfits could quickly adapt to slumbering while their comrades fired their weapons. This ability was key, given the difficulty of daytime rest amid the insects and high temperatures. Half of a unit's manpower would fill the lines while the other half dozed, but the entire outfit needed to be ready for combat between 2:00 and 6:00 a.m. and around 9:00 p.m. daily, when a Confederate assault was most apt to occur. On four occasions Union troops had to remain awake throughout the night in case they needed to oppose a rumored attack.[25]

Trench warfare exposed the later arrivals to a constant barrage of enemy cannon, mortar, and rifle musket fire that dwindled their numbers. During this period, the Vermonters lost thirty-six men killed, wounded, or captured, while the Mainers suffered twenty-eight officers and men killed or wounded. The high volume of missiles could be traced partly to Confederate anger at the presence of the Fourth Division, which consisted of U.S. Colored Troops. In addition, the Federals spent their days within range of Rebel arms, including cannon capable of striking them in enfilade. Since the graybacks held a commanding position on higher ground, they could easily fire at anyone who left the protection of the Federal fieldworks. Hartshorn observed that upon exiting the trenches, "bullets fall around us like hail." The Union soldiers had to continuously watch for enemy activity, which proved difficult because their antagonists rarely left their own defenses. Still, the bluecoats fired back whenever they spotted Rebels, improving their marksmanship through exchanges that ranged from single shots to firing en masse. As Captain Kenfield of the 17th recalled, "we lay, night and day, watching each other waiting ready to send a bullet through the brain of the first rebel that showed his head above the works." Occasionally, the contending troops would shoot at one another for periods of one to two hours, each convinced the other side was about to attack.[26]

The Vermonters and Mainers enjoyed uneven protection in their entrenchments. Occupants of the picket line sometimes had to crouch since those defenses ranged between four and eight feet in height. Cummings observed that anyone who raised his "head, hand or foot . . . [would have it] perforated," while Quartermaster Sgt. A. W. Wilder of the 17th declared that "it was almost sure death for either side to lift a head." Merriam echoed this point, recalling that the Confederate "sharpshooters never lost an opportunity to bring down any one who in the slightest way exposed himself." Adding sandbags to the earthworks provided more cover, although the impact of minié balls showered both the Federals and their food with sand. The rifle pits, however, proved useless against incoming mortar shells, which Sheahan remembered "flying round like humingbirds." Regardless, these trying circumstances were preferable to the plight of troops on fatigue duty. Such soldiers risked the fire of Rebel artillery crews whenever they stood in the open to perform their tasks. Even those Federals filling the main line were vulnerable to enemy projectiles, despite being situated atop an elevation roughly three-quarters of a mile away. The later arrivals sometimes needed to travel between the picket and main lines during the day, but typically they did so at night to present less visible targets. Linking these field fortifications together with a covered way enabled the Union soldiers to move in greater safety from Confederate marksmen, although Merriam admitted that "many a poor fellow paid with his life or limb for a little carelessness."[27]

Individual examples underscored the ever-present risk of injury or death for these Federals. First Lt. Calvin Boston of the 31st Maine once left his rifle pit to shake out a blanket, only to be killed by a Rebel shell exploding overhead. In a different instance a sergeant in the 6th New Hampshire was roughhousing with a captain from the same unit when the former inadvertently broke cover and the enemy immediately shot him dead. A second lieutenant in the 32nd Maine relayed a story about another second lieutenant and a corporal in his outfit who were arranging a blanket to create a canopy when a Confederate bullet pierced the fabric. The second lieutenant warned his comrade, noting the tear, to which the corporal "jokingly replied, 'Why, Lieut., that bullet hole in my blanket don't hurt you any,'" and as he laughed was mortally wounded by a second round. Even when sheltered, these combatants remained vulnerable, as Colonel White exemplified by receiving a wrist wound while he slept in his tent. The case of a few Maine officers reveals that those in the main line could be in danger. These Federals assumed they were safe from Rebel projectiles and chatted while enemy pickets fired away, one of whom ultimately killed Capt. William R. Currier. Understandably, the troops became increasingly inured to these conditions with time. One 6th New Hampshire captain fled just before a Confederate shell detonated in his sleeping area, and a soldier spontaneously appeared to repair the damage with a shovel so the officer could resume his repose. Nevertheless, the resolve of the Union soldiers began to deteriorate. Some of the men opted to make illicit truces with the graybacks, which could be dangerous, given that an enemy sharpshooter struck down one Federal during such a cessation in hostilities. Contrasting with the violence of trench life, these pauses enabled the troops to trade food items and newspapers. The Vermonters and possibly the Mainers counted among those who witnessed the spectacle of Rebels washing their clothes nearby and did not react. As Cummings opined: "After more than 70 days of fighting the rank and file to say nothing of some of the officers gets tired of picket firing and dodging and laying in hot pits day after day. And who wonders? It is unnatural."[28]

The 17th Vermont and 31st Maine regularly fell back to a wood line to spend time in safer environs. Hartshorn relished this opportunity for rest every two days, yet the schedule could be unpredictable. At one time the men remained in the trenches for seventy-two hours and on other occasions spent between twenty-four and less than forty-eight hours in the rear. Moving to the timber, however, was not without peril, for the Federals sustained casualties while making these transits of at least 1,000 feet over fairly open terrain. They relocated to the rear at night, when the Confederates would have greater difficulty spotting them, but using the covered way only shielded them for part of the distance. As Merriam recalled, Union soldiers spent roughly half an hour during one of these trips lying prone amid the "howling of the solid shot and . . . [canister] around us, and the crash of the shells exploding above us." The Rebels could not see these Union troops once they reached the rear line since it lay in a wooded ravine. Regardless, the New Englanders still contended with incoming shells and infrequent minié balls from the graybacks, the small arms rounds having expended much of their energy en route and thus inflicting injury more often than death. Once in the rear, the men entrenched to defend against these missiles, which struck them as they ate, slept, lined up for roll call, or even completed a company payroll. Moreover, Federal efforts to gain protection from the hot sun left these combatants more vulnerable to enemy fire. The woods lacked undergrowth and foliage, so the Vermonters and Mainers built shelters that unfortunately prevented them from spotting arching mortar shells. The bluecoats thus had to remain alert for the recognizable sound of these projectiles to avoid them. Considering the dangers of life in this forested area, the troops likely benefited most from this rearward location to engage in drill, inspections, and dress parade as well as division and brigade review. They even had a chance to wash themselves.[29]

Regardless of the soldiers' physical and mental condition, some participants insisted they were ready for battle. Loring declared "the ardour of the men is not affected nor their confidence lessened," while Potter claimed that the troops were "looking well and in good heart." White briefly praised the quality of those Mainers present, yet the Vermonters were more verbose. Cummings cited his battalion's "reputation for doing its full duty" and agreed with Hartshorn that the army was in fine shape for combat. Wilder of the 17th, writing to a local newspaper, emphasized the need to finish recruitment for the remaining companies of this outfit and for Randall to reach the front with the additional troops, serving as colonel. Then, he maintained, the unit would "win such a record as has never been achieved by any other regiment since the Rebellion began." Pvt. Mark Slayton wrote confidently: "We are getting the rebels in close quarters. We will fix them yet." One anonymous Vermonter, expressing optimism about the capture of Petersburg in another newspaper, declared that it was "the firm belief of every officer and soldier of the Army of the Potomac." He and his comrades undoubtedly drew encouragement from the news that their ninth company, traveling from the Green Mountain State to Petersburg, had reached Alexandria, Virginia.[30]

The later arrivals surely depended on strong leadership during this period and would do so in future combat. In the 17th Vermont Corporal Manson enthused over "some first rate Officers better than we had before," and Wilder regarded them as courageous. Likewise, Asst. Surgeon Richard R.

Ricker of the 31st Maine described White as "calm efficient and brave," while a newspaper correspondent from the unit lauded him as considerate and fearless. An unnamed sergeant complimented the "experience, courage and industry" of the staff officers. Sgt. Charles O. Pendexter insisted that First Lieutenant Boston, who received a deadly wound in the lines around Petersburg, had enjoyed "the confidence and good will of every man in the regiment." Peer pressure likely contributed to the ability of officers to persevere amid such trying conditions. The desire to develop a good reputation back home was in the thoughts of First Lieutenant Sheahan. He wrote his father asking whether friends and family expressed opinions about his service, namely, "how I am liked as Lt or if I do well in a fight and what kind of an officer I make."[31]

Some noncommissioned officers, nonetheless, fell short of the mark in carrying out their responsibilities. Cummings did not hold Orderly Sgt. Cassius Ellsworth in high regard, insisting that his subordinate did not "command obedience to orders in his company," was "no disciplinarian, and . . . heedless of the ordinary duties and responsibilities of a commanding officer." He claimed that Ellsworth could not effectively lead the company when it numbered a mere ten soldiers. In another example Sheahan lamented that the acting orderly sergeant in his company did not "know so much as a dead dog about his duty." Such instances of incompetence offer a reminder that the New Englanders approached their next fight with uneven leadership.[32]

Ultimately, toiling around Petersburg for weeks on end caused the later arrivals to replace rookie enthusiasm with a realistic view of the bloody task ahead. Brig. Gen. J. G. Barnard, chief engineer of the Union armies in the field, summarized the perilous plight of the Ninth Corps as "lying in trenches close up to the enemy, carrying on a quasi siege—not decided enough to accomplish anything, but by heat and sharpshooters losing men every day." Near the end of June, Cummings lamented that "no tongue nor pen can give any adequate idea of the sufferings and privations of this long, continuous and to be continued campaign." As he further complained a month later, "a majority of both officers and men would like to get out of the service and go home." The lieutenant colonel blamed this development on loved ones who frequently "urged [them] . . . to get out of the service." Merriam aptly pointed to "homesickness (an awfully fatal disease)," and Wagoner King of the 17th confessed he was "as homesick as a dog." Captain

Knapp took a longer view of the Vermonters' experiences in uniform. He summed up their daily existence from the Overland Campaign onward as "monotonously uniform, like our rations." Sheahan marveled, "Never has history recorded such battles as these battles with no ends all join together and make one . . . continual battle." Following the end of the First Union Offensive, the Maine officer insisted he had "become quite accustomed to the hum of the little leaden messenger and so no mind them unless they come very near." After a few days, however, he bemoaned there was "no rest for the weary soldier . . . [who was] at no time . . . free from danger." Some two weeks later, Sheahan grimly admitted, "while I am out here . . . I have no assurance that I will live from one hour to another." The lieutenant's letters reveal how fatalism could replace determination in the minds of combatants over time in the trenches.[33]

THE CRUCIBLE OF COHESION

JULY 30, 1864

On July 30 the Army of the Potomac launched an assault to capture Petersburg that would come to be known as the Battle of the Crater, the climactic end of the Third Union Offensive. Four days earlier the Second Corps, three cavalry divisions, and troops of the Tenth and Nineteenth Corps from the Army of the James had advanced along the north side of the eponymous river in a movement past the Confederate left. These bluecoats had had a slim chance of taking Richmond but hoped to at least dismantle the Virginia Central Railroad to its north. Although they failed on both counts during the First Battle of Deep Bottom (July 26–29, 1864), Grant decided to capitalize on the fact that Lee had shifted much of his manpower out of the Petersburg earthworks to oppose this Union drive north of the James. The upcoming large-scale assault would test the later arrivals more severely than the fighting of the First Union Offensive. Burnside's men faced Elliott's Salient, a section of the Confederate defenses that extended forward a short distance from the rest of the entrenchments. The bluecoats were to explode a mine excavated underneath this location, which the 48th Pennsylvania had already charged with about 8,000 pounds of gunpowder. Then, the troops would push through the resulting cavity and breach in the Rebel line to take Cemetery Hill, the high ground before the city. This crest lay 500 yards to the rear of the salient. According to Meade's orders, "promptitude, rapidity of execution, and cordial cooperation are essential to success," bringing to the forefront the need for a rapid advance immediately after the explosion sowed disorder among the enemy. The assailants would not be able to afford the delay of arranging their formations since a failure to quickly seize Cemetery Hill would allow the graybacks time to open artillery and rifle musket fire capable of driving them from the breach. Conversely, establishing control over the crest would enable the Federals to threaten the rest of the Confederate positions around Petersburg. Victory here would likely presage the capture of the city and control of the Appomattox River's south bank.[34]

Federal leaders held mixed opinions about the prospects of this operation. Burnside and a few others were optimistic it would succeed. This stood in contrast to those officers, including Meade, who argued, "it is not the numbers of the enemy which oppose our taking Petersburg; it is their artillery and their works which can be held by reduced numbers against direct assault." Still, the army commander decided this effort could produce a win after learning that the Confederates had merely a battery or two on the crest and had reduced the number of their forces in the city. Meade also took confidence in Burnside's opinion that the Rebels were unaware of the mine's precise location.[35]

A change of plans afforded the New Englanders little opportunity to prepare for the impending clash. As of July 26, Burnside had intended to lead his assault with the Black Fourth Division. He wanted to offer these troops a chance to prove their mettle and believed such fresh combatants were more suitable than exhausted veterans. Other than some prior skirmishing, these Black troops had neither taken part in intense combat nor fatigued themselves manning the trenches. Under his plan, the white troops would follow the Black soldiers into battle. Meade rejected Burnside's proposal two days later, asserting that he could not put confidence in such inexperienced troops, while the seasoned white men were "perfectly reliable." He also feared lest a potential defeat of the Black soldiers imply that the Union leadership had sent them recklessly to their deaths. Echoing Grant's expectations for the attack, Meade further insisted that the Ninth Corps push for Cemetery Hill, rather than Burnside's idea of moving a portion of the advancing bluecoats out on the flanks to expand the gap in the enemy line. Securing Grant's agreement, Meade confirmed on the morning of July 29 that Burnside should begin the attack with white soldiers and focus on seizing the crest. This presented the Ninth Corps commander with a conundrum. He struggled to select one of his other three divisions to spearhead the movement because they varied in suitability based on their proximity to the point of attack, degree of fatigue, and exposure to the graybacks. Since Burnside was friends with Potter, he also wanted to avoid the appearance of playing favorites. As Griffin explained, Burnside had these generals "draw lots," after which he assigned the role to Brig. Gen. James H. Ledlie, in command of the First Division. Potter was caught off guard by the need to even make the assault, for he believed that "all idea of attacking on our front had been abandoned, at any rate for the present." He tellingly warned that "unless the dispositions are commenced early and made with celerity I fear some confusion." Although Burnside familiarized him with the plan that afternoon, Potter complained that he did not receive "written orders . . . until evening." The Second Division commander griped about the difficult terrain over which his men would have to advance, their limited room for maneuver, and the minimal time they had to ready themselves, though at least Griffin's men were already acquainted with the area's topography. But as it was, Ninth Corps headquarters was compelled to make last-minute adjustments throughout the night.[36]

The later arrivals contended with several disadvantages in this assault. They would have to advance uphill to reach the area of Elliott's Salient, which several Union officers regarded as formidable, most notably Grant. Trees and bushes dotted the swampy terrain directly in front of the position. The general in chief found these defenses to be "as strong as they can be made, and the ground . . . very broken and favorable for defense." Enemy entrenchments dotted with batteries extended from both flanks of the salient, enabling the Rebels to open a cross and rear fire on any attackers. As historian Earl J. Hess explains, "it was a reentrant angle formed by bending the line back as it continued south of Pegram's [Elliott's] position." The Vermonters and Mainers, however, enjoyed some protection from incoming fire thanks to a slight ridge on the left flank that extended most of the way to the crest.[37]

Making a headlong attack would be difficult for the white soldiers of the Ninth Corps, whose service in the Overland and Petersburg Campaigns had taken its toll. Burnside noted the long trench duty of these troops, during which they had learned to hide within the earthworks to avoid Confederate fire. As the general recognized, the white soldiers had tallied losses, only eaten food available from the rear, lacked many chances to wash, "and . . . were not in condition to make a vigorous charge." He cited Loring for support and explained that the Black troops "had been drilled for and expected to make the charge." Period accounts differ regarding how much training the USCT regiments received, and they may have had considerably less preparation than some participants claimed or even none. Regardless, Potter agreed that his soldiers were in poor shape, while Merriam considered the Vermonters and Mainers "worn out . . . and somewhat demoralized by six weeks hiding behind the trenches." Thus, the men were more likely to seek cover. Brig. Gen. Edward Ferrero, commanding the Fourth Division, aptly observed that "it had become a second nature . . . to dodge a bullet." Admittedly, the destructive potential of the mine may have bolstered the confidence of some later arrivals. Alluding to the Confederates, Cummings mused that "somebody will be surprised and hurt." Sheahan echoed this perspective, anticipating that the explosion would "astonish them when they find themselves gently raised into the air a couple hundred feet or more and before they have time to come down there will be some Yankee bayonetts waiting for them." This was a contrarian viewpoint, however, given the widespread Federal belief that the mine detonation would injure the bluecoats themselves. In fact, many officers doubted the attack would succeed.[38]

Although the 17th Vermont and the 31st Maine had good commanding officers, they lacked the numbers to make an effective assault. The Shand House fight had reaffirmed the need for sufficient troops to absorb the high cost of a frontal attack. Fortunately, the well-liked Major Reynolds assumed command of the Vermonters for this assault in place of Cummings, who was sick, while the Mainers would report to the popular Colonel White. Such leadership suggested that these two outfits could fight well despite their thinned ranks. First Lieutenant Lucia counted only 128 officers and soldiers present for duty in the 17th, a low figure probably due to the rampant diseases endemic to life in the trenches. Based on the July 20 morning report, this would have equaled 23 percent of the whole unit. The deficit included an ailing adjutant and two captains, plus two other captains who were on detached service. Within the 31st, disease was also likely the chief reason for its reduction in manpower. A newspaper correspondent from this outfit claimed some 135 soldiers were present for duty without specifying the number of officers. Only the morning report for one out of the nine Maine companies is available for July 29, in which 21 percent of officers and men were present for duty. Such rough estimates provide evidence that the later arrivals were more depleted than the Ninth Corps in general, of which 49 percent was present for duty that month.[39]

Hours of trepidation preceded the fight. The Vermonters and Mainers remained in a state of readiness from roughly nightfall to midnight, when they started moving into position. By 3:00 a.m., two men per company in each of the two units helped fill the front line as skirmishers, while the remainder formed in a ravine behind them. A small number of troops slumbered or conversed, while the others stayed awake in fear, knowing they would soon find themselves in a costly engagement. One unnamed participant chided two cooks debating food choices by declaring that "canister, spiced with bullets, are on the bill of fare for our next meal." Capt. Horace H. Burbank of the 31st Maine recalled that the combatants had their weapons at hand and that "many occupied the weary, wakeful, watchful hours in writing brief messages homeward." Making this restless night more taxing, the later arrivals had spent the previous twenty-four hours in the rear, waiting to change their location in response to a Confederate assault that failed to occur. Knapp recalled that "thoughts of the horrors and uncertainties of the battlefield came vividly before them." As Kenfield remembered, "all knew that the morrow was soon to bring for them a hard fought battle and that to many this was their last night on earth, or what was worse to be wounded and suffer and die in rebel prisons." The soldiers attempted to stay quiet, although Provost Marshal General Patrick complained that he "slept very little, as there was a constant bumming kept up all night" by these troops. As the time of the explosion approached, however, a second lieutenant in the 32nd Maine noted "a deathly silence among the men."[40]

The battle started inauspiciously for the Federals. When the mine failed to explode around sunrise at 3:30 a.m., the Union troops grew more apprehensive. This setback was concerning, given that Meade had intended the attackers to push to the crest while concealed in the predawn darkness. To prevent the Confederates from catching sight of the massed and waiting assailants, these troops lay prone. With sunrise approaching, they could not count on many of the Rebels remaining asleep. Not only had the opposing pickets been shooting at one another throughout the night, but

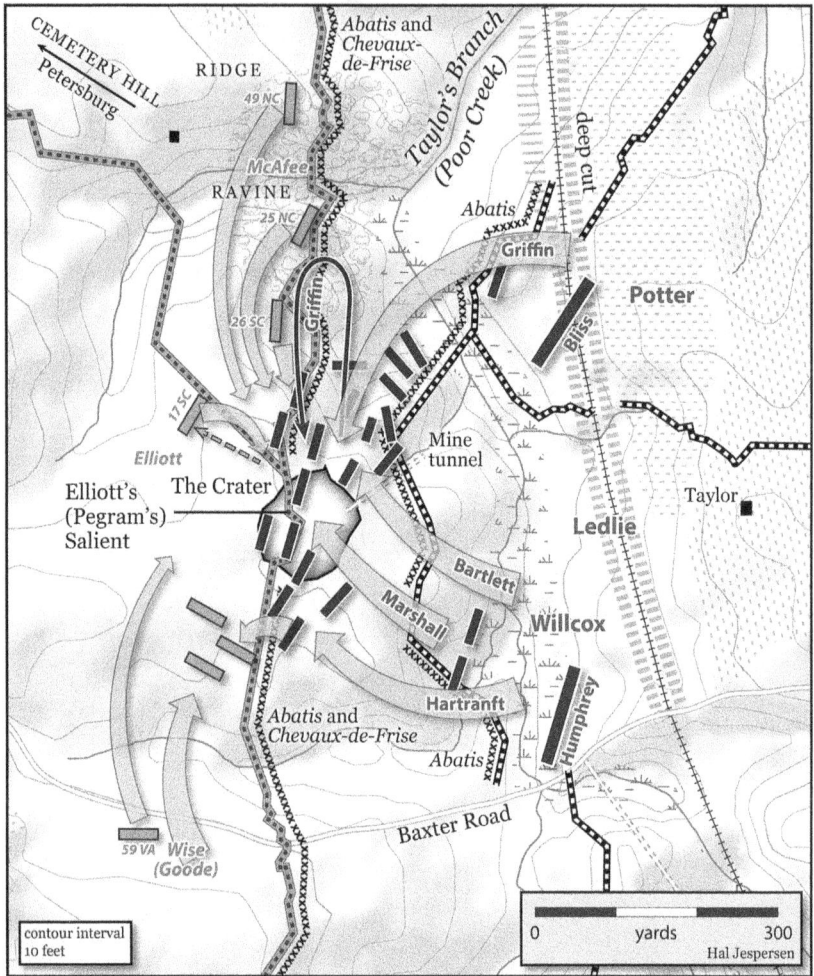

Battle of the Crater, July 30, 1864.

snoring graybacks also started to awaken at 4:00 a.m., with the opposing sharpshooters resuming their grim task. Following the repair of a faulty fuse, the mine finally detonated under a sunlit sky forty-four minutes afterward. It launched chunks of soil upward, some of which landed less than 100 feet away from the Ninth Corps troops. This blast also projected forth artillery pieces, caissons, wood, rocks, camp equipment, and what Knapp described as "a frightful shower of mangled corpses, severed limbs and decapitated trunks." Witnessing this unnerving spectacle, the later arrivals would now have to fight for hours amid high humidity and temperatures reaching 105°F, which would sap their strength.[41]

Poor discipline stymied the intricate plan for the assault. Burnside intended for the First Division to launch the offensive when the mine detonated, driving through the cavity that became known as the Crater and on toward Cemetery Hill. The Third Division would then press forward, guarding the left flank of the First Division as its men entered the Confederate line. The Second Division was to protect the First Division's right flank, waiting to ensure that its own efforts did not impede the progress of the Third Division. And yet Potter did not want his troops to delay their advance, as they would forfeit the opportunity to attack while the Rebels fell into disarray following the explosion. He thus instructed Griffin around 12:00 a.m. to advance a line of skirmishers when the First Division went forward, then proceed with the rest of his men. Pioneers wielding axes would progress simultaneously to clear a path through Confederate abatis. If Rebel opposition proved weak, he was to move the Second Brigade ahead roughly in line with Ledlie's division. Griffin's men would focus on an objective unique to the Second Division: the capture of a ridge overlooking a ravine that stretched between the main enemy line and Cemetery Hill. When the mine exploded, however, Griffin was not actually onsite to lead his soldiers because he was speaking with Grant and Burnside in the rear. Fortunately, he had already informed the regimental commanders of the plan and ordered White, the most senior among his subordinates, to take charge in his absence. Despite such elaborate arrangements, the movement of the troops degenerated into confusion when the leading brigade of the First Division hesitated and drew back out of shock at the detonation, a desire to avoid the resulting debris that included human remains, and fear of a potential enemy countermine. The men of this brigade then went on to clamber over the works, jamming their rifle muskets into the entrenchments to serve as makeshift steps, and dismantled the Union abatis so they could enter no-man's-land. All these complications stalled the start of the attack for approximately five minutes.[42]

The later arrivals fell into disorder while advancing across the intervening ground. Around 5:00 a.m. and against the backdrop of Federal cannon fire, White ordered the troops to fix their bayonets and charge. Hindering a rapid sortie, the skirmishers had to scale their own entrenchments while the rest of this command, standing in any spot they could find amid the

Union defenses, worked through a covered way to follow suit. A member of the Second Brigade recalled of the skirmishers that "no regimental organization was preserved, and the men that could run the fastest mixed in with other regiments." Those following in their wake fell into a line of battle before traversing the fieldworks and re-formed upon reaching the no-man's-land. The shouting Vermonters and Mainers sped about 150 yards across the field at the double-quick with their bayonets at the ready. Only some of the later arrivals and comrades in their brigade went straight into the Crater, for White and the rest headed to its right. Those who pushed toward the cavity moved in small clusters of two to four men. Smoke and dust helped conceal their movement but made it difficult for the Union troops to breathe and reduced their ability to see even three feet away. The Confederates had either frozen in place out of shock or, as Merriam recalled, began "running like sheep, in an utter panic" after the explosion. Only Rebel artillery and infantry more than 200 feet away from the great pit began firing sporadically at their assailants. The higher intensity of enemy projectiles from the right, combined with the poor visibility, caused these Union soldiers to turn leftward. They began to intermingle with those First Division combatants who had mistakenly headed right during their own transit. The 2nd Maryland was spearheading the advance along the left flank of the brigade when it suffered the loss of its commanding officer upon reaching the Confederate entrenchments. This produced chaos as the troops throughout the command began to misunderstand their orders. Surely restoring order to a degree, Griffin arrived among his men sometime during the attack and would remain in close proximity to the action. In contrast, Burnside spent most of the battle approximately a mile distant from the Crater, while Potter stayed 80 yards away. The absence of these leaders doubtless exacerbated the disarray among their men.[43]

The Union assault soon ground to a halt. Those later arrivals entering the Crater did so by scaling a roughly 12-foot incline to pile into the hole. Measuring 150–180 feet long, 40 feet wide, and 20–25 feet in depth, this depression was large enough to contain 4,000–6,000 Federals. The Vermonters were positioned toward the rear of the advancing column, while the Mainers were in the forefront. This included Sgt. Edward A. Sprague, color bearer of the 31st Maine, who planted the regiment's national flag in the massive pit. The jumbled terrain defied the soldiers' efforts to move forward in formation. Burnside explained that the hole was an "obstacle of great formidableness," featuring "sides of loose pulverized sand piled up precipitately, from which projected huge blocks of clay." Besides shattered munitions and armaments, Captain Kenfield wrote that the Crater was "filled with dead and dying men torn and mangled in every form." The later arrivals lingered to capture surviving Confederates buried in the debris and sought cover instead of following orders to advance. To restore the forward momentum, an officer in the 31st ordered Sprague to spur his fellows onward, so the sergeant hefted the flag and planted it atop the Rebels' next entrenched line on the other side of the cavity. This fieldwork was a cavalier, a type of trench with a parapet several feet higher than the front line to afford defenders an advantageous firing position. Inspired by Sprague's feat, the other Federals proceeded in his wake and spread across the rest of the area by 5:10 a.m., twenty-five minutes after the mine explosion. Enemy resistance soon stiffened, with Confederate infantry and cannon massing in front of these bluecoats and along their flanks. Despite Griffin's best efforts, he could not drive his men through the crowd of other Federals. Although the topography shielded these combatants from minié balls, they remained vulnerable to case, canister, solid shot, and shell. Second Lt. Worthington Pierce of the 17th remembered that the Vermonters' "advance was checked by a murderous fire," and in response these men resumed their efforts to entrench. As a First Division officer put it, the Federal assault force was "a perfect mob" in which every soldier believed he would be attacking on his own.[44]

Instead of entering the Crater, a large part of the Second Brigade, including much of the 17th Vermont and 31st Maine, pushed to the right. Available sources provide no evidence that Brigadier General Griffin split the command of his troops with Colonel White during the fighting. And yet the Mainer led the part of this brigade that entered the area to the right of the great pit, probably because Griffin was not present to do so. These Federals negotiated the Confederate abatis and chevaux-de-frise, both of which remained in place since they stood beyond the blast radius. Traversing such obstacles jumbled the ranks of the later arrivals, who found that the defenders had largely abandoned their front line of rifle pits for up to 300 yards. As Griffin recalled, the area was "covered with pits and traverses, and intrenched lines running in every conceivable direction." Comingled with soldiers of the First Division, the New Englanders struggled to advance over this ground, which hindered the movement of soldiers in large numbers. Still, these bluecoats pressed on to reach the Rebel cavalier and engaged in melee combat with its occupants. They seized roughly 200 yards of these defenses as they progressed toward the ridge and, at some point afterward, helped squelch a minor enemy counterattack. Between 5:15 and 5:30 a.m., the Confederates mounted an increasingly fierce opposition by unleashing minié balls, canister, and case shot from straight ahead. They also poured more artillery fire into their assailants' right flank. The Federals reacted by withdrawing to either the nearby fieldworks or to the Crater. White reorganized the soldiers hunkering down within the fortifications, who were not only disordered but also running low on ammunition. He then ordered them to renew the attack by progressing through the other Union troops surrounding them, which only worsened the prevailing turmoil.[45]

Around 7:00 a.m. the later arrivals and their comrades headed toward the targeted ridge. They were still mixed with First Division troops, hampering this effort, but Griffin was finally able to leave the Crater and reach the area with the rest of his command. The Mainers managed to disentangle themselves from the mass of bluecoats, gaining more room to arrange their formation as they advanced, but the Vermonters failed to do so and remained in a covered way. Although both New England units kept firing at the enemy, the 31st Maine counted among the outfits in the brigade that forged ahead 200 yards after twice attempting to take the ridge. These bluecoats had difficulty moving forward under a storm of iron and lead from Confederate mortars, cannon, and rifle muskets. As Griffin admitted, "the terrible fire of musketry from every direction, with . . . canister from our front, rendered the formation of lines from such confused masses lying in pits an impossibility." Adding pressure, Rebel guns loosed upon them from the right flank, and at last the bluecoats fell back to take shelter in the covered way.[46]

The actions of the USCT regiments inadvertently increased the chaos in the ranks of Potter's Second Brigade. Originally, Ferrero's Fourth Division was to promptly advance once the Third Division did so, waiting only until the white soldiers had progressed sufficiently to leave the Crater unobstructed. Even though this area remained crowded, Meade ordered Burnside during the battle to include the USCT division in the drive to Cemetery Hill. Around 8:00 a.m. these men commenced their headlong assault. Unfortunately, the Black troops mistook some of Griffin's men for the enemy, firing at them until the white soldiers displayed their flags. Ferrero's men then jammed into the rifle pits alongside their former targets and captured ground farther ahead. After several minutes the Confederates arrayed themselves less than 160 yards away from the Federals on the right flank. With artillery booming, these graybacks fired their rifle muskets and made a charge that caused the Black troops to fall back to the rifle pits where their white comrades lay in support. Some of Griffin's men then unleashed a point-blank volley to drive back the cheering enemy infantry, who pushed forward again and outflanked the Second Division's First Brigade along the right side of the pits. Griffin now ordered his men to charge but to no avail. Instead, the Confederate onslaught and the spectacle of white Federals in flight spurred a headlong retreat of numerous Black soldiers into the pits on the left side. With fixed bayonets, these troops crammed up to four men deep in the entrenchments, leaving the closely packed occupants unable to use their weapons let alone move. As a 9th New Hampshire sergeant related, bluecoats "were bayoneted, crushed, and trampled."[47]

A brutal melee coincided with the flight of the Fourth Division. As the Black troops returned to the Ninth Corps starting line, they drew a number of white Federals with them back through the Crater and entrenchments to the right of it. Some stood with white comrades who held their ground, with Captain Burbank noting that the "men jumped from the trenches and made the best resistance possible." Now the opposing combatants fired their rifle muskets at one another, and as a soldier in the 11th New Hampshire stated, the Rebels used "bayonets, butts of muskets, swords, pistols, fists, and every possible means for defense." What another 9th New Hampshire sergeant termed "human butchery" took place as enemy minié balls and artillery projectiles slammed into the Union soldiers from their flanks. Both the Vermonters and Mainers managed to rescue their colors from the enemy, although the men of the 31st lost the outfit's national flag. Griffin noted that the troops of the Pine Tree State "fought heroically for their colors, tearing them to pieces and breaking the staves in the mêlée." Around 8:45 a.m. and after some twenty minutes of combat, the Confederates managed to retake the rifle pits and capture some of their Union occupants, including Colonel White. Ending up as a prisoner, Kenfield counted himself among those who "had to . . . beg for mercy at the hands of the rebels." Most of the other regimental commanders in the Second

Brigade had already become casualties, leaving some captains to lead the brigade's roughly 400 remaining bluecoats. Many of Griffin's losses that day occurred during this clash. His diminished force headed toward the Crater, struggling from a lack of food and water amid the day's high temperatures. The men only fired sporadically at the Confederates in keeping with Potter's observation that "it was physically impossible to get any work out of them."[48]

The 17th Vermont and 31st Maine would now endure the most challenging combat conditions of the day. A portion of the Mainers who had originally gone to the right entered the Crater, while the rest and the Vermonters as a whole filled the fieldworks to its right. Combatants from multiple divisions of the Ninth Corps were massed in the deep hole, from which it proved almost impossible to escape. One 9th New Hampshire captain described the hellish landscape as "nearly filled with the wounded, the dead and the dying, to such an extent that many were trampled to death who were otherwise unharmed." Around this time Confederate artillery along Cemetery Hill and on either flank of the depression bombarded the Crater. When the Mainers to its right withdrew into this hole, Adjutant and First Lieutenant Allyn exhorted the men to reverse course and advance again on the graybacks. As this officer pushed forward, however, he crumpled from a mortal wound. Enemy fire grew more intense, as sharpshooters took aim at the Federals and mortars lobbed shells into their midst. Rebel gun crews blasted these bluecoats with case and canister but struggled to lower their cannon sufficiently to strike the closest targets.[49]

Over the next few hours, the later arrivals helped defeat several Confederate assaults on the Crater and the adjacent entrenchments. Shortly after the repulse of Griffin's troops, they drove back a weak attack and took prisoners. Yet the fatigue of crowding together on this hot day served to undermine the Union soldiers' determination. Moreover, a continuous hail of enemy minié balls, shells from mortars and cannon alike, and solid shot detached Federal heads and limbs. The resulting carnage of body parts spattered these men with brains, skin, and blood. At 10:30 a.m. the Mainers assisted in repelling another Rebel advance, but since the Vermonters were not situated in the great pit, they did not take part in this fighting. The difficult combat conditions, rather than cowardice or indiscipline, explain the gradual withdrawal of roughly ten to twenty Federals at a time back to their starting line across the no-man's-land. They had good reason to fight for as long as possible since retreating exposed them to enemy artillery and infantry that would shoot down about a third of the men over the course of the battle. Although most of the uninjured bluecoats fled, the wounded could not easily clamber up the steep walls of the Crater to get away. The soldiers who still stood demonstrated their courage by trying to allay the thirst of their wounded comrades, which involved going back to the Union position to refill canteens. They then either succeeded in returning to their brethren under fire or died trying, moving Griffin to declare this "one of the noblest and bravest acts . . . [he] saw during the whole war."[50]

The Vermonters and Mainers contributed to pushing back another enemy attack at 11:00 a.m. Attesting to the desperate fighting, Major Reynolds personally slew three graybacks and urged his men to stand firm against the Confederates, only to receive a fatal gunshot wound. First Lt. William E. Martin also fell with a mortal wound while bravely spurring his troops onward from the front. A sergeant in the 31st Maine shot at the enemy from his perch along the edge of the Crater, using rifle muskets that his fellow soldiers handed to him, until he received a bullet in the hand. Federal success in delaying the Rebels' progress proved fleeting, for Meade decided it was time to retreat. He obtained the agreement of Grant, who did not want "to take the chances of a slaughter sure to occur if another [Confederate] assault was made." At 12:20 p.m. the brigade commanders in the Crater received Meade's command to fall back when safe to do so. A majority of the Ninth Corps had already departed the area, hence a 9th New Hampshire sergeant's recollection that it was now "every man for himself." This left behind a fatigued and dehydrated core of troops still in disarray who grew even more dejected upon hearing of the retreat order. Still, those unfortunate Federals kept fighting until they were too wedged together to use their weapons.[51]

A Confederate onslaught precipitated the end of the Union withdrawal around 2:30 p.m. The shouting graybacks emerged from a ravine approximately 100 feet in front of the Crater and caught the Federals unaware. According to Griffin, it was impossible to "see them till they appeared on the rising ground immediately in front." These Rebels soon massed along the right side of the great cavity. Griffin instructed his remaining men to fall back under cover of a Federal artillery bombardment. Unlike the bluecoats in the Crater, the Vermonters and Mainers holding the entrenchments to its right retreated with greater discipline and only suffered minimal casualties. Union troops still within enemy lines included the wounded, those who misunderstood the order to withdraw, and others unable to rapidly move through the jumbled mass of bluecoats. During a brief melee, the Confederates bayoneted some of them, taking the rest prisoner. Most of the casualties suffered by the Ninth Corps throughout the battle took place during this time. The Rebels now regained control of their original lines, although two of Potter's outfits did not abandon their efforts to silence an enemy battery until roughly 4:00 p.m.[52]

AN INDELIBLE MARK

WEIGHING THE CONSEQUENCES OF THE CRATER

The 17th Vermont and 31st Maine emerged from the Crater as gutted fighting organizations. No other engagement in their history had imposed so many stresses on these units, which began the day barely fit for combat and ended it nearly destroyed. This battle proved so traumatizing that Knapp could not discuss "the horrors" years afterward "without emotion." The Vermonters lost forty-four officers and men killed, wounded, or captured—a casualty ratio of about one-third. This blow prompted Adj. James S. Peck to lament that "little is left of the brave men who from the Rapidan to the James were accustomed to see only the back of the enemy." The Mainers sustained an even worse seventy-nine officers and men killed, wounded, missing, or captured, equaling a casualty rate of over one-half. Their drive for the ridge probably explains this higher toll. The veterans who joined these outfits appear to have suffered unduly in comparison to their less seasoned comrades. Men with prior military experience represented 36 percent of the Vermont losses, which was substantially higher than the roughly 20 percent of such officers and men who ever fought in the 17th. Among the Mainers, about 25 percent of the casualties consisted of combatants with previous stints in uniform, which was also higher than their 12-percent representation in the 31st during its history.[53]

Courageous leadership helped the later arrivals survive this catastrophe. Lieutenant Colonel Cummings, First Lieutenant Lucia, and Surgeon P. O'Meara Edson lauded Major William Reynolds for providing such a fearless example to the men. Sadly, the major died at the head of his troops, as did two lieutenants. Cpl. Arthur W. Bartle survived the battle to receive a recommendation for the Medal of Honor. This was in recognition of what Potter, writing in February 1865, termed "faithful service and disciplined bravery" during the Petersburg Campaign. In particular, he cited Bartle's role at the Crater, where he ably defended the colors and showed courage that steeled the resolve of his fellow Vermonters. The Mainers also witnessed heroic displays. Griffin echoed the view of a newspaper correspondent from the 31st who enthused that, prior to White's capture, the colonel "maintained his reputation for coolness and bravery." Sgt. William H. H. Ware, aided by some comrades, achieved the feat of overcoming Rebel efforts to take the Maine state flag, while Color Cpl. George H. Hoyt would receive a promotion to lance sergeant for his valor that day. It may have been at this point in the fighting that Sgt. Alexander Crawford earned his recommendation for the Medal of Honor. As Potter related, Crawford "distinguished himself in a hand to hand encounter with the enemy, in which he was disabled by a blow on the head; was captured and sent to the rear, but finally succeeded in making his escape, though severely wounded in the shoulder while so doing." Potter also noted Crawford's courage and steadiness throughout the Overland and Petersburg Campaigns. Merriam offered an anecdote that illustrated how this kind of behavior could galvanize the rank and file. Sometime before the Crater battle, Burnside had scrutinized the Confederate defenses around Petersburg without concern for incoming fire. This display of boldness led Merriam to declare, "if we had been ordered to assault the works in our front . . . all of the money the government paid out to crush the rebellion would not have tempted me to do what I saw done without any show or bluster by the General."[54]

Regardless, most officers at the Crater had not felt the need to spur on their men by leading from the front, where they would have suffered disproportionately high casualties. There is likewise no evidence to indicate that these leaders stayed behind their troops to force them onward, which would have also reduced their exposure to danger. In any case, the tumultuous nature of the fighting arguably made it impossible for the officers to avoid intermingling with the rank and file. Consulting the casualty statistics is therefore telling. Officers equaled 16 percent of Vermont losses and 11 percent of Maine casualties compared to the officer loss rate of 11 percent throughout the Second Brigade. Perhaps the Vermonters, who spent a good portion of the engagement mired in the enemy works, depended more heavily on their leaders to drive them forward. More important is the fact that the share of officer casualties among the later arrivals was, depending on the unit, either little different or not at all from the norm across the brigade. These New Englanders were thus much like their peers insofar as their reliance on leaders was concerned.[55]

Bleak commentary on the crushing defeat at the Crater stands in contrast to the praise that officers bestowed on the men for their valorous sacrifice. Grant regarded this battle as a "disaster," while Meade judged it to be a "most unfortunate and not very creditable operation." The later arrivals shared this grim perspective. Cummings lamented that "nothing [was] accomplished," Captain Hartshorn insisted the "poor boys were slaughtered like sheep," and Merriam bemoaned that his outfit "was nearly annihilated in that frightful calamity." Such disheartening remarks put the combat performance of these New Englanders in doubt. Indeed, Lieutenant Colonel Lyman declared of the Federals broadly that they "did not fight hard enough." This was a dissenting opinion, however, for some of these same quoted individuals shared the views of others who extolled the conduct of the troops under fire. Meade alluded to "heroic fighting" by the Second Division, and Burnside claimed these "officers and men, did all that gallant men could do under the circumstances." Likewise, Brigadier General Potter affirmed that his bluecoats "knew it was a hopeless case, never fought better, and charged as if to certain victory." Even Brigadier General Griffin insisted that the men of his command did their utmost, a sentiment with which Cummings agreed, while White in later years boasted of their courage.[56]

The later arrivals did commendably according to the three measures of combat performance. It was remarkable that they maintained any level of cohesion, given that this assault began in a fragmented way and grew more disorganized when the Federals entered the enemy earthworks. Neither outfit was able to retain its formation, with some of their number fighting in the Crater and the rest to the right outside of it. The Second Brigade functioned under two commanders, each overseeing part of the whole, which may have complicated the execution of orders. These New Englanders could not be blamed for the limited progress they made toward accomplishing the objective of seizing the ridge. Their delayed attack was due to the tardy advance of the First Division, while the combination of intricate Confederate entrenchments and intense enemy fire presented a serious obstacle. And yet these men still helped seize sections of two Rebel lines and resisted the graybacks even after the death or capture of their commanding officers. The Vermonters and Mainers showed determination by continuing to fight regardless of sustaining casualties unprecedented in their service amid battlefield conditions equally unparalleled.

Preceding experiences in uniform reduced the combat performance of the later arrivals during the first six weeks of the Petersburg Campaign. The Vermonters and Mainers began the period by completing the most difficult march of their service, which proved especially trying after the ordeal of the Overland Campaign. This left them in poor shape to fight in the First Union Offensive, but they still managed to assault entrenched Confederates at the Shand House. Tactical success that day did not mean the New Englanders were unfazed by their prior exertions or keen to pit themselves against a fortified enemy. Rather, Griffin had decided upon a bayonet charge, which caught most of the Rebels unawares, introducing an element of surprise that compensated for the Federals' deteriorating condition. Lieutenant Colonel Comstock expressed a contrarian view by insisting that the Union soldiers had shown no decline in their fighting ability. More plausible was Grant's own admission that the rank and file of the Army of the Potomac had reached the end of their tether by contending that "all has been done that could be done." Meade agreed and further remarked that these men had progressively lost energy and gumption since the Wilderness. Contemporary historian John C. Ropes expanded on this point, alluding to "the opinion of many observers that the constant attacks . . . did . . . demoralize the troops," which implies that the surviving combatants had grown reluctant to take the offensive. Lyman blamed the heavy casualties among the better officers and the men, plus the exhaustion of these soldiers, for having reduced "morale and discipline and skill."[57]

Siege warfare left the New Englanders in an even more dismal state to fight at the Crater. This extended time in the trenches reinforced a risk-averse mindset they had developed over past stints within earthworks. As Burnside observed of the battle, "after the training of the previous six weeks it is not to be wondered at that the men should have sought shelter in these defenses." The U.S. congressional Joint Committee on the Conduct of the War similarly concluded that the troops had followed old habits by seeking the cover of entrenchments. Despite this tendency, the soldiers were expected to traverse mostly open ground under enemy fire. They also had to navigate intricate field fortifications that made organized maneuver impossible, which augured poorly for Union victory since Civil War regiments were accustomed to fighting shoulder to shoulder in dense formations. Consequently, the Federal leadership expected too much of their men at the Crater. Major General Humphreys, chief of staff for the Army of the Potomac, overstated by declaring that the Union soldiers as a whole had been combat ready. The Vermonters and Mainers could not be expected to charge with the vigor of fresh, unbloodied greenhorns eager to prove themselves under fire. Meade, Burnside, and Comstock each admitted the Ninth Corps had diminished in vigor. For such grizzled Union combatants, the resolution borne of experience had replaced the foolhardiness typical of rookies. Early in July, Lieutenant Colonel Cummings had fittingly opined, "It is no ordinary job to carry by open assault a strong earthworks defended by men who are disposed to obey orders and hold the place at all hazards."[58]

The 17th Vermont and 31st Maine helped sustain the Army of the Potomac as it alternately assaulted and besieged Petersburg. Reflecting on the record of the Ninth Corps from the Wilderness to the Crater, Burnside declared that his "new infantry regiments . . . soon became as steady and reliable as the older regiments, displaying a courage which rendered them honorable associates of the veterans." Though valiant, the New Englanders were too physically and mentally taxed to take Petersburg with a headlong charge so early in the campaign. These considerations should not overshadow the chief accomplishment of these later arrivals—namely, their perseverance against all odds. During the summer of 1864, the Vermonters and Mainers marched, entrenched, fought, and died in moving testimony to the willpower of Billy Yank.[59]

5

THE BATTLE OF PEEBLES FARM
AND THE NINTH UNION OFFENSIVE
AT PETERSBURG

Peebles' Farm . . . was one of the most
desperately fought little battles of the war.

—Sgt. Maj. Leander Otis Merriam, 31st Maine

If you only knew what I had been through in the
last 48 hours [during the Ninth Union Offensive] we
have had one of the hardest fights of the war.

—Cpl. Charles A. Manson, 17th Vermont

Grant made a telling admission after the Federal defeat at the Crater. Reflecting on the enemy defenses, he concluded, "Our experience of to-day proves that fortifications come near holding themselves without troops." The soldiers in the Army of the Potomac were already well versed in the difficulty of attacking entrenchments, but the Crater still left an imprint on the men of the Ninth Corps. Under Burnside's leadership, they had borne the brunt of the battle against the Army of Northern Virginia. The long hours of intense fire and gruesome, hand-to-hand combat found few parallels throughout the Civil War. Brigadier General Potter accentuated its human cost by describing his Second Division of the Ninth Corps as "nearly annihilated." This elicits a key question about the Union drive to victory in the Petersburg Campaign: could the later arrivals keep fighting effectively after the Crater? The 17th Vermont and 31st Maine provided an answer during the last eight months of the campaign with their participation in two major engagements: Peebles Farm and the Ninth Union Offensive.[1]

The Vermonters and Mainers performed unevenly under fire during this stage of the war. At Peebles Farm they collapsed before a Confederate onslaught but nevertheless went on to defend ground that other Federals had already won from a renewed attack. Conversely, the later arrivals capably assaulted earthworks during the Ninth Union Offensive, even though some of them may have joined the men from their brigade who retreated to avoid fierce Rebel fire. The New Englanders admittedly showed worse cohesion than in months past and only partially achieved their objectives, but casualty figures offer further insight into these battles. Although many later arrivals were taken prisoner at Peebles Farm, others fell killed or wounded, proof of their determination to fight. The remaining New Englanders went on to sustain less severe losses during the Ninth Union Offensive, reflecting the limited scope of the Federal effort rather than a reluctance to engage the enemy.

Though well prepared for combat, the 17th Vermont and 31st Maine faced setbacks under fire attributable to higher-level command decisions. Before each engagement, these units spent considerable time in the Union lines around Petersburg that enabled them to recuperate, incorporate reinforcements, and drill. Such respites were important, for the two outfits started this last phase of the war after having suffered through a half-dozen battles, almost 300 miles of grueling marches, and six weeks of siege warfare. The humble private's duty was to endure these trials unflinchingly and keep fighting bravely to achieve Union victory. In December 1864 Captain Yale of the 17th addressed this reality by lamenting, "Grant . . . has fought all the way inch by inch from Fredricksburgh to the south side [rail]road and left his trail literly piled with Northern boys." Even such sacrifices were not enough to ensure success on the battlefield, for the choices that Union generals made exerted a greater influence on the outcome. These military leaders erred while coordinating the movement of large formations at Peebles Farm. They also miscalculated by conducting a probing attack before the beginning of the Ninth Union Offensive that denied their troops the element of surprise against a well-defended enemy position. Regardless, these decisions lay beyond the purview of the later arrivals. To emerge triumphant from the campaign, these men had a bleak yet essential task: to withstand the dangerous tedium of the siege while proving they could still achieve heroic feats under fire.[2]

WITH THE SPADE, ONCE MORE

JULY 31–SEPTEMBER 29, 1864

Following the Crater, Grant abandoned the effort to take Petersburg by assault. Now the Army of the Potomac would target the Rebel lines of communication connecting this city to the rest of the Confederacy, which included the Weldon Railroad, Boydton Plank Road, and South Side Railroad. Lincoln approved of Grant's determination to continue the investment of Petersburg, exhorting the general in chief to "hold on with a bulldog grip, and chew and choke as much as possible." The Ninth Corps would struggle to sustain this pressure on the enemy despite having already spent a lengthy period in the trenches around the city. Burnside felt that his troops, exhausted and depleted in number after the recent battle, were only capable of keeping the graybacks occupied along a given portion of the line. Supporting this grim prognosis, many of the Mainers present for duty on August 1 were not even physically able to march ten miles a day. Grant instructed Meade that Burnside's men should "leave a very thin line in the works and have the bulk . . . in reserve, [which] . . . will rest them very much." Potter alluded to the Crater when he recalled that "very little occurred before Petersburg, after the mine affair, for some time." The spent 17th Vermont and 31st Maine were fortunate that the operational tempo slowed, for the men could finally recover from their previous trials in uniform.[3]

The Ninth Corps experienced a change in its leadership at this stage in the war. Meade believed that Burnside had failed as a commander at the Crater, and in early August he called for this subordinate's relief, having advanced charges and specifications against him. Ten days later Grant accepted Meade's request, and Burnside promptly departed on a leave of absence. Brevet Major General Willcox, commanding the Third Division, briefly led the Ninth Corps before its chief of staff and most senior officer, Major General Parke, assumed command on August 14. He was not without experience in this role, for he had temporarily led the corps on two previous occasions. The rank and file probably took confidence in Parke, for Griffin described him as "one of the brightest, ablest, and most agreeable young officers in the army."[4]

Over the next two months, the 17th Vermont and 31st Maine served under a succession of unit commanders. Initially, Adjutant Peck led the 17th because Lieutenant Colonel Cummings was in poor health, sleep deprived from neuralgia, and only able to complete tasks while sitting, which caused him to take leave in early August. After Peck, Captain Knapp and Capt. Henry A. Eaton commanded the Vermonters in turn as each came back from periods of detached service until Cummings returned to duty in mid-September. Likewise, the 31st began this stretch in need of a commander since Colonel White had been taken prisoner at the Crater. Captain Dean led the Mainers except for a period when Griffin temporarily replaced him with Captain Jones of the 6th New Hampshire, as the 31st lacked available officers. In a further change within the 31st, Major Talbot resigned in early August after his promotion to lieutenant colonel because of an unspecified "physical disability." Merriam insisted that Talbot's rank change gave him "an easy way to get . . . out" to avoid addressing his unsuitability for the field due to "cannon fever."[5]

The grisly aftermath of the Crater would have weighed heavily on the psyches of the Vermonters and Mainers. According to the editor of the 9th New Hampshire regimental history, the no-man's-land remained dotted with "dead and wounded men, dead and wounded horses, dismounted guns, and scattered sabres, swords, muskets, and accoutrements." To bury the fallen and transport the wounded, the Federals and Confederates began slow-paced negotiations on July 30 but did not agree to a truce until August 1. A sole three-hour ceasefire punctuated the talks. The landscape continued to grow more macabre over these few days, for a 6th New Hampshire captain found the corpses of once-familiar comrades difficult to "recognize . . . so much had they changed." Compounding these horrors, wounded Federals lying among the moldering dead continued to suffer from the wrath of the victorious Confederates. A captain in the 9th New Hampshire remembered that the helpless fellows were "targets for rebel bullets, and no opportunity to shoot one of the wounded was allowed to pass unimproved." He further recalled that the graybacks repulsed those who dragged themselves in the direction of the enemy defenses "by tossing among them bunches of cartridges with a slow match attached that they might more easily become victims of rebel hate." Incredibly, eight wounded bluecoats were still alive when their brethren reached them. Those stricken survived on only diluted milk and water that members of the U.S. Sanitary Commission provided upon daring to enter no-man's-land. These kind visitors improvised shelter for the injured by using rifle muskets to hold up tenting to shield them from the sun.[6]

The later arrivals needed time to rebuild their shattered units. At first Cummings decried "the present deplorable condition of things" in the 17th Vermont, but he felt obliged to concentrate on paperwork in Peck's brief absence because there was no one else to assume this task. Once he returned, the adjutant alluded to the unit's "trimmed enfeebled ranks" and bemoaned that the Vermonters were "disorganized and discouraged, without officers and almost without Sergts." Under these circumstances Peck found his duties nearly overwhelming, with "everything . . . in a state bordering close upon confusion and disorganization." Quartermaster Buel J. Derby went so far as to assert that the unit would last just one more battle without reinforcements. Referring to the Crater, a newspaper editor from the Green Mountain State demanded to know whether it was typical for an outfit to enter "the fight so as to use it up in this way." Despite these bleak comments, the 17th gained in number with the addition of its ninth company in August. The 31st Maine faced a similar predicament. Sergeant Major Merriam served as adjutant to handle regimental administration, for Adjutant and First Lieutenant Allyn had been killed at the Crater and no remaining officer had the knowledge to complete his duties. Attesting to inadequate numbers, Captains Dean and Bolton informed Adjutant General Hodsdon of Maine that "it would be for the good of the Service as well as the Regt if it could be withdrawn from the Field and its thined Ranks filled." A journalist anticipated that "the 31st . . . having been reduced . . . below the minimum standard of members in the service, will be ordered home to recruit very shortly." Nevertheless, this unit remained at the front just like the 17th. Both outfits derived additional strength from the return of convalescents, even though at least some of the men would have lacked the combat experience of their peers. Two dozen recruits further bolstered the ranks, benefiting the Vermonters. Such influxes of manpower surely lifted the later arrivals' spirits.[7]

Light duty in the trenches facilitated the recovery of the New Englanders. Originally, they rotated between the front, main, and rear lines every few days, but the men stayed mostly in the rear from late August onward. When facing the enemy, up to half of each unit kept watch overnight, with the rest joining their comrades on alert for several hours in the early morning. The Confederate positions lay between less than 1,000 yards and just over a mile distant, variations reflecting the Federals' repeated shifts in position as Grant lengthened their line around Petersburg. In response, the Rebels extended their own earthworks, which obliged the contending forces to distribute themselves more sparsely within the trenches. In a reprieve from the rifle pits, the Vermonters briefly garrisoned an earthen fort that offered superior protection from enemy fire. The later arrivals also enjoyed improved lodgings to the rear, even staying in log cabins for up to two weeks. As Cummings enthused, this was the "best time" the Vermonters had had since they entered the field, while Merriam insisted these quarters were "the least unpleasant, of . . . my active service." The ample nourishment of provisions, including fruits and vegetables, helped the New Englanders regain their physical strength. These soldiers were limited to well water, however, given the lack of a whiskey ration. Officers could not purchase this alcohol unless they made a specific request for their own use, albeit with subsequent limitations on the quantity and frequency of sale.[8]

The 17th Vermont and 31st Maine prosecuted the siege in various ways. Besides picket duty, scouting, and skirmishing, they periodically readied for a change in position or potential clash with advancing Confederates, day or night. In addition, these bluecoats labored continuously on the fortifications and on reinforcing the roadways with logs, known as corduroying. This fatigue duty was necessary not only to extend the Federal line around Petersburg but also to compensate for a dearth of manpower by making their fieldworks more formidable. Manson boasted that these entrenchments were so strong, it would be "almost impossible to drive us away." Mortar shells alone were effective against such defenses, which Merriam judged to be "about the best that I had seen." A 9th New Hampshire sergeant ensconced within a reinforced bunker-like structure known as a bombproof even bragged that he was "as much at . . . ease as though the enemy were miles instead of rods away." In any case, the later arrivals had other demands on their time in the rear. Sometimes awakening early, they went on to complete dress parade, brigade or division review, guard duty, drill, and inspections.[9]

Service in the Union lines exposed the later arrivals to varying enemy fire from cannons, mortars, and rifle muskets. These Federals tallied minimal losses from combat, as the 17th Vermont sustained only one soldier captured and the 31st Maine counted five men killed or wounded. Helping explain the low figures, Griffin's soldiers initially proved reluctant to continue the bitter exchanges typical of mid-June through July. A captain in the 6th New Hampshire discouragingly alluded to "our dead that lay but a few rods in front of us" and the dispiriting results of the Crater. A few days after the fighting of July 30, the graybacks temporarily increased the volume of their fire to express enmity over the involvement of the Black troops in that battle. The soldiers of the Ninth Corps were growing exhausted from this exposure, as Burnside noted prior to his leave of absence. A 9th New Hampshire sergeant thus decried the Confederates' lobbing "of rotten iron and such like missiles." Likewise, Army of the Potomac medical director Doctor McParlin called attention to the enemy "sharpshooters, whose skill and vigilance severely taxed the energies and health of the men at the midsummer season." But not all later arrivals were equally anxious about rifle musket and cannon fire, for Manson noted how he had "got used to [it] now so that I like to hear it." Conversely, Corporal Whitehill of the 17th fearfully opined, "I somtimes feel as David did that is but one step betwen me and death." Even in the rear the bluecoats faced these dangers, especially in mid-August, when a portion of the Second Division lacked adequate defenses in their camps to block minié balls. Fortunately, such incoming projectiles were not particularly lethal at these distances.[10]

Frequent bouts of inclement weather worsened the plight of the soldiers. A major in the 48th Pennsylvania remarked of mid-August, "the rainy weather continued, and the men of the regiment had an exceedingly rough time." Between late August and the end of September, the clay-rich soil struggled to absorb the frequent rains. McParlin judged that this precipitation left the "roads . . . almost impracticable for loaded trains." The downpours even grew intense enough to slow entrenching and fill the defenses with water, hindering the men from moving freely within them. Although some days were cooler, the troops also suffered through dry conditions and a stretch of high temperatures that frequently reached 90°F. Bombproofs provided their occupants with some protection from the sun. The editor of the 9th New Hampshire regimental history, however, complained about "the swarms of flies that seemed to be determined to devour them."[11]

For the New Englanders, the most trying episode over these two months was the Battle of Globe Tavern (August 18–21, 1864). This engagement represented the culmination of the Fourth Union Offensive (August 14–25, 1864), which had begun when parts of the Second and Tenth Corps, along with a cavalry division, fought north of the James in the Second Battle of

Deep Bottom (August 14–20, 1864). The clash at Globe Tavern occurred when Grant decided to attack and sever an enemy supply line, the Weldon Railroad, while the graybacks were distracted by operations north of the James. The Fifth Corps seized this railroad near the intersection with Vaughan Road, then engaged with the Confederates close to Six-Mile Station and Globe (Yellow) Tavern. It appears that the prospect of more combat could still strike fear in the hearts of some later arrivals. On August 18 Cpl. Alexander G. Allen of the 17th Vermont was found guilty of cowardly behavior and reduced to the rank of private. Such trepidation notwithstanding, Potter's Second Division supported the Fifth Corps by starting a trek that same afternoon. Once halted for the evening, the Vermonters and Mainers threw out picket lines and dug in overnight. They reached the battlefield at Blick's Station late the following afternoon after finishing their journey at the double-quick despite adverse weather. Repeated downpours lowered the temperature and drenched the roads, moving Potter to state that his troops were having "the most horrible week of wet and mud I think I ever knew." A soldier in the 32nd Maine claimed the men had "marched through mud and water sometimes waist-deep, and in a pouring rain-storm." While the Fifth Corps contended with a Rebel assault, the 17th Vermont and 31st Maine composed part of the Federals' second line. These outfits were not directly engaged but remained exposed to enemy fire. Once the fighting ended, they entrenched, skirmished, and watched for graybacks. Soaked by rain that evening and the following day, the later arrivals doubtless felt the effects of poor rest over the previous ten nights. Once they returned to the Union lines around Petersburg, they would be able to recuperate. Ultimately, this clash at the Weldon Railroad ended successfully for the Army of the Potomac, which would hold that position until war's end.[12]

During this two-month period, disease did more to weaken the 17th and 31st than Confederate missiles. Although the proportion of those sick declined in both units, it continued to represent a large part of the whole. Among the Vermonters, the rate plunged from 68 percent on August 10 to 50 percent by September 25. Fragmentary morning reports provide less complete information on the Mainers. In Company C the ratio fluctuated between 56 and 60 percent from August 1 to September 29, whereas the share of Company D incapacitated by illness only dropped from 80 percent on August 1 to 72 percent a month later. These examples demonstrate that the 31st suffered greatly from poor health, as 1st Lt. E. Brookings Jr. confirmed in August by reporting that the unit had "in Hospital about (600) men." The entire army contended with diarrhea and what Doctor McParlin termed "biliary disorder." Poor camp sanitation contributed to the spread of disease, for the New Englanders struggled to keep the trenches clean while hunkering down to stay out of harm's way. According to Lt. Col. R. Charleton Mitchell, assistant adjutant general of the Ninth Corps, the defenses were frequently "used as sinks and . . . very filthy . . . in consequence." A division officer of the day even alluded to unspecified "sources of disease" that likely included human waste. He also took note of "stagnant and putrid water," a significant issue given that standing water in the earthworks enabled malaria-transmitting mosquitoes to proliferate. Regardless, the actual guilt of the Vermonters and Mainers remains unclear. Owing to these unhygienic conditions, Parke's men did not fare as well as other Federals under medical treatment and frequently required more extensive care in hospitals at City Point, the Union supply base. The transition to cooler autumn weather, which would have lessened the presence of mosquitoes and bacteria, probably contributed to the reduction in the sick rate.[13]

A REVERSAL OF FORTUNE

SEPTEMBER 30–OCTOBER 2, 1864

The later arrivals would play a prominent role in the fighting at Peebles Farm. Grant initiated this battle, part of his Fifth Union Offensive, when he decided the Federals should push west toward Poplar Spring Church to capture the Boydton Plank Road and South Side Railroad. Accomplishing this would render Petersburg useless as a supply hub and prompt its defenders to withdraw. The Confederates protecting Richmond would thus depend for resupply on the James River Canal as well as the Richmond and Danville and the Virginia Central Railroads. Simultaneously, the Army of the James would try to take the Rebel capital, an effort that would culminate in the Battle of Chaffin's Bluff (September 29–30, 1864). Grant waited until Lee reduced his manpower around Poplar Spring Church to order Meade's drive south of Petersburg, in which two divisions of the Fifth Corps would advance straight ahead while two divisions of the Ninth Corps outflanked the Confederates. The bluecoats would toil in high temperatures, but at least the Poplar Spring Church Road on which they were to march was in fine shape. Grant was optimistic about this engagement, for he believed the graybacks near the church were "weak enough at one or the other place" to enable a penetration of their line. Although the lieutenant general believed the Federals might be able to capture Petersburg, Meade was more doubtful, contrasting the now-reduced number of soldiers at his disposal with "the enemy in position and in force."[14]

Despite a few naysayers, the New Englanders had enjoyed fine spirits over most of the two months preceding the battle. A soldier in the 11th New Hampshire, reflecting on his difficult service right after the Crater, griped that some high-ranking officer wanted to ensure the Second Brigade was "wiped out entirely." Adjutant Peck complained of doubtful morale among the Vermonters, and the conduct of the later arrivals while serving on picket supports this view. These men spoke with the Confederates, once traded bread for tobacco, and established an illicit ceasefire at one point. Yet it likely boosted their confidence to learn that Rebel deserters, according to the same 11th New Hampshire private, believed "no corps in the Union army . . . fought them with such determined resistance as did the Ninth, and there was none they feared so much." Cummings and Capt. Daniel Conway of the 17th insisted the Vermonters were primed for action. Conway further expressed hope that they would "ere long see the end of this accursed rebellion, the Union restored, and peace once more reign over the land." Similarly, one or more unnamed newspaper correspondents from the 31st asserted that the Mainers were prepared to "fight for the old flag" and that both Petersburg and Richmond would soon fall to the Federals. Merriam, alluding to the Mainers' resolve at Globe Tavern, declared they "had been stopping bullets all summer and were not frantic for more of the same, but ready if needs must." Griffin surely lifted the mood in the ranks of his command when he issued a celebratory announcement to extoll

> their gallantry and noble conduct as soldiers, whether displayed at a mere review, on the bloody field of battle, or amidst the harassing fatigue of the march. Never did troops display higher qualities as soldiers than have those of this command since crossing the Rapidan on the 5th of May last, and never did patriots win a nobler record than those who have endured the hardships and braved the perils of this memorable Campaign. Every soldier and every officer has a right to feel—as your General does—a just pride in his regiment and in his Brigade.[15]

The 17th Vermont and 31st Maine would enter this battle under leadership of differing effectiveness. Although seasoned, Lieutenant Colonel Cummings had not led the Vermonters in combat since North Anna. He was in less than top physical condition due to persistent neuralgia that produced stiffness in his legs "after lying on the ground all night." A malcontent, Adjutant Peck informed Adjutant and Inspector General Washburn of Vermont that "Cummings . . . does not command the respect of the Regt, neither officers nor men." Captain Knapp likewise carped about him, writing to Washburn that Cummings's "opinion . . among us . . . is regarded of but little value." Such negative commentary was the first of its kind in the extant source material about Cummings. In contrast, the Mainers appear to have benefited from the able leadership of Captain Dean. Although Capt. Joseph S. Harlow was the most senior officer available, he ceded command to Dean on account of his own poor health. Limited evidence points to flaws in Dean's conduct, for Sergeant Major Merriam twice noted his affinity for drink, while Lt. Col. Edward L. Getchell accused him of harboring "secessionist proclivities." Despite this criticism, more compelling were positive allusions to Dean's aptitude for leadership. Pvt. William E. Burn felt this captain was a "brave & faithful officer" who should be promoted to major, an impression supported by his inspiring example at Globe Tavern. As Merriam recalled, the captain had motivated his noncommissioned officers by declaring, "Now, boys, we are in for a hell of a fight to-day, and I want every one of you to do his duty." The rank and file drew confidence from Dean's previous combat experience alongside them. On a different occasion in the siege lines, he had exhorted the Mainers to hold their ground as they readied for an unrealized attack. In Dean's fiery words, "If they try to come across there, we'll show them there is a God in Israel."[16]

Though well drilled, the New Englanders were obliged to fight without adequate manpower or rest. Over the past two months, they had spent much time training in the rear. Regardless, only 214 officers and men in the 17th Vermont were present for duty as of September 25, which equaled one-third of its total strength. A mere 116 Mainers were present for duty on September 30, or one-fifth of the whole 31st Regiment. These later arrivals reached the periphery of the battlefield west of Weldon Railroad on September 28, and from midnight onward, kept up a tiring routine of watching for Confederate activity and staying ready for combat over the next two days.[17]

The Vermonters and Mainers would not engage the enemy until late on

September 30. That morning the Fifth Corps proceeded along the road to Poplar Spring Church in order to capture the intersection with Squirrel Level Road. Griffin's troops did not move until about 10:30 a.m., owing to what Merriam described as "the usual halts and delays in starting a long column on the narrow roads." The 17th and 31st departed their bivouac close to the Aiken House and the Weldon Railroad on a sluggish trek of roughly seven miles via the same Poplar Spring Church Road. Hindering the movement of Parke's troops, the two Fifth Corps divisions did not provide a gap through which they could advance. The task before the rank and file inspired trepidation. As Merriam recalled, "The fact that the Johnnies were forced back 'to the last ditch' and would fight desperately for the [South Side Railroad] . . . didn't make the outlook more of a holiday kind to the men of the divisions which had been selected for the picnic." During this transit, Dean noted a hill covered with undergrowth and trees in front of the 31st. According to Merriam, Dean worried lest "a regiment of Johnnies . . . [appear] within a hundred feet of us in that bush without our seeing them." He ordered Merriam to scout this high ground with a half-dozen skirmishers. On hands and knees, these intrepid Federals forced through the foliage, observed no graybacks, and returned to their comrades. Merriam felt the bloodless effort had proven "more trying to the nerves than being actually under fire." The sound of intermittent rifle musket shots ahead also left the men anxious about their impending role in the fight. Just prior to midday, the two divisions of the Fifth Corps seized the Confederate entrenchments near the Peebles Farm and Squirrel Level Road, moving forward enough so Parke's troops could finally pass. Reaching that property, Potter waited for the First Division of the Ninth Corps to catch up. When Griffin's command mistakenly headed too far leftward, it had to shift right more than a mile before continuing forward. Further contributing to the delay, Parke adopted the defensive, reflecting concern about previous indications of a large Rebel concentration nearby.[18]

Around 3:00 p.m. Potter's troops began their movement to outflank the enemy right. With the Second Brigade in the lead, they departed the Peebles Farm and traversed the wood line that separated it from the adjoining Pegram House. Griffin deployed skirmishers, who fired upon their Confederate counterparts near the home, causing them to fall back across the rolling terrain. Since the soldiers of the Fifth Corps did not progress as quickly, at least a fourth of a mile separated the flanks of the two

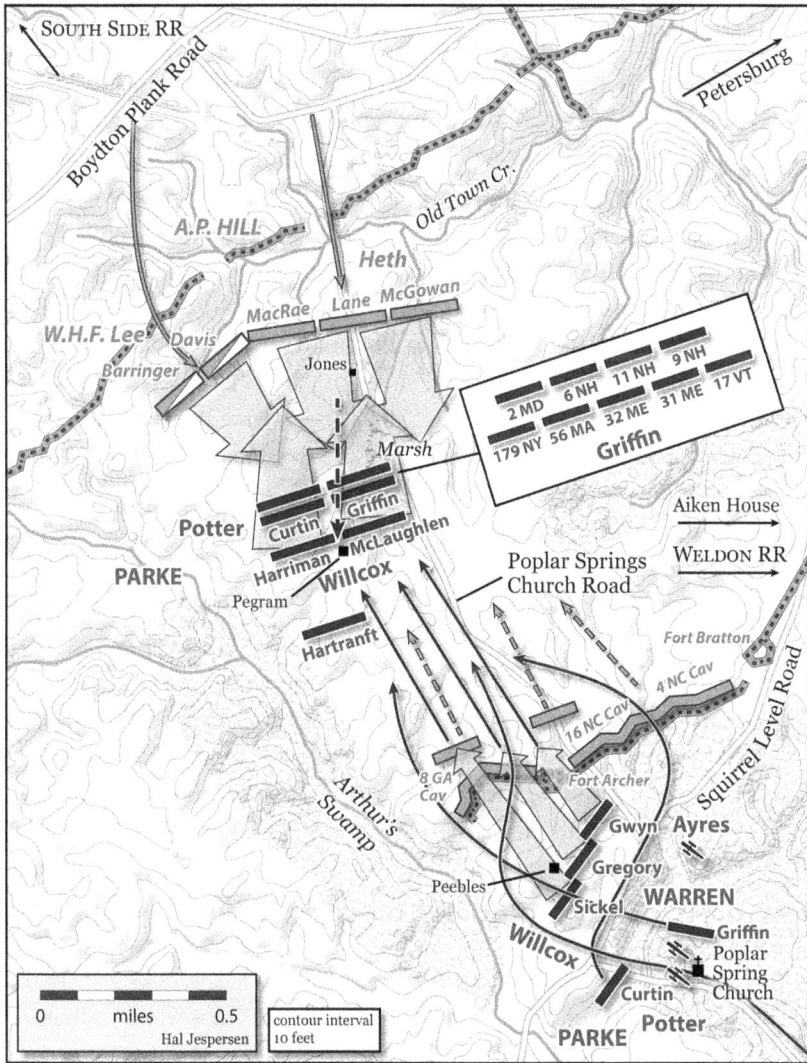

Battle of Peebles Farm, September 30, 1864.

Union forces. This gap left the right side of the Second Brigade column vulnerable to a potential Rebel counterattack. To defeat the increasing opposition of enemy skirmishers at the Pegram House, Griffin advanced one regiment out to each side of his column, selecting neither the 17th nor the 31st. The bluecoats wheeled rightward while advancing to align with a marsh along Old Town Creek that could hinder any assailants. Before reaching more trees, Griffin arranged his column into two lines of battle, with the Vermonters on the right flank of the second line and the Mainers to their left. The later arrivals, unlike their comrades on the left side of Griffin's formation, now entered the boggy area. Despite Rebel artillery fire enfilading Poplar Spring Church Road, the Union troops expelled the graybacks from a ravine that the creek had rendered swampy. Before traversing this wet terrain, Dean warned Griffin that a gap had developed between the Mainers and the Vermonters to their right, yet the brigade commander chastised him for questioning the movement and ordered the captain to proceed.[19]

The fighting began to intensify. Traversing a fence and emerging from the next wood line, the later arrivals halted on a ridge bordering the Jones Farm, then Potter commanded his First Brigade to deploy left of the Second Brigade and attack in tandem. Around 5:00 p.m. Griffin's skirmishers pushed forward after previously suffering a repulse at the Jones farmhouse. The brigade's front line followed suit to help drive the Confederate skirmishers across the uneven terrain of the farmyard, which featured a fence and orchard. Meanwhile, the later arrivals and the rest of the second line lay prone in the woods, having covered two miles from the Peebles Farm. As a Vermonter remarked, "the shells from the enemy's batteries were bursting all around us, accompanied by an incessant shower of bullets." For Griffin's advancing men, what a 6th New Hampshire captain termed "broken ground and other obstructions" limited visibility, causing those in the center of the formation to outpace their comrades on the flanks. Finally, these troops neared the main Rebel line near the Boydton Plank Road, only for the enemy to push through a wooded, mucky area and a ravine choked with undergrowth. Rising from behind a stone wall along the Poplar Spring Church Road, they shot at the unsuspecting bluecoats. Merriam remembered seeing three lines of Rebels who offered "a splendid mark for the boys on our side." Regardless, the numerically superior mass of enemy troops presented a formidable sight that led the Mainer to confess, "my heart went rapidly downward as I saw their strength and knew how thin and light was the line."[20]

For the Union soldiers, this Confederate onslaught proved overwhelming. The Rebels enveloped Griffin's right almost all the way back to Poplar Spring Church Road, threatening to block the later arrivals' retreat. Graybacks also started passing over the farmyard fence to attack the Union left. In response, Griffin ordered most of his second line to bolster the men in front. The Mainers reinforced their comrades near the Jones farmhouse, while the Vermonters lay prone along the fence south of it and defended the right flank. As a member of the 17th remembered, "a solid column were almost upon us," so Cummings ordered his men to stand and loose a volley. These men of the Green Mountain State unknowingly shot at fellow bluecoats, leading Cummings to cancel the order and instruct his men to fix bayonets. The onrushing Rebels, however, preempted their recourse to melee combat by shearing the unit in half while also outflanking it. Confederates drove between Potter's First Brigade and Griffin's Second Brigade, which suffered from inadequate flank support along its right. The expected Fifth Corps division had not advanced far enough to hold the terrain, and only one regiment from Parke's First Division appeared instead of an entire brigade.[21]

The Federal formation now disintegrated. Merriam admitted that the Confederates "thoroughly broke" Potter's command, and it was probably around this time that the Vermonters experienced a blow to their leadership. Lieutenant Colonel Cummings was struck down in front of the 17th while urging his men, "Look out for the colors." During this battle, Major Eaton and 2nd Lt. George W. Tobin also died after demonstrating courage to the men. The Mainers held their ground the longest of the brigade before withdrawing, at which point the oncoming Rebels loomed less than 500 feet away. Potter insisted that "every possible effort was made to rally the troops and check the enemy's advance, but they were in so much force and so close that it could not be done." Some bluecoats managed to shelter in the basement of the Jones farmhouse, while the wounded counted heavily among those who fell prisoner. The Rebel pursuit sowed chaos among the retreating Union troops, moving the editor of the 9th New Hampshire regimental history to write, "it became 'Legs versus Liberty.'" A number of Federals struggled back through the marsh via a bridge, which slowed their egress. As First Lieutenant Lucia explained, owing to "the confusion into which the troops had already been thrown by the appearance of the enemy in their rear, they became inextricably mixed." The remainder of the men poured across the more open ground of the farm, leaving them vulnerable to enemy fire. According to Merriam, a blizzard of projectiles was "threatening the entire extinction of every blue uniform in sight," to which a Rebel battery added by unleashing canister, case, and shells. Peck, along with Captain Conway and Lt. William H. Norton, re-formed some Vermonters around the flags to protect a section of Federal artillery during its withdrawal. Conway boldly shot down three enemy color guards while the Vermonters' own color sergeant, G. W. Bacon, defended his standard resolutely despite ill health. Knapp corralled another portion of the 17th and joined Peck's band, then assumed command of the reunited outfit.[22]

During the final hours of combat, the later arrivals collected themselves to repulse the Confederates. The efforts of Griffin and his staff officers helped restore the formation of the Second Brigade. This belied the claim of Maj. Charles J. Mills, assistant adjutant general of the Ninth Corps, who observed that "it was, as a rule, a nearly fruitless amusement of trying to rally a lot of frightened men under heavy fire." Corporal Inman of the 17th Vermont likewise provided a heroic example while wounded by encouraging his comrades to resist, partially justifying his later receipt of the Medal of Honor. When the Rebels opened with rifle musket and artillery fire on these bluecoats from higher ground, the Vermonters and Mainers lay prone to shield themselves, Manson recalling how "the Shell and balls came in there merry." Griffin's men went on to briefly resist in the woods, delivering three volleys before gradually falling back over a mile to reach the Pegram House. The 17th and probably the 31st Maine kept fighting, bolstered by the timely arrival of a Fifth Corps division and Parke's First Division. Some of the Vermonters gathered to fight back alongside comrades from other Federal units thanks to the efforts of the 7th Rhode Island Volunteer Infantry Regiment's commander. These additional troops launched a counterattack that caused the enemy to retreat from the right flank of the Second Brigade line to the protection of nearby trees. This combat finally ended at nightfall. During an overnight downpour, some Vermonters and Mainers went out to serve as pickets, while their brethren manned and improved the defenses near the Peebles Farm. The troops' morale was surely at a low point. As a 32nd Maine soldier lamented, "Miserable in body and mentally filled with regret and anger, we sullenly counted the hours of that dreary night." Despite the tumultuous reverse, Manson celebrated visual evidence of Union progress that day by mentioning the welcome sight of "the Steeples in Petersberg."[23]

Inconclusive combat persisted over the next two days. On October 1 the Vermonters and Mainers established a picket line behind a fence at the Pegram House amid low temperatures and an all-day rainfall. This was in response to Meade's order to Parke that he advance scouts and ready for a potential drive on the Boydton Plank Road. A Confederate battery began firing at these Federals around 8:00 a.m. from atop the hill separating the Pegram House from the Jones Farm. As a 6th New Hampshire captain admitted, the bombardment transformed "the rail-fence into kindling-wood in a manner more lively than agreeable." The Union soldiers anticipated a Rebel assault upon their position, which was too long and thinly manned to defend, so a number withdrew. A sergeant in the 9th New Hampshire recalled that such bluecoats had to bolt "across a field raked with deadly precision by canister." The remainder held their ground as the graybacks attacked, with the majority falling prisoner. Those retreating reached the Peebles Farm and dug in, comforted only by a meager repast that the same sergeant described as "'tack' with raw pork, a piece of codfish, and a cup of cold coffee once or twice." That evening the men struggled to stay warm beneath rubber blankets during the ongoing rainfall, while the prospect of another enemy onslaught loomed. The next morning the later arrivals sought to reconnoiter the Confederate defenses and capture part of the Boydton Plank Road near the South Side Railroad or even drive toward Petersburg. To accomplish this objective, Meade planned for the Fifth and Ninth Corps to hold the enemy's attention by attacking near the Pegram House while a Second Corps division flanked right around the graybacks. Just prior to 8:00 a.m., amid warm weather and low fog, Griffin's command advanced on soggy terrain to reach the structure while the Rebels pulled back to their own main line. Deploying pickets close to the enemy, these Union troops dug in at the house. Near midday on October 2, Meade concluded that the Army of Northern Virginia would not fight in the open, and Grant approved of his decision not to assault its strong earthworks. This marked the end of the engagement.[24]

THE PRICE OF VICTORY

ASSESSING THE AFTERMATH
OF PEEBLES FARM

The New Englanders suffered heavy casualties at Peebles Farm, nearly all on September 30. Among the Vermonters, seventy-two officers and men were killed, wounded, or captured, whereas the Mainers tallied thirty-seven officers and men killed, wounded, missing, or captured. The present-for-duty strength in both outfits consequently dropped by about one-third. Even though Manson lamented "that many a poor boy has bit the dust," numerous unfortunates had actually been taken prisoner. The officer-loss rate in these two units closely matched the 4-percent ratio across the entire Second Brigade, which suggests that officers generally fled the battlefield as quickly as their men. Conversely, the 17th Vermont and 31st Maine differed significantly in terms of the casualties that members with prior wartime service suffered relative to their less experienced comrades. The more seasoned Vermonters equaled 36 percent of the losses, which far outweighed their share in the ranks. This contrasted with the Mainers, among whom the more grizzled Federals equaled 11 percent of the casualties, on par with the proportion of comparable combatants throughout the outfit. Perhaps the explanation for this disparity reflects the position of the two units in Griffin's formation on September 30. Once the Rebel onslaught shattered the brigade, both outfits faced attacks from multiple directions. Initially, the Mainers were situated left of center, so they were not exposed to attacks on either flank. Since the Vermonters held the right flank, however, they faced enemy pressure from two directions. Those in the 17th without a previous stint in uniform may have struggled to fight effectively under such stressful conditions. It is plausible that they bolted prior to their more experienced comrades, who offered resistance for a longer period.[25]

Eyewitness commentary about this battle focused on the fighting of September 30. Grant highlighted the fact that the Federals lengthened their line two miles west of the Weldon Railroad. And yet Potter confessed to being "extremely grieved and mortified" at what proved to be "the severest loss I ever had" up to that time. Describing the combat of both September 30 and October 1, Manson affirmed the view of "old Soldiers . . . that it was the heaviest fire they was ever under." According to Mills, "Meade has expressed himself satisfied with the very small result we have achieved." The staff officer had a different viewpoint reminiscent of prior observations about these troops in the field. He felt that the bluecoats' insistence on entrenchment "has hurt our men's style of fighting much, and they feel no confidence except behind works." Yet several officers complimented the conduct of the rank and file at September's end. Potter lauded a majority of soldiers in his division while regretting that "the recruits (mostly substitutes, and many unable to speak English) behaved badly" and "seemed perfectly panic-stricken." This claim may have applied to individual recruits who had recently joined the later arrivals. It could have equally reflected upon the tenth company in the 17th Vermont but not the 31st Maine, for all of its companies had already served throughout the Overland and Petersburg Campaigns. Nevertheless, Griffin insisted that his men had "fought bravely, and with a determination to hold." The two generals even singled out the Mainers, while Adjutant and Inspector General Washburn praised the troops from the Green Mountain State for "their cool and determined bravery in action."[26]

The later arrivals turned in a mixed record at Peebles Farm based on the three measures of combat performance. These New Englanders had been tired but not dispirited when they entered the battle. The fighting of September 30 marked the first time that they engaged in a stand-up clash with the Confederates outside of entrenchments or natural cover. The Vermonters and Mainers also faced the challenge of resisting a larger number of Rebels, who outflanked them on both sides. Under these circumstances, it is unsurprising that the cohesion of the 17th and 31st crumbled. Although these units failed to achieve their objective of getting around the enemy's flank, they managed to hold a defensive line at the Pegram House. In this way the two outfits solidified some of the Union gains while incurring heavy casualties. The fact that so many men were captured rather than killed or wounded is no evidence of cowardice but instead speaks to the power of the enemy assault. Ultimately, the New Englanders fought admirably under circumstances that compelled a retreat. They did not commit to another large-scale attack on either October 1 or October 2 due to higher-level command decisions.

DUG IN TO THE END

OCTOBER 3, 1864–MARCH 28, 1865

Following Peebles Farm, the later arrivals resumed their pattern of life in the Union fortifications around the city. Early in this period, Grant explained that "the operations in front of Petersburg . . . until the spring campaign of 1865, were confined to the defense and extension of our lines and to offensive movements for crippling the enemy's lines of communication and to prevent his detaching any considerable force to send south." The

Vermonters and Mainers continued to move and dig in around Petersburg. They departed the Pegram Farm and spent much of the next few months in earthen forts rather than trenches, as the Union leadership believed the garrisons of these emplacements could unleash interlocking fields of fire to stop advancing Confederates. In addition, the 17th and 31st labored on fortifications, making them so formidable that a 9th New Hampshire sergeant declared, "every inch of the ground we have gained is being fortified in the strongest manner possible." Though important to sustain pressure on the Rebels, this repetitive duty caused the Federals to complain of boredom. Captain Yale decried "so much monotony to the life of a soljer" and wrote letters "to kill time." Brigadier General Potter summed up the routine between December 1864 and March 1865 by declaring that "little was done of an offensive character, besides the prosecution of the siege and preparing for the spring campaign."[27]

Service in the fieldworks was disquieting for these men. They performed picket duty regularly, remaining in front for one to three days at a time. When on picket duty overnight, one-third of each unit had to keep watch. In addition, the troops repeatedly prepared to either move or fight, but the alarms generally proved to be false. Nevertheless, these soldiers skirmished with the enemy, sometimes exceeding their standard issue of roughly twenty rounds to fire up to 100 times per night. As a journalist admitted, this use of ammunition was "more than usual—more than is necessary, perhaps." Instead of carefully aiming at targets, the Federals tried to relieve campaign stresses by unleashing a high volume of fire on the graybacks. Offering respite from their repetitive and tiring duties, these bluecoats were able to rest in bombproofs and tents while they garrisoned the forts.[28]

Periodically, the troops gained a measure of relief by rotating to the rear. They completed assorted tasks that led a 9th New Hampshire sergeant to bemoan the "daily programme in which 'fatigue' was the principal item, with a small margin for grumbling." The later arrivals typically awakened early and passed a large portion of their days on brigade review, dress parade, guard duty, and inspections. Officers and noncommissioned officers alike studied army regulations and tactics. Meanwhile, the soldiers trained, with the greenhorns among them engaging in target practice. This preparation was a needed change of pace, given Mills's claim that "our troops . . . need rest and drill badly." Lieutenant Colonel Lyman referred to instruction in early November when writing that "the 9th Corps, in particular, have gone into the evolutions to an alarming extent." Despite such rigorous activity, life in the rear offered improved living conditions in comparison to frontline service. Several Federals commented on their lodgings, which transitioned from cozy tents to wood huts complete with beds. In this vein Captain Yale enthused over one "tip top camping ground" that proved "a great deal more healthy, than an old camp." On several occasions officers in the two outfits even had the opportunity to play ball.[29]

The later arrivals witnessed changes in leadership. Knapp led the Vermonters after the death of Cummings at Peebles Farm. With the formation of the tenth company, Randall officially assumed his post as colonel. He had long been recruiting for the 17th in the Green Mountain State and finally joined this outfit around Petersburg in October. When Randall took a leave of absence in March 1865, previously promoted Major Knapp assumed command. The Mainers underwent a more tumultuous experience. Following Dean's capture at Peebles Farm, a sergeant led the unit until Bolton assumed the role in October. Lieutenant Colonel Getchell arrived that month to take command, only to fall wounded while in a fort the following month. Bolton, who received a promotion to major, temporarily replaced Getchell until the lieutenant colonel returned to lead the 31st around February 1865.[30]

The Vermonters approved of the officers now commanding them. Randall had broad popularity in the 17th, even going back to April 1864, when a visitor to the unit had noted a widespread desire for his leadership. That July, Quartermaster Sergeant Wilder also looked forward to Randall's presence, as did Yale, prior to the arrival of the colonel in October. Manson considered Randall to be a fatherly figure, declaring, "we have got a man to look out for us and not afraid to intersede in our behalf a little we never had a man that did yet." In contrast to this implicit criticism of Cummings, Knapp earned plaudits from Surgeon Rutherford, who stated that he was "very much pleased with" those officers present for duty. According to a newspaper correspondent from this outfit, Adjutant Peck was "always at his post . . . and . . . indefatigable in the discharge of his duties."[31]

The Mainers served under well-liked officers as well. According to newspaper correspondence, the 31st boasted many leaders "whose faithful discipline and upright character command the obedience and respect of the men." Individuals from all ranks held Major Bolton in high esteem. This included Griffin, who justified Bolton's promotion to major by insisting he knew "of no officer in this reg't. better qualified to fill the vacancy . . . and none in the army more worthy." The Mainers expressed their support for Bolton by giving an address in his honor and offering him the gift of a horse. Second Lieutenant A. R. Wescott, noting that he was in then-Captain Bolton's mess, judged him to be "a fine officer." Getchell was also "universally beloved," according to the unit correspondence, while Adjt. R. G. Rollins proved to be "the right man in the right place" and Captain Rogers, formerly a lieutenant, was "a very efficient officer." When Rollins was absent on leave, 1st Lt. G. I. Brown likewise distinguished himself by temporarily filling the role, such that "a better and more soldierly appearing man for the place it would have been difficult to find." Another Mainer to receive a promotion was Wescott, who as of February 1865 rose to first lieutenant in recognition of his "meritorious services" during the Overland Campaign.[32]

Popularity aside, the officers of the 17th and 31st needed time to replenish the depleted ranks. Merriam tellingly referred to the Mainers as "the little squad," an allusion to their diminished size and equally applicable to the Vermonters. Between October and December 1864, however, the gradual return of healing combatants and the addition of recruits increased the number of New Englanders present for duty. During this time, the tenth company of the 17th also reached the front, making the Vermont unit a proper regiment. Two companies of unassigned infantry reinforced the 31st, with which the 32nd Maine was then consolidated. This influx of manpower enabled the Vermonters and Mainers to compensate for the severe losses they had incurred during past service.[33]

Throughout the war's six remaining months, the enemy intermittently fired upon the later arrivals using cannons, mortars, and rifle muskets. When these Union soldiers once returned temporarily to the frontage of the Crater, Manson derided the area as "the meanest hole on the whole line," given the intensity of Confederate fire. The Vermonters and Mainers rarely fell victim to incoming projectiles, however, and did not engage in combat other than light skirmishing. Wescott, while a second lieutenant in the 31st, noted on October 7 that it was "very quiet now & but little piquet . . . firing." Still, he admitted that "the Reb lines are very near to us." Near year's end, Potter ordered his pickets to only shoot at Confederates during the day who changed position or were performing fatigue duty. Conversely, these bluecoats were expected to keep up sufficient fire over-

night to maintain their own alertness and to hinder Rebel efforts at bolstering their lines or pushing them forward. This contrasted with the ferocious
exchanges of the summer months, even though the opposing pickets now
lay at various times only between sixty feet and a quarter-mile apart. The
17th suffered no losses, while the 31st tallied a mere six officers and men
killed, wounded, missing, or captured. Helping explain these low figures,
the contending forces established several unofficial ceasefires, one of which
lasted as long as two weeks. Captain Yale alluded to "verry friendly" pickets, and Manson remarked of the enemy that "to keep peace in the family
they wont fire on us." As a 9th New Hampshire sergeant admitted, "there
was little to remind one of the proximity of the foe." The men in the front
line even conversed with their counterparts. By early November, however,
Union authorities forbid the trading of newspapers for Confederate tobacco. Meade reiterated at month's end that the Federals could not exchange goods with the graybacks, yet Grant allowed the troops to obtain
the most recent periodicals from the enemy as of mid-March 1865. Further
contributing to modest casualties, the later arrivals remained mostly in
forts or in rear areas. Manson downplayed the risk of Rebel projectiles by
dismissively writing, "once in a while a shell will come a little nearer than
is pleasant." He discounted enemy artillery fire as "nothing only to make
us dodge behind the Breast Works." Wescott likewise remarked that the
spectacle of a Confederate artillery bombardment "looked a bit natural"
and expressed the belief that he would survive the night ahead "if the jon-
nies don't get me." Despite such bravado, Getchell suffered his wounding
within the protection of a fort, while one Maine soldier was struck down
fatally while in his tent and a second suffered injury from a stray bullet.[34]

Even when enemy fire diminished, the New Englanders continued to
be subjected to the miseries of inclement weather. Throughout autumn,
intermittently high temperatures and limited rainfall left the soil so dry
that moving artillery and wagons ground the road surfaces into dust. There
were still some cold snaps, however, leading Mills to once claim that the
temperature dropped up to 50°F in a single day in early October. A shift to
wet conditions heralded winter. Writing to a local newspaper, an unnamed
member of the 31st Maine declared after a three-week dousing, "Let no man
who has never been in Virginia during these past four years flatter himself
that he has seen mud." Both in front and in rear, Union positions lacked
sufficient drainage to evacuate rainwater, moving the 9th New Hampshire

sergeant to complain that a powerful deluge "came near drowning out the camp." The southern climate taxed the troops physically and mentally. As the editor of the 9th New Hampshire regimental history observed, it was not "easy for men to see that lying in a mud-hole a month at a time was doing anything towards subduing the Rebellion." Temperatures now fluctuated between a few comfortably warm days and those sufficiently cold to freeze the muck. Reflecting a New Englander's hardiness to chilly conditions, Private Gould of the 17th Vermont regarded the season as mild, proclaiming it "the greatest winter that I ever experienced." From mid-January 1865 onward, the bluecoats were exposed to heavier sleet, snowfall, and frigid air, leading Manson to complain, "our pitts was all mud and watter so we could have no fire." Come spring the soldiers faced alternating heat and rain that dried and soaked the roadways. Rutherford lamented the occasional presence of abundant dust, making "it . . . almost suffocating to go out." Then in late March high winds troubled the Federals by spreading a fire within the camp of the 17th. Manson noted the destruction of the "quartermaster's tents and a large amount of camp equipage" as well as the quarters of "every officer but one," while the gusts also ripped "the roof of my Shanty and Scattered the Stuff all over Creation."[35]

As a further hardship, the later arrivals had to make do with inconsistent rations. Between October and November 1864, they enjoyed abundant food except for inadequate vegetables, which they resolved by substituting onions and potatoes for a portion of their coffee allocation from Federal stocks. Around this time an officer could only obtain whiskey if he affirmed that it was intended for his personal consumption or that of his troops. The men did receive additional sustenance by mail from loved ones for Thanksgiving. Yet even with the completion of a nearby railroad to facilitate the transport of goods in December, the rank and file lacked bread. Lieutenant Colonel Loring wrote late that month about the "insufficiency of rations" and the absence of fresh produce, a problem addressed shortly thereafter by a distribution of vegetables. Then in February 1865, the Federals again suffered a shortage of bread along with low levels of sugar and meat. Loring aptly complained that the quantity of food was "insufficient even for troops in camp when the picket and fatigue duty demanded of them is as arduous as it now is." Following access to a second railroad in early March, Asst. Surgeon Samuel Adams, the medical inspector of the Ninth Corps, found "the supply of fresh vegetables entirely sufficient" again.[36]

Disease continued to plague the New Englanders. Among the Vermonters, 36–51 percent of the troops were sick at any given time from November 1864 to March 1865. The Mainers also suffered heavily from sickness. Based on morning reports available for five to seven companies per month, the rate of disease fluctuated 42–51 percent between October and December 1864. Consolidated morning reports detail the first three months of 1865, indicating that Mainers with maladies equaled 40–44 percent of the entire unit. Notably, disease little affected the newest companies in the 31st. The sick rate in Company L stood at 4–11 percent between October and December 1864, while Company M tallied between 0 and 14 percent in November and December. This difference was surprising, given that rookie soldiers across the Union army generally suffered more heavily from illness because their immune systems were unready for crowded camp conditions. Medical Director Doctor McParlin blamed the poor health in the Army of the Potomac at this time on campaign rigors and the grueling weather. Perhaps as a result of such wear and tear, the original ten companies in the 31st experienced higher rates of disease than newly formed Companies L and M. Between the end of September and November, about half of unwell Federals throughout the army contended with malaria and diarrhea. Among the Mainers, however, McParlin emphasized the prevalence of typhoid fever in addition to malaria. By way of explanation, he noted that the men camped in marshy conditions and endured substandard nutrition due to the lack of vegetables. Such compromised health exacerbated the dearth of officers in the two New England units. The case of Adjutant Peck demonstrates the relationship between bad weather, meager food, and illness. After spending the early days of October in soaking rain without proper nourishment, he contracted pneumonia. Although having partially recovered while on leave, Peck went on to die from an undescribed affliction. Likewise underscoring this issue, Surgeon Preston Fisher of the 31st had to resign after twice coming down with malaria. Between October 1864 and January 1865, Lieutenant Colonel Getchell and Major Bolton repeatedly noted the paucity of officers in their regiment. Even when bathhouses were available, their use did not appear to reduce the sick rate in the two units.[37]

The later arrivals were determined to keep fighting, realizing that more bloody conflict lay ahead. In the 17th Vermont Rutherford expected Petersburg to soon fall: "Every soldier is tip toe with excitement and ready to power upon the enemy with a will." Likewise, Captain Yale judged that most Federals anticipated the city's capture: "the grand 'finale' of the so-thern confederacy is near at hand." Regardless, he predicted that the keen rookies in the 17th who had "seen but verry little of the hardships of war" would "change thier tune before many days." Manson insisted the Vermont-ers were "all well and anxious for the fight," although he fatalistically "be-lieved that if it so orderd that a man is to be killed he will be let him sneak as much as he likes but if not he may go through a dozen hard fights and not get a scratch." He further declared, "if I should happen to fall it will be in my Countrys Service." Many in the 17th believed the war would end shortly, but Gould expected 1865 to bring "a hard campaign this summer [worse] than ever was fought." A newspaper editor reported that 1st Sgt. Henry A. Jordan perceived this outfit to be "in an excellent condition." A similar mindset prevailed in the 31st Maine, as Getchell "found the Regt in good condition, and leaving an enviable reputation throughout the Corps." A newspaper correspondent from that unit declared "the men are in good spirits, and more than ever ready when the propitious moment comes." Even Loring maintained that the 31st was "especially praised for Military ap-pearance." Surely boosting morale, the mayor of Bangor, Maine, delivered an address that galvanized the rank and file. And yet the Mainers were not naïve about the dangers they were to face. As a second lieutenant, Wescott informed his parents that he "found the boys in the best of spirits," yet he still sent home "a piece of our tattered banner . . . [which was] more than ⅓ gone & is smoked & stained with blood." Based on newspaper corre-spondence, most graybacks would keep resisting despite their inevitable defeat and "absolute extermination." Still, the outfit remained steadfast, for "wherever its glorious old colors, torn and rent by the iron hail, and dyed in the heart's blood of more than one brave soldier, shall lead the way, there will the gallant veterans of the 31st be found, ready to die, if need be."[38]

IMMORTALIZED COURAGE

MARCH 29–APRIL 2, 1865

The Vermonters and Mainers would face a final test of their willingness to assault entrenchments in the Ninth Union Offensive (April 2, 1865). Grant's plan for this headlong attack on the city reflected his concerns about the outcome of the preceding Eighth Union Offensive (March 29–

April 1, 1865), which had culminated in Major General Sheridan's victory in the Battle of Five Forks (April 1, 1865). Now the general in chief worried that Lee would strike at Sheridan to enable a Confederate withdrawal and head south to link up with Gen. Joseph E. Johnston's army. The Union commander opted to hinder the Rebels' potential flight by advancing on their entrenchments, which he believed vulnerable to attack because the graybacks were only sparsely defending them. As part of this effort, Meade allowed Parke the freedom to arrange his men into the formation of his choosing and select a portion of the enemy line to strike. Consequently, Parke decided that the Second Division should target the Rebel fieldworks that lay on the Jerusalem Plank Road before Fort Sedgwick. In preparation for this advance, now–Brevet Major General Potter's pickets would remain in place along with the garrisons of various forts. The rest of the division concentrated behind and on the left side of Fort Sedgwick.[39]

Past experience suggested the New Englanders might struggle to capture these formidable fieldworks. In early March, Meade predicted that the outcome of an assault would rely principally "on the views of the enlisted men . . . among [whom] . . . there is great indisposition to attack intrenchments." The Rebel position in question consisted of the most imposing fortifications surrounding Petersburg, with ample cannon dotting the line. As journalist William Swinton explained, this "portion of the Confederate defences [was the] longest held and most strongly fortified." For the later arrivals in particular, the advance would entail crossing an area with an entrenched enemy line extending along the left flank. Griffin insisted this location was the most suitable for an assault, presumably reflecting Parke's observation that the graybacks were neither ready to oppose a Federal advance nor fully manning the works in that area. Notably, Griffin still feared "his chance of survival [was] not good." The rank and file respected the strength of their own defenses and probably believed they faced bleak odds in attempting to capture the Rebel fortifications. Rutherford had previously declared, "if the enemy should attempt to take our works we could completely destroy him while he was trying to get through the obstructions." Manson had shared this perspective, insisting that oncoming graybacks "would only get slaughterd in heaps." Whereas the Union leadership questioned the bluecoats' ability to take the offensive, the Confederates had good cause to fight strenuously for their main line, without which they could not hold Petersburg.[40]

The later arrivals faced a grim challenge, but a combination of good leadership, increased manpower, and unshaken resolve suggested they could still fight well in their last battle. Major Knapp commanded the 17th, having formerly shown he could rally the troops at Peebles Farm. The Vermonters boasted their largest numbers since the Wilderness, with 408 officers and men present for duty as of March 31. Conversely, the well-liked Lieutenant Colonel Getchell led the 31st in battle for the first time. Back on March 29, this unit totaled 622 officers and men. Numbers aside, the New Englanders probably drew confidence knowing they would move only a short distance over terrain they knew well to reach the enemy fieldworks. Rutherford insisted the entire army was excited "at the speedy prospects of the downfall of the rebellion," and the Vermonters in particular were "confident and determined." Echoing this mindset, Getchell and a newspaper correspondent agreed that the Mainers were keen to see the Confederacy destroyed, and likewise Capt. Alvan D. Brock hoped that "this foul rebellion shall have been crushed forever."[41]

The days preceding this engagement, however, taxed the 17th Vermont and 31st Maine. Between March 29 and April 1, these regiments stayed ready for combat while the Army of the Potomac got into position to assault the city's defenses during the preceding Eighth Union Offensive. Grant desired the Army of the Potomac and Army of the James to "be moved by our left . . . turning the enemy out of his present position around Petersburg." This would take place in coordination with Sheridan's cavalry force, "which [sought] . . . to reach and destroy the South Side and [the Richmond and] Danville Railroads." Foreshadowing the logic behind the Ninth Union Offensive, the general in chief anticipated the Army of Northern Virginia would attempt to retreat southward to join with other Confederates, in which case these two railroads would constitute "the last avenues left to the enemy." The New Englanders were expected to display what Meade termed "a threatening attitude" and advance on the Confederate earthworks if there proved to be "any weakness," an expectation that persisted even after the attack was delayed. Grant blamed the nearly incessant rain for "horrid road[s]" that hindered movement and therefore "prevented the execution of my designs." Emphasizing the tiresome cycle of false starts due to weather, Manson fumed of one episode, "I never was so mad in my life as I was to come away for I have no Idea but we might have gone Straight to Petersburg."[42]

The later arrivals went on to fight a large-scale nighttime skirmish with the enemy on April 1, just prior to the Ninth Union Offensive. Grant decided to have Parke advance his troops to test the viability of an assault on the Confederate lines that night. This preliminary action was intended to keep the Rebels from shifting manpower to confront Sheridan's forces. These Ninth Corps soldiers were to drive ahead into the defenses if the graybacks started to retreat. Without the benefit of moonlight, Griffin formed his command approximately a half mile left of Fort Sedgwick, arraying the troops into two lines of battle and with a single regiment as a reserve. The 17th Vermont held the right flank of the front line, yet it is unclear where the 31st Maine was positioned. Against the backdrop of a Federal artillery bombardment, these bluecoats advanced at 10:00 p.m. They stormed the Rebel frontage between Union Forts Hays and Howard, capturing 249 surprised graybacks and the picket line for approximately a half mile, which caused Griffin to praise his men for fighting in "a very handsome manner." The later arrivals and their comrades then continued forward, locating the main Confederate fieldworks and their numerous vigilant defenders. Here the Federals halted amid enemy artillery fire that started prior to 12:20 a.m. and continued for roughly an hour in response to the Union guns, which finally quieted around 1:00 a.m. The Vermonters and Mainers had sustained no casualties as of yet. Without an assault in the offing, they did not push forward.[43]

This clash lessened the New Englanders' odds of success in the morning onslaught of April 2. Griffin did not learn that the 4:00 a.m. attack was still scheduled to occur until an hour beforehand, for he previously thought the 10:00 p.m. advance had negated it. This realization led the brigadier general to admit that he broke out in "a cold sweat" as he worried about moving his men efficiently into position across one mile of uneven terrain dotted with felled trees, tree stumps, and abatis. During their transit, the Federals had to relinquish control of the picket line they had just taken. The later arrivals managed to reach their appointed spot punctually, along the left side of the Jerusalem Plank Road behind and left of Fort Sedgwick. They were now situated some 200 yards away from the well-defended Confederate earthworks. Parke nevertheless doubted the morning offensive could prevail, for the bluecoats' "only hope of success in the assault . . . was in a surprise . . . entirely lost" due to the preceding skirmish. Further warning the enemy that night, a 6th New Hampshire captain recalled that the exchange of Federal and Confederate artillery fire over the preceding hours had left "the air . . . filled with rockets, bombs, shot, and exploding shells."[44]

The later arrivals had a significant part to play in the assault. Griffin's men composed the vanguard of the Second Division, with a storming party of 108 Mainers in front. These troops were to push right until they reached the Jerusalem Plank Road, using that as a guide to approach the Confederate defenses. They would enter a gap in the abatis while ax-bearing pioneers along both flanks removed these wooden obstructions from the sides of the road to facilitate the column's movement. Meanwhile, the storming party would help the pioneers dismantle the chevaux-de-frise that lay closer to the enemy line. These Mainers would then lead the effort to take the Confederate entrenchments and artillery pieces that commanded the road. Given this objective, Federal artillerymen would press forward to operate any captured cannon. The Second Brigade was organized into a column by regiments—the units would advance one behind the other—except for two outfits that stayed behind to hold forts and another regiment that composed the reserve. The remainder of the 31st Maine held the second position in this column, while the 17th Vermont was the next-to-last regiment. Capt. Thomas P. Beals of the 31st, who led the storming party, recalled that "to get all these troops into their proper positions, with their accoutrements on, without noise sufficient to attract the attention of the enemy, especially in the gloom of night, was a delicate and difficult task which took considerable time." The men worried that the Confederates might preempt the offensive with an advance of their own, and Beals counted himself among the majority who feared the outcome of this battle, asserting "that few . . . expected to emerge alive."[45]

For the New Englanders, the offensive started promisingly. Around the designated time of 4:00 a.m., soldiers from the First Division of the Ninth Corps launched a diversionary attack to reinforce the enemy's expectation that the Federal onslaught would strike near Fort Stedman. The Confederates duly shifted some manpower away from the frontage of the Second Division to counter these efforts. Simultaneously, Union artillery began a preliminary bombardment that lasted for several minutes. At 4:30 a.m. Griffin's men moved forward in orderly ranks through mist and under a dawn sky that illuminated the terrain merely a couple of paces ahead. The Mainers shifted to advance at the double-quick as they neared the Rebel picket line, whose occupants only caught sight of the bluecoats as

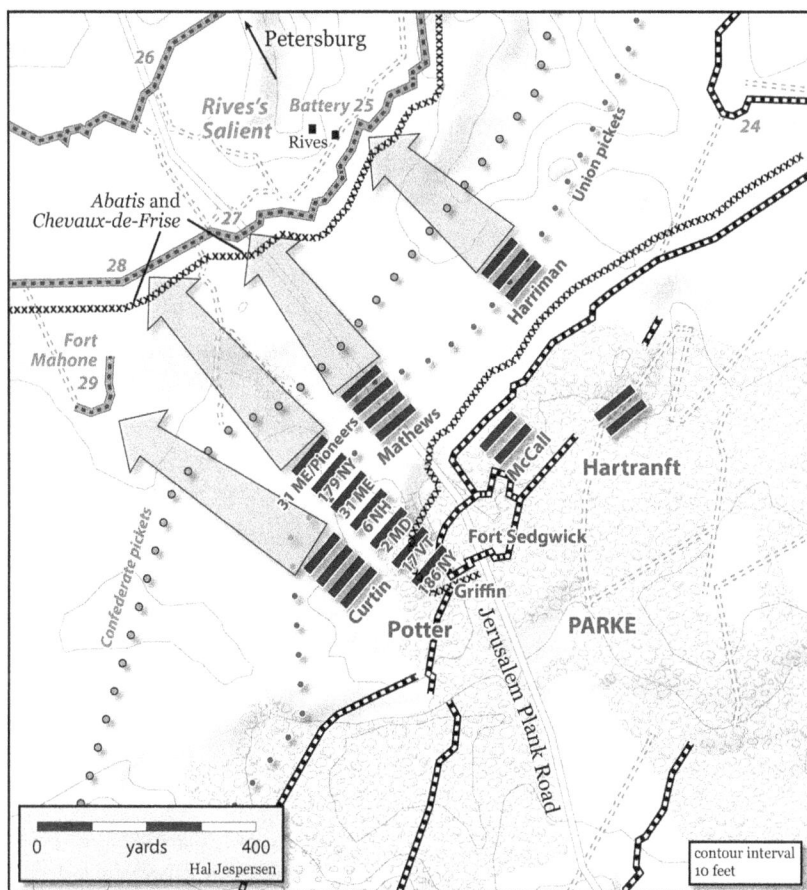

Ninth Union Offensive at Petersburg, April 2, 1865.

they entered the rifle pits. These graybacks briefly resisted by opening fire, then fell back. Continuing onward, the storming party shortly reached the road and the gap in the abatis. They resumed the double-quick and loosed a battle cry that elicited an enemy reply in the form of canister, case, mortar shells, and minié balls. The Mainers stopped in front of the chevaux-de-frise, re-formed their line, and lay prone to avoid the enemy projectiles while waiting for the rest of the brigade to catch up. They then took advantage of the growing sunlight to shoot at the embrasures dotting Battery No. 28, which Beal remarked "produced a good effect in distract-ing somewhat the fire of the Confederates and diverting the attention of my own men from their exposed condition." The captain lamented the delayed arrival of the assault column, for "it seemed as if an hour had passed," although it was likely a few minutes but felt longer owing to the furious Rebel fire. According to early Ninth Corps historian Augustus B. Woodbury, this barrage of lead and iron "made dreadful rents in the attacking column." Now the pioneers and storming party advanced on hands and knees to remove part of the chevaux-de-frise for the passage of Griffin's column. The Mainers attempted to cross a deep trench, although a number slipped on the opposite slope and drowned in the rainwater partially filling it. Blocked from advancing, the Mainers flanked left to reach the main enemy position. The column joined in this assault to expel the defenders of Battery No. 28 with the bayonet and take hundreds more Rebels prisoner along with numerous cannon. Still, a large number of graybacks sought refuge within the lines to the rear. Griffin boasted of his command that "nothing could exceed the coolness and intrepidity with which both officers and men, under a terrific fire, advanced to the attack." Several of the participants inspired the Vermonters and Mainers to go forth and help seize Confederate Fort Mahone. Knapp persevered despite multiple wounds, while 2nd Lt. J. Edwin Henry of the 17th Vermont was struck down while leading his men from the front of the formation. Parke claimed that 1st Sgt. George F. Goldthwait of the 31st Maine "was the first to enter . . . [Fort Mahone] and was wounded while assisting in turning one of the enemy's guns upon them," a feat partially justifying his subsequent recommendation for the Medal of Honor. Likewise, Bolton praised Pvt. Julius Rhodes of the same unit for pushing his fellow soldiers to overrun this emplacement. Since the fort had no protection at its rear, the occupying bluecoats became vulnerable to incoming Rebel cannon fire.[46]

After only fifteen minutes, Parke's assault degenerated into a stalemate. Beals fell, temporarily incapacitated by an exploding enemy shell, but he recalled that the men conducted "a series of charges and the organizations became intermingled, although fighting with a will." The 17th Vermont and 31st Maine drove down the left flank of this Confederate position, engaging in melee combat to slowly expel the Rebels from consecutive traverses for roughly a quarter mile. Graybacks manning detached fieldworks farther to the rear unleashed a storm of projectiles, bolstered by additional troops. Such resistance stymied the bluecoats. It was probably now that Sgt. Warren Boothby of the 31st motivated his comrades to keep fighting under adverse conditions. As Parke put it, this Mainer was eligible to receive a Medal of Honor, for "he seized the colors and, amid a shower of shot and shell, planted them upon the rebel works and stood by them until the action was ended. Whenever the men wavered he would grasp the colors, wave them in the face of the enemy, and call on the men to stand by him. By his brave example and words of encouragement he contributed all possible for one in his position to do toward the success of the day." Another soldier from the 31st recommended for a Medal of Honor was Cpl. Leonard Trafton, whom Parke broadly credited with being "first and foremost in every battle in which he was engaged, and particularly in the engagement of April 2." These efforts notwithstanding, incoming rifle musket and artillery fire produced what a 6th New Hampshire captain called a "murderous slaughter." This sowed chaos among the Federals, leading Griffin to decry a "flood of terror stricken fugitives . . . [who] took to the rear." Despite these culprits, who may have included some later arrivals, Beals observed that the Federals were clinging to "the outside of the works and . . . still holding them." Worsening their confusion, Potter was wounded by a shell while in the rear at Fort Sedgwick, so Griffin had to take command of the Second Division. Parke recalled that "attention was turned to securing what we had gained, and restoring the organization of the troops. . . . This was rendered the more difficult by the great loss we had sustained in officers . . . and by the very exposed position occupied." Lieutenant Colonel Getchell presumably suffered his nonfatal wound around this time, leaving Bolton to assume command.[47]

For the rest of the day, the later arrivals helped repulse Confederate counterattacks. They also worked on improving their defenses since Battery No. 28, like Fort Mahone, lacked protection in the rear. Around 7:40 a.m. the Rebels prepared to make a charge, yet only a small number exited their works due to the intensity of Federal fire. The graybacks nevertheless went on to surge forward multiple times between midday and late evening, and the New Englanders were likely among those driving back such assaults. In addition to these infantry assaults, the enemy continued to advance more cannon into position while their marksmen maintained what Parke termed "an incessant and murderous fire." Griffin proudly watched as his soldiers braved this storm of projectiles and held the captured ground "without yielding an inch." Despite this impressive effort, Parke admitted around 5:00 p.m. that his soldiers were in an "exhausted condition." The

Mainers faced an additional challenge when Bolton suffered a wound after Getchell's own, leaving Capt. Ebenezer S. Kyes to lead the men for the remainder of the fighting. Regardless of the Union troops' eroding condition, they kept trading intermittent fire with the Confederates through much of the evening.[48]

On April 3 the New Englanders awakened to find themselves in control of the battlefield. They were unaware that the Confederates had largely exited Petersburg under the cover of night. The Federal skirmishers scouted the terrain around 4:00 a.m., captured the handful of Rebel pickets holding the line, and then entered the city with the rest of the corps. The previous evening a lieutenant in the 11th New Hampshire had rightly opined, "We have whipped the rebels as though God's hand was smiting them." After nine and a half months, this citadel of the Confederacy had fallen to the later arrivals and their Union brethren. The Petersburg Campaign was at an end.[49]

A FINAL LIST OF WOE

WEIGHING THE TOLL OF
THE NINTH UNION OFFENSIVE

The 17th Vermont and 31st Maine suffered modest losses in their final engagement of the Civil War. Among the Vermonters, forty-three officers and men fell killed or wounded, or 11 percent of those present for duty. The Mainers suffered thirty-four officers and men killed, wounded, or missing, a casualty ratio of only 5 percent. These low figures reflect that the later arrivals spent most of this battle on the defensive and stayed within the cover of the captured enemy main line. Under these circumstances, the proportionally few losses that officers tallied indicate that many of them also sheltered in entrenchments rather than expose themselves unduly to Confederate fire. This behavior appears to have been typical of the entire brigade. Officers made up 5 percent of the Vermont casualties and 6 percent of those among the Mainers compared to a 7-percent rate throughout Griffin's command. Despite such statistics, the later arrivals demonstrated bravery that helped their comrades keep fighting. Knapp and Getchell counted among the nine officers in the two units who received brevets. A few other officers and soldiers earned plaudits for their courage, including three Maine officers in the storming party. These examples of valor outweighed the conduct of two noncommissioned officers in the 31st who acted cowardly in battle and were subsequently reduced to the rank of private. Turning to Federals with prior wartime service reveals a stark contrast between the 17th and 31st. Among the Vermonters, such combatants made up 30 percent of the losses, far exceeding the ratio of those Federals who ever served in the 17th. The situation differed sharply for the Mainers. Prior veterans totaled 6 percent of the casualties in contrast to their higher proportion in the 31st. It is unclear why these two outfits differed so markedly in terms of casualties among the most seasoned participants. Notably, the Vermonters started this battle near the back of the column, whereas the Mainers were situated toward the front, with some composing the storming party. This enabled the officers and men of the 31st to charge without much encumbrance from their comrades. Conversely, the members of the 17th had to force their way through the ranks of those units ahead of them, a task particularly difficult for less tenured combatants who would have been somewhat protected from projectiles by the bodies of their brethren.[50]

Eyewitnesses fittingly lauded the fighting prowess of the later arrivals. Meade highlighted the contribution of the Ninth Corps, declaring that "too much praise cannot be bestowed upon . . . [it] for the gallantry displayed in this daring and successful assault." Parke shared this view, proclaiming that his men had shown "steadiness which reflects the greatest credit." Most expansive was Griffin, who asserted, "great praise is due to both officers and men." He further proclaimed, "the daring deeds of this day. . . . will live in history and in the hearts of your countrymen, while time shall last."[51]

Against the three measures of combat performance, the New Englanders performed well. Admittedly, some likely broke formation after reaching the third Confederate line in evidence of weakening cohesion, and they only achieved their objective in part. The majority, nonetheless, helped maintain a strong defensive position. This ensured that the Federals kept a foothold along the most formidable section of Rebel fortifications surrounding Petersburg. It was only natural that the Vermonters and Mainers sought the protection of the captured fieldworks, for they had repeatedly learned the perils of attacking a dug-in enemy in previous engagements. Still, the men managed to accomplish much, given their minimal losses. Their efforts contributed to the achievement of the Ninth

Corps that day, which entailed seizing 400 yards of Confederate frontage along either flank of the Jerusalem Plank Road, including two forts, two redans, and two redoubts. Parke's men also captured twelve cannon, two battle flags, and 800 graybacks.[52]

After the Crater the later arrivals continued to fight well during the Petersburg Campaign. They began this period on the last day of July 1864 by manning the Union lines around the city in a less taxing stretch of time than what they had experienced over the previous months. Unpleasant weather proved more troublesome than enemy fire, as the Vermonters and Mainers suffered few casualties. They could now rest, replenish their numbers, and train for their next battle, Peebles Farm, which took place nearly two months later. Notwithstanding this preparation, the Union soldiers fled before the graybacks during this engagement, which proved to be the most embarrassing reverse of their field service. The bluecoats showed perseverance, however, by ultimately recovering to defend Union gains. The later arrivals had not retreated simply because they lacked the resolve to withstand the Rebel onslaught. Rather, the fighting of September 30 tested these Federals in ways that they had not previously experienced. For the first time, they fought in the open against a larger number of Confederates who attacked from straight ahead and along both flanks. No soldiers could be reasonably expected to endure such pressure, especially given that this predicament was attributable to poor command decisions. Recalling the events, Brevet Major General Potter explained that he had informed Meade and Parke about the vulnerable flanks of his command. He even told the Ninth Corps commander, "if I advanced any further, it must be distinctly understood that I protested against doing so." This warning was for naught: "Meade . . . was anxious that we should push on, and I was ordered to advance." The Vermonters and Mainers could only do so much to compensate for the tactical blunder that ensued.[53]

The New Englanders proved their mettle in the struggle for control of Petersburg. Before confronting the enemy anew, they returned to the trenches and readied themselves once more for combat in the longest stretch they ever spent between engagements. The effects of harsh and varied weather again outweighed the nominal losses that these bluecoats sustained from Rebel fire. Nevertheless, the Vermonters and Mainers were arguably in the best condition of their field service when they fought in the Ninth Union Offensive. At the start of this engagement, the later arrivals progressed forward quickly to seize the enemy picket and main lines. Stiffening resistance from graybacks holding another set of entrenchments farther back compelled the Federals to adopt the defensive for the rest of the battle. The limited progress of this Union attack is unsurprising, given Parke's warnings during the early morning of April 2, 1865, which pointed to the faulty decision-making of the Union leadership. He had remarked, "unless we find a weak place the attack ordered at 4 will not be attended with success." The Ninth Corps commander maintained that his troops had not located a vulnerable spot, in contrast to his optimistic assessment of the area prior to the 10:00 p.m. skirmish. Parke thus recognized that his men would be charging a well-defended position. Admittedly, some Confederates there shifted position to oppose the diversionary effort made by the First Division of the Ninth Corps. Despite such movements, the later arrivals would confront an ample number of Rebels in formidable earthworks. Reminiscent of Potter's disregarded admonition on September 30, once more the troops had to fight under conditions that placed them at a disadvantage.[54]

Ultimately, the later arrivals advanced the cause of Union victory in both engagements. Brevet Brigadier General Adam Badeau, Grant's military secretary, after the war observed, "the test of troops is—not their willingness to rush blindly into a charge, but their ability to recover themselves and continue a movement under fire, when once the advance has been checked, and the first impetus, physical and moral, has been lost." In both battles the New Englanders did not press forward continually in the manner Badeau described. They did, however, show remarkable determination given the severity of their previous defeat at the Crater. Understanding the course of these engagements and the campaign as a whole consequently depends on a reckoning with the willpower of these often-derided later arrivals. Writing after the Civil War, Maj. Gen. John A. Logan, one-time commander of the Fifteenth Corps in the Army of the Tennessee, asserted:

> Official leadership is a prime factor in the issue of battles, but much of the interest of the engagement clusters around the common soldier, as well as about the officer. No estimate of battle results can be consid-

ered wholly safe that fails to include both officers and men. Indeed, it may be broadly alleged that there has been no battle fought since the beginning of human contention, where the common soldiers did not largely outnumber the officers, not alone in the ranks of the contestants, but also in the lists of the killed and wounded. . . . Soldiers, then, have fought the battles of the world. The officers have directed them.

The humble privates in the 17th Vermont and 31st Maine knew this truth all too well. Repeatedly, they risked their lives for the sake of Federal success even as their generals could dismiss the mounting human toll as inevitable. In late November 1864, Brigadier General Griffin reflected on the course of events since the start of the Overland Campaign. He acknowledged that the "losses were frightful but it was the only way to defeat a powerful and determined antagonist who had the advantage of choosing his position mostly fortified in advance previously, etc." The fighting at Peebles Farm and during the Ninth Union Offensive bore out Griffin's words, yet this combat also revealed a bleaker reality about the Union war effort. Even when the later arrivals proved themselves worthy of comradeship with the vaunted "Boys of '61," upper-level command woes could put the New Englanders in predicaments that cast an unjustified shadow on their legacy.[55]

CONCLUSION

Considering . . . [the 17th Vermont's] period of service,
it is a record which tells of duty faithfully performed
and one of which any Vermonter may well be proud.

—1st Lt. Joel H. Lucia, 17th Vermont

It may well be doubted if any of the old and veteran regiments
can show such an appalling story of desperate fighting and
frightful loss as . . . [the 31st Maine,] which crowded its story
into less than one half the term for which it was mustered.

—Sgt. Maj. Leander Otis Merriam, 31st Maine

For too long the reputation of the later arrivals has languished in obscurity. Contemporary observers and historians alike have judged these troops inferior to the celebrated "Boys of '61," who enlisted when the Civil War began. According to this broadly held interpretation, the 1863 Enrollment Act (the U.S. draft law) diluted the fighting ability of the Union army. Critics maintain that most of the men signing up after passage of this legislation did so out of greed, in contrast to the patriotism of their predecessors. Recruits drawn into the ranks by the newly available large cash bounties supposedly lacked the physical and mental fitness for soldiering. Proponents of this bleak depiction allege that the later arrivals were unreliable in combat. Such claims pertain especially to the Army of the Potomac, which depended upon a steady influx of manpower to sustain its costly offensives during the Overland and Petersburg Campaigns of 1864–65.

The consensus on the later arrivals has endured because it is intuitive. For students of the conflict, it is a truism that the contending armies only grew more effective in combat by suffering heavy casualties. The bloody process transformed their naïve and eager greenhorns into battle-hardened veterans who developed the tactical skill to fight while protecting themselves from enemy fire. Arguably, the later arrivals faced greater difficulty in entering military service than other soldiers in blue or gray, for they did so during the most trying stage of the Civil War. Describing the eve of the Overland Campaign, historian Mark Grimsley emphasizes the disparity between the large share of rookies in the Army of the Potomac and the predominantly seasoned Confederates in the Army of Northern Virginia.[1]

Using the 17th Vermont and 31st Maine as a case study, the later arrivals actually proved to have fought with valor to destroy the Confederacy. These Federals overcame challenges in recruitment and training to perform well in eight major engagements. This finding does not speak to the experiences of all later arrivals, a population of some 820,000 men who donned the blue uniform between 1863 and 1865. Rather, it calls for more small-unit analysis to restore the agency of the rank and file instead of relying on generalizations from high-ranking officials, officers, outsiders, and previous historians. Doing so is necessary if these overlooked soldiers are to finally receive the attention they deserve. The story of the New Englanders reveals that the struggle for Union victory intertwined triumph and tragedy. From the perspective of the Vermonters and Mainers, there was nothing preordained about the downfall of the southern rebellion. With each engagement they put their lives in the balance to defeat the enemy, long after Americans learned that the horrendous conflict many had envisioned had become a grisly reality. As historian Jason Phillips asserts: "Civil War Americans did not descend into a war that was unexpected in length and bloodshed. Instead, they realized a horrible conflict that many of them had anticipated from the start." In a comment equally applicable to the 31st, Adjutant and Inspector General Washburn of Vermont tellingly wrote of the 17th, "[its] record . . . is one of honor, and yet one of blood through out."[2]

To contribute to Union victory, the Vermonters and Mainers needed to play a meaningful role in repeated engagements over an eleven-month period. After the conflict Brevet Colonel Livermore of the 18th New Hampshire expressed an opinion that ran counter to the later-arrival stereotype. Pondering the record of such troops during the Overland Campaign, he observed of the Ninth Corps "that two thirds of its strength was in raw soldiers, but they fought well." To accomplish this feat, it was not enough to evince the foolhardiness and enthusiasm typical of greenhorns engaging in combat. Journalist William Swinton gave a representative example of Federal heavy artillerymen under fire on May 19, 1864, at Spotsylvania: "The foot artillerists had not before been in battle, but it was found that once under fire, they displayed an audacity surpassing even the old troops. In these murderous wood-fights, the veterans had learned to employ all the Indian devices that afford shelter to the person; but these green battalions, unused to this kind of craft, pushed boldly on, firing furiously. Their loss was heavy, but the honor of the enemy's repulse belongs to them." Despite this enthusiastic narration, fearlessness borne of inexperience could not last amid the grueling conditions of the two campaigns in Virginia. Soldiers who behaved in this way would quickly suffer losses so grievous as to greatly reduce their effectiveness during future clashes. Grant initially sought to defeat the Army of Northern Virginia in the field, depending on the bluecoats to march, fight, and entrench at a relentless pace to maintain pressure on the Rebels. He then shifted to siege warfare so as to break the resolve of the Confederates dug in around Petersburg and extending north to Richmond. The New Englanders showed the necessary endurance to perform well in combat under varied conditions.[3]

Eyewitnesses and scholars have overemphasized the negative consequences of the Enrollment Act on the quality of incoming manpower. In fact, recruiting advocates depicted military service as a socially acceptable way to advance oneself financially. Working-class men responded well to such appeals and consequently filled most of the ranks in the 17th Vermont and 31st Maine. Although the allure of cash prompted many individuals to sign up, their doing so often reflected need rather than mere self-interest. This does not mean that the later arrivals were uniquely impoverished in comparison to earlier recruits, for the lower classes had always represented the majority of the Federal rank and file. Besides, the availability of sizable bonuses was an effective and justifiable means of securing enlistees when the Union army's demand for more troops was most acute. These bounties were not even as exorbitant as they appeared since paper-currency inflation reduced their dollar value. Moreover, monetary temptations paled in comparison to the human cost of the Civil War that was plain to all by 1863. It took considerable bravery to don the uniform at this stage of the conflict, unlike the heady days of 1861, when numerous Americans anticipated the fighting would quickly end without much bloodshed. Newspapers disabused their readers of the notion that military service could be a grand adventure by regularly publishing casualty information. As a result, those individuals pondering whether to join the army would have known that many soldiers perished on the battlefield or in the hospital, never to go home. The combatants who returned, either absent on leave or having reached the end of their service terms, frequently suffered from wounds or poor health that humanized the painful statistics of the war's mounting toll. Against this backdrop bounties provided legitimate compensation for civilians willing to assume the risks of soldiering. They were not simply a reward for mercenaries.[4]

Limitations in the source material make it all too easy to misjudge the motivations of the later arrivals to serve. Firsthand accounts generally cast aspersions on the character of these men, reflecting their authors' prejudices against the working class and immigrants. Such people made up the bulk of the troops, who themselves frequently left unmentioned their reasons for signing up. Whereas officers tended to write expansively, the rank and file favored a semiliterate prose that has made it more difficult to decipher their meaning. These soldiers focused on topics germane to their everyday lives, musing on the weather, food, and clothing or inquiring after loved ones and friends. Every so often, however, they hinted at reasons other than money that drew them into service, including a sense of patriotism, youthful exuberance, peer pressure, and a desire to avoid the draft.

The Vermonters and Mainers underwent a jarring transition from civilian life to soldiering. Bureaucratic confusion hindered recruitment, more so in the 17th than in the 31st, and both units received only limited training before heading to the front. Although a majority of officers and men behaved well, some were guilty of poor discipline prior to and during their field service. This included scuffles, drunkenness, thievery, and disobedience, conduct not atypical for volunteers resistant to authority. Desertion was the most notable crime, yet only a fraction of the culprits left evidence for why they fled. Apart from those simply intent on pocketing a bounty, others absconded due to personal reasons, disgruntlement over unit identity, or to duck grueling service. Some were simply tardy in rejoining their outfits. Thus, even the soldiers generally deemed most emblematic of the later-arrival stereotype—deserters—cannot be dismissed categorically as unpatriotic ne'er-do-wells. Ultimately, closer study of these men reveals that detractors have unduly emphasized the relationship between enlistment motivation and fighting ability. This implies that the later arrivals could not be expected to perform well, given the supposedly discreditable circumstances of their enlistment. In actuality, most of the 17th and 31st chose to join the army after thoughtfully evaluating their options and had the potential to become dependable soldiers. They went on to fight admirably during the Overland and Petersburg Campaigns based on the three measures of combat performance: cohesion, completing tactical objectives as a form of combat power, and casualty rates.

HOW THE LATER ARRIVALS
MEASURED UP

Throughout most engagements, the New Englanders maintained moderate to high levels of cohesion. They broke before the enemy on three occasions, but the circumstances warrant further scrutiny. When these troops received their baptism of fire at the Wilderness, they charged headlong at entrenched Confederates and only retreated once the seasoned Federals around them began falling back. Rookies could not be fairly judged as substandard combatants for recoiling when their experienced comrades were doing the same. At Peebles Farm the Vermonters and Mainers again withdrew when the entire Second Division of the Ninth Corps collapsed. Finally, some of the soldiers in these two units may have fallen back in the course of the Ninth Union Offensive in evidence of crumbling resolve across the Second Brigade. While these instances of retreat were unfortunate, in no battle did the later arrivals run away collectively while their brethren stayed to fight.

The New Englanders also showed their determination to accomplish battlefield objectives. These soldiers did not always achieve their goals, but this was not solely their fault because such tasks were invariably shared by most or all of the Second Brigade. The early morning assault upon the Shand House during the First Union Offensive exemplified this dynamic. When the 17th Vermont and the rest of the Second Brigade's front line hesitated to advance, the 31st Maine along with the other units in the second line pushed forward. This movement enabled the entire body of Federals to seize the Confederate defenses. The efforts of both outfits, though important to the outcome, only influenced the result insofar as they related to broader efforts by the whole formation. At the Crater these two units persisted in a brigade-level push to occupy high ground. Whereas the 31st strove to take the ridge that lay ahead and to the right of the yawning hole, the 17th sheltered within the captured enemy fieldworks while firing at the Rebels. From the soldiers' vantage point, they did their utmost to defeat the graybacks.

Combat exacted a heavy toll from the later arrivals. The 17th Vermont suffered 399 officers and men killed, wounded, missing, or captured, which equaled 36 percent of those who served in the unit during the war. The 31st Maine counted 505 commissioned and enlisted losses, or 45 percent of those serving in that outfit. This carnage attested to the New Englanders' perseverance amid Confederate fire, although casualty rates ranged widely depending on their role in a particular battle. For instance, these Federals suffered sizable losses in severe combat at Spotsylvania on May 12, 1864; during the First Union Offensive; and at Peebles Farm. They incurred lower casualties when they tentatively advanced at Spotsylvania on May 18, played a modest role at North Anna, and remained largely within earthworks during the Ninth Union Offensive. Comparing the outcomes of each engagement also reveals a contrast between the Vermonters and Mainers according to their position on the field and the intensity of Rebel resistance. The 17th accrued greater casualties at the Wilderness, whereas the 31st had more losses at Cold Harbor and the Crater. Although these statistics testify to the dangers of the later arrivals' service, they hold greater meaning within the context of a given battle and the role these men played in it.

The officers of the 17th and 31st tallied casualties generally proportional to those of officers throughout the Second Brigade. This suggests the later arrivals could be depended upon in battle. If these troops had been reluctant to engage the Confederates, their leaders might have felt greater pressure to spur them on from the front. This would have left the officers more vulnerable to enemy fire and thus liable to suffer higher losses than those typical in long-serving regiments. But there is also little evidence that the officers resorted to coercion, in which case they would have remained behind their men to drive them onward and direct their fighting as a unit.

Federal veterans who enlisted in the 17th Vermont and 31st Maine often bore an outsized toll relative to their representation. This bloodshed indicates that both units looked to their most experienced members to bear the brunt of Confederate resistance. Complicating this finding, officers and men in the 17th with past Civil War service sustained disproportionately high casualties in six battles, while those in the 31st only did so in three engagements. It is unclear whether the Vermonters' greater reliance on veteran officers and men reflected inadequate qualities among the new troops, shortcomings among their leaders, or even local variables on the battlefield that exposed some individuals to greater fire than others. In any case, those later arrivals without prior military service grew seasoned over time, lessening the distinction between themselves and their more grizzled comrades. Perhaps the repeat enlistees proved somewhat more resolute because they had benefited from a more gradual introduction to field service. The fast-paced battles of the Overland Campaign and continual stress of trench warfare during the Petersburg Campaign surely hindered the transformation of greenhorns into steadfast troops.

The scholarship on the Civil War soldier's experience has long maintained that recruits learned the intricacies of military life from their veteran comrades. This was the means by which a depleted regiment could transform fresh manpower into an asset on the battlefield. Unfortunately, the available sources for the 17th and 31st are silent about this key element of cohesion within both units. It is difficult to imagine that these novice New Englanders could have survived—much less done well—in the most grueling campaigns of the Civil War without such assistance. Old campaigners would have struggled, however, amid the unprecedented conditions they faced, leaving them poorly positioned to advise their new brothers in arms. This, in turn, suggests that the often-quoted veterans' quips about clueless and unpatriotic greenhorns should not be taken at face value. Perhaps the more experienced men in these two outfits realized that helping the rookies would be to their own advantage; a soldier unprepared for the travails of the march, camp, and battlefield was hardly the sort on which to depend in matters of life and death. Alternatively, these troops may have forged strong interpersonal bonds because of their collective exposure to tremendous physical and psychological stresses. Without letters, diaries, or other primary sources to shed light on this question, it is only possible to make educated guesses about how the later arrivals interacted with their seasoned fellows.

The service of the 17th Vermont and 31st Maine offers evidence to question the conventional wisdom that a rookie became a veteran upon surviving his first battle. This distinction is arguably too simplistic, considering the gulf of experience between a novice combatant and one who endured multiple engagements. Furthermore, historians frequently allude to "battle-hardened" troops, implying that men exposed to combat proved more reliable and capable under fire. This assumption also falters upon closer examination. The pacing of both the Overland and Petersburg Campaigns, the rest and preparation between clashes, and the challenges of each battle played a larger role in determining how well these later arrivals fought than any strengths they developed through their time in the ranks.

Many factors influenced the combat performance of the later arrivals. The most apparent ones were the quality of leadership and training, available manpower, physical condition, and morale, all of which helped determine their readiness for each battle. And yet disease also exerted a persistent influence on both units by reducing their present-for-duty strength throughout the two campaigns. Rookie New Englanders would have begun their service with immune systems unaccustomed to unhygienic, crowded life in camp. The long-term consequences of sickness, however, reflected the grueling nature of life in uniform even after such acclimation. Less quantifiable but equally prevalent, poor weather tested the mettle of the Vermonters and Mainers on the battlefield. Finally, officers at the upper echelons of command exerted a greater influence on the outcome of a clash by deciding upon the coordination and timing of movements as well as the objectives. Thus, to closely associate the results of a battle with the quality of these small units unfairly insinuates that the men composing them had complete control over their circumstances. The New Englanders had a narrowly defined yet essential task: to stand and fight, following orders to the best of their ability. Whether their efforts could produce victory was another matter entirely.

A MEANINGFUL LEGACY

It is remarkable that the Vermonters and Mainers fought as well as they did for so long. Like previous waves of recruits, they learned that headlong charges against entrenched Confederates tended to produce a grievous cost among the attackers for little gain. The New Englanders showed some reluctance to assume the offensive under such conditions, but this did not greatly reduce their role in combat. From the viewpoint of the rank and file, Grant's efforts to crush the Confederacy depended on their own sacrifice. It was one thing to muster enough courage to fight in a single battle, but to do so repeatedly speaks volumes about the determination of these troops.

The later arrivals deserve acknowledgement for their efforts to secure Federal victory. In 1873 Brig. Gen. Charles Devens, who had commanded the Third Division of the Twenty-Fourth Corps in the Army of the James, delivered a speech at a veterans' reunion in Rutland, Vermont. Now grand commander of the Grand Army of the Republic, the Union veterans' organization, Devens told his audience that "the heroes of '61" donned the uniform in the early days of the conflict to protect the achievements of the generation that had fought the War of Independence. These Federals were, in his words, "the bronzed re-cast of the heroic ages" whose conduct would inspire future generations. A reappraisal of the later-arriving Vermonters and Mainers justifies the recognition of these men on the same terms as the storied bluecoats who preceded them.[5]

Perhaps one brave Mainer's example best testifies to the character of these later arrivals. When the conflict began, civilian Edward A. Sprague resided in a southern state and found himself drafted to wear the Rebel gray. He promptly deserted the Confederacy to enlist in the Union army but suffered capture during his first engagement and spent a few months at the Confederate prisoner-of-war camp known as Andersonville. Sprague escaped and reached his hometown in Maine, whereupon he received a discharge from military service due to poor health. Several months later he had recovered sufficiently to sign up in another unit, the 31st Maine. Serving as sergeant and color bearer, Sprague later distinguished himself at the Crater by pushing across this great pit under enemy fire, inspiring hesitant bluecoats to follow suit. Following such bravery, he then paid the ultimate price when he fell mortally wounded at Peebles Farm.

Sprague's moving story departs from the general depiction of later arrivals, who largely await recognition in scholarship to come. It is time to bring to light the contributions that the forgotten boys in blue made and acknowledge how well they fought. As Maj. William Reynolds of the 17th Vermont so poignantly stated after the trials of the Wilderness and Spotsylvania, "Our losses have been heavy, but we trust our sacrifices have not been in vain."[6]

Notes

ABBREVIATIONS

17th VS	17th Vermont Volunteer Infantry Regiment Soldiers Spreadsheet, in author's possession
31st MS	31st Maine Volunteer Infantry Regiment Soldiers Spreadsheet, in author's possession
HSCC	Historical Society of Cheshire County, Keene, NH
LOC	Library of Congress, Washington, DC
MHS	Maine Historical Society, Portland
MSA	Maine State Archives, Augusta
NA	National Archives and Records Administration, Washington, DC
NYHS	New-York Historical Society, New York City
OR	U.S. War Department, *The War of the Rebellion: A Compilation of the Official Records of the Union and Confederate Armies,* 70 vols. in 128 pts. (Washington, DC: Government Printing Office, 1880–1901); all citations to ser. 1 unless otherwise noted
RG	Record Group
UVM	Silver Special Collections Library, University of Vermont, Burlington
UVMLDC	University of Vermont Libraries Digital Collections
VHS	Vermont Historical Society, Barre
VSARA	Vermont State Archives and Records Administration, Middlesex

INTRODUCTION

1. *National Tribune,* 15 May 1890, Chronicling America, https://chroniclingamerica.loc.gov.

2. Theda Skocpol, *Protecting Soldiers and Mothers: The Political Origins of Social Policy in the United States* (Cambridge, MA: Harvard University Press, 1992), 102, 107, EBSCOhost; *National Tribune,* 6 July 1893, 26 December 1895, 18 February 1897, 23 April 1903, Chronicling America.

3. Skocpol, *Protecting Soldiers and Mothers,* 151.

4. Ulysses S. Grant, *Personal Memoirs of U. S. Grant* (New York, 1885; repr., 2 vols. in 1, Project Gutenberg, 2004), 509, https://www.gutenberg.org/files/4367/old/4367

-pdf/4367-pdf.pdf; John J. Hennessy, "I Dread the Spring: The Army of the Potomac Prepares for the Overland Campaign," in *The Wilderness Campaign,* ed. Gary W. Gallagher (Chapel Hill: University of North Carolina Press, 1997), 81, 85–86, https://doi.org/10.5149/9780807835890_gallagher; *Vermont Watchman and State Journal* (Montpelier), 15 April 1864, Chronicling America; William Marvel, *Burnside* (Chapel Hill: University of North Carolina Press, 1991), 474n39; William H. Powell, "The Battle of the Petersburg Crater," in *Battles and Leaders of the Civil War,* ed. Robert Underwood Johnson and Clarence Clough Buel, vol. 4 (New York: Century, 1888), 547.

5. Allen C. Guelzo, *Fateful Lightning: A New History of the Civil War & Reconstruction* (New York: Oxford University Press, 2012), 262–63; Carol Reardon, "A Hard Road to Travel: The Impact of Continuous Operations on the Army of the Potomac and the Army of Northern Virginia in May 1864," in *The Spotsylvania Campaign,* ed. Gary W. Gallagher (Chapel Hill: University of North Carolina Press, 1998), 175, https://doi.org/10.5149/9780807898376_gallagher; Judith Lee Hallock, "The Role of the Community in Civil War Desertion," *Civil War History* 29, no. 3 (June 1983): 123–24, https://doi.org/10.1353/cwh.1983.0013. I selected the 17th Vermont and 31st Maine Volunteer Infantry Regiments after consulting Frederick H. Dyer, *A Compendium of the War of the Rebellion* (Des Moines, IA: Dyer Publishing, 1908). To verify when these units began their service in the Army of the Potomac, see American Civil War Research Database, Historical Data Systems, http://civilwardata.com/.

To assess many aspects of the 17th Vermont's soldiery, I created a spreadsheet to tabulate all the officers and men who served in the regiment. This document (cited as 17th VS) includes name, company, rank upon entry, town and county of residence, birthplace, immigrant status, age, occupation, and enlistment date. It also lists whether each individual commuted his state pay, served as a substitute, deserted, joined the Rebels, returned from desertion, suffered a reduction in rank, had previous military experience, and was killed, wounded, missing, or captured. To compensate for incomplete official records, I cross-checked the following sources to produce as accurate a final accounting as possible: Theodore S. Peck, comp., *Revised Roster of Vermont Volunteers and Lists of Vermonters Who Served in the Army and Navy of the United States [. . .]* (Montpelier, VT: Watchman, 1892; repr., Newport, VT: Civil War Enterprises, 1996), 575–97; Ancestry, Civil War Service Records (CMSR), Union, Vermont 17th Volunteer Infantry, Fold3; Reels F26082, F26083, F26084, F26085, Records of the Adjutant and Inspector General, VSARA, microfilm; Ethan Bisbee, finding aid, September 2000, Lyman E. Knapp Papers, 1862–87, Folder 15, MSA 189, VHS; Bisbee, finding aid, June 2009, Matthew and Moses Whitehill Letters, 1859–78, MSA 520, VHS; finding aid, no date, Inventory Folder, Box 1, John Yale Papers, UVM; enlistment contract, Folder 2, Box 1, ibid.; Descriptive Book, 17th Vermont (Volunteer) Infantry, Entry 114: Civil War Regimental Books, RG 94: Records of the Adjutant General's Office, NA; Regimental Consolidated Morning Report & Order Book, 17th Vermont (Volunteer) Infantry, Entry 115: Civil War Regimental Books, ibid. In cases of conflicting information, I deferred to Peck, *Revised Roster.*

Likewise, I created a spreadsheet that tabulates all the officers and men who served in the 31st Maine (cited as 31st MS). It includes name, company, rank upon entry, town and county of residence, birthplace, immigrant status, age, occupation, and enlistment date. It also lists whether each individual deserted, joined the Rebels, returned from desertion, suffered a reduction in rank, had previous military experience, and was killed, wounded, missing, or captured. To compensate for incomplete records, I cross-checked the following sources to produce as accurate a final accounting as possible: John S. Hodsdon, *Appendix D of the Report of the Adjutant General of the State of Maine, for the Years 1864 and 1865* [. . .] (Augusta, ME: Stevens & Sayward, Printers to the State, 1866), 733–67; Descriptive Book, Companies A to F, and Descriptive Book, Companies G to M, 31st Maine (Volunteer) Infantry, Entry 114, RG 94, NA; and Enlistment Papers, 1864, Container 321200, 31st Maine Infantry Records, 1861–65, Civil War—Regimental Records, 1861–65, Office of the Adjutant General, 1753–1971, RG 15: Department of Defense, Veterans, and Emergency Management, MSA. Information on Thomas Hight's service prior to enlistment in the 31st came from "Thomas Hight," Bill Thayer's Web Site, updated 17 February 2013, https://penelope .uchicago.edu/Thayer/E/Gazetteer/Places/America/United_States/Army/USMA /Cullums_Register/1587*.html.

Note that regimental books for the 17th Vermont and 31st Maine were rebound after the war, so pages may be missing. The researcher is obliged to draw inferences on this subject.

6. John Lynn, *Battle: A History of Combat and Culture* (Boulder, CO: Westview, 2003), xvi; Daniel E. Sutherland, review of *Hood's Texas Brigade: The Soldiers and Families of the Confederacy's Most Celebrated Unit,* by Susannah J. Ural, *Journal of the Civil War Era* 8, no. 4 (December 2018): 710, https://doi.org/10.1353/cwe.2018.0079; Eugene C. Murdock, *One Million Men: The Civil War Draft in the North* (Madison: State Historical Society of Wisconsin, 1971), 344; Gregory J. W. Urwin, "'The Lord Has Not Forsaken Me and I Won't Forsake Him': Religion in Frederick Steele's Union Army, 1863–1864," *Arkansas Historical Quarterly* 52 (Autumn 1993): 320, https://doi.org/10.2307/40030853; Peter S. Carmichael, *The War for the Common Soldier* (Chapel Hill: University of North Carolina Press, 2018), 12; Kanisorn Wongsrichanalai, *Northern Character: College-Educated New Englanders, Honor, Nationalism, and Leadership in the Civil War Era* (New York: Fordham University Press, 2016), 201n26, JSTOR; Adrian R. Lewis, *The American Culture of War: The History of U.S. Military Force from World War II to Operation Iraqi Freedom* (New York: Routledge, 2007), 11. For an example of a unit history dealing with later arrivals, see Edwin P. Rutan II, *"If I Have Got to Go and Fight, I Am Willing": A Union Regiment Forged in the Petersburg Campaign: The 179th New York Volunteer Infantry, 1864–1865* (Park City, UT: RTD, 2015). Other scholarly studies of Civil War regiments include Leslie J. Gordon, *A Broken Regiment: The 16th Connecticut's Civil War* (Baton Rouge: Louisiana State University Press, 2014); Joseph C. Fitzharris, *The Hardest Lot of Men: The Third Minnesota Infantry in the Civil War* (Norman: University of Oklahoma Press, 2019); David W. Mellott and Mark A. Snell, *The Seventh West Virginia Infantry: An Embattled Union Regiment from the Civil War's Most Divided State* (Lawrence: University Press of Kansas, 2019); and Brian Matthew Jordan, *A Thousand May Fall: Life, Death, and Survival in the Union Army* (New York: Liveright, 2021).

7. Mark Grimsley, *And Keep Moving On: The Virginia Campaign, May–June 1864*

(Lincoln: University of Nebraska Press, 2002), 224–25; Steven E. Sodergren, *The Army of the Potomac in the Overland and Petersburg Campaigns: Union Soldiers and Trench Warfare, 1864–1865* (Baton Rouge: Louisiana State University Press, 2017), 39; Earl J. Hess, *Trench Warfare under Grant and Lee: Field Fortifications in the Overland Campaign* (Chapel Hill: University of North Carolina Press, 2007), 209; Hess, *The Union Soldier in Battle: Enduring the Ordeal of Combat* (Lawrence: University Press of Kansas, 1997), 64–67; William Marvel, *Tarnished Victory: Finishing Lincoln's War* (Boston: Houghton Mifflin Harcourt, 2011), 74–75; Earl J. Hess, *In the Trenches at Petersburg: Field Fortifications and Confederate Defeat* (Chapel Hill: University of North Carolina Press, 2009), 280. The term "operations tempo" can be defined as "the rate of military actions or missions." Carl A. Castro and Amy B. Adler, "OPTEMPO: Effects on Soldier and Unit Readiness," *Parameters* 29, no. 3 (Autumn 1999): 86, https://press.armywarcollege.edu/cgi/viewcontent.cgi?article=1939&context=parameters.

8. *OR,* 36(2):810; Steven E. Woodworth, *This Great Struggle: America's Civil War* (Lanham, MD: Rowman & Littlefield, 2011), 250; Grimsley, *And Keep Moving On,* 224–25; Russell F. Weigley, *A Great Civil War: A Military and Political History, 1861–1865* (Bloomington: Indiana University Press, 2000), 328–29; Joseph T. Glatthaar, *General Lee's Army: From Victory to Collapse* (New York: Free Press, 2008), 469; Murdock, *One Million Men,* 344; Grant, *Personal Memoirs,* 502; John H. Brinton, *Personal Memoirs of John H. Brinton* (New York: Neale, 1914), 273; A. Wilson Greene, *A Campaign of Giants: The Battle for Petersburg—Volume One: From the Crossing of the James to the Crater* (Chapel Hill: University of North Carolina Press, 2018), 202, 204; Hess, *Trench Warfare under Grant and Lee,* 210; James M. McPherson, *Battle Cry of Freedom: The Civil War Era* (New York: Oxford University Press, 1988), 732; Brent Nosworthy, *The Bloody Crucible of Courage: Fighting Methods and Combat Experience of the Civil War* (New York: Carroll & Graf, 2003), 553–54; Gordon C. Rhea, *On to Petersburg: Grant and Lee, June 4–15, 1864* (Baton Rouge: Louisiana State University Press, 2017), 19; George Meade, *The Life and Letters of George Gordon Meade, Major-General United States Army,* ed. George Gordon Meade, vol. 2 (New York: Charles Scribner's Sons, 1913), 208, 210–11, 225, 247, 251, 255, 262–63. This book follows the naming conventions for the various engagements of the Petersburg Campaign proposed in Hess, *In the Trenches at Petersburg,* xvii–xx.

9. Charles Royster, *A Revolutionary People at War: The Continental Army and American Character, 1775–1783* (Chapel Hill: University of North Carolina Press, 1979), 25; Earl J. Hess, *Liberty, Virtue, and Progress: Northerners and Their War for the Union,* 2nd ed. (New York: Fordham University Press, 1997), viii–ix; Ricardo A. Herrera, *For Liberty and the Republic: The American Soldier, 1775–1861* (New York: New York University Press, 2015), 163, EBSCOhost; James M. McPherson, *For Cause and Comrades: Why Men Fought in the Civil War* (New York: Oxford University Press, 1997), 16.

10. Carol Reardon, *With a Sword in One Hand & Jomini in the Other: The Problem of Military Thought in the Civil War North* (Chapel Hill: University of North Carolina Press, 2012), 89, 92, 134–35, EBSCOhost; Lorien Foote, *The Gentlemen and the Roughs: Violence, Honor, and Manhood in the Union Army* (New York: New York University Press, 2010), 6, 119–21, 129, 139, 141, 172–73, Kindle; Carmichael, *War for the Common Soldier,* 57.

11. Allan Nevins, ed., *A Diary of Battle: The Personal Journals of Colonel Charles S.*

Wainwright, 1861–1865 (New York: Harcourt, Brace, and World, 1962), 221, 223, 345; Francis A. Walker, *History of the Second Army Corps in the Army of the Potomac* (New York: Charles Scribner's Sons, 1886), 315; Stephen W. Sears, ed., *Mr. Dunn Browne's Experiences in the Army* (New York: Fordham University Press, 1998), 132–34, EBSCOhost; James I. Robertson Jr., ed., *The Civil War Letters of General Robert McAllister* (New Brunswick, NJ: Rutgers University Press, 1965), 464–65; Ulysses S. Grant to Abraham Lincoln, 19 June 1863, in *The Papers of Ulysses S. Grant,* ed. John Y. Simon (Carbondale: Southern Illinois University Press, 1984), 8:395, https://scholarsjunction.msstate.edu/usg-volumes/. Volunteer officers, like their regular army counterparts, were eligible to receive brevet promotions.

12. Walker, *Second Army Corps,* 353, 488, 538, 541–42, 651; *OR,* 36(3):6; Augustus Woodbury, *Major General Ambrose E. Burnside and the Ninth Army Corps* [. . .] (Providence, RI: Sidney S. Rider & Brother, 1867), 389, 409–10; Greene, *Campaign of Giants,* 398; William Swinton, *Campaigns of the Army of the Potomac* [. . .], rev. ed. (New York: Charles Scribner's Sons, 1882), 457, 480–81, 533, 577; Andrew A. Humphreys, *The Virginia Campaign of 1864 and 1865: The Army of the Potomac and the Army of the James* (New York: Charles Scribner's Sons, 1883), 114, 319; Horace Porter, *Campaigning with Grant* (New York: Century, 1906), 127, 129; Grant, *Personal Memoirs,* 356; Nevins, *Diary of Battle,* 378–79, 504; Martin T. McMahon, "Cold Harbor," in Johnson and Buel, *Battles and Leaders,* 218–19; Robertson, *Letters of General Robert McAllister,* 424, 446, 511–12; Committee on the Conduct of the War, *Report of the Committee on the Conduct of the War on the Attack on Petersburg, on the 30th Day of July, 1864* (Washington, DC: Government Printing Office, 1865), 125; Henry Goddard Thomas, "The Colored Troops at Petersburg," in Johnson and Buel, *Battles and Leaders,* 563; John F. Hartranft, "The Recapture of Fort Stedman," in Johnson and Buel, *Battles and Leaders,* 586–89; Robert Hunt Rhodes, ed., *All for the Union: A History of the 2nd Rhode Island Volunteer Infantry in the War of the Great Rebellion* [. . .] (Lincoln, RI: Andrew Mowbray, 1985), 212, 221; George R. Agassiz, ed., *Meade's Headquarters, 1863–1865: Letters of Colonel Theodore Lyman from the Wilderness to Appomattox* (Boston: Atlantic Monthly Press, 1922), 323; Frank Wilkeson, *Recollections of a Private Soldier in the Army of the Potomac* (New York: G. P. Putnam's Sons, 1887), 86.

13. Nevins, *Diary of Battle,* 320, 327, 342, 391, 464; Rhodes, *All for the Union,* 187–88; Robertson, *Letters of General Robert McAllister,* 454, 504, 513; Walker, *Second Army Corps,* 398, 483; Meade, *Life and Letters,* 196; Sears, *Dunn Browne's Experiences,* 175.

14. Simon, ed., *Papers of Ulysses S. Grant,* 12:37, 128, 146, 298; Meade to Lincoln, 14 December 1864, in John Y. Simon and John F. Marzalek, eds., *The Papers of Ulysses S. Grant Digital Edition* (Charlottesville: University of Virginia Press, 2018), https://rotunda.upress.virginia.edu/founders/GRNT.html; Walker, *Second Army Corps,* 317; Humphreys, *Virginia Campaign,* 283n; Martin T. McMahon, "From Gettysburg to the Coming of Grant," in Johnson and Buel, *Battles and Leaders,* 91, 93; Meade, *Life and Letters,* 251, 368–69; Agassiz, *Meade's Headquarters,* 177–78, 209; Nevins, *Diary of Battle,* 271, 275, 279, 319–20, 327–28, 475–76; David S. Sparks, ed., *Inside Lincoln's Army: The Diary of Marsena Rudolph Patrick, Provost Marshal General, Army of the Potomac* (New York: Thomas Yoseloff, 1964), 290–91, 471; Robertson, *Letters of General Robert*

McAllister, 503, 509, 523; Sears, *Dunn Browne's Experiences,* 143–44, 150–52, 163, 170, 175, 192, 197; Survivor's Association, *History of the Corn Exchange Regiment: 118th Pennsylvania Volunteers, from Their First Engagement at Antietam to Appomattox* [. . .] (Philadelphia: J. L. Smith, 1888), 296; Wilkeson, *Recollections of a Private,* 2–3.

15. Humphreys, *Virginia Campaign,* 283n; Meade, *Life and Letters,* 247; Sparks, *Inside Lincoln's Army,* 444–45, 471; Nevins, *Diary of Battle,* 279, 476; Robertson, *Letters of General Robert McAllister,* 509, 523; Agassiz, *Meade's Headquarters,* 177–78, 209; Sears, *Dunn Browne's Experiences,* 143–44, 150–52, 163, 173, 175–76, 192, 195–98; William Marvel, *Lincoln's Mercenaries: Economic Motivation among Union Soldiers during the Civil War* (Baton Rouge: Louisiana State University Press, 2018), 45–46, 218; Wilkeson, *Recollections of a Private,* 3, 188; *OR,* ser. 3, 5:673.

16. Agassiz, *Meade's Headquarters,* 199–201, 208, 224, 238, 257–58, 273; Andrew A. Humphreys, *From Gettysburg to the Rapidan: The Army of the Potomac, July 1863, to April, 1864* (New York: Charles Scribner's Sons, 1883), 35; Meade, *Life and Letters,* 368–69; Sparks, *Inside Lincoln's Army,* 374, 376, 378, 384–85, 405; Humphreys, *Virginia Campaign,* 46, 270, 281–83, 283n, 292n; Walker, *Second Army Corps,* 419, 594, 596–97; *OR,* 36(2):921, 42(1):72; Nevins, *Diary of Battle,* 357, 379, 385, 458, 469, 475; Robertson, *Letters of General Robert McAllister,* 424; Porter, *Campaigning with Grant,* 174, 210, 282; Powell, "Petersburg Crater," 548, 550; Orlando B. Willcox, "Actions on the Weldon Railroad," in Johnson and Buel, *Battles and Leaders,* 573; Swinton, *Army of the Potomac,* 521–22, 525n, 530n2, 576; Wilkeson, *Recollections of a Private,* 185, 188–89.

17. Agassiz, *Meade's Headquarters,* 131, 135–36, 208–9, 214; Robertson, *Letters of General Robert McAllister,* 509, 512; Meade, *Life and Letters,* 247, 251; Willcox, "Actions on the Weldon Railroad," 573; Humphreys, *Virginia Campaign,* 283; Nevins, *Diary of Battle,* 529–30; "Grand Review," U.S. Army Heritage & Education Center, accessed 11 June 2022, https://ahec.armywarcollege.edu/exhibits/CivilWarImagery/edwards_Grand_Review.cfm; Christian B. Keller, *Chancellorsville and the Germans: Nativism, Ethnicity, and Civil War Memory* (New York: Fordham University Press, 2007), 6, JSTOR; Wilkeson, *Recollections of a Private,* 188.

18. Rhodes, *All for the Union,* 237; Swinton, *Army of the Potomac,* 404, 410; Humphreys, *Virginia Campaign,* 11–12; Porter, *Campaigning with Grant,* 72, 407, 507, 512; Agassiz, *Meade's Headquarters,* 141, 238; Robertson, *Letters of General Robert McAllister,* 408; Sears, *Dunn Browne's Experiences,* 248–49; Meade, *Life and Letters,* 193; Grant, *Personal Memoirs,* 372; Grant to Stanton, 20 June 1865, in Simon and Marzalek, *Papers of Ulysses S. Grant Digital Edition; OR,* 42(2):1045–46.

19. Anthony King, *The Combat Soldier: Infantry Tactics and Cohesion in the Twentieth and Twenty-First Centuries* (Oxford: Oxford University Press, 2013), 359–61, EBSCOhost.

20. Bruce Catton, *This Hallowed Ground: The Story of the Union Side of the Civil War* (Garden City, NY: Doubleday, 1956), 317–18, 333–34; Bell Irvin Wiley, *The Life of Billy Yank: The Common Soldier of the Union* (Indianapolis: Bobbs-Merrill, 1952), 345; Wiley, "A Portrait of Plain Americans," in *The Bell Irvin Wiley Reader,* ed. Hill Jordan, James I. Robertson Jr., and J. H. Segars (Baton Rouge: Louisiana State University Press, 2001), 70; Allan Nevins, *The War for the Union,* vol. 4, *The Organized War to Victory, 1864–1865* (New York: Scribner, 1959), 227, 273; Nevins, *Diary of Battle,* 318n**; Carmichael, *War*

for the Common Soldier, 190–91; Edward Steere, *The Wilderness Campaign* (Harrisburg, PA: Stackpole, 1960), 315; Zachery A. Fry, *A Republic in the Ranks: Loyalty and Dissent in the Army of the Potomac* (Chapel Hill: University of North Carolina Press, 2020), 157–58; Weigley, *Great Civil War,* 323; Woodworth, *This Great Struggle,* 228, 249–50; Bruce Catton, *Grant Takes Command: 1863–1865* (Boston: Little, Brown, 1969), 368; James I. Robertson Jr., *Soldiers Blue and Gray* (Columbia: University of South Carolina Press, 1998), 37–40, 135; Gerald F. Linderman, *Embattled Courage: The Experience of Combat in the American Civil War* (New York: Free Press, 1987), 172–73, 225, 229; Marvel, *Lincoln's Mercenaries,* 208–9, 220; Bruce Catton, "Billy Yank and the Army of the Potomac," *Military Affairs* 18, no. 4 (Winter 1954): 174, https://doi.org/10.2307 /1983083; Richard J. Sommers, *Richmond Redeemed: The Siege at Petersburg: The Battles of Chaffin's Bluff and Poplar Spring Church, September 29–October 2, 1864,* rev. ed. (El Dorado Hills, CA: Savas Beatie, 2014), 230–31; Gordon C. Rhea, *The Battle of the Wilderness, May 5–6, 1864* (Baton Rouge: Louisiana State University Press, 1994), 34–35, 243–44; Randall C. Jimerson, *The Private Civil War: Popular Thought during the Sectional Conflict* (Baton Rouge: Louisiana State University Press, 1988), 196; Marvin A. Kreidberg and Merton G. Henry, *History of Military Mobilization in the United States Army, 1775–1945* (Washington, DC: Department of the Army, 1955): 109–12, 123; Robertson, *Letters of General Robert McAllister,* 509n19; J. G. Randall and David Donald, *The Civil War and Reconstruction* (Lexington, MA: D. C. Heath, 1969), 328–29; Peter J. Parish, *The American Civil War* (New York: Holmes & Meier, 1974), 467; James M. McPherson, *Ordeal by Fire: The Civil War and Reconstruction* (New York: Alfred A. Knopf, 1982), 251–52, 356–57; Hallock, "Role of the Community," 124–26; McPherson, *Battle Cry of Freedom,* 720, 732, 780; Noah Andre Trudeau, *Bloody Roads South: The Wilderness to Cold Harbor, May–June 1864* (Boston: Little, Brown, 1989), 15–16, 80; James W. Geary, *We Need Men: The Union Draft in the Civil War* (DeKalb: Northern Illinois University Press, 1991), 13–15, 17, 75, 113, 157, 161–62; Marvel, *Burnside,* 369; Robert Garth Scott, *Into the Wilderness with the Army of the Potomac,* rev. and enlarged ed. (Bloomington: Indiana University Press, 1992), 132; Hess, *Union Soldier in Battle,* 90; McPherson, *For Cause and Comrades,* 8–9; Grimsley, *And Keep Moving On,* 21–22, 186; Gordon C. Rhea, *The Battles for Spotsylvania Court House and the Road to Yellow Tavern, May 7–12, 1864* (Baton Rouge: Louisiana State University Press, 2005), 66; Hess, *Trench Warfare under Grant and Lee,* 201, 208–9; Hess, *In the Trenches at Petersburg,* 227–28; Guelzo, *Fateful Lightning,* 459; Stephen W. Sears, *Lincoln's Lieutenants: The High Command of the Army of the Potomac* (Boston: Houghton Mifflin Harcourt, 2017), 623–24, 746; Sodergren, *Army of the Potomac in the Overland and Petersburg Campaigns,* 81, 226; Reardon, "Hard Road to Travel," 176; Michael F. Holt, "An Elusive Synthesis: Northern Politics during the Civil War," in *Writing the Civil War: The Quest to Under-stand,* ed. James M. McPherson and William J. Cooper Jr. (Columbia: University of South Carolina Press, 1998), 131; Greene, *Campaign of Giants,* 13.

21. Jason Phillips, *Looming Civil War: How Nineteenth-Century Americans Imagined the Future* (New York: Oxford University Press, 2018), 7, https://doi.org/10.1093/oso /9780190868161.001.0001; Earl J. Hess, "Revitalizing Traditional Military History in the Current Age of Civil War Studies," in *Upon the Fields of Battle: Essays on the Military*

History of America's Civil War, ed. Andrew S. Bledsoe and Andrew F. Lang (Baton Rouge: Louisiana State University Press, 2018), 24; Geary, *We Need Men,* 13, 47, 65, 159, 196; Guelzo, *Fateful Lightning,* 458; Hallock, "Role of the Community," 124; Marvel, *Tarnished Victory,* 122–23, 126; Sears, *Lincoln's Lieutenants,* 528; Wiley, *Life of Billy Yank,* 38; Murdock, *One Million Men,* 4; Gregory J. W. Urwin, *The United States Infantry: An Illustrated History, 1775–1918* (Norman: University of Oklahoma Press, 1988), 104; Weigley, *Great Civil War,* 235; Allan R. Millett, Peter Maslowski, and William Feis, *For the Common Defense: A Military History of the United States from 1607 to 2012,* 3rd ed. (New York: Free Press, 2012), loc. 3757, Kindle; Mark E. Neely Jr., *Lincoln and the Democrats: The Politics of Opposition in the Civil War* (Cambridge: Cambridge University Press, 2017), 26; J. Matthew Gallman, *Defining Duty in the Civil War: Personal Choice, Popular Culture, and the Union Home Front* (Chapel Hill: University of North Carolina Press, 2015), 15; McPherson, *Ordeal by Fire,* 357; Mark A. Snell, "'If They Know What I Know It Would Be Pretty Hard to Raise One Company': Recruiting, the Draft, and Society's Response in York County, Pennsylvania, 1861–1865," in *Union Soldiers and the Northern Home Front: Wartime Experiences, Postwar Adjustments,* ed. Paul A. Cimbala and Randall M. Miller (New York: Fordham University Press, 2002), 108.

22. Maris A. Vinovskis, "Have Social Historians Lost the Civil War? Some Preliminary Demographic Speculations," in *Toward a Social History of the American Civil War: Exploratory Essays,* ed. Maris A. Vinovskis (Cambridge: Cambridge University Press, 1990), 17; Thomas R. Kemp, "Community and War: The Civil War Experience of Two New Hampshire Towns," in Vinovskis, *Toward a Social History,* 61–62, 65–66; Tyler Anbinder, "Which Poor Man's Fight? Immigrants and the Federal Conscription of 1863," *Civil War History* 52, no. 4 (December 2006): 372, https://doi.org/10.1353/cwh .2006.0068; McPherson, *Battle Cry of Freedom,* 603–5, 607–8; Geary, *We Need Men,* 170; Phillip Shaw Paludan, "What Did the Winners Win? The Social and Economic History of the North during the Civil War," in McPherson and Cooper, *Writing the Civil War,* 193; Robertson, *Soldiers Blue and Gray,* 38; Guelzo, *Fateful Lightning,* 239; Carmichael, *War for the Common Soldier,* 190; Jimerson, *Private Civil War,* 196; Russell L. Johnson, "'Volunteer While You May': Manpower Mobilization in Dubuque, Iowa," in Cimbala and Miller, *Union Soldiers and the Northern Home Front,* 66–67; Snell, "If They Know What I Know," 107, 112–13.

23. Dora L. Costa and Matthew E. Kahn, *Heroes & Cowards: The Social Face of War* (Princeton, NJ: Princeton University Press, 2008), 52; Marvel, *Lincoln's Mercenaries,* x, 8, 10, 140–41, 164, 236; Fitzharris, *Hardest Lot of Men,* 19.

24. Charles Patrick Neimeyer, *America Goes to War: A Social History of the Continental Army* (New York: New York University Press, 1997), xiii–xiv, 25, 116; Royster, *Revolutionary People at War,* 268; Marvel, *Lincoln's Mercenaries,* xiii; Beth Bailey, *America's Army: Making the All-Volunteer Force* (Cambridge, MA: Harvard University Press, 2009), 258, EBSCOhost.

25. Randall and Donald, *Civil War and Reconstruction,* 329; Kreidberg and Henry, *Military Mobilization in the United States Army,* 110–11; Marvel, *Tarnished Victory,* 79; Carmichael, *War for the Common Soldier,* 190–91; Royster, *Revolutionary People at War,*

374, 378; Guelzo, *Fateful Lightning,* 276; Gallman, *Defining Duty,* 129; Johnson, "Volunteer While You May," 42, 45; Snell, "If They Know What I Know," 111.

26. John Lynn, *The Bayonets of the Republic: Motivation and Tactics in the Army of Revolutionary France* (New York: Routledge, 2019), 20, 35, https://doi.org/10.4324 /9780429309052; Kenneth W. Noe, *Reluctant Rebels: The Confederates Who Joined the Army after 1861* (Chapel Hill: University of North Carolina Press, 2010), 3–7, EBSCO-host; Aaron Sheehan-Dean, "The Blue and the Gray in Black and White: Assessing the Scholarship on Civil War Soldiers," in *The View from the Ground: Experiences of Civil War Soldiers,* ed. Aaron Sheehan-Dean (Louisville: University Press of Kentucky, 2007), 16; Costa and Kahn, *Heroes & Cowards,* 54; Rutan, *"If I Have Got to Go and Fight,"* 10.

27. Marvel, *Burnside,* 387, 411–12; Michael A. Cavanaugh and William Marvel, *The Petersburg Campaign: The Battle of the Crater, "the Horrid Pit"* (Lynchburg, VA: H. E. Howard, 1989), 42; Scott, *Into the Wilderness,* 132; Rhea, *Wilderness,* 305, 436; Gordon C. Rhea, *To the North Anna River: Grant and Lee, May 13–25, 1864* (Baton Rouge: Louisiana State University Press, 2000), 142; Hess, *Trench Warfare under Grant and Lee,* 201–2; Hess, *In the Trenches at Petersburg,* 140; Trudeau, *Bloody Roads South,* 101–2; Sears, *Lincoln's Lieutenants,* 736; Fry, *Republic in the Ranks,* 160.

28. Williamson Murray and Wayne Wei-Siang Hsieh, *A Savage War: A Military History of the Civil War* (Princeton, NJ: Princeton University Press, 2016), 355, 385–89; Sears, *Lincoln's Lieutenants,* 667–73.

29. Susannah Ural Bruce, *The Eagle and the Harp: Irish-American Volunteers and the Union Army, 1861–1865* (New York: New York University Press, 2006), 136, 187, 199–200, 203, 207, 209, 211; Phillip Shaw Paludan, *"A People's Contest": The Union & Civil War, 1861–1865* (Lawrence: University Press of Kansas, 1988), 233, 235, 283; Weigley, *Great Civil War,* 194; Carol Reardon, "'We Are All in This War': The 148th Pennsylvania and Home Front Dissension in Centre County during the Civil War," in Cimbala and Miller, *Union Soldiers and the Northern Home Front,* 27–28; Timothy J. Orr, "'A Viler Enemy in Our Rear': Pennsylvania Soldiers Confront the North's Antiwar Movement," in Sheehan-Dean, *View from the Ground,* 181.

30. Don H. Doyle, *The Cause of All Nations: An International History of the American Civil War* (New York: Basic Books, 2015), 160, 169–70; William W. Swan, "Battle of the Wilderness," in *The Wilderness Campaign, May–June 1864,* vol. 4 of *Papers of the Military Historical Society of Massachusetts,* comp. Military Historical Society of Massachusetts (Boston: Military Historical Society of Massachusetts, 1905), 121.

31. Paludan, *"A People's Contest,"* 168, 284; Jimerson, *Private Civil War,* 235; Hallock, "Role of the Community," 125–26, 128–29, 131–34; Geary, *We Need Men,* 38; Costa and Kahn, *Heroes & Cowards,* 100–102, 104, 106; Carmichael, *War for the Common Soldier,* 176, 225–28.

32. Randall and Donald, *Civil War and Reconstruction,* 417, 420; Marvin R. Cain, "A 'Face of Battle' Needed: An Assessment of Motives and Men in Civil War Historiography," *Civil War History* 28, no. 1 (March 1982): 25, https://doi.org/10.1353/cwh.1982 .0059; Joseph T. Glatthaar, "The Common Soldier of the Civil War," in *New Perspectives on the Civil War: Myths and Realities of the National Conflict,* ed. John Y. Simon and

Michael E. Stevens (Madison, WI: Madison House, 1998), 120–21; Edward A. Altemos, *From the Wilderness to Appomattox: The Fifteenth New York Heavy Artillery in the Civil War* (Kent, OH: Kent State University Press, 2023), xxviii, xxxiii, 178–79; Carmichael, *War for the Common Soldier,* 191; Michael Fellman, Lesley J. Gordon, and Daniel E. Sutherland, *This Terrible War: The Civil War and Its Aftermath* (Boston: Pearson, 2003), 273, 291; Will Hickox, "The Civil War's 11th-Hour Soldiers," *Disunion* (blog), *New York Times,* 6 April 2015, https://opinionator.blogs.nytimes.com/2015/04/06/the-civil-wars-11th-hour-soldiers/; McPherson, *Ordeal by Fire,* 426; Marvel, *Tarnished Victory,* 35, 177; Reardon, "Hard Road to Travel," 193; Noah Andre Trudeau, "The Walls of 1864," in *With My Face to the Enemy: Perspectives on the Civil War,* ed. Robert Cowley (New York: G. P. Putnam's Sons, 2001), 423, 427; Grimsley, *And Keep Moving On,* 132–33; Earl J. Hess, *Into the Crater: The Mine Attack at Petersburg* (Columbia: University of South Carolina Press, 2010), 4; Marvel, *Burnside,* 388; Fry, *Republic in the Ranks,* 157; Rutan, *"If I Have Got to Go and Fight,"* 10–11.

33. Hess, *Into the Crater,* 4; Glatthaar, *General Lee's Army,* 175, 185; Reardon, *With a Sword in One Hand,* 135; John Keegan, *The Face of Battle* (New York: Viking, 1976), 52; Stephen G. Fritz, *Frontsoldaten: The German Soldier in World War II* (Lexington: University Press of Kentucky, 1995), 6; Edward Coss, "The Vicissitudes of Violence: Fear, Physiology, and Behavior under Fire," in *Technology, Violence, and War: Essays in Honor of Dr. John F. Guilmartin, Jr.,* ed. Robert S. Ehlers Jr., Sarah K. Douglas, and Daniel P. M. Curzon (Leiden, Neth.: Brill, 2019), 283; Scott, *Into the Wilderness,* 128; Robert Garth Scott, ed., *Forgotten Valor: The Memoirs, Journals, & Civil War Letters of Orlando B. Willcox* (Kent, OH: Kent State University Press, 1999), 562, 593; Sears, *Dunn Browne's Experiences,* 248–49.

34. Wayne Wei-Siang Hsieh, review of *A Campaign of Giants: The Battle for Petersburg. Volume 1: From the Crossing of the James to the Crater,* by A. Wilson Greene, *Journal of the Civil War Era* 9, no. 2 (September 2019): 488, https://doi.org/10.1353/cwe.2019.0064; Mark Grimsley, "Why Military History Sucked," *Blog Them Out of the Stone Age: Toward a Broader Vision of Military History and National Security Affairs,* 2 June 2016, http://warhistorian.blogspot.com/2016/06/why-military-history-sucked.html; Hess, "Revitalizing Traditional Military History," 36.

35. Linderman, *Embattled Courage,* 16; Hess, *Union Soldier in Battle,* ix; McPherson, *For Cause and Comrades,* 13; Lynn, *Bayonets of the Republic,* 21, 24, 30; Nora Kinzer Stewart, *Mates & Muchachos: Unit Cohesion in the Falklands/Malvinas War* (Washington, DC: Brassey's, 1991), 2, 133–34; Leonard Wong et al., *Why They Fight: Combat Motivation in the Iraq War* (Carlisle, PA: Strategic Studies Institute, U.S. Army War College, 2003), vii, 3; Ilya Berkovich, *Motivation in War: The Experience of Common Soldiers in Old-Regime Europe* (Cambridge: Cambridge University Press, 2017), 11, 28–29, 198, 229.

36. McPherson, *For Cause and Comrades,* 88; Lynn, *Bayonets of the Republic,* 34; Hess, *Union Soldier in Battle,* 122; Christopher H. Hamner, *Enduring Battle: American Soldiers in Three Wars, 1776–1945* (Lawrence: University Press of Kansas, 2011), 3; Berkovich, *Motivation in War,* 24–26, 28–29; Stewart, *Mates & Muchachos,* 26–30, 136; King, *Combat Soldier,* 26–27; Wong et al., *Why They Fight,* vii, 3–4; Robert E. Hum-

phrey, *Once upon a Time in War: The 99th Division in World War II* (Norman: University of Oklahoma Press, 2008), 119.

37. Costa and Kahn, *Heroes & Cowards,* 95; Hamner, *Enduring Battle,* 11–12; Keegan, *Face of Battle,* 298; Berkovich, *Motivation in War,* 14.

38. Lewis, *American Culture of War,* 42; Allan R. Millett, Williamson Murray, and Kenneth H. Watman, "The Effectiveness of Military Organizations," *International Security* 11, no. 1 (Summer 1986): 37, https://doi.org/10.2307/2538875; Headquarters, Department of the Army, *ADP 3-0: Operations* (Washington, DC: Headquarters, Department of the Army, 2019), 5-1, https://armypubs.army.mil/epubs/DR_pubs /DR_a/ARN18010-ADP_3-0-000-WEB-2.pdf; Stephen Biddle, *Military Power: Explaining Victory and Defeat in Modern Battle* (Princeton, NJ: Princeton University Press, 2004), 6.

39. William F. Fox, *Regimental Losses in the American Civil War, 1861–1865* (Albany, NY: Albany Publishing, 1889), 122; Thomas L. Livermore, *Numbers and Losses in the Civil War in America, 1861–65* (Boston: Houghton, Mifflin, 1900), 64, 70, 72; *OR,* ser. 3, 5:666.

1. RAISING THE REGIMENTS

1. *OR,* 40(3):394–95.

2. *OR,* 42(1):547–48, 42(2):768, 783, 42(3):198, 245; *OR,* ser. 3, 4(2):1059, 5:668, 673–74.

3. John L. Yale to brother, 6 October 1864, Folder 3, Box 1, John Yale Papers, UVM; Peck, *Revised Roster,* 595.

4. Charles Cummings to wife, 17 March, 1 April 1864, Charles Cummings Papers, 1857–73, Folder 9, MSA 28, VHS, transcription; Joel H. Lucia, "Seventeenth Regiment," in Peck, *Revised Roster,* 568; Peter T. Washburn, *Report of the Adjutant & Inspector General's Office of the State of Vermont, from October 1, 1863, to October 1, 1864* (Montpelier, VT: Walton's, 1864), 78; George G. Benedict, *Vermont in the Civil War: A History of the Part Taken by the Vermont Soldiers and Sailors in the War for the Union, 1861–5,* vol. 2 (Burlington, VT: Free Press Association, 1888), 496–98, 507, 520, 525–26; U.S. War Department, *Revised United States Army Regulations of 1861* [. . .] (Washington, DC: Government Printing Office, 1863), 352; 17th VS. For an explanation of my spreadsheet tabulating and detailing the officers and men serving in the 17th Vermont, see introduction, note 5.

5. *OR,* 36(1):113; *OR,* ser. 3, 4(1):557; Leander Otis Merriam, "Personal Recollections of the War for the Union," Collection S-5186, MHS, 34; Henry C. Houston, *The Thirty-Second Maine Regiment of Infantry Volunteers: An Historical Sketch* (Portland, ME: Press of Southworth Brothers, 1903), 56; *Bangor (ME) Daily Whig and Courier,* 2 May 1864, newspapers.com; William E. S. Whitman and Charles H. True, *Maine in the War for the Union: A History of the Part Borne by Maine Troops in the Suppression of the American Rebellion* (Lewiston, ME: Nelson Dingley Jr., 1865), 577, 586; John S. Hodsdon, *Report*

of the Adjutant General of the State of Maine, for the Years 1864 and 1865 (Augusta, ME: Stevens & Sayward, Printers to the State, 1866), 20, 545, 1147; Hodsdon, *Appendix D,* 1362; Hodsdon, *Annual Report of the Adjutant General of the State of Maine, for the Year Ending December 31, 1866* (Augusta, ME: Stevens & Sayward, Printers to the State, 1867), 166; Entry 5011: Letters Sent and Circulars, February–December 1864, RG 393: Records of U.S. Army Continental Commands, pt. 2, NA; 31st MS. For an explanation of my spreadsheet tabulating and detailing the officers and men serving in the 31st Maine, see introduction, note 5. The composition of the Second Brigade changed over time. On May 5, 1864, it included three units composed of later arrivals: the 17th Vermont and the 31st and 32nd Maine Volunteer Infantry Regiments. Three seasoned outfits also served in the brigade, namely the 6th, 9th, and 11th New Hampshire Volunteer Infantry Regiments.

6. Whitman and True, *Maine in the War,* 582; Houston, *Thirty-Second Maine,* 443; *Vermont Phoenix* (Brattleboro), 29 July 1864, Chronicling America; *Vermont Phoenix* (Brattleboro), 12 August 1864, newspapers.com; *Burlington (VT) Free Press,* 5 August 1864, Chronicling America; *Lamoille Newsdealer* (Hyde Park, VT), 17 February 1864, newspapers.com; *Ellsworth (ME) American,* 26 August 1864, Chronicling America; *Loyal Sunrise* (Presque Isle, ME), 7 September 1864, DigitalMaine, https://digitalmaine. com/newspapers/; *Portland (ME) Daily Press,* 25 July, 14 December 1864, Chronicling America; *Bangor (ME) Daily Whig and Courier,* 6, 11 October 1864, newspapers.com; Hodsdon, *Report of the Adjutant General of the State of Maine, . . . 1864 and 1865,* 549; *Maine Democrat* (Biddeford), 10 January 1865, DigitalMaine; Robert B. Potter and Abby Austin Potter, *Personal Experiences of Maj. Gen'l Robert B. Potter in the War of the Rebellion, 1861–1865* (New York: Lotus, 1894), 74; *Biddeford (ME) Union and Journal,* 16 September 1864, Chronicling America; *Rutland (VT) Weekly Herald,* 14 January 1864, newspapers.com; *Burlington (VT) Daily Times,* 6 August 1864, newspapers.com. See also *Burlington (VT) Daily Times,* 2 March 1864; thanks to John J. Hennessy for providing a scan of this newspaper article.

7. Washburn, *Adjutant & Inspector General's Office,* 36; *Loyal Sunrise* (Presque Isle, ME), 25 January 1865, DigitalMaine; *Gardiner (ME) Home Journal,* 2 February 1865, ibid.; *Portland (ME) Daily Press,* 14 December 1864; *Burlington (VT) Daily Times,* 6 August 1864. Thanks to Heather Moran, archivist at the Maine State Archives, for providing the information on Bvt. Lt. Col. Robert McCandless Littler, the acting assistant adjutant general, based on FamilySearch, https://www.familysearch.org/en/.

8. Houston, *Thirty-Second Maine,* 75; Merriam, "Personal Recollections," MHS, 7; *Vermont Phoenix* (Brattleboro), 22 April 1864, newspapers.com; *Bangor (ME) Daily Whig and Courier,* 28 April, 10 November, 17 December 1864, newspapers.com; *Burlington (VT) Daily Times,* 16 January 1864, newspapers.com; Lucia, "Seventeenth Regiment," 574; Peck, *Revised Roster,* 575, 593; Leander W. Cogswell, *A History of the Eleventh New Hampshire Volunteer Infantry in the Rebellion War, 1861–1865* [. . .] (Concord, NH: Republican Press Association, 1891), 264; *Lamoille Newsdealer* (Hyde Park, VT), 17 February 1864; Charles A. Manson to mother, 29 August 1864, Charles A. Manson Papers, 1861–1918, Collection 454, Emory University, microfilm; Yale to brother, 6, 8 October 1864, Folder 3, Box 1, John Yale Papers, UVM; *Rutland (VT) Weekly Herald,* 21

January 1864, Chronicling America; "Joseph Rutherford to [Hannah Rutherford]," 29 March 1865, Joseph Chase Rutherford Correspondence, Vermonters in the Civil War, UVMLDC, https://cdi.uvm.edu/manuscript/uvmcdi-94533.

9. Washburn, *Adjutant & Inspector General's Office*, 26, 28; Hodsdon, *Report of the Adjutant General of the State of Maine, . . . 1864 and 1865*, 20, 546, 560; *Burlington (VT) Free Press*, 1 January 1864, Chronicling America; *Rutland (VT) Weekly Herald*, 25 February 1864, newspapers.com; *Biddeford (ME) Union and Journal*, 1 July 1864, DigitalMaine; *OR*, ser. 3, 3:89; Marvel, *Tarnished Victory*, 122. Tyler Anbinder explains that "the person who hired a substitute was excused from service for the length of the substitute's enrollment . . . whereas someone paying the commutation fee was exempted only from that particular draft." Anbinder, "Which Poor Man's Fight?," 353.

10. *Argus and Patriot* (Montpelier, VT), 25 February 1864, newspapers.com; Washburn, *Adjutant & Inspector General's Office*, 26–28; *Lamoille Newsdealer* (Hyde Park, VT), 17 February 1864; *Vermont Record* (Brandon), 15 April 1864, newspapers.com; *Vermont Standard* (Woodstock), 5 February, 18 March 1864, newspapers.com.

11. *Bangor (ME) Daily Whig and Courier*, 12 August 1864, newspapers.com; *Biddeford (ME) Union and Journal*, 7 October 1864, Chronicling America; *Gardiner (ME) Home Journal*, 9 February 1865, DigitalMaine.

12. Benedict, *Vermont in the Civil War*, 525; *Vermont Phoenix* (Brattleboro), 29 July 1864; *Portland (ME) Daily Press*, 16 August 1864, Chronicling America; *Burlington (VT) Daily Times*, 29 September 1863, 19 July 1865, newspapers.com.

13. *OR*, 33:444; *OR*, ser. 3, 3:888–89.

14. Guelzo, *Fateful Lightning*, 262; *Vermont Watchman and State Journal* (Montpelier), 11 December 1863, Chronicling America; *Vermont Watchman and State Journal* (Montpelier), 19 August 1864, newspapers.com; *Lamoille Newsdealer* (Hyde Park, VT), 20 January 1864, newspapers.com; *Bangor (ME) Daily Whig and Courier*, 4 February, 6 October 1864, newspapers.com.

15. *Green Mountain Freeman* (Montpelier, VT), 5 January 1864, newspapers.com; *OR*, ser. 3, 3:879, 5:672; Lucia, "Seventeenth Regiment," 568; Benedict, *Vermont in the Civil War*, 496; Washburn, *Adjutant & Inspector General's Office*, 27; *Daily Green Mountain Freeman* (Montpelier, VT), 31 August 1863, newspapers.com.

16. Houston, *Thirty-Second Maine*, 34–35; Hodsdon, *Report of the Adjutant General of the State of Maine, . . . 1864 and 1865*, 37, 140–41, 575; Hodsdon, *Annual Report of the Adjutant General of the State of Maine, . . . 1866*, 165.

17. Marvel, *Lincoln's Mercenaries*, x; *Vermont Standard* (Woodstock), 5 February 1864; *Lamoille Newsdealer* (Hyde Park, VT), 17 February 1864; *Burlington (VT) Daily Times*, 6 August 1864; *Maine Democrat* (Biddeford), 10 January 1865.

18. *St. Albans (VT) Daily Messenger*, 24 March 1864, newspapers.com; *OR*, ser. 3, 5:673–74; Washburn, *Adjutant & Inspector General's Office*, 15, 28; Hodsdon, *Report of the Adjutant General of the State of Maine, . . . 1864 and 1865*, 554; *Bangor (ME) Daily Whig and Courier*, 8 April, 6 August 1864, newspapers.com; *Gardiner (ME) Home Journal*, 7 January 1864, DigitalMaine; *Gardiner (ME) Home Journal*, 9 February 1865; *Vermont Watchman and State Journal* (Montpelier), 11 December 1863; *Portland (ME) Daily Press*, 21 September 1864, Chronicling America.

19. *OR,* ser. 3, 5:673, 675; Joseph C. G. Kennedy, *Population of the United States in 1860; Compiled from the Original Returns of the Eighth Census* [. . .] (Washington, DC: Government Printing Office, 1864), 208–9, 499; *Gardiner (ME) Home Journal,* 2 February 1865; *Rutland (VT) Weekly Herald,* 31 December 1863, Chronicling America.

20. *Bangor (ME) Daily Whig and Courier,* 4, 19 February, 8 April, 20 June, 27 July, 4, 8, 26 August, 2, 19 September, 6 October, 5 November 1864, newspapers.com; *Daily Green Mountain Freeman* (Montpelier, VT), 31 August 1863; *Rutland (VT) Weekly Herald,* 31 December 1863, 21 January 1864; *Biddeford (ME) Union and Journal,* 2 September 1864, Chronicling America; *Vermont Watchman and State Journal* (Montpelier), 25 December 1863, newspapers.com; *Lamoille Newsdealer* (Hyde Park, VT), 20 January, 17 February 1864; *Burlington (VT) Daily Times,* 28 September 1863, newspapers.com; *Portland (ME) Daily Press,* 30 May, 21 September, 3 October 1864, Chronicling America; *Gardiner (ME) Home Journal,* 18 August 1864, DigitalMaine; *Burlington (VT) Free Press,* 1 January 1864; *Ellsworth (ME) American,* 29 July 1864, Chronicling America; *Piscataquis Observer* (Dover, ME), 10 March 1864, DigitalMaine; *Walton's Daily Journal* (Montpelier, VT), 27 January 1864, newspapers.com; *Orleans Independent Standard* (Irasburgh, VT), 23 October 1863, newspapers.com. See also *Orleans Independent Standard,* 13 November 1863; thanks to John J. Hennessy for providing a scan of this newspaper article.

21. Richard F. Miller, ed., *States at War,* vol. 1, *A Reference Guide to Connecticut, Maine, Massachusetts, New Hampshire, Rhode Island, and Vermont in the Civil War* (Hanover, NH: University Press of New England, 2013), 153, 557–58.

22. Kennedy, *Population of the United States in 1860,* 208–9, 499; 17th VS; 31st MS. Tyler Anbinder laments that "so many studies have lumped yeoman farmers and menial farm laborers together into a single category." Still, he admits to "variation in age and wealth among farmers . . . [given that] a significant number of farmers (typically younger, possibly less prosperous ones) did enter the army due to conscription." Anbinder, "Which Poor Man's Fight?," 363. I found that the enlistment contracts for the later arrivals featured diverse terminology for each recruit's employment status. For simplicity, Anbinder uses the terms "farmer" and "laborer" to encompass the many variations. Vermonters and Mainers were typically of modest means, which pushes against his emphasis on the gulf between farmers and laborers.

To examine trends in the infantry throughout the Union army, I edited a custom spreadsheet created by Coralee Lewis based on the database called Union Army Data: Early Indicators of Later Work Levels, Disease, and Death (hereafter cited as Early Indicators, Union Army), https://www.nber.org/research/data/union-army-data-data -101. This spreadsheet contains information from Robert W. Fogel et al., Aging of Veterans of the Union Army: Version M-5 (Chicago: Center for Population Economics, University of Chicago Graduate School of Business; Department of Economics, Brigham Young University; and The National Bureau of Economic Research, 2000). The Early Indicators project was supported by the National Institute of Health under award number P01 AG10120. The custom spreadsheet is drawn from the "Unionarmy" files contained in the following zip archives from the Union Army Data—Data 101 webpage: "The Basics," "Socioeconomic," "Pension," "Military," and "Migration."

Thanks to staff members Heather DeSomer, Coralee Lewis, and Noelle Yetter for offering guidance on the analysis of the database. To determine the percentage of farmers and laborers in the 17th Vermont, 31st Maine, and Union army overall, I referred to the number of men who provided their livelihood upon enlistment.

23. *Burlington (VT) Daily Times,* 6 August 1864; Ken Sturtz, ed., *The Civil War Letters of S. R. Emerson: Fighting with the 13th and 17th Vermont Volunteers from Gettysburg to Petersburg* (Amazon Digital Services, 2016), loc. 2719, 2728, 2766, Kindle; Tom Ledoux and Associates, "Civil War Diary of Franklin Temple Carter, Private, Company G," Vermont in the Civil War, updated 9 January 2002, https://vermontcivilwar.org/units /17/frankcarter.php (website discontinued); John P. Sheahan to father, [no date] May, 26 June, 10, 14, 20 July 1864, Folder 9, Box 1, John Parris Sheahan Papers, 1862–65, Collection 184, MHS; Whitman and True, *Maine in the War,* 636; Voranus L. Coffin to wife, 2 May 1864, Lt. Voranus L. Coffin Papers, 1863–65, Container 298408, RG 29: Maine State Archives Gifts, MSA; "Sheahan, John P.," I1029, Civil War Era Soldiers' Portraits, DigitalMaine, https://digitalmaine.com/arc_civilwarportraits/559/; Peck, *Revised Roster,* 586, 590; William Griffin, "1864–65: Gustavus Gould to Family," *Spared & Shared 21* (blog), 18 February 2020, transcription, https://sparedcreative21.art.blog /2020/02/18/1864-65-gustavus-gould-to-family/; Griffin, "1863: William Elmore Howard to George Sumner Howard," *Spared & Shared 4* (blog), accessed 27 April 2022, transcription, https://sparedshared4.wordpress.com /letters/1863-william-elmore -howard-to-george-sumner-howard/; Manson to mother, 10, 18 July, 3, [no date] August, 30 September, 11 November, 2, 11 December 1864, Collection 454, Emory University, microfilm; Moses Whitehill to brother, 15 February, 21 June 1863, 15 March, 20, 24 April, 1 May, 13, 22 June 1864, Matthew and Moses Whitehill Letters, MSA 520, VHS; Horatio Fox Smith, journal, 4, 6 July 1863, Folder 12, Box 1, Journal of Horatio Fox Smith, July 4, 1863–November 11, 1863, Civil War Miscellany, M131.2, George J. Mitchell Department of Special Collections & Archives, Bowdoin College Library, transcription; Alpheus Hardy to Assistant Adjutant General of Maine, 28 March 1865, 31st Maine Regiment, 1862–66, Container 353956, Civil War—Incoming Military Correspondence, 1861–68, Office of the Adjutant General, RG 15, MSA; James H. Belcher to John Hodsdon, no date, ibid.; Solomon Anderson to unknown, 1865, ibid.; Henry W. Lancaster to wife, 9, 16, 17 March (first of two letters), 17 April 1864, Folder 2, Misc. Box 263, Lancaster Family Letters, Collection S-7464, MHS; Cummings to wife, 17 March, 5 June, 3 July, 18 September 1864, Folder 9, MSA 28, VHS; Yale to parents, 10 November 1864, Folder 3, Box 1, John Yale Papers, UVM; Yale to mother, 4 March 1865, ibid.; Hodsdon, *Appendix D,* 735; "Joseph Rutherford to Son," 8 March 1865, Rutherford Correspondence, Vermonters in the Civil War, UVMLDC, https://cdi.uvm.edu /manuscript/uvmcdi-94527; *Bangor (ME) Daily Whig and Courier,* 15 March 1865, newspapers.com; Paul G. Zeller, "'My Soldier Boy Mark': The Civil War Letters of Pvt. Mark B. Slayton," *Vermont History* 82, no. 1 (Winter/Spring 2014): 49, Mark B. Slayton Civil War Letters, 1863, Folder 15, MSA 518, VHS; Box 2011, Court-Martial Case Files, 1809–94, RG 153: Records of the Office of the Judge Advocate General (Army), NA.

24. 17th VS; Hodsdon, *Report of the Adjutant General of the State of Maine, . . . 1864*

and 1865, 142; Phillips, *Looming Civil War,* 190; George W. Sargent to unknown, 4
February 1865, Incoming Military Correspondence, Office of the Adjutant General,
RG 15, MSA.

25. *Portland (ME) Daily Press,* 3 February 1864, Chronicling America; *Bangor (ME)
Daily Whig and Courier,* 9 July, 26 August, 2 September, 6 October 1864, newspapers
.com; *Gardiner (ME) Home Journal,* 30 June 1864, DigitalMaine, https://digitalmaine
.com/newspapers/; *Gardiner (ME) Home Journal,* 18 August 1864; *Orleans Independent
Standard* (Irasburgh, VT), 23 October 1863; *Lamoille Newsdealer* (Hyde Park, VT),
17 February 1864; *Ellsworth (ME) American,* 26 August 1864; *Loyal Sunrise* (Presque Isle,
ME), 7 September 1864; *Vermont Phoenix* (Brattleboro), 12 August 1864; *Vermont
Watchman and State Journal* (Montpelier), 11 December 1863; *Rutland (VT) Weekly
Herald,* 25 February 1864; *Burlington (VT) Free Press,* 1 January 1864; 31st MS.

26. Smith to Samuel Cony, 25 June 1864, Incoming Military Correspondence,
Office of the Adjutant General, RG 15, MSA; 17th VS; grandmother to Manson, 29
January 1863, Collection 454, Emory University, microfilm; Manson to mother, 9
October, 18 December 1864, 5 January, 1 February, 13 March 1865, ibid.; "Joseph
Rutherford to [Hannah Rutherford]," 9 September 1864, Rutherford Correspondence,
Vermonters in the Civil War, UVMLDC, https://cdi.uvm.edu/manuscript/uvmcdi
-94383; Yale to brother, 8 October 1864, Folder 3, Box 1, John Yale Papers, UVM; Yale
to mother, 21 February 1865, ibid.; Coffin to wife, 27 May 1864, Container 298408, RG
29, MSA; *Bangor (ME) Daily Whig and Courier,* 2 December 1864, 25 February, 15 March
1865, newspapers.com; Edward L. Getchell to Samuel Cony, [no date] February 1865,
Incoming Military Correspondence, Office of the Adjutant General, RG 15, MSA;
George Hodgkins to unknown, no date, ibid.; Zeller, "My Soldier Boy Mark," 58,
Folder 15, MSA 518, VHS; Lancaster to wife, no date, Folder 11, Misc. Box 263,
Collection S-7464, MHS; Whitehill to brother, 23 January, 20 February, 30 March
1863, 24 April 1864, MSA 520, VHS; "Joseph Rutherford to [Hannah Rutherford],"
13 March 1864, Rutherford Correspondence, Vermonters in the Civil War, UVMLDC,
https://cdi.uvm.edu/manuscript/uvmcdi-94306; "Joseph Rutherford to [Hannah
Rutherford]," 25 April 1864, ibid., https://cdi.uvm.edu/manuscript/uvmcdi-94374;
"Joseph Rutherford to [Hannah Rutherford]," 14 April 1864, ibid., https://cdi.uvm
.edu/manuscript/uvmcdi-94368; "Joseph Rutherford to [Hannah Rutherford],"
9 September 1864, ibid., https://cdi.uvm.edu/manuscript/uvmcdi-94383.

27. Merriam, "Personal Recollections," MHS, 9, 76; Sheahan to father, 25 January,
[no date] February, 7 June 1864 (first of two letters), Folders 3, 9, Box 1, Collection 184,
MHS; Cummings to wife, 5 June, 11 July 1864, Folder 9, MSA 28, VHS.

28. *Gardiner (ME) Home Journal,* 18 August 1864; Hodsdon, *Report of the Adjutant
General of the State of Maine, . . . 1864 and 1865,* 32–33; *Bangor (ME) Daily Whig and
Courier,* 19 February, 20 June, 27 July, 26 August 1864; *Burlington (VT) Daily Times,*
6 August 1864; *Orleans Independent Standard* (Irasburgh, VT), 13 November 1863;
Sturtz, *Civil War Letters of S. R. Emerson,* loc. 2283, Kindle; Manson to mother, 29
August 1864, Collection 454, Emory University, microfilm.

29. *Vermont Watchman and State Journal* (Montpelier), 19 August 1864.

30. Maine State Museum, "Transcripts of Letters in *Maine Voices from the Civil War,*"

December 2017, 38, https://mainestatemuseum.org/wp-content/uploads/2017/12
/Transcripts-of-letters-in-Maine-Voices-from-the-Civil-War.pdf; Maine State Museum,
"Biographies of People Included in the Museum's Exhibit [Maine Voices from the
Civil War]," December 2017, 44, https://mainestatemuseum.org/wp-content/uploads
/2017/12/alphabeticalbios.pdf; Seaver Howard to Peter T. Washburn, 12 February 1864,
Reel F26085, Records of the Adjutant and Inspector General, VSARA, microfilm;
Julius and Sophia T. Granger, notarized statement, no date, ibid.; Almond Worester to
Washburn, 8 December 1863, ibid.; Almond and Emmaline Worester to Washburn, 16
December 1863, ibid.; *Green Mountain Freeman* (Montpelier, VT), 16 August 1864,
newspapers.com; *Vermont Standard* (Woodstock), 15 January 1864, newspapers.com;
Portland (ME) Daily Press, 3 February, 7 May 1864, Chronicling America; Cogswell,
Eleventh New Hampshire, 584.

31. 17th VS; 31st MS; Early Indicators, Union Army.

32. 17th VS; 31st MS; Lucia, "Seventeenth Regiment," 568; Kennedy, *Population of
the United States in 1860,* 207, 498; *OR,* ser. 3, 3:802; *Ellsworth (ME) American,* 19 August
1864, Chronicling America.

33. *Bangor (ME) Daily Whig and Courier,* 6 October 1864; *OR,* ser. 3, 4(1):34, 43;
Ledoux and Associates, "Civil War Diary of Franklin Temple Carter"; Enlistment
Papers, 1864, Container 321200, 31st Maine, Civil War—Regimental Records, Office of
the Adjutant General, RG 15, MSA; *Maine Democrat* (Biddeford), 10 January 1865;
Anbinder, "Which Poor Man's Fight?," 370.

34. 17th VS; 31st MS. To examine trends relating to company demographics
throughout the Union army, I used another custom spreadsheet based on the same
Early Indicators sample. Thanks to Coralee Lewis for creating this file.

35. Kennedy, *Population of the United States in 1860,* 207, 498; Early Indicators,
Union Army; *Burlington (VT) Daily Times,* 19 March 1864, www.newspapers.com;
Burlington (VT) Weekly Sentinel, 15 April 1864, newspapers.com; 17th VS; 31st MS; *OR,*
25(1):176. Enlistment contracts do not indicate when a foreign-born recruit immigrated
to this country. Using the U.S. census, it may be possible to estimate the arrival date
for such individuals, but the results of such a labor-intensive approach would be less
valuable for this book than determining the overall composition of the 17th Vermont
and 31st Maine.

36. 17th VS; 31st MS; Merriam, "Personal Recollections," MHS, 50. Officers and
men who previously served in other units could have done so without gaining actual
combat experience before they entered the 17th or the 31st. This book follows the
commonsense position that this would have been the exception rather than the rule.

37. Sturtz, *Civil War Letters of S. R. Emerson,* loc. 2335, Kindle; 17th VS; Cummings
to wife, 12 February 1864, Folder 9, MSA 28, VHS; *OR,* 27(1):174; Merriam, "Personal
Recollections," MHS, 5–7, 45–46, 61, 63–64, 66, 78; Sheahan to father, 6 July 1864,
Folder 9, Box 1, Collection 184, MHS; Hodsdon, *Appendix D,* 733; *Portland (ME) Daily
Press,* 15 August 1864, Chronicling America; Benedict, *Vermont in the Civil War,* 498;
Lucia, "Seventeenth Regiment," 569; *Springfield (MA) Republican,* 4 October 1886;
thanks to John J. Hennessy for providing a scan of this newspaper article. "Cannon
fever" is "severe anxiety and stress caused by exposure to cannon fire on the battle-

field; a fear of battle arising from this [experience]." "Cannon Fever," Oxford English Dictionary, accessed 24 February 2024, subscription website. Gerald F. Linderman cites this term as an example of how the Civil War generation downplayed negative connotations by making "occasional metaphorical references to cowardice as an illness." Linderman, *Embattled Courage,* 31.

38. Ledoux and Associates, "Civil War Diary of Franklin Temple Carter"; James Pollard, diary, 25–27 February, 1–3, 14–15, 22, 30–31 March, 2, 4, 5–6, 8–9, 12–13 April 1864, Reel F2850, Records of the Vermont Civil War Centennial Committee, Microfilm Collections, Civil War Era, VSARA; Cummings to wife, 26 February, 11 March, 1, 4 April 1864, Folder 9, MSA 28, VHS; Lucia, "Seventeenth Regiment," 569; Zeller, "My Soldier Boy Mark," 47, Folder 15, MSA 518, VHS.

39. Merriam, "Personal Recollections," MHS, 9; Houston, *Thirty-Second Maine,* 36–37, 39; *Bangor (ME) Daily Whig and Courier,* 10 November 1864; Charles W. Roberts to Governor of Maine, 24 September 1864, Incoming Military Correspondence, Office of the Adjutant General, RG 15, MSA.

40. Mark W. Johnson, "Emory Upton's Twenty-Six: Desertion and Divided Loyalty of U.S. Army Soldiers, 1860–1861," *Journal of Military History* 81, no. 3 (July 2017): 755; 17th VS; 31st MS; Early Indicators, Union Army. I developed this sample of 205 infantry, sharpshooter, and heavy artillery regiments, with corresponding data including the desertion rate, using "Three Hundred Fighting Regiments—Statistical and Historical Sketch of Each," chapter 10 in Fox, *Regimental Losses;* and American Civil War Research Database. Note that Fox included the 17th and 31st in his list of hard-fighting units, although I have excluded them from the sample.

In this section I only address those cases of unruly behavior that occurred between the creation of these outfits and the capture of Petersburg on April 3, 1865, reflecting the book's focus on combat performance.

41. Hallock, "Role of the Community," 134; 17th VS; 31st MS; Anbinder, "Which Poor Man's Fight?," 368.

42. *Portland (ME) Daily Press,* 10 December 1864, Chronicling America; 17th VS; Boxes 734, 857, 859, 861, 1042, Court-Martial Case Files, RG 153, NA.

43. Box 2011, RG 153, Court-Martial Case Files, NA; 17th VS; 31st MS.

44. Box 1955, Court-Martial Case Files, RG 153, NA; Howard to Washburn, 12 February 1864, Reel F26085, Records of the Adjutant and Inspector General, VSARA, microfilm; Luther Pease et al. to Washburn, 13 February 1864, ibid.; notarized statement from Grangers, ibid.; Francis V. Randall to unknown, 7 September 1864, ibid.; 17th VS.

45. Box 1042, Court-Martial Case Files, RG 153, NA.

46. Stephen F. Brown, untitled essay, no date, Stephen F. Brown Civil War Papers, 1864–1903, 973.78 B815, VHS, 2, 4; *Argus and Patriot* (Montpelier, VT), 17 March 1864, newspapers.com.

47. Houston, *Thirty-Second Maine,* 431; *Bangor (ME) Daily Whig and Courier,* 17 December 1864.

48. Boxes 1723, 1758, 2088, Court-Martial Case Files, RG 153, NA; Pollard, diary, 29 December 1864, Reel F2850, Records of the Vermont Civil War Centennial

Committee, VSARA, microfilm; Manson to mother, 11 August, 14 September 1864, Collection 454, Emory University, microfilm; 17th VS; *Vermont Phoenix* (Brattleboro), 29 July 1864; Descriptive Books, 31st Maine, Entry 114: Civil War Regimental Books, RG 94: Records of the Adjutant General's Office, NA; Merriam, "Personal Recollections," MHS, 43.

49. 17th VS; Merriam, "Personal Recollections," MHS, 6–7, 55; Smith to mother, 15 April 1864, Folder 6, Box 1, 1864 Apr 15–Jul 10, Horatio Fox Smith Letters, Civil War Miscellany, M131.1, George J. Mitchell Department of Special Collections & Archives, Bowdoin College Library, transcription; Lancaster to wife, 17 March 1864 (second of two letters), Folder 11, Misc. Box 263, Collection S-7464, MHS; *Burlington (VT) Weekly Free Press,* 15 April 1864, newspapers.com; Hodsdon, *Appendix D,* 750; Pollard, diary, 19 February, 3 March, 5 April 1864, Reel F2850, Records of the Vermont Civil War Centennial Committee, VSARA, microfilm; Manson to mother, 31 March 1865, Collection 454, Emory University, microfilm; Yale to brother, 6 October 1864, Folder 3, Box 1, John Yale Papers, UVM; Daniel Read Larned to sister, 1 May 1864, Box 4, Daniel Read Larned Papers, 1861–78, MSS29470, LOC, microfilm; Foote, *Gentlemen and the Roughs,* 6; Entry 4985: Circulars Issued by the Assistant Inspector General, July 1864–May 1865, RG 393: Records of U.S. Army Continental Commands, pt. 2, NA; Morning Report, Companies A–G, I, K, 17th Vermont (Volunteer) Infantry, Entry 115: Civil War Regimental Books, RG 94, NA; Morning Report & Order Book, 17th Vermont, ibid.

50. *Lamoille Newsdealer* (Hyde Park, VT), 27 April 1864, Chronicling America; *Rutland (VT) Weekly Herald,* 21 April 1864, Chronicling America; Sturtz, *Civil War Letters of S. R. Emerson,* loc. 2943, Kindle; Ledoux and Associates, "Civil War Diary of Franklin Temple Carter"; Pollard, diary, 14 April 1864, Reel F2850, Records of the Vermont Civil War Centennial Committee, VSARA, microfilm. The members of a court of inquiry found no need to hold a general court-martial in the case of Private Sweeny.

51. Morning Report & Order Book, 17th Vermont, Entry 115, RG 94, NA; Ledoux and Associates, "Civil War Diary of Franklin Temple Carter"; Ancestry, Vermont 17th Volunteer Infantry, Fold3; *Orleans Independent Standard* (Irasburgh, VT), 12 August 1864, newspapers.com; *Green Mountain Freeman* (Montpelier, VT), 29 March 1864, newspapers.com.

52. Boxes 1038, 2022, Court-Martial Case Files, RG 153, NA.

53. Merriam, "Personal Recollections," MHS, 7–8; 31st MS.

54. Boxes 858, 874, 872, 1042, 1767, 1944, 1971, 1989, 1989, 1990, 2086, Court-Martial Case Files, RG 153, NA; Morning Report & Order Book, 17th Vermont, Entry 115, RG 94, NA; Morning Reports, Companies A to M, 31st Maine (Volunteer) Infantry, ibid.; 31st Maine Infantry Consolidated Morning Reports, 1864, Container 43327, 31st Maine Infantry Records, 1861–65, Civil War—Regimental Records, 1861–65, Office of the Adjutant General, RG 15, MSA. Owing to incomplete records for the 31st Maine, I drew on both consolidated morning reports and company-level morning reports to calculate as accurate a percentage as possible.

55. Morning Reports, 31st Maine, Entry 115, RG 94, NA; Consolidated Morning Reports, Container 43327, 31st Maine, Regimental Records, Office of the Adjutant General, RG 15, MSA; 17th VS; 31st MS; Peck, *Revised Roster,* 575–76; Boxes 858, 872,

874, 1042, 1243, 1767, 1944, 1971, 1989, 1990, 2086, Court-Martial Case Files, RG 153, NA; Regimental Order Book, 31st Maine (Volunteer) Infantry, Entry 113: Civil War Regimental Books, RG 94, NA; Morning Report & Order Book, 17th Vermont, Entry 115, ibid.

56. Cummings to wife, 23 July 1864, Folder 9, MSA 28, VHS; Yale to brother, 6 October 1864, Folder 3, Box 1, John Yale Papers, UVM; Sheahan to father, 6 July 1864, Folder 9, Box 1, Collection 184, MHS; Maine State Museum, "Transcripts of Letters," 38.

57. Reunion Society of Vermont Officers, *Proceedings of the Reunion Society of Vermont Officers, 1864–1884, with Addresses Delivered at Its Meetings* [. . .] (Burlington, VT: Free Press Association, 1885), 89; *Bangor (ME) Daily Whig and Courier,* 4 February 1870, newspapers.com; Marvel, *Lincoln's Mercenaries,* 10.

58. Ancestry, Vermont 17th Volunteer Infantry, Fold3; Bisbee, finding aid, Folder 15, MSA 189, VHS; Lyman E. Knapp, "1887 speech," Folder 16, MSA 189, VHS.

59. *Dedication of the Soldiers' Monument, at Gorham, Maine, Thursday, October 18th, 1866* [. . .] (Portland, ME: Press of B. Thurston, 1866), 3–4, 17, https://www.maine .gov/civilwar/books/Dedication_of_the_Soldiers__monument__at.pdf; *Portland (ME) Daily Press,* 27 July 1865, Chronicling America; *OR,* 46(1):584.

2. THE BATTLES OF THE WILDERNESS AND SPOTSYLVANIA COURT HOUSE

1. George F. Williams, "Lights and Shadows of Army Life," *Century Magazine,* October 1884, 812–13; Meade, *Life and Letters,* 196.

2. Merriam, "Personal Recollections of the War for the Union," Collection S-5186, MHS, 15; *OR,* 36(1):113–14.

3. Although historians have produced extensive treatments of the Overland and Petersburg Campaigns, the focused nature of this study precludes a comprehensive narrative of individual engagements here and in subsequent chapters. Notable examples of operational histories covering the campaigns include Hess, *Trench Warfare under Grant and Lee;* Rhea, *Wilderness;* Rhea, *Battles for Spotsylvania;* Rhea, *North Anna;* Gordon C. Rhea, *Cold Harbor: Grant and Lee, May 26–June 3, 1864* (Baton Rouge: Louisiana State University Press, 2002); Rhea, *On to Petersburg;* Hess, *In the Trenches at Petersburg;* Greene, *Campaign of Giants;* Hess, *Into the Crater;* A. Wilson Greene, *The Final Battles of the Petersburg Campaign: Breaking the Backbone of the Rebellion,* 2nd ed. (Knoxville: University of Tennessee Press, 2008); and Sommers, *Richmond Redeemed.* To every extent possible, this chapter and those following depend upon the sources closest to the action involving the men in the 17th Vermont and 31st Maine. When required, the research drew on additional writings, including those of other combatants in the same brigade.

4. Merriam, "Personal Recollections," MHS, 22; and *Burlington (VT) Free Press,* 5 August 1864; *Vermont Phoenix* (Brattleboro), 6 May 1864, America's Historical Newspapers. This unsigned article in the *Phoenix* is attributable to Cummings based on the highly literate writing style and the fact that he was the editor of the newspaper

in question. Further references to Cummings as the author of anonymous material from the *Phoenix* follow this logic.

5. Merriam, "Personal Recollections," MHS, 16.

6. *OR,* 36(1):934; Merriam, "Personal Recollections," MHS, 9–11; Lancaster to wife, 22 April 1864, Folder 11, Misc. Box 263, Lancaster Family Letters, Collection S-7464, MHS; Cummings to wife, 22, 30 April 1864, Charles Cummings Papers, Folder 9, MSA 28, VHS, transcription; Whitman and Charles, *Maine in the War,* 578; Ledoux and Associates, "Civil War Diary of Franklin Temple Carter"; James Pollard, diary, 23, 25 April 1864, Reel F2850, Records of the Vermont Civil War Centennial Committee, Microfilm Collections, Civil War Era, VSARA.

7. *OR,* 36(1):113, 148, 905, 934, 36(3):169; Whitman and True, *Maine in the War,* 578; Houston, *Thirty-Second Maine,* 71; Merriam, "Personal Recollections," MHS, 12; Simon G. Griffin, journal, Folder 1, Box 1, Journal of Simon G. Griffin (excerpts), MG257, HSCC, 34, transcription.

8. Merriam, "Personal Recollections," MHS, 10; *Vermont Watchman and State Journal* (Montpelier), 6 May 1864; Peck, *Revised Roster,* 581; Hodsdon, *Appendix D,* 750; Lancaster to wife, 22 April 1864, Folder 11, Misc. Box 263, Collection S-7464, MHS; *Lamoille Newsdealer* (Hyde Park, VT), 4 May 1864, Chronicling America.

9. *OR,* 36(1):16–17; Adam Badeau, *Military History of Ulysses S. Grant, from April, 1861, to April, 1865* (New York: D. Appleton, 1882), 2:95–96; Grant, *Personal Memoirs,* 316.

10. Houston, *Thirty-Second Maine,* 77–79; *Rutland (VT) Weekly Herald,* 12 May 1864, Chronicling America; Lancaster to wife, 29 April 1864, Folder 11, Misc. Box 263, Collection S-7464, MHS; Smith to mother, [no date] April 1864, Folder 6, Box 1, Horatio Fox Smith Letters, M131.1, Bowdoin College Library, transcription; Hodsdon, *Appendix D,* 750; *Lamoille Newsdealer* (Hyde Park, VT), 8 June 1864; Cogswell, *Eleventh New Hampshire,* 288–89; Merriam, "Personal Recollections," MHS, 12; Moses Whitehill to brother, 1 May 1864, Matthew and Moses Whitehill Letters, MSA 520, VHS.

11. Houston, *Thirty-Second Maine,* 76–78.

12. *OR,* 33:955, 36(1):18; Cummings to wife, 30 April 1864, Folder 9, MSA 28, VHS; Ledoux and Associates, "Civil War Diary of Franklin Temple Carter"; Merriam, "Personal Recollections," MHS, 12–13; Cogswell, *Eleventh New Hampshire,* 299.

13. Glatthaar, *General Lee's Army,* 67; Morning Report & Order Book, 17th Vermont, Entry 115: Civil War Regimental Books, RG 94: Records of the Adjutant General's Office, NA; *Portland (ME) Daily Press,* 13 February 1864, Chronicling America; *Biddeford (ME) Union and Journal,* 26 February 1864, Chronicling America; Kennedy, *Population of the United States in 1860,* 200–207, 494–97. I have determined the disease fatality rate with reference to the 205-regiment sample described in chapter 1, note 40. Thanks to Dick Dobbins of Historical Data Systems for providing the spreadsheets used to establish the relationship between length of time and mortality from disease.

14. *OR,* 36(1):18, 927, 36(2):380; Potter and Potter, *Personal Experiences,* 80; Ledoux and Associates, "Civil War Diary of Franklin Temple Carter"; Cogswell, *Eleventh New Hampshire,* 260, 311, 314, 316, 327, 359; *Lamoille Newsdealer* (Hyde Park, VT), 8 June 1864; Merriam, "Personal Recollections," MHS, 14; Benedict, *Vermont in the Civil War,*

499; Lyman Jackman, *History of the Sixth New Hampshire Regiment in the War for the Union*, ed. Amos Hadley (Concord, NH: Republican Press Association, 1891), 214; Houston, *Thirty-Second Maine*, 92; Pollard, diary, 4 May 1864, Reel F2850, Records of the Vermont Civil War Centennial Committee, VSARA, microfilm; Perry, diary, 4 May 1864, Henry O. Perry Diaries, 1864 January–1866 April, MS 2187, NYHS; Rhea, *Wilderness*, 92–93. Maj. Gen. Robert B. Potter referred to the Spotswood House as Spotswood Tavern, which may reflect confusion over the similarly named Spotswood Inn located near Spotsylvania Court House.

15. Box 1767, Court-Martial Case Files, 1809–94, RG 153: Records of the Office of the Judge Advocate General (Army), NA; Cogswell, *Eleventh New Hampshire*, 332; *Lamoille Newsdealer* (Hyde Park, VT), 8 June 1864; Jackman, *Sixth New Hampshire*, 214; A. P. Horne, "Andersonville and Florence," in *History of the Ninth Regiment New Hampshire Volunteers in the War of the Rebellion*, ed. Edward O. Lord (Concord, NH: Republican Press Association, 1895), 619; Rhea, *Wilderness*, 185.

16. *OR*, 36(1):906, 36(2):412, 425; Badeau, *Military History of Ulysses S. Grant*, 2:115; Thomas L. Livermore, "Grant's Campaign against Lee," in Military Historical Society, *Wilderness Campaign*, 425; Hazard Stevens, "The Sixth Corps in the Wilderness," in Military Historical Society, *Wilderness Campaign*, 195; Alexander S. Webb, "Through the Wilderness," in Johnson and Buel, *Battles and Leaders*, 158n; Morris Schaff, *The Battle of the Wilderness* (Boston: Houghton Mifflin, 1910), 228; Rhea, *Wilderness*, 324.

17. *OR*, 36(2):404–5; Schaff, *Wilderness*, 225–26.

18. Charles Lawrence Peirson, "The Operations of the Army of the Potomac, May 7–11, 1864," in Military Historical Society, *Wilderness Campaign*, 208; John C. Ropes, "Grant's Campaign in Virginia in 1864," ibid., 378; Badeau, *Military History of Ulysses S. Grant*, 2:119, 123; *OR*, 36(1):222, 325; Houston, *Thirty-Second Maine*, 99–100; Cogswell, *Eleventh New Hampshire*, 335, 347; Regis de Trobriand, *Four Years with the Army of the Potomac*, trans. George K. Dauchy (Boston: Ticknor, 1889), 571; Porter, *Campaigning with Grant*, 72; Webb, "Through the Wilderness," 154.

19. *Burlington (VT) Daily Times*, 21 May 1864, newspapers.com; Schaff, *Wilderness*, 101; Charles H. Porter, "Opening of the Campaign of 1864," in Military Historical Society, *Wilderness Campaign*, 23; Peck, *Revised Roster*, 578; Cummings to wife, 26 April 1864, Folder 9, MSA 28, VHS; Merriam, "Personal Recollections," MHS, 6; Lucia, "Seventeenth Regiment," 569; Benedict, *Vermont in the Civil War*, 499; Ledoux and Associates, "Civil War Diary of Franklin Temple Carter"; Whitman and True, *Maine in the War*, 578; *Bangor (ME) Daily Whig and Courier*, 13 July 1864, newspapers.com; *Lewiston (ME) Daily Sun*, 15 March 1894, newspapers.com; Morning Report & Order Book, 17th Vermont, Entry 115, RG 94, NA; Regimental Order Book, 31st Maine, Entry 113: Civil War Regimental Books, ibid.; Morning Reports, 31st Maine, Entry 115, ibid.; "Morris Schaff," Bill Thayer's Web Site, last updated 7 October 2013, https://penelope .uchicago.edu/Thayer/E/Gazetteer/Places/America/United_States/Army/USMA /Cullums_Register/1975*.html.

20. U.S. Army Center of Military History, File:WILDERNESS May6.jpg, Wikipedia, accessed 28 February 2022, https://en.wikipedia.org/wiki/File:WILDERNESS _May6.jpg; Lucia, "Seventeenth Regiment," 569; *OR*, 36(1):906, 927, 934, 36(2):425;

Cogswell, *Eleventh New Hampshire,* 337, 340, 359; Benedict, *Vermont in the Civil War,* 499; Merriam, "Personal Recollections," MHS, 21–22; Ropes, "Grant's Campaign in Virginia," 380.

21. Pollard, diary, 6 May 1864, Reel F2850, Records of the Vermont Civil War Centennial Committee, VSARA, microfilm; Margaret E. Wagner, Gary W. Gallagher, and Paul Finkelman, eds., *The Library of Congress Civil War Desk Reference* (New York: Simon & Schuster Paperbacks, 2002), 467; Cogswell, *Eleventh New Hampshire,* 311, 335; David W. Lowe, ed., *Meade's Army: The Private Notebooks of Lt. Col. Theodore Lyman* (Kent, OH: Kent State University Press, 2013), 136; Peirson, "Operations of the Army of the Potomac," 210–11; *Lamoille Newsdealer* (Hyde Park, VT), 8 June 1864; Badeau, *Military History of Ulysses S. Grant,* 2:118–19; Houston, *Thirty-Second Maine,* 96; Schaff, *Wilderness,* 233; "Morris Schaff," Bill Thayer's Web Site; *OR,* 36(1):934, 36(2):460, 463; Rhea, *Wilderness,* 325–26; Merriam, "Personal Recollections," MHS, 22. The troops marched for 18.75 out of 33.5 hours, estimating that the five-minute breaks during the journey totaled a half hour. For May 6, the New Englanders started marching around 2:00 a.m. and ended around 9:00 a.m. This estimate includes an hour for navigating obstacles en route and the time needed for breakfast, with the troops covering twelve miles in six hours. For the sources used in making these calculations, see note 18.

22. *OR,* 36(1):934; *Burlington (VT) Daily Times,* 21 May 1864; Jackman, *Sixth New Hampshire,* 215–17; Potter and Potter, *Personal Experiences,* 57; Merriam, "Personal Recollections," MHS, 22; Smith to mother, 16 May 1864, Folder 6, Box 1, M131.1, Bowdoin College Library; Griffin, journal, Folder 1, Box 1, MG257, HSCC, 19; Swinton, *Army of the Potomac,* 435; U.S. Army Center of Military History, File:WILDERNESS May6.jpg; Rhea, *Wilderness,* 328. Sources occasionally refer to the use of grapeshot, which was strictly applicable to naval warfare. My inference whether the actual projectile was case or canister (here and elsewhere) is informed by eyewitness descriptions of the fighting. I did not find evidence to support Gordon Rhea's contention that the Confederates repulsed the Vermonters from this rail fence.

23. *OR,* 36(1):322; Swinton, *Army of the Potomac,* 435, 436n; Rhea, *Wilderness,* 329.

24. *OR,* 36(1):934; *Lamoille Newsdealer* (Hyde Park, VT), 8 June 1864; Cummings to wife, 15 May 1864, Folder 9, MSA 28, VHS; Merriam, "Personal Recollections," MHS, 23–24; Cogswell, *Eleventh New Hampshire,* 356; Smith to mother, 16 May 1864, Folder 6, Box 1, M131.1, Bowdoin College Library.

25. Nevins, *Diary of Battle,* 352; Benedict, *Vermont in the Civil War,* 500; *OR,* 36(1):906, 928, 36(2):461.

26. Merriam, "Personal Recollections," MHS, 24; *OR,* 36(1):906; Potter and Potter, *Personal Experiences,* 57; Porter, *Campaigning with Grant,* 61; Cogswell, *Eleventh New Hampshire,* 350.

27. Jackman, *Sixth New Hampshire* 219, 221; *OR,* 36(1):928; Merriam, "Personal Recollections," MHS, 25; Benedict, *Vermont in the Civil War,* 500; Cogswell, *Eleventh New Hampshire,* 344.

28. *OR,* 36(1):928, 36(2):461; Benedict, *Vermont in the Civil War,* 500–501, 500n2; Merriam, "Personal Recollections," MHS, 25; Cogswell, *Eleventh New Hampshire,* 341, 352, 356; Houston, *Thirty-Second Maine,* 97; *Lamoille Newsdealer* (Hyde Park, VT), 8

June 1864; Cummings to wife, 15 May 1864, Folder 9, MSA 28, VHS; Simon G. Griffin, *A History of the Town of Keene: From 1732, When the Township Was Granted by Massachusetts, to 1874, When It Became a City* (Keene, NH: Sentinel Printing, 1904), 496; Jackman, *Sixth New Hampshire,* 221.

29. Benedict, *Vermont in the Civil War,* 501; Merriam, "Personal Recollections," MHS, 26; Cogswell, *Eleventh New Hampshire,* 341, 343; Pollard, diary, 6 May 1864, Reel F2850, Records of the Vermont Civil War Centennial Committee, VSARA, microfilm; Potter and Potter, *Personal Experiences,* 57; Hodsdon, *Report of the Adjutant General of the State of Maine, . . . 1864 and 1865,* 484; Hodsdon, *Appendix D,* 279; Jackman, *Sixth New Hampshire,* 224; 31st MS.

30. Merriam, "Personal Recollections," MHS, 26–27; Benedict, *Vermont in the Civil War,* 500–501; Jackman, *Sixth New Hampshire,* 222–24; Cogswell, *Eleventh New Hampshire,* 342–43, 355–56, 358; *OR,* 36(1):928, 934, 953, 36(2):461; Cummings to wife, 15 May 1864, Folder 9, MSA 28, VHS; Potter and Potter, *Personal Experiences,* 57; Ledoux and Associates, "Civil War Diary of Franklin Temple Carter"; Houston, *Thirty-Second Maine,* 98–99; 31st MS; 17th VS.

31. *OR,* 36(1):132; 17th VS; 31st MS. For simplicity's sake, I have opted to use the overall percentage of officers and men in both outfits with prior service experience rather than determining the ratio of such individuals present for duty in each battle. The primary sources that enable a count of the Vermonters' casualties do not provide dates to indicate when a soldier was captured. Likewise, the available data for Maine casualties do not specify when twenty-two of those men were wounded and another forty-eight taken prisoner. This contributes to an artificially low total of Vermont and Maine losses in each engagement. See the conclusion for a comprehensive total of the two regiments' casualties. The regimental spreadsheets, not the *OR,* inform these and subsequent casualty calculations. This reflects the assumption that officers attempting to tally their losses in the chaotic aftermath of a battle would probably struggle to generate accurate figures, especially during an ongoing campaign. For the sources informing the spreadsheets, see introduction, note 5.

32. *OR,* 36(1):133, 198, 915; Louis C. Duncan, *The Medical Department of the United States Army in the Civil War* (Washington, DC: U.S. Surgeon-General's Office, c. 1916), chap. 9, p. 2.

33. *OR,* 36(1):190, 540, 906–7, 934–35, 36(2):462; Lowe, *Meade's Army,* 139, 146; Swan, "Battle of the Wilderness," 160; Stevens, "Sixth Corps in the Wilderness," 201; Ropes, "Grant's Campaign in Virginia," 381; Henry Alexander White, "Lee's Wrestle with Grant in the Wilderness," in Military Historical Society, *Wilderness Campaign,* 53; Porter, *Campaigning with Grant,* 61; Swinton, *Army of the Potomac,* 435; Badeau, *Military History of Ulysses S. Grant,* 2:125; Humphreys, *Virginia Campaign,* 46–47; Agassiz, *Meade's Headquarters,* 96; Schaff, *Wilderness,* 287; Potter and Potter, *Personal Experiences,* 57; Benedict, *Vermont in the Civil War,* 500–501; *Burlington (VT) Free Press,* 21 July 1865, Chronicling America; *Burlington (VT) Daily Times,* 21 May 1864; Washburn, *Adjutant & Inspector General's Office,* 74; Lucia, "Seventeenth Regiment," 569–70; Cummings to wife, 15 May 1864, Folder 9, MSA 28, VHS; *Burlington (VT) Daily Times,* 19 July 1865; *Lamoille Newsdealer* (Hyde Park, VT), June 8, 1864; unknown newspaper and issue

date, Lieutenant Colonel Charles Cummings Papers, 1863–65, Folder 9, MSA 829, VHS; *Lewiston (ME) Daily Sun,* 15 March 1894.

34. Houston, *Thirty-Second Maine,* 76, 162. Gettysburg casualty rate calculated by referring to the Army of the Potomac's present-for-duty strength as of June 30, 1863. *OR,* 27(1):151, 187.

35. Webb, "Through the Wilderness," 162; Humphreys, *Virginia Campaign,* 72; Rhea, *Wilderness,* 437; *OR,* 36(1):113, 908; Jackman, *Sixth New Hampshire,* 233n; Houston, *Thirty-Second Maine,* 99; Swinton, *Army of the Potomac,* 446. As of May 8, 1864, a detachment of the 2nd Maryland Veteran Volunteer Infantry Regiment joined the Second Brigade.

36. *OR,* 36(1):907–8, 928; Cogswell, *Eleventh New Hampshire,* 361; Jackman, *Sixth New Hampshire,* 234–35; Houston, *Thirty-Second Maine,* 99, 108–10; Merriam, "Personal Recollections," MHS, 20; Peirson, "Operations of the Army of the Potomac," 219; Perry, diary, 8–9 May 1864, MS 2187, NYHS; Pollard, diary, 7–8 May 1864, Reel F2850, Records of the Vermont Civil War Centennial Committee, VSARA, microfilm.

37. Peirson, "Operations of the Army of the Potomac," 220–21; *OR,* 36(1):908–9, 36(2):549; Houston, *Thirty-Second Maine,* 111, 113–14, 117, 120–21; Ledoux and Associates, "Civil War Diary of Franklin Temple Carter"; Jackman, *Sixth New Hampshire,* 240–41; Cogswell, *Eleventh New Hampshire,* 363; Lord, *Ninth Regiment,* 370; C. W. Wilcox, "Prisoners-of-War, at Macon and Savannah, Georgia, and Charleston and Columbia, South Carolina," in Lord, *Ninth Regiment,* 563; 17th VS; 31st MS; Peck, *Revised Roster,* 581; Ancestry, Vermont 17th Volunteer Infantry, Fold3; Pollard, diary, 9–10 May 1864, Reel F2850, Records of the Vermont Civil War Centennial Committee, VSARA, microfilm; Perry, diary, 11 May 1864, MS 2187, NYHS; Merriam, "Personal Recollections," MHS, 30; Larned to sister, 10 May 1864, Box 4, Daniel Read Larned Papers, MSS29470, LOC, microfilm.

38. Ropes, "Grant's Campaign in Virginia," 384; *OR,* 36(1):192, 36(2):643; Houston, *Thirty-Second Maine,* 126; G. Norton Galloway, "Hand-to-Hand Fighting at Spotsylvania," in Johnson and Buel, *Battles and Leaders,* 174; Wilcox, "Prisoners-of-War," 564; Merriam, "Personal Recollections," MHS, 30.

39. *OR,* 36(2):629, 643, 677–79; Merlin E. Sumner, ed. and comp., *The Diary of Cyrus B. Comstock* (Dayton, OH: Morningside, 1987), 266; Badeau, *Military History of Ulysses S. Grant,* 2:177.

40. Potter and Potter, *Personal Experiences,* 58, 80; Jackman, *Sixth New Hampshire,* 240–41; Badeau, *Military History of Ulysses S. Grant,* 2:179; Merriam, "Personal Recollections," MHS, 31; Woodbury, *Burnside and the Ninth Army Corps,* 383; Galloway, "Hand-to-Hand Fighting," 172; Ledoux and Associates, "Civil War Diary of Franklin Temple Carter."

41. Jackman, *Sixth New Hampshire,* 240–41, 243; Merriam, "Personal Recollections," MHS, 34–35; Cogswell, *Eleventh New Hampshire,* 363; *OR,* 36(1):909, 935; Houston, *Thirty-Second Maine,* 121, 133–34; Lord, *Ninth Regiment,* 370; *Burlington (VT) Free Press,* 21 July 1865; Morning Report & Order Book, 17th Vermont, Entry 115, RG 94, NA; Lucia, "Seventeenth Regiment," 570; Hodsdon, *Report of the Adjutant General of the State of Maine, . . . 1864 and 1865,* 484.

42. Jackman, *Sixth New Hampshire,* 241–43; *OR,* 36(1):335, 909, 935; Houston, *Thirty-Second Maine,* 126, 133–34; Lord, *Ninth Regiment,* 371; Cogswell, *Eleventh New Hampshire,* 364; Badeau, *Military History of Ulysses S. Grant,* 2:174; Lucia, "Seventeenth Regiment," 570; Rhea, *Battles for Spotsylvania,* 244.

43. Merriam, "Personal Recollections," MHS, 31; *OR,* 36(1):909; Jackman, *Sixth New Hampshire,* 242; Potter and Potter, *Personal Experiences,* 80; Cogswell, *Eleventh New Hampshire,* 368.

44. Merriam, "Personal Recollections," MHS, 31–32; *OR,* 36(1):935; Jackman, *Sixth New Hampshire,* 242, 245; Houston, *Thirty-Second Maine,* 131; Wilcox, "Prisoners-of-War," 564; Smith to mother, 14 May 1864, Folder 6, Box 1, M131.1, Bowdoin College Library.

45. Merriam, "Personal Recollections," MHS, 31–32; *OR,* 36(1):935–36; Lord, *Ninth Regiment,* 372; Benedict, *Vermont in the Civil War,* 503n; Woodbury, *Burnside and the Ninth Army Corps,* 383; Perry, diary, 12 May 1864, MS 2187, NYHS; Coffin to wife, 15 May 1864, Container 298408, Lt. Voranus L. Coffin Papers, RG 29: Maine State Archives Gifts, MSA.

46. Merriam, "Personal Recollections," MHS, 33; *OR,* 36(1):936; Perry, diary, 12 May 1864, MS 2187, NYHS; Entry 4993: Letters Sent, Jan. 1864–July 1865, RG 393: Records of U.S. Army Continental Commands, pt. 2, NA.

47. *OR,* 36(1):681, 910, 928, 36(2):680; Jackman, *Sixth New Hampshire,* 246–47; Lord, *Ninth Regiment,* 374; Potter and Potter, *Personal Experiences,* 80; Merriam, "Personal Recollections," MHS, 33; Coffin to wife, 15 May 1864, Container 298408, RG 29, MSA; Houston, *Thirty-Second Maine,* 136–37.

48. Cogswell, *Eleventh New Hampshire,* 369; Houston, *Thirty-Second Maine,* 133; *OR,* 36(1):72, 929, 936, 36(2):680; Lord, *Ninth Regiment,* 374; Ledoux and Associates, "Civil War Diary of Franklin Temple Carter"; Griffin, journal, Folder 1, Box 1, MG257, HSCC, 20–21; Jackman, *Sixth New Hampshire,* 242–43; Lowe, *Meade's Army,* 157; Smith to mother, 14 May 1864, Folder 6, Box 1, M131.1, Bowdoin College Library; Merriam, "Personal Recollections," MHS, 34–35; Badeau, *Military History of Ulysses S. Grant,* 2:192; Woodbury, *Burnside and the Ninth Army Corps,* 388; Whitehill to mother and brothers, 16 May 1864, MSA 520, VHS; Perry, diary, 14–16 May 1864, MS 2187, NYHS.

49. Houston, *Thirty-Second Maine,* 151–52, 154; Jackman, *Sixth New Hampshire,* 247; Merriam, "Personal Recollections," MHS, 34–35; Whitehill to mother and brothers, 16 May 1864, MSA 520, VHS; Larned to Henry A. Howe, 17 May 1864, Box 4, MSS29470, LOC; Perry, diary, 14 May 1864, MS 2187, NYHS.

50. Sumner, *Diary of Cyrus B. Comstock,* 267; Ledoux and Associates, "Civil War Diary of Franklin Temple Carter"; *OR,* 36(1):72; Jackman, *Sixth New Hampshire,* 247, 251; Larned to sister, 13 May 1864, Box 4, MSS29470, LOC; Larned to unknown, 20 May 1864, ibid.; Perry, diary, 13 May 1864, MS 2187, NYHS; Hodsdon, *Appendix D,* 746; Pollard, diary, 13–15 May 1864, Reel F2850, Records of the Vermont Civil War Centennial Committee, VSARA, microfilm; Smith to mother, 14 May 1864, Folder 6, Box 1, M131.1, Bowdoin College Library; Coffin to wife, 15, 18 May 1864, Container 298408, RG 29, MSA; Cogswell, *Eleventh New Hampshire,* 368; Lord, *Ninth Regiment,* 375; Houston, *Thirty-Second Maine,* 153–54.

51. *Bangor (ME) Daily Whig and Courier,* 23 May 1864, newspapers.com; Hodsdon, *Appendix D,* 733; Cummings to wife, 20 May 1864, Folder 9, MSA 28, VHS; Larned to sister, 13 May 1864, Box 4, MSS29470, LOC; *OR,* 36(2):826.

52. Houston, *Thirty-Second Maine,* 154; Lord, *Ninth Regiment,* 375–76; Peirson, "Operations of the Army of the Potomac," 266; William P. Shreve, "The Operations of the Army of the Potomac, May 13–June 2, 1864," in Military Historical Society, *Wilderness Campaign,* 295; Jackman, *Sixth New Hampshire,* 250; *OR,* 36(2):870; Lowe, *Meade's Army,* 162; Sumner, *Diary of Cyrus B. Comstock,* 268; Badeau, *Military History of Ulysses S. Grant,* 2:179; Coffin to wife, 18 May 1864, Container 298408, RG 29, MSA; *Burlington (VT) Free Press,* 21 July 1865.

53. Lowe, *Meade's Army,* 162; Ledoux and Associates, "Civil War Diary of Franklin Temple Carter"; Jackman, *Sixth New Hampshire,* 250–51; Lord, *Ninth Regiment,* 383; Houston, *Thirty-Second Maine,* 154; White, "Lee's Wrestle with Grant," 67.

54. Jackman, *Sixth New Hampshire,* 251–52; Lord, *Ninth Regiment,* 375–76, 383; Cogswell, *Eleventh New Hampshire,* 370; Benedict, *Vermont in the Civil War,* 505; Houston, *Thirty-Second Maine,* 156; Rhea, *North Anna,* 140; Committee of the Regimental Association, *History of the Thirty-Fifth Massachusetts Volunteers, 1862–1865* (Boston: Mills, Knight, Printers, 1884), 232.

55. Charles Carleton Coffin, *The Boys of '61; or, Four Years of Fighting* [. . .] (Boston: Estes and Lauriat, 1881), 330; Jackman, *Sixth New Hampshire,* 252–53, 254n, 255; Ledoux and Associates, "Civil War Diary of Franklin Temple Carter"; Lowe, *Meade's Army,* 162; Houston, *Thirty-Second Maine,* 154–55, 157; Merriam, "Personal Recollections," MHS, 36; Perry, diary, 18 May 1864, MS 2187, NYHS; *OR,* 36(1):929; Lord, *Ninth Regiment,* 376.

56. *OR,* 36(1):148; Jackman, *Sixth New Hampshire,* 255; Benedict, *Vermont in the Civil War,* 504; Morning Report & Order Book, 17th Vermont, Entry 115, RG 94, NA; Merriam, "Personal Recollections," MHS, 34.

57. Lucia, "Seventeenth Regiment," 570; Theodore Gerrish and John S. Hutchinson, *The Blue and the Gray: A Graphic History of the Army of the Potomac and that of Northern Virginia* [. . .] (Bangor, ME: Brady, Mace, 1884), 497; Grant, *Personal Memoirs,* 353; Shreve, "Operations of the Army of the Potomac," 295; *OR,* 36(1):68, 192, 910–11, 929, 936; Woodbury, *Burnside and the Ninth Army Corps,* 383, 388; Potter and Potter, *Personal Experiences,* 59; Cummings to wife, 15 May 1864, Folder 9, MSA 28, VHS; Coffin to wife, 15 May 1864, Container 298408, RG 29, MSA; Hodsdon, *Appendix D,* 737; *Burlington (VT) Free Press,* 21 July 1865; J. H. Stine, *History of the Army of the Potomac* (Philadelphia: J. B. Rodgers Printing, 1892), 625; Ropes, "Grant's Campaign in Virginia," 391; Livermore, "Grant's Campaign against Lee," 438–39; Swinton, *Army of the Potomac,* 453; Badeau, *Military History of Ulysses S. Grant,* 2:179; Lowe, *Meade's Army,* 156.

58. Peck, *Revised Roster,* 575; "Joseph Rutherford to [Hannah Rutherford]," 18 November 1864, Joseph Chase Rutherford Correspondence, Vermonters in the Civil War, UVMLDC, https://cdi.uvm.edu/manuscript/uvmcdi-94446.

59. Sumner, *Diary of Cyrus B. Comstock,* 266; *OR,* 36(1):231; Potter and Potter, *Personal Experiences,* 59.

60. Potter and Potter, *Personal Experiences,* 59.

1. *New York Herald,* 26 May 1864, Chronicling America; Ropes, "Grant's Campaign in Virginia," in Military Historical Society, *Wilderness Campaign,* 405.

2. Woodbury, *Burnside and the Ninth Army Corps,* 429.

3. Perry, diary, 19, 21–22 May 1864, Henry O. Perry Diaries, MS 2187, NYHS; Rhea, *North Anna,* 157, 246; Cummings to wife, 20 May 1864, Folder 9, MSA 28, VHS; Jackman, *Sixth New Hampshire,* 266n; Cogswell, *Eleventh New Hampshire,* 371, 471; Houston, *Thirty-Second Maine,* 164; Shreve, "Operations of the Army of the Potomac," in Military Historical Society, *Wilderness Campaign,* 301; *OR,* 36(1):19, 75, 929; Hess, *Trench Warfare under Grant and Lee,* 121. The primary sources lack sufficient mileage information, so I estimated the straight-line distance between Bethel Church and Ox Ford, the start and end points for the movement of May 23, and rounded up for the total since the winding nature of the roads would have equaled a longer mileage than a straight-line measure. "Civil War in Central Virginia: On to Richmond," Civil War Trails, accessed 3 November 2022, https://www.civilwartrails.org/docs/Central -brochure.pdf.

4. Perry, diary, 20 May 1864, MS 2187, NYHS; *OR,* 36(1):75–76, 929; Ledoux and Associates, "Civil War Diary of Franklin Temple Carter"; Lord, *Ninth Regiment,* 377, 392–95; Shreve, "Operations of the Army of the Potomac," 296, 305; Cummings to wife, 20 May 1864, Charles Cummings Papers, Folder 9, MSA 28, VHS, transcription.

5. Perry, diary, 19–22 May 1864, MS 2187, NYHS; Larned to sister, 20, 22 May 1864, Box 4, Daniel Read Larned Papers, MSS29470, LOC, microfilm; *OR,* 36(1):912; Cummings to wife, 20 May 1864, Folder 9, MSA 28, VHS; Ledoux and Associates, "Civil War Diary of Franklin Temple Carter"; Jackman, *Sixth New Hampshire,* 255; Cogswell, *Eleventh New Hampshire,* 370–71; Lord, *Ninth Regiment,* 376–77; Houston, *Thirty-Second Maine,* 166.

6. *OR,* 36(3):96, 135, 229; Lowe, *Meade's Army,* 169, 173; Sparks, *Inside Lincoln's Army,* 376; Ledoux and Associates, "Civil War Diary of Franklin Temple Carter"; Cummings to wife, 20 May 1864, Folder 9, MSA 28, VHS; James W. Lathe, "Told in Home Letters," in Lord, *Ninth Regiment,* 431; Shreve, "Operations of the Army of the Potomac," 301.

7. 31st MS; 17th VS; *OR,* 36(1):78; Cummings to wife, 20, 31 May 1864, Folder 9, MSA 28, VHS; Regimental Order Book, 31st Maine, Entry 113: Civil War Regimental Books, RG 94: Records of the Adjutant General's Office, NA; Morning Report & Order Book, 17th Vermont, Entry 115: Civil War Regimental Books, ibid.; *Burlington (VT) Free Press,* 21 July 1865; Livermore, "Grant's Campaign against Lee," in Military Historical Society, *Wilderness Campaign,* 412.

8. Shreve, "Operations of the Army of the Potomac," 309; *OR,* 36(1):19, 21, 78, 543; Cummings to wife, 31 May 1864, Folder 9, MSA 28, VHS; Ledoux and Associates, "Civil War Diary of Franklin Temple Carter"; Houston, *Thirty-Second Maine,* 171; Perry, diary, 25–26 May 1864, MS 2187, NYHS; Lord, *Ninth Regiment,* 408; Merriam, "Personal Recollections of the War for the Union," Collection S-5186, MHS, 38.

9. *OR,* 36(1):912, 36(3):166; Lord, *Ninth Regiment,* 408.

10. *OR,* 36(1):341, 912, 36(3):129, 134; Cummings to wife, 30 May 1864, Folder 9, MSA 28, VHS; Perry, diary, 24 May 1864, MS 2187, NYHS; Lord, *Ninth Regiment,* 408; Cogswell, *Eleventh New Hampshire,* 371; Houston, *Thirty-Second Maine,* 169, 180; Larned to Henry A. Howe, 25 May 1864, Box 4, MSS29470, LOC; Nevins, *Diary of Battle,* 142.

11. Cummings to wife, 30 May 1864, Folder 7, MSA 28, VHS; Houston, *Thirty-Second Maine,* 169; Cogswell, *Eleventh New Hampshire,* 372; Merriam, "Personal Recollections," MHS, 37; Shreve, "Operations of the Army of the Potomac," 308.

12. *OR,* 36(1):363, 36(3):169; Merriam, "Personal Recollections," MHS, 37; Cummings to wife, 31 May 1864, Folder 9, MSA 28, VHS; Lord, *Ninth Regiment,* 409; Woodbury, *Burnside and the Ninth Army Corps,* 394.

13. *OR,* 36(1):21, 77, 364, 36(3):213; Cummings to wife, 31 May 1864, Folder 9, MSA 28, VHS; Merriam, "Personal Recollections," MHS, 38–39; Perry, diary, 25–26 May 1864, MS 2187, NYHS; Ledoux and Associates, "Civil War Diary of Franklin Temple Carter"; Lord, *Ninth Regiment,* 404; Shreve, "Operations of the Army of the Potomac," 310; Rhea, *North Anna,* 157.

14. Houston, *Thirty-Second Maine,* 187–88; Cummings to wife, 31 May 1864, Folder 9, MSA 28, VHS.

15. Houston, *Thirty-Second Maine,* 170; Merriam, "Personal Recollections," MHS, 38; Cogswell, *Eleventh New Hampshire,* 575; Cummings to wife, 31 May 1864, Folder 9, MSA 28, VHS.

16. 17th VS; 31st MS; *OR,* 36(1):162. Casualty figures for May 22 to June 1, which encompass the fighting at North Anna and a portion of the clash at Cold Harbor, are from the *OR.*

17. Badeau, *Military History of Ulysses S. Grant,* 2:232; *OR,* 36(1):913; Woodbury, *Burnside and the Ninth Army Corps,* 392–93.

18. *OR,* 36(3):206.

19. *OR,* 36(1):21, 36(3):598; Jackman, *Sixth New Hampshire,* 271n; Cogswell, *Eleventh New Hampshire,* 471; Cummings to wife, 31 May 1864, Folder 9, MSA 28, VHS; Ledoux and Associates, "Civil War Diary of Franklin Temple Carter"; Perry, diary, 26 May 1864, MS 2187, NYHS; Grant, *Personal Memoirs,* 364.

20. *OR,* 36(1):79, 930, 36(3):206; Lord, *Ninth Regiment,* 409–10; Ledoux and Associates, "Civil War Diary of Franklin Temple Carter"; Cogswell, *Eleventh New Hampshire,* 372, 471, 575; Humphreys, *Virginia Campaign,* 161; Grant, *Personal Memoirs,* 363–64; Houston, *Thirty-Second Maine,* 196–99, 211; Cummings to wife, 31 May 1864, Folder 9, MSA 28, VHS; Perry, diary, 26 May 1864, MS 2187, NYHS; Jackman, *Sixth New Hampshire,* 273.

21. Lord, *Ninth Regiment,* 410; Houston, *Thirty-Second Maine,* 196–200; *OR,* 36(1):83, 36(3):309; Cummings to wife, 31 May, 4 June 1864, Folder 9, MSA 28, VHS; Agassiz, *Meade's Headquarters,* 139; Ledoux and Associates, "Civil War Diary of Franklin Temple Carter."

22. Merriam, "Personal Recollections," MHS, 39; *OR,* 36(1):83–84, 87, 930; Ledoux and Associates, "Civil War Diary of Franklin Temple Carter"; Houston, *Thirty-Second Maine,* 204, 212; Lord, *Ninth Regiment,* 410–11; Perry, diary, 31 May, 1–2 June 1864, MS 2187, NYHS; Cogswell, *Eleventh New Hampshire,* 471, 496; Cummings to

wife, 2 June 1864 (second letter of same date), Folder 9, MSA 28, VHS; Jackman, *Sixth New Hampshire,* 274; Lucia, "Seventeenth Regiment," 570.

23. Merriam, "Personal Recollections," MHS, 44; *OR,* 36(1):930; Houston, *Thirty-Second Maine,* 204, 212; Lord, *Ninth Regiment,* 405, 411; Newell T. Dutton, "Tolopotomoy [*sic*] from Another Point of View," ibid., 423–24; Cogswell, *Eleventh New Hampshire,* 471; Cummings to wife, 2 June 1864 (second letter of same date), Folder 9, MSA 28, VHS.

24. Swinton, *Army of the Potomac,* 483–84; *OR,* 36(1):933; Benedict, *Vermont in the Civil War,* 506; Cummings to wife, 4 June 1864, Folder 9, MSA 28, VHS; Merriam, "Personal Recollections," MHS, 39; Ledoux and Associates, "Civil War Diary of Franklin Temple Carter"; Jackman, *Sixth New Hampshire,* 274–75; Cogswell, *Eleventh New Hampshire,* 496; Dutton, "Tolopotomoy [*sic*]," 424; Humphreys, *Virginia Campaign,* 179. As of June 2, 1864, the entire 2nd Maryland (rather than solely a detachment) served in the Second Brigade, Second Division, Ninth Corps. *OR,* 36(1):176.

25. Lord, *Ninth Regiment,* 405–6; Theodore Lyman, "Operations of the Army of the Potomac, June 5–15, 1864," in *Petersburg, Chancellorsville, Gettysburg,* vol. 5 of *Papers of the Military Historical Society,* comp. Military Historical Society (1906; repr., Wilmington, NC: Broadfoot, 1989), 5; Thomas L. Livermore, "The Failure to Take Petersburg, June 15, 1864," ibid., 37; Merriam, "Personal Recollections," MHS, 42; Agassiz, *Meade's Headquarters,* 148n; Badeau, *Military History of Ulysses S. Grant,* 2:287; Houston, *Thirty-Second Maine,* 207, 214–15; Gerrish and Hutchinson, *Blue and the Gray,* 511; Cummings to wife, 4 June 1864, Folder 9, MSA 28, VHS.

26. Badeau, *Military History of Ulysses S. Grant,* 2:290, 305; *OR,* 36(3):494; Lucia, "Seventeenth Regiment," 570; Grant, *Personal Memoirs,* 368.

27. Lyman, "Operations of the Army of the Potomac," 5; Shreve, "Operations of the Army of the Potomac," 317.

28. Merriam, "Personal Recollections," MHS, 39, 44; *OR,* 36(3):501; Shreve, "Operations of the Army of the Potomac," 316; Cummings to wife, 2 June 1864 (two letters of same date), Folder 9, MSA 28, VHS.

29. Livermore, "Grant's Campaign against Lee," 412; Lyman, "Operations of the Army of the Potomac," 19; Morning Report & Order Book, 17th Vermont, Entry 115, RG 94, NA.

30. Hodsdon, *Appendix D,* 733; Merriam, "Personal Recollections," MHS, 44; *Burlington (VT) Free Press,* 21 July 1865; Regimental Descriptive Book, 31st Maine, Entry 114: Civil War Regimental Books, RG 94, NA; Cummings to wife, 2 June 1864 (second letter of same date), Folder 9, MSA 28, VHS; *OR,* 36(1):936. The roster for the 31st Maine does not provide the name of the individual who served as acting major while Daniel White commanded the unit before his promotion to colonel on 8 July 1864.

31. Merriam, "Personal Recollections," MHS, 40; Badeau, *Military History of Ulysses S. Grant,* 2:289–90, 290n; Cummings to wife, 31 May, 2 June 1864 (second letter of same date), Folder 9, MSA 28, VHS.

32. Houston, *Thirty-Second Maine,* 218; Jackman, *Sixth New Hampshire,* 275n, 276–77; Merriam, "Personal Recollections," MHS, 41; Lucia, "Seventeenth Regiment,"

570; *OR,* 36(1):946, 952, 36(3):494; Rhea, *Cold Harbor,* 369; Benedict, *Vermont in the Civil War,* 506.

33. Houston, *Thirty-Second Maine,* 220, 223, 228; *OR,* 36(1):930; Merriam, "Personal Recollections," MHS, 41–42; Frances Coffin Sullivan, untitled biographical sketch, 1979, Container 298408, Lt. Voranus L. Coffin Papers, RG 29: Maine State Archives Gifts, MSA, typescript; Cummings to wife, 4 June 1864, Folder 7, MSA 28, VHS; Lathe, "Told in Home Letters," 430.

34. Rhea, *Cold Harbor,* 380; *OR,* 36(1):937; Cummings to wife, 4 June 1864, Folder 7, MSA 28, VHS; Merriam, "Personal Recollections," MHS, 42. During the Battle of the Crater (July 30, 1864), Brigadier General Griffin temporarily gave authority over his troops to Col. Daniel White of the 31st Maine. That instance lends credibility to the assertion that Griffin acted similarly at Cold Harbor. For more on the Crater, see chapter 4.

35. *OR,* 36(1):88, 544, 36(3):526, 528–29; Houston, *Thirty-Second Maine,* 225; Merriam, "Personal Recollections," MHS, 42; Cummings to wife, 4 June 1864, Folder 7, MSA 28, VHS; Ledoux and Associates, "Civil War Diary of Franklin Temple Carter"; Perry, diary, 4 June 1864, MS 2187, NYHS.

36. Ledoux and Associates, "Civil War Diary of Franklin Temple Carter"; *OR,* 36(1):930; Cogswell, *Eleventh New Hampshire,* 497; Houston, *Thirty-Second Maine,* 225, 233; Jackman, *Sixth New Hampshire,* 277; Rhea, *Cold Harbor,* 376; Perry, diary, 4 June 1864, MS 2187, NYHS; Swinton, *Army of the Potomac,* 487; Agassiz, *Meade's Headquarters,* 140; Meade, *Life and Letters,* 201.

37. *OR,* 36(1):11, 22; Cummings to wife, 5 June 1864, Folder 7, MSA 28, VHS; Merriam, "Personal Recollections," MHS, 43; Swinton, *Army of the Potomac,* 498; Benedict, *Vermont in the Civil War,* 507; Houston, *Thirty-Second Maine,* 233.

38. Ledoux and Associates, "Civil War Diary of Franklin Temple Carter"; Griffin, journal, Folder 1, Box 1, MG257, HSCC, 21; Lucia, "Seventeenth Regiment," 570; Lord, *Ninth Regiment,* 407; Lathe, "Told in Home Letters," 433–34; Merriam, "Personal Recollections," MHS, 43; Houston, *Thirty-Second Maine,* 239–40; Cummings to wife, 5–6 June 1864, Folder 7, MSA 28, VHS.

39. Merriam, "Personal Recollections," MHS, 43–44; Nevins, *Diary of Battle,* 406; Ledoux and Associates, "Civil War Diary of Franklin Temple Carter"; Jackman, *Sixth New Hampshire,* 278; Houston, *Thirty-Second Maine,* 240; McMahon, "Cold Harbor," in Johnson and Buel, *Battles and Leaders,* 219; Lathe, "Told in Home Letters," 433.

40. Humphreys, *Virginia Campaign,* 190–91; Ledoux and Associates, "Civil War Diary of Franklin Temple Carter"; *OR,* 36(1):96; Lyman, "Operations of the Army of the Potomac," 18; Rhea, *On to Petersburg,* 58; Lord, *Ninth Regiment,* 414; Lathe, "Told in Home Letters," 433; McMahon, "Cold Harbor," 219; Larned to sister, 9 June 1864, Box 4, MSS29470, LOC; Houston, *Thirty-Second Maine,* 242; Cummings to wife, 31 May 1864, Folder 9, MSA 28, VHS; Cummings to wife, 6 June 1864, Folder 7, MSA 28, VHS.

41. Cummings to wife, 6 June 1864, Folder 7, MSA 28, VHS; Jackman, *Sixth New Hampshire,* 278, 280; Perry, diary, 4 June 1864, MS 2187, NYHS; *OR,* 36(3):711; Ledoux and Associates, "Civil War Diary of Franklin Temple Carter"; Lathe, "Told in Home

Letters," 433; Houston, *Thirty-Second Maine,* 241; Lucia, "Seventeenth Regiment," 570; Potter and Potter, *Personal Experiences,* 61; Cogswell, *Eleventh New Hampshire,* 406; Lauren K. Thompson, *Friendly Enemies: Soldier Fraternization throughout the American Civil War* (Lincoln: University of Nebraska Press, 2020), 15, 168, https://doi.org /10.2307/j.ctv125jvdv.

42. Woodbury, *Burnside and the Ninth Army Corps,* 401; McMahon, "Cold Harbor," 219; Ledoux and Associates, "Civil War Diary of Franklin Temple Carter"; Lathe, "Told in Home Letters," 433; Lyman, "Operations of the Army of the Potomac," 15, 17–18; *OR,* 36(1):248; Cummings to wife, 5 June 1864, Folder 7, MSA 28, VHS; Cogswell, *Eleventh New Hampshire,* 406.

43. 31st MS; 17th VS; Morning Report & Order Book, 17th Vermont, Entry 115, RG 94, NA; Merriam, "Personal Recollections," MHS, 43; *OR,* 36(1):176.

44. Nevins, *Diary of Battle,* 401; Merriam, "Personal Recollections," MHS, 40, 42; Gerrish and Hutchinson, *Blue and the Gray,* 513; Grant, *Personal Memoirs,* 368; Badeau, *Military History of Ulysses S. Grant,* 2:281–82, 305; Cummings to wife, 4 June 1864, Folder 7, MSA 28, VHS.

45. Cummings to wife, 6 June 1864, Folder 7, MSA 28, VHS; *OR,* 36(1):914, 937; Potter and Potter, *Personal Experiences,* 60; Cogswell, *Eleventh New Hampshire,* 496; *Bangor (ME) Daily Whig and Courier,* 20 June 1864; *Burlington (VT) Free Press,* 21 July 1865; *Lewiston (ME) Daily Sun,* 15 March 1894; Woodbury, *Burnside and the Ninth Army Corps,* 398; Jackman, *Sixth New Hampshire,* 275n; Badeau, *Military History of Ulysses S. Grant,* 2:299.

46. Cummings to wife, 4 June 1864, Folder 7, MSA 28, VHS.

47. Woodbury, *Burnside and the Ninth Army Corps,* 402.

48. *OR,* 36(1):12, 22; Meade, *Life and Letters,* 201.

49. Nevins, *Diary of Battle,* 406; Badeau, *Military History of Ulysses S. Grant,* 2:324.

4. THE FIRST UNION OFFENSIVE AT PETERSBURG
AND THE BATTLE OF THE CRATER

1. *OR,* ser. 3, 5:668; Sheahan to father, 21 June 1864, Folder 9, Box 1, John Parris Sheahan Papers, Collection 184, MHS; *Rutland (VT) Weekly Herald,* 30 June 1864, Chronicling America.

2. *OR,* 36(1):22–23, 25, 235; Hess, *In the Trenches at Petersburg,* 285; Rhea, *On to Petersburg,* 63, 311; Badeau, *Military History of Ulysses S. Grant,* 2:341.

3. Lucia, "Seventeenth Regiment," 570; Rhea, *On to Petersburg,* 180; *OR,* 36(1):253, 36(3):749, 40(1):521–22, 568; Frank S. Ritter, "A Drummer Boy's Service in the Ranks," in Lord, *Ninth Regiment,* 420; Newell T. Dutton, "The Camp on the James River," ibid., 428; Cummings to wife, 15 June 1864, Charles Cummings Papers, Folder 9, MSA 28, VHS, transcription; Cumming to wife, 18 June 1864, Folder 7, ibid.; Perry, diary, 14–15 June 1864, Henry O. Perry Diaries, MS 2187, NYHS; Cogswell, *Eleventh New Hampshire,* 472; Houston, *Thirty-Second Maine,* 254–56; Porter, *Campaigning with Grant,* 197; Lyman, "Operations of the Army of the Potomac," in Military Historical Society,

Petersburg, Chancellorsville, Gettysburg, 23; Merriam, "Personal Recollections of the War for the Union," Collection S-5186, MHS, 47; Eldin J. Hartshorn, diary, 15 June 1864, Civil War Diary of Eldin J. Hartshorn, 1864, Folder 17, MSC 209, VHS; Ledoux and Associates, "Civil War Diary of Franklin Temple Carter."

4. Cogswell, *Eleventh New Hampshire,* 376; John C. Ropes, "The Failure to Take Petersburg on June 15–18, 1864," in Military Historical Society, *Petersburg, Chancellorsville, Gettysburg,* 167; *Green Mountain Freeman* (Montpelier, VT), 12 July 1864, Chronicling America; Lucia, "Seventeenth Regiment," 570–71; Peck, *Revised Roster,* 590; *OR,* 36(1):253, 40(1):196, 40(2):65–66; Dutton, "Camp on the James River," 429; Hartshorn, diary, 16 June 1864, Folder 17, MSC 209, VHS; Kathryn Shively, *Nature's Civil War: Common Soldiers and the Environment in 1862 Virginia* (Chapel Hill: University of North Carolina Press, 2013), 5, https://doi.org/10.5149/9781469610771_meier; Morning Report & Order Book, 17th Vermont, Entry 115: Civil War Regimental Books, RG 94: Records of the Adjutant General's Office, NA.

5. Cogswell, *Eleventh New Hampshire,* 472, 497; Lowe, *Meade's Army,* 207; Lucia, "Seventeenth Regiment," 570–71; *OR,* 36(1):25, 40(1):522, 544, 568, 40(2):97; Greene, *Campaign of Giants,* 130; Hartshorn, diary, 16 June 1864, Folder 17, MSC 209, VHS; Perry, diary, 16 June 1864, MS 2187, NYHS; Cummings to wife, 18 June 1864, Folder 7, MSA 28, VHS; William H. King to wife, 22 June 1864, William H. King Letters, 1856–70, Folder 5, MSA 677, VHS; Smith to aunt, 20 June 1864, Folder 6, Box 1, Horatio Fox Smith Letters, M131.1, Bowdoin College Library; Smith to unknown, no date, ibid.; Charles Carleton Coffin, *Redeeming the Republic: The Third Period of the War of the Rebellion in the Year 1864* (New York: Harper & Brothers, 1890), 325; Dutton, "Camp on the James River," 429; Lord, *Ninth Regiment,* 444; Houston, *Thirty-Second Maine,* 269–70; Humphreys, *Virginia Campaign,* 216–17; Merriam, "Personal Recollections," MHS, 49.

6. Ropes, "Failure to Take Petersburg," 163, 167; Lord, *Ninth Regiment,* 444–45, 671; Franklin J. Burnham, "In the Trenches," ibid., 459; Cogswell, *Eleventh New Hampshire,* 376; *OR,* 40(1):522, 545, 568; Coffin, *Redeeming the Republic,* 325; Greene, *Campaign of Giants,* 147.

7. Meade, *Life and Letters,* 204; *OR,* 40(1):569; *OR,* ser. 3, 5:668; Smith to unknown, 18 June 1864, Folder 6, Box 1, M131.1, Bowdoin College Library; Lucia, "Seventeenth Regiment," 570; Morning Report & Order Book, 17th Vermont, Entry 115, RG 94, NA.

8. Cummings to wife, 18 June 1864, Folder 7, MSA 28, VHS; Smith to unknown, undated, Folder 6, Box 1, M131.1, Bowdoin College Library; Merriam, "Personal Recollections," MHS, 48; Ropes, "Failure to Take Petersburg," 164, 167.

9. Charles C. Cummings to Adjutant and Inspector General of Vermont, 15 June 1864, Reel F26085, Records of the Adjutant and Inspector General, VSARA, microfilm; Hodsdon, *Appendix D,* 733; Smith to unknown, 18 June 1864, Folder 6, Box 1, M131.1, Bowdoin College Library; Merriam, "Personal Recollections," MHS, 49; William R. Currier et al. to Governor of Maine and Council, 11 June 1864, approved by Simon G. Griffin on 12 June 1864, 31st Maine Regiment, Container 353956, Incoming Military Correspondence, Office of the Adjutant General, RG 15, MSA.

10. *OR,* 40(1):545, 569; Lucia, "Seventeenth Regiment," 571; Cummings to wife,

18 June 1864, Folder 7, MSA 28, VHS; Greene, *Campaign of Giants*, 149; Potter and Potter, *Personal Experiences*, 61; Merriam, "Personal Recollections," MHS, 49; *Bangor (ME) Daily Whig and Courier*, 25 June 1864, newspapers.com; Coffin, *Boys of '61*, 365.

11. Lord, *Ninth Regiment*, 445–46; S. H. Perry, "Establishing a Claim," ibid., 481; *OR*, 40(1):318, 569, 42(2):809; Greene, *Campaign of Giants*, 150; Peck, *Revised Roster*, 575; Smith to unknown, 18 June 1864, Folder 6, Box 1, M131.1, Bowdoin College Library; Cummings to wife, 18 June, 11 July 1864, Folder 7, MSA 28, VHS; Woodbury, *Burnside and the Ninth Army Corps*, 409; Benedict, *Vermont in the Civil War*, 509, 509n1, 519n; Merriam, "Personal Recollections," MHS, 49; Houston, *Thirty-Second Maine*, 279; Joseph S. Harlow to Governor of Maine, 12 July 1864, Incoming Military Correspondence, Office of the Adjutant General, RG 15, MSA; H. Gilmore to Governor of Maine, 25 June 1864, ibid.; Zeller, "My Soldier Boy Mark," 55, Mark B. Slayton Civil War Letters, 1863, Folder 15, MSA 518, VHS; 17th VS.

12. *OR*, 40(1):522, 545; Merriam, "Personal Recollections," MHS, 49–50; Houston, *Thirty-Second Maine*, 276, 280; Perry, diary, 17 June 1864, MS 2187, NYHS; Cummings to wife, 18 June 1864, Folder 7, MSA 28, VHS; Sheahan to father, 18 June 1864, Folder 9, Box 1, Collection 184, MHS; King to wife, 22 June 1864, Folder 5, MSA 677, VHS; Cummings to wife, 11 July 1864, Folder 9, MSA 28, VHS; Cogswell, *Eleventh New Hampshire*, 377; Humphreys, *Virginia Campaign*, 218.

13. *OR*, 40(1):196, 523, 545, 40(2):191; Peck, *Revised Roster*, 583, 595; Ancestry, Vermont 17th Volunteer Infantry, Fold3; Hartshorn, diary, 18 June 1864, Folder 17, MSC 209, VHS; Perry, diary, 18 June 1864, MS 2187, NYHS; Lord, *Ninth Regiment*, 453; Jackman, *Sixth New Hampshire*, 295; J. N. Jones, "Advancing the Pickets," ibid., 297–99; Woodbury, *Burnside and the Ninth Army Corps*, 412.

14. *OR*, 40(2):157, 253; Meade, *Life and Letters*, 206; Potter and Potter, *Personal Experiences*, 61; 17th VS; 31st MS.

15. *OR*, 40(1):531, 545, 569, 40(2):157; Cogswell, *Eleventh New Hampshire*, 377; Lucia, "Seventeenth Regiment," 571; *Bangor (ME) Daily Whig and Courier*, 25 June 1864; Smith to unknown, 18 June 1864, Folder 6, Box 1, M131.1, Bowdoin College Library; Woodbury, *Burnside and the Ninth Army Corps*, 410.

16. *Bangor (ME) Daily Whig and Courier*, 20, 25 June 1864; *Burlington (VT) Daily Times*, 2 July 1864, newspapers.com; *Green Mountain Freeman* (Montpelier, VT), 5 July 1864, newspapers.com; *OR*, 40(1):530, 569; Cummings to wife, 18 June 1864, Folder 7, MSA 28, VHS; Larned to sister, 20 June 1864, Box 4, Daniel Read Larned Papers, MSS29470, LOC, microfilm; James Dean and George A. Bolton to Governor of Maine, 1 August 1864, Incoming Military Correspondence, Office of the Adjutant General, RG 15, MSA; Badeau, *Military History of Ulysses S. Grant*, 2:366; Cogswell, *Eleventh New Hampshire*, 386.

17. Woodbury, *Burnside and the Ninth Army Corps*, 410–11.

18. Lucia, "Seventeenth Regiment," 571; *OR*, 36(1):254, 40(2):156–57, 431; Smith to aunt, 20 June 1864, Folder 6, Box 1, M131.1, Bowdoin College Library; Cummings to wife, 27 June 1864, Folder 9, MSA 28, VHS; J. B. Mitchell to Governor of Maine, 7 July 1864, Incoming Military Correspondence, Office of the Adjutant General, RG 15, MSA; Sheahan to father, 10 July 1864, Folder 9, Box 1, Collection 184, MHS; Badeau,

Military History of Ulysses S. Grant, 2:382; Cogswell, *Eleventh New Hampshire,* 386; Meade, *Life and Letters,* 206, 210; Lord, *Ninth Regiment,* 448; Merriam, "Personal Recollections," MHS, 53.

19. Merriam, "Personal Recollections," MHS, 55, 57; Sturtz, *Civil War Letters of S. R. Emerson,* loc. 2708–2719, Kindle; King to wife, 27 June 1864, Folder 5, MSA 677, VHS; Cummings to wife, 27 June, 11, 18, 23 July 1864, Folder 9, MSA 28, VHS; *OR,* 36(1):254–55, 40(3):444, 446; Houston, *Thirty-Second Maine,* 296–97, 308; Hartshorn, diary, 2, 13 July 1864, Folder 17, MSC 209, VHS; Humphreys, *Virginia Campaign,* 243; J. J. Chase, *The Charge at Daybreak: Scenes and Incidents at the Battle of the Mine Explosion, near Petersburg, Va., July 30th, 1864* (Lewiston, ME: Journal Office, 1875), 4, 9, 12; *Vermont Phoenix* (Brattleboro), 29 July 1864; Peck, *Revised Roster,* 586, 593; Committee on the Conduct of the War, *Report . . . on the Attack on Petersburg,* 17.

20. Merriam, "Personal Recollections," MHS, 51, 53; Cummings to wife, 3, 11, 18, 23 July 1864, Folder 9, MSA 28, VHS; Sheahan to father, 21, 26 June 1864 (second of two letters), Folder 9, Box 1, Collection 184, MHS; *OR,* 40(1):523, 40(3):238, 414; Griffin, journal, Folder 1, Box 1, MG257, HSCC, 22; *Green Mountain Freeman* (Montpelier, VT), 12 July 1864; Benedict, *Vermont in the Civil War,* 511; Ervin T. Case, "Battle of the Mine," in *Personal Narratives of Events in the War of the Rebellion, Being Papers Read before the Rhode Island Soldiers and Sailors Historical Society,* comp. Rhode Island Soldiers and Sailors Historical Society, vol. 1 (1878–79; repr., Wilmington, NC: Broadfoot, 1993), 281.

21. *OR,* 36(1):255, 40(1):271, 40(3):529, 611; Lord, *Ninth Regiment,* 455; Cummings to wife, 3, 18 July 1864, Folder 9, MSA 28, VHS; Potter and Potter, *Personal Experiences,* 63; Entry 4986: Inspection Reports, RG 393: Records of U.S. Army Continental Commands, pt. 2, NA.

22. Spreadsheet provided by Dick Dobbins of Historical Data Systems; *OR,* 36(1):259, 40(1):271; Theodore Lyman, "Crossing of the James and Advance on Petersburg, June 13–16, 1864," in Military Historical Society, *Petersburg, Chancellorsville, Gettysburg,* 29; Morning Report & Order Book, 17th Vermont, Entry 115, RG 94, NA; Morning Reports, 31st Maine, ibid.

23. *OR,* 36(1):259, 40(1):570; Hartshorn, diary, 12, 22–25 June, 2–4, 7, 15, 21, 23–24, 26, 28, 30 July 1864, Folder 17, MSC 209, VHS; Cummings to wife, 27, 28 June, 11, 14, 18, 23, 31 July 1864, Folder 9, MSA 28, VHS; Albert Camp Raymond to family, 3 July 1864, Civil War Letters of Albert Camp Raymond, 1862–74, Folder 4, MSA 773, VHS, transcription; Sheahan to father, 10, 14, 20, 27 July 1864, Folder 9, Box 1, Collection 184, MHS; Peck, *Revised Roster,* 580; Morning Report & Order Book, 17th Vermont, Entry 115, RG 94, NA.

24. Merriam, "Personal Recollections," MHS, 55; Griffin, "1863: William Elmore Howard to George Sumner Howard"; *OR,* 36(1):255; Tim Leno and Gail Wiese, finding aid, August 2013, Folder 0, MSA 677, VHS; King to wife, 22, 27 June 1864, Folder 5, ibid.; Raymond to family, 3 July 1864, Folder 4, MSA 773, VHS; Cummings to wife, 3, 11, 18 July 1864, Folder 9, MSA 28, VHS; Lord, *Ninth Regiment,* 454; James W. Lathe, "Bits of Home Letters," ibid., 465.

25. Lord, *Ninth Regiment,* 455; Newell T. Dutton, "Along with the Colors," ibid.,

457–58; Burnham, "In the Trenches," 462; Lathe, "Bits of Home Letters," 467; Hartshorn, diary, 22 June, 18, 22 July 1864, Folder 17, MSC 209, VHS; *OR,* 40(3):353–54; Chase, *Charge at Daybreak,* 11–12.

26. 17th VS; 31st MS; *OR,* 40(1):523, 40(2):319; Merriam, "Personal Recollections," 52–53; Lucia, "Seventeenth Regiment," in Peck, *Revised Roster,* 571; Hartshorn, diary, 21 June 1864, Folder 17, MSC 209, VHS; Cummings to wife, 3 July 1864, Folder 9, MSA 28, VHS; Burnham, "In the Trenches," 460, 463–64; Lathe, "Bits of Home Letters," 465; Frank Kenfield, "Captured by Rebels: A Vermonter at Petersburg, 1864," *Vermont History* 36, no. 4 (August 1968): 231.

27. *OR,* 40(3):526; Merriam, "Personal Recollections," MHS, 52–53, 55; Cummings to wife, 3 July 1864, Folder 9, MSA 28, VHS; Sheahan to father, 23 July 1864, Folder 9, Box 1, Collection 184, MHS; Case, "Battle of the Mine," 280; *Green Mountain Freeman* (Montpelier, VT), 12 July 1864; Chase, *Charge at Daybreak,* 12; Dutton, "Along with the Colors," 457; E. C. Babb, "Clippings from Major Chandler's Correspondence," in Lord, *Ninth Regiment,* 473; Agassiz, *Meade's Headquarters,* 199.

28. *Gardiner (ME) Home Journal,* 7 July 1864, DigitalMaine; *Bangor (ME) Daily Whig and Courier,* 14 July 1864, newspapers.com; Jackman, *Sixth New Hampshire,* 304, 307–8; Hartshorn, diary, 10 July 1864, Folder 17, MSC 209, VHS; Cummings to wife, 11, 14 July 1864, Folder 9, MSA 28, VHS; Chase, *Charge at Daybreak,* 13; Merriam, "Personal Recollections," MHS, 53.

29. Jackman, *Sixth New Hampshire,* 301–3; Hartshorn, diary, 21, 23 June, 4–5, 20, 24–26, 28 July 1864, Folder 17, MSC 209, VHS; Cummings to wife, 27 June, 11, 14, 18, 23 July 1864, Folder 9, MSA 28, VHS; Chase, *Charge at Daybreak,* 7, 12–13; Babb, "Clippings from Major Chandler's Correspondence," 472; Merriam, "Personal Recollections," MHS, 51, 53–54; Burnham, "In the Trenches," 459, 462; Case, "Battle of the Mine," 281.

30. *Green Mountain Freeman* (Montpelier, VT), 12 July 1864; *Rutland (VT) Weekly Herald,* 4 August 1864, newspapers.com; Cummings to wife, 3 July 1864, Folder 9, MSA 28, VHS; Daniel White to Governor of Maine, 13 July 1864, Incoming Military Correspondence, Office of the Adjutant General, RG 15, MSA; Potter and Potter, *Personal Experiences,* 62; Benedict, *Vermont in the Civil War,* 511; Entry 4986, RG 393, NA; Zeller, "My Soldier Boy Mark," 55, Folder 15, MSA 518, VHS; Peck, *Revised Roster,* 582; Hartshorn, diary, 14 July 1864, Folder 17, MSC 209, VHS.

31. Manson to mother, 10 July 1864, Charles. A. Manson Papers, Collection 454, Emory University, microfilm; Sheahan to father, 10 July 1864, Folder 9, Box 1, Collection 184, MHS; *Gardiner (ME) Home Journal,* 7 July 1864; *Green Mountain Freeman* (Montpelier, VT), 12 July 1864; *Bangor (ME) Daily Whig and Courier,* 13, 19 July 1864, newspapers.com; Hodsdon, *Appendix D,* 733, 758; 31st MS; Peck, *Revised Roster,* 593.

32. Cummings to Adjutant and Inspector General of Vermont, 26 August 1864, Reel F26085, Records of the Adjutant and Inspector General, VSARA, microfilm; Sheahan to father, 10, 20 July 1864, Folder 9, Box 1, Collection 184, MHS.

33. *OR,* 40(2):584; Sheahan to father, 21, 26 June (second of two letters), 10 July 1864, Folder 9, Box 1, Collection 184, MHS; King to wife, 27 June 1864, Folder 5, MSA 677, VHS; Cummings to wife, 28 June 1864, Folder 9, MSA 28, VHS; Houston,

Thirty-Second Maine, 331; Merriam, "Personal Recollections," MHS, 55; *Vermont Phoenix* (Brattleboro), 29 July 1864.

34. *OR,* 40(1):47, 126, 166, 241, 244–45, 286, 309–10, 527, 40(3):125, 597, 636; Hess, *In the Trenches at Petersburg,* 79, 82; Humphreys, *Virginia Campaign,* 250; Zeller, "'My Soldier Boy Mark,'" 56, Folder 15, MSA 518, VHS; Houston, *Thirty-Second Maine,* 329; Korff Brothers, *Battles of the Crater and of June 22nd,* 52 x 68 cm (New York, 1864), LOC, accessed 19 February 2024, http://hdl.loc.gov/loc.gmd/g3884p.cw10170000/.

35. *OR,* 40(1):46, 78, 40(3):424, 458, 460, 476; C. B. Comstock, diary, 2 July 1864, Reel 1, Box 1, C. B. Comstock Papers, 1847–1908, MSS16527, LOC, microfilm.

36. Griffin, journal, Folder 1, Box 1, MG257, HSCC, 23; *OR,* 40(1):136–37, 165, 424, 524, 527, 40(3):612–13; Potter and Potter, *Personal Experiences,* 64–65, 68; Hess, *Into the Crater,* 57; Woodbury, *Burnside and the Ninth Army Corps,* 428; Committee on the Conduct of the War, *Report . . . on the Attack on Petersburg,* 17–18, 56–57, 125; Lord, *Ninth Regiment,* 454.

37. *OR,* 40(1):45, 121–22, 164, 40(3):125–26, 428, 636; Hess, *Into the Crater,* 5; Badeau, *Military History of Ulysses S. Grant,* 3:130n*; Humphreys, *Virginia Campaign,* 250; Committee on the Conduct of the War, *Report . . . on the Attack on Petersburg,* 116; Nevins, *Diary of Battle,* 440.

38. Merriam, "Personal Recollections," MHS, 58; Potter and Potter, *Personal Experiences,* 63; Woodbury, *Burnside and the Ninth Army Corps,* 428; Greene, *Campaign of Giants,* 398; Sheahan to father, 6 July 1864, Folder 9, Box 1, Collection 184, MHS; Cummings to wife, 11 July 1864, Folder 9, MSA 28, VHS; *OR,* 40(1):524; Committee on the Conduct of the War, *Report . . . on the Attack on Petersburg,* 17, 158; Scott, *Forgotten Valor,* 554.

39. Lucia, "Seventeenth Regiment," 571; Benedict, *Vermont in the Civil War,* 515n; *Portland (ME) Daily Press,* 11 August 1864, Chronicling America; *OR,* 40(1):570, 40(3):728; Morning Report & Order Book, 17th Vermont, Entry 115, RG 94, NA; Morning Reports, 31st Maine, ibid.; Daniel Conway to Adjutant and Inspector General of Vermont, 23 August 1864, Reel F26085, Records of the Adjutant and Inspector General, VSARA, microfilm.

40. Lord, *Ninth Regiment,* 490, 495, 502; George L. Wakefield, "Why the Ninth Was the First Regiment to Float Its Colors over the Crater," ibid., 499; Chase, *Charge at Daybreak,* 13, 15–16, 29; Knapp, "1887 speech," Folder 16, MSA 189, VHS; Sparks, *Inside Lincoln's Army,* 404; *OR,* 40(3):525–26; Horace H. Burbank, "The Battle of 'The Crater,'" in *War Papers Read before the Commandery of the State of Maine, Military Order of the Loyal Legion of the United States,* comp. Military Order of the Loyal Legion of the United States, vol. 1 (1898; repr. Wilmington, NC: Broadfoot, 1992), 285; Kenfield, "Captured by Rebels," 232.

41. *OR,* 40(1):164, 527; *Vermont Christian Messenger,* 4 August 1864, newspapers.com; Woodbury, *Burnside and the Ninth Army Corps,* 436; Knapp, "1887 speech," Folder 16, MSA 189, VHS; Chase, *Charge at Daybreak,* 16, 29; Hess, *Into the Crater,* xi; Jackman, *Sixth New Hampshire,* 320; Benedict, *Vermont in the Civil War,* 515; Burbank, "Battle of 'The Crater,'" 286; Agassiz, *Meade's Headquarters,* 196.

42. Charles H. Houghton, "In the Crater," in Johnson and Buel, *Battles and*

Leaders, 561; *OR,* 40(1):88–89, 527, 40(3):611–12; Hess, *Into the Crater,* 60, 81; Woodbury, *Burnside and the Ninth Army Corps,* 438; Benedict, *Vermont in the Civil War,* 515; Case, "Battle of the Mine," 297; Lord, *Ninth Regiment,* 496.

43. Potter and Potter, *Personal Experiences,* 65; *OR,* 40(1):84, 527–28, 547, 567, 40(3):126; *Portland (ME) Daily Press,* 11 August 1864; Scott, *Forgotten Valor,* 553; Case, "Battle of the Mine," 280; Hess, *Into the Crater,* 67, 92; Agassiz, *Meade's Headquarters,* 199–200; Merriam, "Personal Recollections," MHS, 59–60; Committee on the Conduct of the War, *Report . . . on the Attack on Petersburg,* 18, 118, 130, 192, 194; Howard Coffin, *Full Duty: Vermonters in the Civil War* (Woodstock, VT: Countryman, 1995), 329; *Chicago Tribune,* 7 August 1864, Chronicling America; William I. Brown, "A Letter to Major Chandler," in Lord, *Ninth Regiment,* 494; Wakefield, "Why the Ninth Was the First Regiment," 499; Lord, *Ninth Regiment,* 142 (appendix), 504–5; Griffin, journal, Folder 1, Box 1, MG257, HSCC, 23–24; Chase, *Charge at Daybreak,* 29; Woodbury, *Burnside and the Ninth Army Corps,* 437–39. Since there were three units in front during the charge, I deduced that the unit to lose its commanding officer at this time was the 2nd Maryland. Later in the fighting, Colonel White was captured and the captain leading the 9th New Hampshire fell with a fatal wound.

44. *OR,* 40(1):126, 164, 527, 567; Committee on the Conduct of the War, *Report . . . on the Attack on Petersburg,* 39, 171; Coffin, *Full Duty,* 329; Peck, *Revised Roster,* 580, 583; A. Sprague to Governor of Maine, 8 August 1864, Incoming Military Correspondence, Office of the Adjutant General, RG 15, MSA; Hodsdon, *Appendix D,* 752; *Bangor (ME) Daily Whig and Courier,* 8 August 1864; *National Tribune,* 21 June 1883, Chronicling America; Lord, *Ninth Regiment,* 505; Chase, *Charge at Daybreak,* 19–20, 29–30; Benedict, *Vermont in the Civil War,* 516n; Stephen M. Weld, "The Petersburg Mine," in Military Historical Society, *Petersburg, Chancellorsville, Gettysburg,* 209; Griffin, journal, Folder 1, Box 1, MG257, HSCC, 23; Houston, *Thirty-Second Maine,* 346; Benjamin Perley Poore, *The Life and Public Services of Ambrose E. Burnside, Soldier—Citizen—Statesman* (Providence, RI: J. A. & R. A. Reid, 1882), 244; Hess, *In the Trenches at Petersburg,* 86.

45. *OR,* 40(1):90, 97, 547, 567, 569; Burbank, "Battle of 'The Crater,'" 288; Potter and Potter, *Personal Experiences,* 65–66; Houston, *Thirty-Second Maine,* 346; Committee on the Conduct of the War, *Report . . . on the Attack on Petersburg,* 192; *National Tribune,* 21 June 1883; Benedict, *Vermont in the Civil War,* 517; Weld, "Petersburg Mine," 209.

46. *OR,* 40(1):89, 528, 547–48, 567, 40(3):646; Burbank, "Battle of 'The Crater,'" 288–89; Potter and Potter, *Personal Experiences,* 65; *National Tribune,* 21 June 1883; Benedict, *Vermont in the Civil War,* 517.

47. *OR,* 40(1):107, 164, 528, 548, 567, 40(3):612; Hodsdon, *Appendix D,* 738; Lord, *Ninth Regiment,* 498; Wakefield, "Why the Ninth Was the First Regiment," 502; Moses Whitehill to brother, 9 August 1864, Whitehill Letters, MSA 520, VHS; *Chicago Tribune,* 7 August 1864; *Lamoille Newsdealer* (Hyde Park, VT), 10 August 1864, Chronicling America; Burbank, "Battle of 'The Crater,'" 289; Committee on the Conduct of the War, *Report . . . on the Attack on Petersburg,* 8.

48. *OR,* 40(1):90, 165, 528, 548, 567–68; Burbank, "Battle of 'The Crater,'" 289; Hess, *Into the Crater,* 166, 168, 204; Coffin, *Full Duty,* 329; Lord, *Ninth Regiment,* 506; *Lamoille Newsdealer* (Hyde Park, VT), 10 August 1864; Powell, "Petersburg Crater," 558.

49. *OR,* 40(1):165, 529, 548; Committee on the Conduct of the War, *Report . . . on the Attack on Petersburg,* 193; *Bangor (ME) Daily Whig and Courier,* 6 August 1864; *Chicago Tribune,* 7 August 1864; Case, "Battle of the Mine," 299; Benedict, *Vermont in the Civil War,* 517; Hodsdon, *Appendix D,* 733; Potter and Potter, *Personal Experiences,* 66; Burbank, "Battle of 'The Crater,'" 290.

50. *OR,* 40(1):165, 529; Potter and Potter, *Personal Experiences,* 68; Powell, "Petersburg Crater," 557; Jackman, *Sixth New Hampshire,* 316–17; Houston, *Thirty-Second Maine,* 349; Lord, *Ninth Regiment,* 489, 511; Wakefield, "Why the Ninth Was the First Regiment," 501; Porter, *Campaigning with Grant,* 264; Swinton, *Army of the Potomac,* 524.

51. *OR,* 40(1):165, 570, 40(3):636, 663, 706; Reunion Society of Vermont Officers, *Proceedings,* 469; Benedict, *Vermont in the Civil War,* 517; *Vermont Watchman and State Journal* (Montpelier), 12 August 1864, newspapers.com; Lord, *Ninth Regiment,* 492; Peck, *Revised Roster,* 585; Hess, *Into the Crater,* 176. A. Wilson Greene concedes that there may have been a separate attack, as described here, although he maintains that most sources do not indicate this was a distinct stage of the fighting. Conversely, Earl J. Hess asserts that there were three assaults in total. I found evidence of five Confederate attacks spanning from the early morning to midafternoon. This discrepancy over number and timing probably reflects the especially chaotic conditions of the Crater and the vague, contradictory nature of both wartime and postwar descriptions of the fighting there. What appeared to be an attack from one vantage point could have been a minor probing action by a small body of troops. Consistent with the rest of this book, however, I have described the events from the perspective of the Federals. Greene, *Campaign of Giants,* 486; Hess, *Into the Crater,* xii.

52. *OR,* 40(1):100, 102, 529, 546, 549, 568, 570, 40(3):706; Jackman, *Sixth New Hampshire,* 318; Powell, "Petersburg Crater," 558; Committee on the Conduct of the War, *Report . . . on the Attack on Petersburg,* 193; 17th VS.

53. Knapp, "1887 speech," Folder 16, MSA 189, VHS; James S. Peck to Adjutant and Inspector General of Vermont, 1 August 1864, Reel F26085, Records of the Adjutant and Inspector General, VSARA, microfilm; 17th VS; 31st MS.

54. *OR,* 40(1):567, 570; *Portland (ME) Daily Press,* 11 August 1864; *Vermont Watchman and State Journal* (Montpelier), 12 August 1864; *Enterprise and Vermonter (Vergennes),* 19 August 1864, newspapers.com; Benedict, *Vermont in the Civil War,* 519n; Lucia, "Seventeenth Regiment," 571; Peck, *Revised Roster,* 575; Morning Report & Order Book, 17th Vermont, Entry 115, RG 94, NA; Merriam, "Personal Recollections," MHS, 54; Entry 4993, Letters Sent, Jan. 1864–July 1865, RG 393, NA; Entry 5011: Letters Sent and Circulars, February–December 1864, ibid.

55. 17th VS; 31st MS; *OR,* 40(1):247.

56. *OR,* 36(1):27, 40(1):165, 529, 568, 570; Cummings to wife, 31 July 1864, Folder 9, MSA 28, VHS; Hartshorn, diary, 31 July 1864, Folder 17, MSC 209, VHS; Scott, *Forgotten Valor,* 557; Agassiz, *Meade's Headquarters,* 201; Potter and Potter, *Personal Experiences,* 71; *National Tribune,* 21 June 1883.

57. *OR,* 40(1):25, 40(2):117, 157; Ropes, "Failure to Take Petersburg," in Military Historical Society, *Petersburg, Chancellorsville, Gettysburg,* 182–83; Agassiz, *Meade's Headquarters,* 179.

58. *OR,* 40(1):527; Committee on the Conduct of the War, *Report . . . on the Attack on Petersburg,* 8, 39; Humphreys, *Virginia Campaign,* 264; Comstock, diary, 30 July 1864, Reel 1, Box 1, MSS16527, LOC; Cummings to wife, 3 July 1864, Folder 9, MSA 28, VHS.

59. *OR,* 40(1):525.

5. THE BATTLE OF PEEBLES FARM AND THE
NINTH UNION OFFENSIVE AT PETERSBURG

1. Besides the Ninth Corps, the Second Division of the Tenth Corps in the Army of the James advanced to participate in the Crater battle shortly after the USCT regiments pushed forward at 8:00 a.m., yet many of these bluecoats fell back when the Black troops retreated. Brig. Gen. John W. Turner, commanding this Tenth Corps division, determined there was not enough room for his troops to fight effectively, marking the end of their involvement in the battle. Hess, *Into the Crater,* 134. See also *OR,* 40(3):638, 667, 42(1):158, 42(2):11, 434, 668. As of August 1, 1864, the 48th Pennsylvania joined the Second Brigade, but it returned to the First Brigade on August 23. Several more later-arrival units then joined the Second Brigade, starting with the 2nd New York Mounted Rifles Volunteer Cavalry Regiment that same day. The 56th Massachusetts and 179th New York Volunteer Infantry Regiments followed suit on September 2, and the 186th New York Volunteer Infantry Regiment arrived on October 27.

2. Yale to mother, 18 December 1864, Folder 3, Box 1, John Yale Papers, UVM; Peck, *Revised Roster,* 595.

3. De Trobriand, *Four Years with the Army,* 625; *OR,* 40(3):704, 42(2):169, 243; Potter and Potter, *Personal Experiences,* 68, 76; Dean and Bolton to Adjutant General of Maine, 1 August 1864, 31st Maine Regiment, Container 353956, Civil War—Incoming Military Correspondence, Office of the Adjutant General, RG 15, MSA.

4. *OR,* 40(1):172–74, 42(2):142, 155, 177–78; Potter and Potter, *Personal Experiences,* 68; Griffin, journal, Folder 1, Box 1, MG257, HSCC, 34; Entry 5011: Letters Sent and Circulars, February–December 1864, RG 393: Records of U.S. Army Continental Commands, pt. 2, NA; Sommers, *Richmond Redeemed,* 228.

5. Cummings to wife, 31 July, 18 September 1864, Charles Cummings Papers, Folder 9, MSA 28, VHS, transcription; James S. Peck to Adjutant and Inspector General of Vermont, 1 August 1864 (first of two letters), Reel F26085, Records of the Adjutant and Inspector General, VSARA, microfilm; Cummings to Adjutant and Inspector General of Vermont, 12 August 1864, ibid.; *Portland (ME) Daily Press,* 1 September 1864, Chronicling America; Merriam, "Personal Recollections of the War for the Union," Collection S-5186, MHS, 7, 62; Lucia, "Seventeenth Regiment," 572; Peck, *Revised Roster,* 575; Benedict, *Vermont in the Civil War,* 520; Hodsdon, *Appendix D,* 733; Dean and Bolton to Adjutant General of Maine, 1 August 1864, Incoming Military Correspondence, Office of the Adjutant General, RG 15, MSA; War Department, Adjutant General's Office, Special Orders No. 261, 6 August 1864, ibid.

6. Jackman, *Sixth New Hampshire,* 330; Lord, *Ninth Regiment,* 513–14; *Lamoille*

Newsdealer (Hyde Park, VT), 10 August 1864; Case, "Battle of the Mine," in Soldiers and Sailors Historical Society, *Personal Narratives,* 306; *OR,* 40(3):704.

7. Peck to Adjutant and Inspector General of Vermont, 1 August 1864 (two letters of same date), Reel F26085, Records of the Adjutant and Inspector General, VSARA, microfilm; Cummings to wife, 31 July 1864, Folder 9, MSA 28, VHS; Merriam, "Personal Recollections," MHS, 61–62, 67; Benedict, *Vermont in the Civil War,* 520; Peck, *Revised Roster,* 575; *Bangor (ME) Daily Whig and Courier,* 13 August 1864, newspapers.com; *Enterprise and Vermonter (Vergennes),* 19 August 1864; Dean and Bolton to Adjutant General of Maine, 1 August 1864, Incoming Military Correspondence, Office of the Adjutant General, RG 15, MSA; 31st MS; 17th VS.

8. Merriam, "Personal Recollections," MHS, 55, 62, 65; Jackman, *Sixth New Hampshire,* 330; Lord, *Ninth Regiment,* 515–18, 520–22; Cogswell, *Eleventh New Hampshire,* 577; Oliver Christian Bosbyshell, *The 48th in the War: Being a Narrative of the Campaigns of the 48th Regiment, Infantry* [. . .] (Philadelphia: Avil Printing, 1895), 180, https://digital.libraries.psu.edu/digital/collection/digitalbks2/id/71070; Manson to mother, 9, 14, 21, 24 September 1864, Charles A. Manson Papers, Collection 454, Emory University, microfilm; *OR,* 42(1):186, 544–45, 42(2):494, 533, 642, 837, 1042; Cummings to wife, 18, 25, 30 September 1864, Folder 9, MSA 28, VHS; De Trobriand, *Four Years with the Army,* 626; Lucia, "Seventeenth Regiment," 572; Entry 4986: Inspection Reports, RG 393, NA. See also Entry 4993: Letters Sent, Jan. 1864–July 1865, ibid.; and Entry 5011, ibid.

9. Merriam, "Personal Recollections," MHS, 64–65; Jackman, *Sixth New Hampshire,* 333; Lord, *Ninth Regiment,* 517–18, 521–22; Cogswell, *Eleventh New Hampshire,* 426, 473, 577; Houston, *Thirty-Second Maine,* 373, 387–89; Bosbyshell, *48th in the War,* 180; Daniel Conway to Adjutant and Inspector General of Vermont, 23 August 1864, Reel F26085, Records of the Adjutant and Inspector General, VSARA, microfilm; Manson to mother, 9 September 1864, Collection 454, Emory University, microfilm; Cummings to wife, 18, 25 September 1864, Folder 9, MSA 28, VHS; James Pollard, diary, 23, 28 September 1864, Reel F2850, Records of the Vermont Civil War Centennial Committee, Microfilm Collections, Civil War Era, VSARA; *OR,* 42(2):153, 406, 434, 494, 497, 533–34, 666, 1008; De Trobriand, *Four Years with the Army,* 626; Entry 5011, RG 393, NA; Peck, *Revised Roster,* 593.

10. 17th VS; 31st MS; Jackman, *Sixth New Hampshire,* 330–31; Lord, *Ninth Regiment,* 516; *OR,* 42(1):186; Bosbyshell, *48th in the War,* 179, 181; Houston, *Thirty-Second Maine,* 372; *OR,* 42(2):154, 156, 279, 706, 725; Moses Whitehill to brother, 9 August 1864, Whitehill Letters, MSA 520, VHS; Conway to Adjutant and Inspector General of Vermont, 23 August 1864, Reel F26085, Records of the Adjutant and Inspector General, VSARA, microfilm; Manson to mother, 9, 14 September 1864, Collection 454, Emory University, microfilm.

11. *OR,* 42(1):186, 42(2):292, 316, 434; Lord, *Ninth Regiment,* 515–17; Houston, *Thirty-Second Maine,* 373–74; Bosbyshell, *48th in the War,* 179, 193; Pollard, diary, 20–24, 26–28 September 1864, Reel F2850, Records of the Vermont Civil War Centennial Committee, VSARA; Cummings to wife, 25 September 1864, Folder 9, MSA 28, VHS; Meade, *Life and Letters,* 228; Merriam, "Personal Recollections," MHS, 63–65.

12. Merriam, "Personal Recollections," MHS, 63; Lord, *Ninth Regiment,* 519–20; Cogswell, *Eleventh New Hampshire,* 426–28, 577; Hess, *In the Trenches at Petersburg,* 124, 128; Greene, *Final Battles of the Petersburg Campaign,* 9; Houston, *Thirty-Second Maine,* 376; Potter and Potter, *Personal Experiences,* 68–69, 81; *OR,* 42(1):76, 42(2):242–44, 292; Grant, *Personal Memoirs,* 393; 17th VS; Morning Report & Order Book, 17th Vermont, Entry 115: Civil War Regimental Books, RG 94: Records of the Adjutant General's Office, NA.

13. *OR,* 42(1):186, 203, 42(2):120; E. Brookings Jr. to Governor of Maine, 19 August 1864, Incoming Military Correspondence, Office of the Adjutant General, RG 15, MSA; Entry 4986, RG 393, NA; Morning Report & Order Book, 17th Vermont, Entry 115, RG 94, NA; Morning Reports, 31st Maine, ibid.

14. *OR,* 42(1):31, 545, 42(2):1046–47, 1094, 1118; Cummings to wife, 30 September 1864, Folder 9, MSA 28, VHS; Sommers, *Richmond Redeemed,* 176, 203; Humphreys, *Virginia Campaign,* 290–91. Much of the Second Cavalry Division also took part in the Battle of Peebles Farm, but its movements and actions did not intersect with those of the later arrivals and thus are beyond the scope of this discussion.

15. Lord, *Ninth Regiment,* 518; Cogswell, *Eleventh New Hampshire,* 425–26, 577; Peck to Adjutant and Inspector General of Vermont, 1 August 1864, Reel F26085, Records of the Adjutant and Inspector General, VSARA, microfilm; Conway to Adjutant and Inspector General of Vermont, 23 August 1864, ibid.; Cummings to wife, 30 September 1864, Folder 9, MSA 28, VHS; Merriam, "Personal Recollections," MHS, 63; Entry 5011, RG 393, NA; *Bangor (ME) Daily Whig and Courier,* 13 August 1864; *Portland (ME) Daily Press,* 11 August, 1 September 1864. See also *Springfield (MA) Republican,* 31 January 1887; thanks to John J. Hennessy for providing a scan of this newspaper article.

16. Peck to Adjutant and Inspector General of Vermont, 1 August 1864, Reel F26085, Records of the Adjutant and Inspector General, VSARA, microfilm; Knapp to Adjutant and Inspector General of Vermont, 13 August 1864, ibid.; William E. Burn to Governor of Maine, 26 September 1864, Incoming Military Correspondence, Office of the Adjutant General, RG 15, MSA; Cummings to wife, 30 September 1864, Folder 9, MSA 28, VHS; Getchell to Governor of Maine, 27 October 1864, Incoming Military Correspondence, Office of the Adjutant General, RG 15, MSA; Merriam, "Personal Recollections," MHS, 63–64, 66–67; 17th VS; "'Lyman E. Knapp, LL. D.,' *Civic Progress,*" no date, Lyman E. Knapp Papers, 1862–87, Folder 15, MSA 189, VHS; Hodsdon, *Appendix D,* 752, 760.

17. *OR,* 42(2):1047–48, 1070; Houston, *Thirty-Second Maine,* 390; Entry 5011, RG 393, NA; Cummings to wife, 30 September 1864, Folder 9, MSA 28, VHS; Pollard, diary, 29 September 1864, Reel F2850, Records of the Vermont Civil War Centennial Committee, VSARA, microfilm; Morning Report & Order Book, 17th Vermont, Entry 115, RG 94, NA.

18. Manson to mother, 3 October 1864, Collection 454, Emory University, microfilm; *OR,* 42(1):31, 545–46, 578; Merriam, "Personal Recollections," MHS, 67–68; Lucia, "Seventeenth Regiment," 572; Sommers, *Richmond Redeemed,* 253.

19. Merriam, "Personal Recollections," MHS, 69; *OR,* 42(1):546, 578–79, 587;

Potter and Potter, *Personal Experiences,* 72; Jackman, *Sixth New Hampshire,* 335; Lord, *Ninth Regiment,* 524; Sommers, *Richmond Redeemed,* 243, 265–66.

20. Merriam, "Personal Recollections," MHS, 69; *OR,* 42(1):77, 546, 579, 587; Jackman, *Sixth New Hampshire,* 335–36; Lord, *Ninth Regiment,* 524; W. A. McGarrett, "Sufferings at Salisbury," ibid., 614; Sommers, *Richmond Redeemed,* 272, 274; *Lamoille Newsdealer* (Hyde Park, VT), 19 October 1864, newspapers.com.

21. Newell T. Dutton, "Under the Old Flag," in Lord, *Ninth Regiment,* 527; *OR,* 42(1):546, 579, 587–88; *Lamoille Newsdealer* (Hyde Park, VT), 19 October 1864; Sommers, *Richmond Redeemed,* 275. Lucia, "Seventeenth Regiment," 573.

22. Simon G. Griffin to wife of Cummings, 10 October 1864, Lieutenant Colonel Charles Cummings Papers, Folder 9, MSA 829, VHS; Merriam, "Personal Recollections," MHS, 67, 70–71; Lord, *Ninth Regiment,* 525; Dutton, "Under the Old Flag," 527; McGarrett, "Sufferings at Salisbury," 614; *OR,* 42(1):546, 579; Potter and Potter, *Personal Experiences,* 72; Hodsdon, *Report of the Adjutant General of the State of Maine, . . . 1864 and 1865,* 293; Lucia, "Seventeenth Regiment," 573; Peck, *Revised Roster,* 575, 593; *Lamoille Newsdealer* (Hyde Park, VT), 19 October 1864; 17th VS.

23. Lucia, "Seventeenth Regiment," 572; Peck, *Revised Roster,* 595; Jackman, *Sixth New Hampshire,* 337; J. Gregory Acken, ed., *Through Blood and Fire: The Civil War Letters of Major Charles J. Mills, 1862–1865,* rev. and exp. ed. (Kent, OH: Kent University Press, 2023), 202; Lord, *Ninth Regiment,* 525; Dutton, "Under the Old Flag," 527; Potter and Potter, *Personal Experiences,* 73; *OR,* 42(1):546, 579, 588; Manson to mother, 30 September, 3 October 1864, Collection 454, Emory University, microfilm; Ancestry, Vermont 17th Volunteer Infantry, Fold3; Sommers, *Richmond Redeemed,* 284, 311.

24. *OR,* 42(1):546, 42(3):26–27, 36; Sommers, *Richmond Redeemed,* 311, 367, 371; Pollard, diary, 1 October 1864, Reel F2850, Records of the Vermont Civil War Centennial Committee, VSARA, microfilm; Hess, *In the Trenches at Petersburg,* 166; Jackman, *Sixth New Hampshire,* 337; Lord, *Ninth Regiment,* 525; Dutton, "Under the Old Flag," 528, 530.

25. 17th VS; 31st MS; Manson to mother, 3 October 1864, Collection 454, Emory University, microfilm; *OR,* 42(1):138n*, 142, 588.

26. Potter and Potter, *Personal Experiences,* 72–74; Manson to mother, 9 October 1864, Collection 454, Emory University, microfilm; *OR,* 42(1):21, 579, 588; Washburn, *Adjutant & Inspector General's Office,* 78; Acken, *Through Blood and Fire,* 203; *Piscataquis Observer* (Dover, ME), 13 October 1864, DigitalMaine.

27. *OR,* 36(1):33, 42(1):71; "1864-10-07 Letter from Lieutenant A. R. Wescott to his parents about the Battle of Peebles' Farm and enclosing a fragment of the regimental flag," DigitalMaine, transcription, accessed 19 June 2023, https://digitalmaine.com /cw_me_31st_regiment_corr/1/; *OR,* 42(3):350; Yale to sister, 16 November, 9 December 1864, Folder 3, Box 1, John Yale Papers, UVM; Yale to mother, 21 February 1865, ibid.; Manson to mother, 17 November 1864, 5 January 1865, Collection 454, Emory University, microfilm; Dutton, "Under the Old Flag," 529, 537; Cogswell, *Eleventh New Hampshire,* 430; Houston, *Thirty-Second Maine,* 444; Potter and Potter, *Personal Experiences,* 76; Benedict, *Vermont in the Civil War,* 524–25; Lucia, "Seventeenth

Regiment," 573; De Trobriand, *Four Years with the Army,* 650; Morning Reports, 31st Maine, Entry 115, RG 94, NA; *Bangor (ME) Daily Whig and Courier,* 25 February 1865.

28. Yale to friends, 26 October 1864, Folder 3, Box 1, John Yale Papers, UVM; Yale to parents, 10 November 1864, ibid.; Yale to sister, 16 November 1864, ibid.; Manson to mother, 4, 17, 22 November, 11, 23 December 1864, 5, 20 January 1865, Collection 454, Emory University, microfilm; "Joseph Rutherford to [Hannah Rutherford]," 29 March 1865, Joseph Chase Rutherford Correspondence, Vermonters in the Civil War, UVMLDC, https://cdi.uvm.edu/manuscript/uvmcdi-94533; Jackman, *Sixth New Hampshire,* 341; Dutton, "Under the Old Flag," 529, 531, 533; Lord, *Ninth Regiment,* 549, 552; Cogswell, *Eleventh New Hampshire,* 500; Griffin, "1864–65: Gustavus Gould to Family"; Benedict, *Vermont in the Civil War,* 525–26; *OR,* 42(1):195, 42(3):968, 46(2):370, 661, 967, 973, 46(3):158, 186; Pollard, diary, 31 December 1864, Reel F2850, Records of the Vermont Civil War Centennial Committee, VSARA, microfilm; *Bangor (ME) Daily Whig and Courier,* 10 November 1864, newspapers.com; Entry 5011, RG 393, NA; Morning Reports, 31st Maine, Entry 115, RG 94, NA; Whitman and True, *Maine in the War,* 581; *Evening Star* (Washington, DC), 17 December 1864, Chronicling America; Entry 5017: Orders and Letters Received, RG 393, NA. See also Entry 5020: Special Orders, Feb. 1864–July 1865, ibid.

29. Dutton, "Under the Old Flag," 529, 533, 535–36; Lord, *Ninth Regiment,* 549; Cogswell, *Eleventh New Hampshire,* 430–31; Acken, *Through Blood and Fire,* 207; Hodsdon, *Report of the Adjutant General of the State of Maine, . . . 1864 and 1865,* 293; Benedict, *Vermont in the Civil War,* 526; Yale to parents, 10 November 1864, Folder 3, Box 1, John Yale Papers, UVM; Yale to father, 10 February 1865, ibid.; Manson to mother, 11, 23 December 1864, Collection 454, Emory University, microfilm; Griffin, "1864–65: Gustavus Gould to Family"; *Bangor (ME) Daily Whig and Courier,* 10 November 1864, 25 February, 15 March 1865; *Vermont Record* (Brandon), 4 March 1865, newspapers.com; Entry 4986, RG 393, NA; Entry 5011, ibid.; Agassiz, *Meade's Headquarters,* 261; Whitman and True, *Maine in the War,* 581.

30. Lucia, "Seventeenth Regiment," 573; Ancestry, Vermont 17th Volunteer Infantry, Fold3; *Bangor (ME) Daily Whig and Courier,* 10 November, 17 December 1864, 25 February 1865; Hodsdon, *Report of the Adjutant General of the State of Maine, . . . 1864 and 1865,* 293–94; Entry 5011, RG 393, NA; Hodsdon, *Appendix D,* 733.

31. *Lamoille Newsdealer* (Hyde Park, VT), 4 May 1864; *Green Mountain Freeman* (Montpelier, VT), 12 July 1864; *Burlington (VT) Times,* 25 March 1865, newspapers.com; Yale to friends, 26 October 1864, Folder 3, Box 1, John Yale Papers, UVM; Manson to mother, 30 October 1864, Collection 454, Emory University, microfilm; "Joseph Rutherford to [Hannah Rutherford]," 29 March 1865, Rutherford Correspondence, Vermonters in the Civil War, UVMLDC; Peck, *Revised Roster,* 575.

32. Simon G. Griffin to Governor of Maine, 22 September 1864, Incoming Military Correspondence, Office of the Adjutant General, RG 15, MSA; "1864-10-07 Letter from Lieutenant A. R. Wescott to his parents," DigitalMaine; 31st MS; *Bangor (ME) Daily Whig and Courier,* 10 November, 2, 17 December 1864, 4, 25 February 1865, newspapers.com; Hodsdon, *Appendix D,* 733, 763, 765; *OR,* 46(1):1026.

33. 17th VS; 31st MS; Merriam, "Personal Recollections," MHS, 73; Benedict,

Vermont in the Civil War, 525; Hodsdon, *Report of the Adjutant General of the State of Maine, . . . 1864 and 1865,* 294; Whitman and True, *Maine in the War,* 589; *OR,* 42(1):580; Houston, *Thirty-Second Maine,* 443.

34. 17th VS; 31st MS; Pollard, diary, 4–6 October, 28 December 1864, Reel F2850, Records of the Vermont Civil War Centennial Committee, VSARA, microfilm; Yale to friends, 26 October 1864, Folder 3, Box 1, John Yale Papers, UVM; "1864-10-07 Letter from Lieutenant A. R. Wescott to his parents," DigitalMaine; Manson to mother, 17 November, 2, 5, 11, 18 December 1864, 5 January 1865, Collection 454, Emory University, microfilm; Dutton, "Under the Old Flag," 531; Lord, *Ninth Regiment,* 552; Cogswell, *Eleventh New Hampshire,* 433; Houston, *Thirty-Second Maine,* 417; Benedict, *Vermont in the Civil War,* 526; *OR,* 42(3):752, 46(2):694, 696, 733, 964; *Bangor (ME) Daily Whig and Courier,* 10 November, 17 December 1864, 4 February 1865; Entry 4993, RG 393, NA; Entry 5017, ibid.; Griffin, journal, Folder 1, Box 1, MG257, HSCC, 25.

35. Yale to friends, 26 October 1864, Folder 3, Box 1, John Yale Papers, UVM; Yale to sister, 16 November, 9–10 December 1864, ibid.; Yale to mother, 4 March 1865, ibid.; 17th VS; Manson to mother, 4, 22 November, 11, 23, 30 December 1864, 5, 20 January, 1 February, 24 March 1865, Collection 454, Emory University, microfilm; "Joseph Rutherford to [Hannah Rutherford]," 9 March 1865, Rutherford Correspondence, Vermonters in the Civil War, UVMLDC, https://cdi.uvm.edu/manuscript/uvmcdi -94528; "Joseph Rutherford to [Hannah Rutherford]," 15 March 1865, ibid., https:// cdi.uvm.edu/manuscript/uvmcdi-94530; Dutton, "Under the Old Flag," 535–37; Cogswell, *Eleventh New Hampshire,* 433; Benedict, *Vermont in the Civil War,* 526; Griffin, "1864–65: Gustavus Gould to Family"; *OR,* 42(1):195, 42(3):789, 46(2):108, 46(3):54; Acken, *Through Blood and Fire,* 205–6; *Bangor (ME) Daily Whig and Courier,* 10 November, 2, 17 December 1864, 4, 25 February, 15 March 1865; Pollard, diary, 4–6 October, 26, 28–31 December 1864, Reel F2850, Records of the Vermont Civil War Centennial Committee, VSARA, microfilm; Entry 4986, RG 393, NA; Scott, *Forgotten Valor,* 578, 585; De Trobriand, *Four Years with the Army,* 664, 688.

36. Yale to sister, 9 December 1864, Folder 3, Box 1, John Yale Papers, UVM; "Joseph Rutherford to Son," 8 March 1865, Rutherford Correspondence, Vermonters in the Civil War, UVMLDC, https://cdi.uvm.edu/manuscript/uvmcdi-94527; Dutton, "Under the Old Flag," 530; Cogswell, *Eleventh New Hampshire,* 500; *OR,* 42(1):195, 46(1):321; Entry 4986, RG 393, NA; Entry 5011, ibid.; Entry 5020, ibid.; *Bangor (ME) Daily Whig and Courier,* 10 November, 2 December 1864.

37. *OR,* 42(1):195, 199; *Bangor (ME) Daily Whig and Courier,* 2 December 1864; Benedict, *Vermont in the Civil War,* 524n1; Hodsdon, *Appendix D,* 733; Morning Report & Order Book, 17th Vermont, Entry 115, RG 94, NA; Morning Reports, 31st Maine, ibid.; Getchell to Governor of Maine, 27 October 1864, Incoming Military Correspondence, Office of the Adjutant General, RG 15, MSA; Getchell to unknown, 28 November 1864, ibid.; Bolton to Adjutant General of Maine, 12 January 1865, ibid.; Consolidated Morning Reports, Container 43327, 31st Maine, Regimental Records, ibid.

38. Manson to mother, 9, 30 October 1864, 13 March 1865, Collection 454, Emory University, microfilm; Yale to friends, 26 October 1864, Folder 3, Box 1, John Yale Papers, UVM; Yale to mother, 21 February 1865, ibid.; Entry 5017, RG 393, NA; Griffin,

"1864–65: Gustavus Gould to Family"; Getchell to Governor of Maine, 27 October 1864, Incoming Military Correspondence, Office of the Adjutant General, RG 15, MSA; *Bangor (ME) Daily Whig and Courier,* 10 November 1864, 4, 25 February, 15 March 1865; *Rutland (VT) Weekly Herald,* 9 February 1865, Chronicling America; "1864-10-07 Letter from Lieutenant A. R. Wescott to his parents," DigitalMaine; "Joseph Rutherford to Son," 8 March 1865, Rutherford Correspondence, Vermonters in the Civil War, UVMLDC; "Joseph Rutherford to [Hannah Rutherford]," 29 March 1865, ibid; Peck, *Revised Roster,* 576; 17th VS.

39. *OR,* 36(1):56–57, 46(1):1015–16, 46(3):397, 429; Potter and Potter, *Personal Experiences,* 76.

40. *OR,* 46(1):1015–16, 1055, 46(2):805–6, 46(3):454; Griffin, journal, Folder 1, Box 1, MG257, HSCC, 27; Manson to mother, 23 December 1864, Collection 454, Emory University, microfilm; "Joseph Rutherford to Son," 8 March 1865, Rutherford Correspondence, Vermonters in the Civil War, UVMLDC; Swinton, *Army of the Potomac,* 602.

41. *OR,* 46(1):1015–16; Lucia, "Seventeenth Regiment," 573; "Joseph Rutherford to [Hannah Rutherford]," 29 March 1865, Rutherford Correspondence, Vermonters in the Civil War, UVMLDC; *Bangor (ME) Daily Whig and Courier,* 2 December 1864, 15 March 1865; Morning Report & Order Book, 17th Vermont, Entry 115, RG 94, NA; Consolidated Morning Reports, Container 43327, 31st Maine, Regimental Records, Office of the Adjutant General, RG 15, MSA; Woodbury, *Burnside and the Ninth Army Corps,* 483; Getchell to Governor of Maine, [no date] February 1865, Incoming Military Correspondence, Office of the Adjutant General, RG 15, MSA; Hodsdon, *Report of the Adjutant General of the State of Maine, . . . 1864 and 1865,* 294; Hodsdon, *Appendix D,* 763.

42. *OR,* 36(1):52, 55–56, 46(3):198–99, 207, 285, 311, 332, 334; Manson to mother, 31 March 1865, Collection 454, Emory University, microfilm; Woodbury, *Burnside and the Ninth Army Corps,* 482.

43. Jackman, *Sixth New Hampshire,* 358; *OR,* 46(1):1016, 1059, 1072, 46(3):397–99, 407, 482; Woodbury, *Burnside and the Ninth Army Corps,* 482; Brett Schulte, ed., "MOLLUS ME V2: In a Charge near Fort Hell, Petersburg, April 2, 1865 by Thomas P. Beals," The Siege of Petersburg Online, accessed 17 May 2024, https://www.beyond thecrater.com/resources/mollus/me-mollus/mollus-me-v2-in-a-charge-near-fort-hell/. Fort Hell was the nickname Union troops gave to Fort Sedgwick.

44. Jackman, *Sixth New Hampshire,* 358–59; Griffin, journal, Folder 1, Box 1, MG257, HSCC, 29; *OR,* 46(1):1016, 1054, 46(3):429, 482–83; Schulte, "MOLLUS ME V2: In a Charge near Fort Hell"; Hodsdon, *Appendix D,* 756.

45. *OR,* 46(1):1016, 1054, 1056, 1059; Schulte, "MOLLUS ME V2: In a Charge near Fort Hell."

46. Jackman, *Sixth New Hampshire,* 359; Greene, *Final Battles of the Petersburg Campaign,* 335; Hess, *In the Trenches at Petersburg,* 268; Woodbury, *Burnside and the Ninth Army Corps,* 483–84; *OR,* 46(1):1016–17, 1035, 1039, 1054, 1059; Benedict, *Vermont in the Civil War,* 528, 528n2; Peck, *Revised Roster,* 595; "Sketch of Life of Lyman E. Knapp," Folder 15, MSA 189, VHS; Box 1234, Court-Martial Case Files, 1809–94, RG

153: Records of the Office of the Judge Advocate General (Army), NA; Reunion Society of Vermont Officers, *Proceedings,* 403; Schulte, "MOLLUS ME V2: In a Charge near Fort Hell."

47. *OR,* 46(1):1017, 1035, 1039, 1054–55, 1060; Griffin, journal, Folder 1, Box 1, MG257, HSCC, 29–30; Jackman, *Sixth New Hampshire,* 360; Potter and Potter, *Personal Experiences,* 77; Schulte, "MOLLUS ME V2: In a Charge near Fort Hell."

48. *OR,* 46(1):574, 1017–18, 46(3):485–86; Woodbury, *Burnside and the Ninth Army Corps,* 485; Schulte, "MOLLUS ME V2: In a Charge near Fort Hell."

49. *OR,* 46(1):1018–19; Lord, *Ninth Regiment,* 546; Cogswell, *Eleventh New Hampshire,* 500.

50. *OR,* 46(1):1056, 1060; 17th VS; 31st MS; Jacob G. Ullery, comp., *Men of Vermont: An Illustrated Biographical History of Vermonters and Sons of Vermont* (Brattleboro, VT: Transcript, 1894), pt. 3, 99; Regimental Order Book, 31st Maine, Entry 113: Civil War Regimental Books, RG 94, NA; Ancestry, Vermont 17th Volunteer Infantry, Fold3; Hodsdon, *Report of the Adjutant General of the State of Maine, . . . 1864 and 1865,* 530–32; Lucia, "Seventeenth Regiment," 573.

51. *OR,* 46(1):1019, 1055, 1060; Entry 5019: General Orders, RG 393, NA.

52. Jackman, *Sixth New Hampshire,* 360; *OR,* 46(1):1017, 46(3):449, 454; *Bangor (ME) Daily Whig and Courier,* 5 April 1865, newspapers.com.

53. Potter and Potter, *Personal Experiences,* 72.

54. *OR,* 46(3):482.

55. Badeau, *Military History of Ulysses S. Grant,* 2:292n; John A. Logan, *The Volunteer Soldier in America* [. . .] (Chicago: R. S. Peale, 1887), 88–89; Griffin, journal, Folder 1, Box 1, MG257, HSCC, 26.

CONCLUSION

1. Grimsley, *And Keep Moving On,* 20–21.

2. Phillips, *Looming Civil War,* 190; Reunion Society of Vermont Officers, *Proceedings,* 94.

3. Livermore, "Grant's Campaign against Lee," in Military Historical Society, *Wilderness Campaign,* 416; Swinton, *Army of the Potomac,* 457.

4. Phillips, *Looming Civil War,* 7. For examples of published casualty lists for the 17th Vermont and the 31st Maine, see *Bangor (ME) Daily Whig and Courier,* 23 May 1864; and *Rutland (VT) Weekly Herald,* 18 August 1864, Chronicling America.

5. *Rutland Daily Globe,* 7, 9 August 1873, Chronicling America.

6. *OR,* 36(1):936; Leander Otis Merriam, "Personal Recollections of the War for the Union," Folder 1990.97, Misc. Collection 111/30, Collection S-5186, MHS, 67; 31st MS; Hodsdon, *Appendix D,* 752.

Bibliography

PRIMARY SOURCES

Archives

Bowdoin College Library, Brunswick, ME
   Horatio Fox Smith Letters, Civil War Miscellany, M131.1 (transcription)
   Journal of Horatio Fox Smith, Civil War Miscellany, M131.2 (transcription)
Emory University, Atlanta, GA
   Charles A. Manson Papers, 1861–1918, Collection 454 (microfilm)
Historical Society of Cheshire County, Keene, NH
   Journal of Simon G. Griffin (excerpts), MG257 (transcription)
Library of Congress, Washington, DC
   C. B. Comstock Papers, 1847–1908, MSS16527 (microfilm)
   Daniel Read Larned Papers, 1861–78, MSS29470 (microfilm)
Maine Historical Society, Portland
   Lancaster Family Letters, Collection S-7464
   Leander Otis Merriam, "Personal Recollections of the War for the Union,"
      Collection S-5186
   John Parris Sheahan Papers, 1862–65, Collection 184
Maine State Archives, Augusta
   Office of the Adjutant General, 1753–1971, Record Group 15: Department of
      Defense, Veterans, and Emergency Management
         Consolidated Morning Reports, 1864, Container 43327, 31st Maine
            Infantry Records, 1861–65, Civil War—Regimental Records,
            1861–65
         Enlistment Papers, 1864, Container 321200, 31st Maine Infantry
            Records, 1861–65, Civil War—Regimental Records, 1861–65
         31st Maine Regiment, 1862–66, Container 353956, Civil War—In-
            coming Military Correspondence, 1861–68
      Record Group 29: Maine State Archives Gifts
         Lt. Voranus L. Coffin Papers, 1863–65, Container 298408
National Archives and Records Administration, Washington, DC
   Record Group 94: Records of the Adjutant General's Office
      Entry 113: Civil War Regimental Books

Entry 114: Civil War Regimental Books
Entry 115: Civil War Regimental Books
Record Group 153: Records of the Office of the Judge Advocate General
(Army)
Court-Martial Case Files, 1809–94
Record Group 393: Records of U.S. Army Continental Commands, Part 2
Entry 4985: Circulars Issued by the Assistant Inspector General,
July 1864–May 1865
Entry 4986: Inspection Reports
Entry 4993: Letters Sent, Jan. 1864–July 1865
Entry 5011: Letters Sent and Circulars, February–December 1864
Entry 5017: Orders and Letters Received
Entry 5019: General Orders
Entry 5020: Special Orders
New-York Historical Society, New York City
Henry O. Perry Diaries, 1864 January–1866 April, MS 2187
Silver Special Collections Library, University of Vermont, Burlington
John Yale Papers
Vermont Historical Society, Barre
Stephen F. Brown Civil War Papers, 1864–1903, 973.78 B815
Charles Cummings Papers, 1857–73, MSA 28
Lieutenant Colonel Charles Cummings Papers, 1863–65, Folder 9, MSA
829
Civil War Diary of Eldin J. Hartshorn, Folder 17, MSC 209
William H. King Letters, 1856–70, MSA 677
Lyman E. Knapp Papers, 1862–87, Folders 15 and 16, MSA 189
Civil War Letters of Albert Camp Raymond, 1862–74, Folder 4, MSA 773
Mark B. Slayton Civil War Letters, 1863, Folder 15, MSA 518
Matthew and Moses Whitehill Letters, 1859–78, MSA 520
Vermont State Archives and Records Administration, Middlesex
Records of the Vermont Civil War Centennial Committee, Microfilm
Collections, Civil War Era, Reel F2850
Records of the Adjutant and Inspector General, Reels F26082, F26083,
F26084, F26085

Databases and Digital Archives

American Civil War Research Database. http://civilwardata.com/.
Ancestry. Fold3. https://www.fold3.com/.
———. Newspapers.com. https://www.newspapers.com/.
Bill Thayer's Web Site. Updated 11 October 2024. https://penelope.uchicago
.edu/Thayer/E/home.html.

Chronicling America. Library of Congress. https://chroniclingamerica.loc
.gov/.
DigitalMaine Repository, Digital Public Library of America. https://digital
maine.com/.
Griffin, William. "1863: William Elmore Howard to George Sumner Howard."
Spared & Shared 4 (blog). Transcription. https://sparedshared4.wordpress
.com/letters/1863-william-elmore-howard-to-george-sumner-howard/.
———. "1864–65: Gustavus Gould to Family." *Spared & Shared 21* (blog).
18 February 2020. Transcription. https://sparedcreative21.art.blog/2020
/02/18/1864-65-gustavus-gould-to-family/.
National Bureau of Economic Research. Union Army Data: Early Indicators of
Later Work Levels, Disease, and Death. https://www.nber.org/research
/data/union-army-data-data-101.
Vermonters in the Civil War. University of Vermont Libraries Digital Collections. https://cdi.uvm.edu/collection/uvmcdi-uvmcdicivilwar.

Published Primary Sources

Agassiz, George R., ed. *Meade's Headquarters, 1863–1865: Letters of Colonel
Theodore Lyman from the Wilderness to Appomattox.* Boston: Atlantic Monthly
Press, 1922.
Badeau, Adam. *Military History of Ulysses S. Grant, from April, 1861, to April, 1865.*
Vols. 2–3. New York: D. Appleton, 1881–82.
Benedict, George G. *Vermont in the Civil War: A History of the Part Taken by the
Vermont Soldiers and Sailors in the War for the Union, 1861–5.* Vol. 2. Burling-
ton, VT: Free Press Association, 1888.
Bosbyshell, Oliver Christian. *The 48th in the War: Being a Narrative of the
Campaigns of the 48th Regiment, Infantry* [. . .] . Philadelphia: Avil Printing,
1895. https://digital.libraries.psu.edu/digital/collection/digitalbks2/id
/71070.
Brinton, John H. *Personal Memoirs of John H. Brinton.* New York: Neale, 1914.
Chase, J. J. *The Charge at Daybreak: Scenes and Incidents at the Battle of the Mine
Explosion, near Petersburg, Va., July 30th, 1864.* Lewiston, ME: Journal Office,
1875.
Coffin, Charles Carleton. *The Boys of '61; or, Four Years of Fighting* [. . .] . Boston:
Estes and Lauriat, 1881.
———. *Redeeming the Republic: The Third Period of the War of the Rebellion in the
Year 1864.* New York: Harper & Brothers, 1890.
Cogswell, Leander W. *A History of the Eleventh New Hampshire Volunteer Infantry
in the Rebellion War, 1861–1865* [. . .] . Concord, NH: Republican Press
Association, 1891.
Committee of the Regimental Association. *History of the Thirty-Fifth Massachu-
setts Volunteers, 1862–1865.* Boston: Mills, Knight, Printers, 1884.

Committee on the Conduct of the War. *Report of the Committee on the Conduct of the War on the Attack on Petersburg, on the 30th Day of July, 1864*. Washington, DC: Government Printing Office, 1865.

Dedication of the Soldiers' Monument, at Gorham, Maine, Thursday, October 18th, 1866 [. . .] . Portland, ME: B. Thurston, 1866. https://www.maine.gov /civilwar/books/Dedication_of_the_Soldiers__monument__at.pdf.

De Trobriand, Regis. *Four Years with the Army of the Potomac*. Translated by George K. Dauchy. Boston: Ticknor, 1889.

Duncan, Louis C. *The Medical Department of the United States Army in the Civil War*. Washington, DC: U.S. Surgeon-General's Office, c.1916.

Dyer, Frederick H. *A Compendium of the War of the Rebellion*. Des Moines, IA: Dyer Publishing, 1908.

Fox, William F. *Regimental Losses in the American Civil War, 1861–1865*. Albany, NY: Albany Publishing, 1889.

Gerrish, Theodore, and John S. Hutchinson. *The Blue and the Gray: A Graphic History of the Army of the Potomac and that of Northern Virginia* [. . .] . Bangor, ME: Brady, Mace, 1884.

Grant, Ulysses S. *Personal Memoirs of U. S. Grant*. New York, 1885. 2 vols. in 1. Project Gutenberg, 2004. https://www.gutenberg.org/files/4367/old/4367 -pdf/4367-pdf.pdf.

Griffin, Simon G. *A History of the Town of Keene: From 1732, When the Township Was Granted by Massachusetts, to 1874, When It Became a City*. Keene, NH: Sentinel Printing, 1904.

Headquarters, Department of the Army. *ADP 3-0: Operations*. Washington, DC: Headquarters, Department of the Army, 2019. https://armypubs.army.mil /epubs/DR_pubs/DR_a/ARN18010-ADP_3-0-000-WEB-2.pdf.

Hodsdon, John S. *Annual Report of the Adjutant General of the State of Maine, for the Year Ending December 31, 1866*. Augusta, ME: Stevens & Sayward, Printers to the State, 1867.

——— . *Appendix D of the Report of the Adjutant General of the State of Maine, for the Years 1864 and 1865* [. . .] . Augusta, ME: Stevens & Sayward, Printers to the State, 1866.

——— . *Report of the Adjutant General of the State of Maine for the Years 1864 and 1865*. Augusta, ME: Stevens & Sayward, Printers to the State, 1866.

Houston, Henry C. *The Thirty-Second Maine Regiment of Infantry Volunteers: An Historical Sketch*. Portland, ME: Southworth Brothers, 1903.

Humphreys, Andrew A. *From Gettysburg to the Rapidan: The Army of the Potomac, July, 1863, to April, 1864*. New York: Charles Scribner's Sons, 1883.

——— . *The Virginia Campaign of 1864 and 1865: The Army of the Potomac and the Army of the James*. New York: Charles Scribner's Sons, 1883.

Jackman, Lyman. *History of the Sixth New Hampshire Regiment in the War for the Union*. Edited by Amos Hadley. Concord, NH: Republican Press Association, 1891.

Johnson, Robert Underwood, and Clarence Clough Buel, eds. *Battles and Leaders of the Civil War*. Vol. 4. New York: Century, 1888.

Kennedy, Joseph C. G. *Population of the United States in 1860: Compiled from the Original Returns of the Eighth Census* [. . .] . Washington, DC: Government Printing Office, 1864.

Livermore, Thomas L. *Numbers and Losses in the Civil War in America, 1861–65*. Boston: Houghton, Mifflin, 1900.

Logan, John A. *The Volunteer Soldier in America* [. . .] . Chicago: R. S. Peale, 1887.

Lord, Edward O., ed. *History of the Ninth Regiment New Hampshire Volunteers in the War of the Rebellion*. Concord, NH: Republican Press Association, 1895.

Lowe, David W., ed. *Meade's Army: The Private Notebooks of Lt. Col. Theodore Lyman*. Kent, OH: Kent State University Press, 2013.

Lucia, Joel H. "Seventeenth Regiment." In Peck, *Revised Roster*, 568–74.

Maine State Museum. "Transcripts of Letters in *Maine Voices from the Civil War*." December 2017. https://mainestatemuseum.org/wp-content/uploads /2017/12/Transcripts-of-letters-in-Maine-Voices-from-the-Civil-War.pdf.

——— . "Biographies of People Included in the Museum's Exhibit [Maine Voices from the Civil War]." December 2017. https://mainestatemuseum .org/wp-content/uploads/2017/12/alphabeticalbios.pdf.

Meade, George. *The Life and Letters of George Gordon Meade, Major-General United States Army*. Vol. 2. Edited by George Gordon Meade. New York: Charles Scribner's Sons, 1913.

Military Historical Society of Massachusetts, comp. *The Wilderness Campaign, May–June 1864*. Vol. 4 of *Papers of the Military Historical Society of Massachusetts*. Boston: Military Historical Society of Massachusetts, 1905.

——— , comp. *Petersburg, Chancellorsville, Gettysburg*. Vol. 5 of *Papers of the Military Historical Society of Massachusetts*. 1906. Reprint, Wilmington, NC: Broadfoot, 1989.

Military Order of the Loyal Legion of the United States, comp. *War Papers Read before the Commandery of the State of Maine, Military Order of the Loyal Legion of the United States,* Vol. 1. 1898. Reprint, Wilmington, NC: Broadfoot, 1992.

Nevins, Allan, ed. *A Diary of Battle: The Personal Journals of Colonel Charles S. Wainwright, 1861–1865*. New York: Harcourt, Brace, and World, 1962.

Peck, Theodore S., comp. *Revised Roster of Vermont Volunteers and Lists of Vermonters Who Served in the Army and Navy of the United States* [. . .] . Montpelier, VT: Watchman, 1892. Reprint, Newport, VT: Civil War Enterprises, 1996.

Poore, Benjamin Perley. *The Life and Public Services of Ambrose E. Burnside, Soldier—Citizen—Statesman*. Providence: J. A. & R. A. Reid, 1882.

Porter, Horace. *Campaigning with Grant*. New York: Century, 1906.

Potter, Robert B., and Abby Austin Potter. *Personal Experiences of Maj. Gen'l Robert B. Potter in the War of the Rebellion, 1861–1865*. New York: Lotus, 1894.

Reunion Society of Vermont Officers. *Proceedings of the Reunion Society of*

Vermont Officers, 1864–1884, with Addresses Delivered at Its Meetings [. . .] . Burlington, VT: Free Press Association, 1885.

Rhode Island Soldiers and Sailors Historical Society, comp. *Personal Narratives of Events in the War of the Rebellion, Being Papers Read before the Rhode Island Soldiers and Sailors Historical Society.* Vol. 1. 1878–79. Reprint, Wilmington, NC: Broadfoot, 1993.

Rhodes, Robert Hunt, ed. *All for the Union: A History of the 2nd Rhode Island Volunteer Infantry in the War of the Great Rebellion* [. . .] . Lincoln, RI: Andrew Mowbray, 1985.

Robertson, James I., Jr., ed. *The Civil War Letters of General Robert McAllister.* New Brunswick, NJ: Rutgers University Press, 1965.

Schaff, Morris. *The Battle of the Wilderness.* Boston: Houghton Mifflin, 1910.

Scott, Robert Garth, ed. *Forgotten Valor: The Memoirs, Journals, & Civil War Letters of Orlando B. Willcox.* Kent, OH: Kent State University Press, 1999.

Sears, Stephen W., ed. *Mr. Dunn Browne's Experiences in the Army: The Civil War Letters of Samuel W. Fiske.* New York: Fordham University Press, 1998. EBSCOhost.

Simon, John Y., ed. *The Papers of Ulysses S. Grant.* Vols. 8 and 12. Carbondale: Southern Illinois University Press, 1984. https://scholarsjunction.msstate .edu/usg-volumes/.

Simon, John Y., and John F. Marzalek, eds. *The Papers of Ulysses S. Grant Digital Edition.* Charlottesville: University of Virginia Press, 2018. https://rotunda .upress.virginia.edu/founders/GRNT.html.

Sparks, David S., ed. *Inside Lincoln's Army: The Diary of Marsena Rudolph Patrick, Provost Marshal General, Army of the Potomac.* New York: Thomas Yoseloff, 1964.

Stine, J. H. *History of the Army of the Potomac.* Philadelphia: J. B. Rodgers Printing, 1892.

Sumner, Merlin E., ed. and comp. *The Diary of Cyrus B. Comstock.* Dayton, OH: Morningside, 1987.

Survivor's Association. *History of the Corn Exchange Regiment: 118th Pennsylvania Volunteers, from Their First Engagement at Antietam to Appomattox* [. . .] . Philadelphia: J. L. Smith, 1888.

Swinton, William. *Campaigns of the Army of the Potomac* [. . .] . Rev. ed. New York: Charles Scribner's Sons, 1882.

Ullery, Jacob G., comp. *Men of Vermont: An Illustrated Biographical History of Vermonters and Sons of Vermont.* Brattleboro, VT: Transcript, 1894.

U.S. War Department. *Revised United States Army Regulations of 1861.* Washing-ton, DC: Government Printing Office, 1863.

———. *The War of the Rebellion: A Compilation of the Official Records of the Union and Confederate Armies.* 70 vols. in 128 pts. Washington, DC: Government Printing Office, 1880–1901.

Walker, Francis A. *History of the Second Army Corps in the Army of the Potomac.* New York: Charles Scribner's Sons, 1886.

Washburn, Peter T. *Report of the Adjutant & Inspector General's Office of the State of Vermont, from October 1, 1863, to October 1, 1864.* Montpelier, VT: Walton's, 1864.

Whitman, William E. S., and Charles H. True. *Maine in the War for the Union: A History of the Part Borne by Maine Troops in the Suppression of the American Rebellion.* Lewiston, ME: Nelson Dingley Jr., 1865.

Wilkeson, Frank. *Recollections of a Private Soldier in the Army of the Potomac.* New York: G. P. Putnam's Sons, 1887.

Williams, George F. "Lights and Shadows of Army Life." *Century Magazine,* October 1884, 803–19.

Woodbury, Augustus. *Major General Ambrose E. Burnside and the Ninth Army Corps* [. . .] . Providence, RI: Sidney S. Rider & Brother, 1867.

Newspapers

Argus and Patriot (Montpelier, VT)
Bangor (ME) Daily Whig and Courier
Biddeford (ME) Union and Journal
Burlington (VT) Daily Times
Burlington (VT) Free Press
Burlington (VT) Times
Burlington (VT) Weekly Free Press
Burlington (VT) Weekly Sentinel
Chicago Tribune
Daily Green Mountain Freeman (Montpelier, VT)
Ellsworth (ME) American
Evening Star (Washington, DC)
Gardiner (ME) Home Journal
Green Mountain Freeman (Montpelier, VT)
Lamoille Newsdealer (Hyde Park, VT)
Lewiston (ME) Daily Sun
Loyal Sunrise (Presque Isle, ME)
Maine Democrat (Biddeford)
National Tribune (Washington, DC)
New York Herald
Orleans Independent Standard (Irasburgh, VT)
Piscataquis Observer (Dover, ME)
Portland (ME) Daily Press
Rutland (VT) Weekly Herald
Springfield (MA) Republican
St. Albans (VT) Daily Messenger
Enterprise and Vermonter (Vergennes)
Vermont Christian Messenger (Montpelier)
Vermont Phoenix (Brattleboro)
Vermont Record (Brandon)
Vermont Standard (Woodstock)
Vermont Watchman and State Journal (Montpelier)
Walton's Daily Journal (Montpelier, VT)

SECONDARY SOURCES

Books

Acken, J. Gregory, ed. *Through Blood and Fire: The Civil War Letters of Major Charles J. Mills, 1862–1865.* Rev. and expanded ed. Kent, OH: Kent University Press, 2023.

Bailey, Beth. *America's Army: Making the All-Volunteer Force*. Cambridge, MA: Harvard University Press, 2009. EBSCOhost.

Berkovich, Ilya. *Motivation in War: The Experience of Common Soldiers in Old-Regime Europe*. Cambridge: Cambridge University Press, 2017.

Biddle, Stephen. *Military Power: Explaining Victory and Defeat in Modern Battle*. Princeton, NJ: Princeton University Press, 2004.

Bledsoe, Andrew S., and Andrew F. Lang, eds. *Upon the Fields of Battle: Essays on the Military History of America's Civil War*. Baton Rouge: Louisiana State University Press, 2018.

Bruce, Susannah Ural. *The Eagle and the Harp: Irish-American Volunteers and the Union Army, 1861–1865*. New York: New York University Press, 2006.

Carmichael, Peter S. *The War for the Common Soldier*. Chapel Hill: University of North Carolina Press, 2018.

Catton, Bruce. *Grant Takes Command: 1863–1865*. Boston: Little, Brown, 1969.

———. *This Hallowed Ground: The Story of the Union Side of the Civil War*. Garden City, NY: Doubleday, 1956.

Cavanaugh, Michael A., and William Marvel. *The Petersburg Campaign: The Battle of the Crater, "the Horrid Pit."* Lynchburg, VA: H. E. Howard, 1989.

Cimbala, Paul A., and Randall M. Miller, eds. *Union Soldiers and the Northern Home Front: Wartime Experiences, Postwar Adjustments*. New York: Fordham University Press, 2002.

Coffin, Howard. *Full Duty: Vermonters in the Civil War*. Woodstock, VT: Countryman, 1995.

Costa, Dora L., and Matthew E. Kahn. *Heroes & Cowards: The Social Face of War*. Princeton, NJ: Princeton University Press, 2008.

Cowley, Robert, ed. *With My Face to the Enemy: Perspectives on the Civil War*. New York: G. P. Putnam's Sons, 2001.

Doyle, Don H. *The Cause of All Nations: An International History of the American Civil War*. New York: Basic Books, 2015.

Ehlers, Robert S., Jr., Sarah K. Douglas, and Daniel P. M. Curzon. *Technology, Violence, and War: Essays in Honor of Dr. John F. Guilmartin, Jr*. Leiden, Neth.: Brill, 2019.

Fellman, Michael, Lesley J. Gordon, and Daniel E. Sutherland. *This Terrible War: The Civil War and Its Aftermath*. Boston: Pearson, 2003.

Fitzharris, Joseph C. *The Hardest Lot of Men: The Third Minnesota Infantry in the Civil War*. Norman: University of Oklahoma Press, 2019.

Fry, Zachery A. *A Republic in the Ranks: Loyalty and Dissent in the Army of the Potomac*. Chapel Hill: University of North Carolina Press, 2020.

Foote, Lorien. *The Gentlemen and the Roughs: Violence, Honor, and Manhood in the Union Army*. New York: New York University Press, 2010. Kindle.

Fritz, Stephen G. *Frontsoldaten: The German Soldier in World War II*. Lexington: University Press of Kentucky, 1995.

Gallman, J. Matthew. *Defining Duty in the Civil War: Personal Choice, Popular*

Culture, and the Union Home Front. Chapel Hill: University of North Carolina Press, 2015.

Gallagher, Gary W., ed. *The Spotsylvania Campaign*. Chapel Hill: University of North Carolina Press, 1998. https://doi.org/10.5149/9780807898376_gallagher.

——, ed. *The Wilderness Campaign*. Chapel Hill: University of North Carolina Press, 1997. https://doi.org/10.5149/9780807835890_gallagher.

Geary, James W. *We Need Men: The Union Draft in the Civil War*. DeKalb: Northern Illinois University Press, 1991.

Glatthaar, Joseph T. *General Lee's Army: From Victory to Collapse*. New York: Free Press, 2008.

Greene, A. Wilson. *A Campaign of Giants: The Battle for Petersburg. Vol. 1, From the Crossing of the James to the Crater*. Chapel Hill: University of North Carolina Press, 2018.

——. *The Final Battles of the Petersburg Campaign: Breaking the Backbone of the Rebellion*. 2nd ed. Knoxville: University of Tennessee Press, 2008.

Grimsley, Mark. *And Keep Moving On: The Virginia Campaign, May–June 1864*. Lincoln: University of Nebraska Press, 2002.

Guelzo, Allen C. *Fateful Lightning: A New History of the Civil War & Reconstruction*. New York: Oxford University Press, 2012.

Hamner, Christopher H. *Enduring Battle: American Soldiers in Three Wars, 1776–1945*. Lawrence: University Press of Kansas, 2011.

Herrera, Ricardo A. *For Liberty and the Republic: The American Soldier, 1775–1861*. New York: New York University Press, 2015. EBSCOhost.

Hess, Earl J. *In the Trenches at Petersburg: Field Fortifications and Confederate Defeat*. Chapel Hill: University of North Carolina Press, 2009.

——. *Into the Crater: The Mine Attack at Petersburg*. Columbia: University of South Carolina Press, 2010.

——. *Liberty, Virtue, and Progress: Northerners and Their War for the Union*. 2nd ed. New York: Fordham University Press, 1997.

——. *Trench Warfare under Grant and Lee: Field Fortifications in the Overland Campaign*. Chapel Hill: University of North Carolina Press, 2007.

——. *The Union Soldier in Battle: Enduring the Ordeal of Combat*. Lawrence: University Press of Kansas, 1997.

Humphrey, Robert E. *Once upon a Time in War: The 99th Division in World War II*. Norman: University of Oklahoma Press, 2008.

Jimerson, Randall C. *The Private Civil War: Popular Thought during the Sectional Conflict*. Baton Rouge: Louisiana State University Press, 1988.

Jordan, Hill, James I. Robertson Jr., and J. H. Segars, eds. *The Bell Irvin Wiley Reader*. Baton Rouge: Louisiana State University Press, 2001.

Keegan, John. *The Face of Battle*. New York: Viking, 1976.

Keller, Christian B. *Chancellorsville and the Germans: Nativism, Ethnicity, and Civil War Memory*. New York: Fordham University Press, 2007. JSTOR.

King, Anthony. *The Combat Soldier: Infantry Tactics and Cohesion in the Twentieth and Twenty-First Centuries*. Oxford: Oxford University Press, 2013. EBSCOhost.

Kreidberg, Marvin A., and Merton G. Henry. *History of Military Mobilization in the United States Army, 1775–1945*. Washington, DC: Department of the Army, 1955.

Lewis, Adrian R. *The American Culture of War: The History of U.S. Military Force from World War II to Operation Iraqi Freedom*. New York: Routledge, 2007.

Linderman, Gerald F. *Embattled Courage: The Experience of Combat in the American Civil War*. New York: Free Press, 1987.

Lynn, John. *Battle: A History of Combat and Culture*. Boulder, CO: Westview, 2003.

—— . *The Bayonets of the Republic: Motivation and Tactics in the Army of Revolutionary France*. New York: Routledge, 2019. https://doi.org/10.4324/9780429309052.

Marvel, William. *Burnside*. Chapel Hill: University of North Carolina Press, 1991.

—— . *Lincoln's Mercenaries: Economic Motivation among Union Soldiers during the Civil War*. Baton Rouge: Louisiana State University Press, 2018.

—— . *Tarnished Victory: Finishing Lincoln's War*. Boston: Houghton Mifflin Harcourt, 2011.

McPherson, James M. *Battle Cry of Freedom: The Civil War Era*. New York: Oxford University Press, 1988.

—— . *For Cause and Comrades: Why Men Fought in the Civil War*. New York: Oxford University Press, 1997.

—— . *Ordeal by Fire: The Civil War and Reconstruction*. New York: Alfred A. Knopf, 1982.

McPherson, James M., and William J. Cooper, eds. *Writing the Civil War: The Quest to Understand*. Columbia: University of South Carolina, 1998.

Miller, Richard F., ed. *States at War*. Vol. 1, *A Reference Guide to Connecticut, Maine, Massachusetts, New Hampshire, Rhode Island, and Vermont in the Civil War*. Hanover, NH: University Press of New England, 2013.

Millett, Allan R., Peter Maslowski, and William Feis. *For the Common Defense: A Military History of the United States from 1607 to 2012*. 3rd ed. New York: Free Press, 2012. Kindle.

Murdock, Eugene C. *One Million Men: The Civil War Draft in the North*. Madison: State Historical Society of Wisconsin, 1971.

Murray, Williamson, and Wayne Wei-Siang Hsieh. *A Savage War: A Military History of the Civil War*. Princeton, NJ: Princeton University Press, 2016.

Neely, Mark E., Jr. *Lincoln and the Democrats: The Politics of Opposition in the Civil War*. Cambridge: Cambridge University Press, 2017.

Neimeyer, Charles Patrick. *America Goes to War: A Social History of the Continental Army*. New York: New York University Press, 1997.

Nevins, Allan. *The War for the Union,* Vol. 4, *The Organized War for Victory, 1864–1865.* New York: Scribner, 1959.

Noe, Kenneth W. *Reluctant Rebels: The Confederates Who Joined the Army after 1861.* Chapel Hill: University of North Carolina Press, 2010. EBSCOhost.

Nosworthy, Brent. *The Bloody Crucible of Courage: Fighting Methods and Combat Experience of the Civil War.* New York: Carroll & Graf, 2003.

Paludan, Phillip Shaw. *"A People's Contest": The Union & Civil War, 1861–1865.* Lawrence: University Press of Kansas, 1988.

Parish, Peter J. *The American Civil War.* New York: Holmes & Meier, 1974.

Phillips, Jason. *Looming Civil War: How Nineteenth-Century Americans Imagined the Future.* New York: Oxford University Press, 2018. https://doi.org /10.1093/oso/9780190868161.001.0001.

Randall, J. G., and David Donald. *The Civil War and Reconstruction.* Lexington, MA: D. C. Heath, 1969.

Reardon, Carol. *With a Sword in One Hand & Jomini in the Other: The Problem of Military Thought in the Civil War North.* Chapel Hill: University of North Carolina Press, 2012. EBSCOhost.

Rhea, Gordon C. *The Battle of the Wilderness, May 5–6, 1864.* Baton Rouge: Louisiana State University Press, 1994.

———. *The Battles for Spotsylvania Court House and the Road to Yellow Tavern, May 7–12, 1864.* Baton Rouge: Louisiana State University Press, 2005.

———. *Cold Harbor: Grant and Lee, May 26–June 3, 1864.* Baton Rouge: Louisiana State University Press, 2002.

———. *On to Petersburg: Grant and Lee, June 4–15, 1864.* Baton Rouge: Louisiana State University Press, 2017.

———. *To the North Anna River: Grant and Lee, May 13–25, 1864.* Baton Rouge: Louisiana State University Press, 2000.

Robertson, James I., Jr. *Soldiers Blue and Gray.* Columbia: University of South Carolina Press, 1998.

Royster, Charles. *A Revolutionary People at War: The Continental Army and American Character, 1775–1783.* Chapel Hill: University of North Carolina Press, 1979.

Rutan, Edwin P., II. *"If I Have Got to Go and Fight, I Am Willing": A Union Regiment Forged in the Petersburg Campaign: The 179th New York Volunteer Infantry, 1864–1865.* Park City, UT: RTD, 2015.

Scott, Robert Garth. *Into the Wilderness with the Army of the Potomac.* Rev. and enlarged ed. Bloomington: Indiana University Press, 1992.

Sears, Stephen W. *Lincoln's Lieutenants: The High Command of the Army of the Potomac.* Boston: Houghton Mifflin Harcourt, 2017.

Sheehan-Dean, Aaron, ed. *The View from the Ground: Experiences of Civil War Soldiers.* Louisville: University Press of Kentucky, 2007.

Shively, Kathryn. *Nature's Civil War: Common Soldiers and the Environment in*

1862 Virginia. Chapel Hill: University of North Carolina Press, 2013. https://doi.org/10.5149/9781469610771_meier.

Simon, John Y., and Michael E. Stevens, eds. *New Perspectives on the Civil War: Myths and Realities of the National Conflict.* Madison, WI: Madison House, 1998.

Skocpol, Theda. *Protecting Soldiers and Mothers: The Political Origins of Social Policy in the United States.* Cambridge, MA: Harvard University Press, 1992.

Sodergren, Steven E. *The Army of the Potomac in the Overland and Petersburg Campaigns: Union Soldiers and Trench Warfare, 1864–1865.* Baton Rouge: Louisiana State University Press, 2017.

Sommers, Richard J. *Richmond Redeemed: The Siege at Petersburg: The Battles of Chaffin's Bluff and Poplar Spring Church, September 29–October 2, 1864.* Rev. ed. El Dorado Hills, CA: Savas Beatie, 2014.

Steere, Edward. *The Wilderness Campaign.* Harrisburg, PA: Stackpole, 1960.

Stewart, Nora Kinzer. *Mates & Muchachos: Unit Cohesion in the Falklands/ Malvinas War.* Washington, DC: Brassey's, 1991.

Sturtz, Ken, ed. *The Civil War Letters of S. R. Emerson: Fighting with the 13th and 17th Vermont Volunteers from Gettysburg to Petersburg.* Amazon Digital Services, 2016. Kindle.

Thompson, Lauren K. *Friendly Enemies: Soldier Fraternization throughout the American Civil War.* Lincoln: University of Nebraska Press, 2020. https://doi.org/10.2307/j.ctv125jvdv.

Trudeau, Noah Andre. *Bloody Roads South: The Wilderness to Cold Harbor, May–June 1864.* Boston: Little, Brown, 1989.

Urwin, Gregory J. W. *The United States Infantry: An Illustrated History, 1775–1918.* Norman: University of Oklahoma Press, 1988.

Wagner, Margaret E., Gary W. Gallagher, and Paul Finkelman, eds. *The Library of Congress Civil War Desk Reference.* New York: Simon & Schuster Paperbacks, 2002.

Weigley, Russell F. *A Great Civil War: A Military and Political History, 1861–1865.* Bloomington: Indiana University Press, 2000.

Wiley, Bell Irvin. *The Life of Billy Yank: The Common Soldier of the Union.* Indianapolis: Bobbs-Merrill, 1952.

Wong, Leonard, et al. *Why They Fight: Combat Motivation in the Iraq War.* Carlisle, PA: Strategic Studies Institute, U.S. Army War College, 2003.

Wongsrichanalai, Kanisorn. *Northern Character: College-Educated New Englanders, Honor, Nationalism, and Leadership in the Civil War Era.* New York: Fordham University Press, 2016. JSTOR.

Woodworth, Steven E. *This Great Struggle: America's Civil War.* Lanham, MD: Rowman & Littlefield, 2011.

Vinovskis, Maris A., ed. *Toward a Social History of the American Civil War: Exploratory Essays.* Cambridge: Cambridge University Press, 1990.

Articles

Anbinder, Tyler. "Which Poor Man's Fight? Immigrants and the Federal Conscription of 1863." *Civil War History* 52, no. 4 (December 2006): 344–372. https://doi.org/10.1353/cwh.2006.0068.

Cain, Marvin R. "A 'Face of Battle' Needed: An Assessment of Motives and Men in Civil War Historiography." *Civil War History* 28, no. 1 (March 1982): 5–27. https://doi.org/10.1353/cwh.1982.0059.

Castro, Carl A., and Amy B. Adler. "OPTEMPO: Effects on Soldier and Unit Readiness." *Parameters* 29, no. 3 (Autumn 1999): 86–95. https://press .armywarcollege.edu/cgi/viewcontent.cgi?article=1939&context=parameters.

Catton, Bruce. "Billy Yank and the Army of the Potomac." *Military Affairs* 18, no. 4 (Winter 1954): 169–75. https://doi.org/10.2307/1983083.

"Grand Review." U.S. Army Heritage & Education Center. https://ahec .armywarcollege.edu/exhibits/CivilWarImagery/edwards_Grand_Review .cfm.

Grimsley, Mark. "Why Military History Sucked." *Blog Them Out of the Stone Age: Toward a Broader Vision of Military History and National Security Affairs.* 2 June 2016. http://warhistorian.blogspot.com/2016/06/why-military-history -sucked.html.

Hallock, Judith Lee. "The Role of the Community in Civil War Desertion." *Civil War History* 29, no. 3 (June 1983): 123–34. https://doi.org/10.1353 /cwh.1983.0013.

Hickox, Will. "The Civil War's 11th-Hour Soldiers." *Disunion* (blog). *New York Times,* 6 April 2015. https://opinionator.blogs.nytimes.com/2015/04/06 /the-civil-wars-11th-hour-soldiers/.

Hsieh, Wayne Wei-Siang. Review of *A Campaign of Giants: The Battle for Petersburg. Volume 1: From the Crossing of the James to the Crater,* by A. Wilson Greene. *Journal of the Civil War Era* 9, no. 2 (September 2019): 486–88. https://doi.org/10.1353/cwe.2019.0064.

Johnson, Mark W. "Emory Upton's Twenty-Six: Desertion and Divided Loyalty of U.S. Army Soldiers, 1860–1861." *Journal of Military History* 81, no. 3 (July 2017): 747–74.

Kenfield, Frank. "Captured by Rebels: A Vermonter at Petersburg, 1864." *Vermont History* 36, no. 4 (August 1968): 230–35.

Millett, Allan R., Williamson Murray, and Kenneth H. Watman. "The Effectiveness of Military Organizations." *International Security* 11, no. 1 (Summer 1986): 37–71. https://doi.org/10.2307/2538875.

Schulte, Brett, ed. "MOLLUS ME V2: In a Charge near Fort Hell, Petersburg, April 2, 1865, by Thomas P. Beals," The Siege of Petersburg Online. https:// www.beyondthecrater.com/resources/mollus/me-mollus/mollus-me-v2-in-a -charge-near-fort-hell/.

Sutherland, Daniel E. Review of *Hood's Texas Brigade: The Soldiers and Families of the Confederacy's Most Celebrated Unit,* by Susannah J. Ural. *Journal of the Civil War Era* 8, no. 4 (December 2018): 710–12. https://doi.org/10.1353/cwe.2018.0079.

Urwin, Gregory J. W. "'The Lord Has Not Forsaken Me and I Won't Forsake Him': Religion in Frederick Steele's Union Army, 1863–1864." *Arkansas Historical Quarterly* 52 (Autumn 1993): 318–40. https://doi.org/10.2307/40030853.

Maps

"Civil War in Central Virginia: On to Richmond." Civil War Trails. Accessed 3 November 2022. https://www.civilwartrails.org/docs/Central-brochure.pdf.

U.S. Army Center of Military History. File:WILDERNESS May6.jpg. Wikipedia. Accessed 28 February 2022. https://en.wikipedia.org/wiki/File:WILDERNESS_May6.jpg.

Index

Aiken House, 180

Alsop's Farm, 83

Battery No. 28, 199–201

battlefield objectives, ability to accomplish: at Cold Harbor, 126–27; at the Crater, 166–67; in the First Union Offensive, 140–41; in the Ninth Union Offensive at Petersburg, 203; at North Anna, 110; at Peebles Farm, 187; throughout the service of the 17th Vermont and 31st Maine, 211–12; at Spotsylvania Court House, 97; at the Wilderness, 82

Bethesda Church, 112–14

Blick's Station, 176

bounties, 35–37, 39–41, 48–49

Boydton Plank Road, 171, 177, 182, 185

Burnside, Ambrose E., 25–26, 66, 108, 171

casualties: and Cold Harbor, 119, 124–26; and the Crater, 161–64–67; and the First Union Offensive at Petersburg, 137–41; and Gettysburg, 82, 241n34; and limitations in source material, 240n31; and the Ninth Union Offensive at Petersburg, 200, 202–3; and North Anna, 109–10, 245n16; throughout the Overland Campaign, 128; and Peebles Farm, 183–87; during the Petersburg Campaign, 146–48, 174, 190–91; throughout the service of the 17th Vermont and 31st

Maine, 212–13; and Spotsylvania Court House, 84, 88–90, 95–97; and the Wilderness, 76, 78–82

Cemetery Hill, 151–52, 157, 160, 162

Chesterfield Bridge, 105–6

Chewning Farm, 71, 74–77, 82

cohesion: and Cold Harbor, 126; and the Crater, 161, 163–64, 166; and the First Union Offensive at Petersburg, 138, 141; and the Ninth Union Offensive at Petersburg, 201, 203; and North Anna, 106–7, 110; and Peebles Farm, 183–85, 187; during recruitment of the 17th Vermont and 31st Maine, 47–49, 53; throughout the service of the 17th Vermont and 31st Maine, 211; and Spotsylvania Court House, 88, 94, 97; and the Wilderness, 78–80, 82

combat performance, methodology of, 26–30

conscription, 4, 35–37

consolidation: of the 31st and 32nd Maine, 33–34, 47, 55, 190

desertion, 52–56, 59, 210–11

disciplinary issues: and Cold Harbor, 112; and the Crater, 157–58; and Globe Tavern, 176; and the First Union Offensive at Petersburg, 133; and the Ninth Union Offensive at Petersburg, 203; and North Anna, 103–4; and Peebles Farm, 179; throughout the service of the 17th Vermont and 31st Maine, 8, 56–60,

and distance calculations, 239n21, 244n3; and the First Union Offensive at Petersburg, 131, 133–35; and Globe Tavern, 176; and North Anna, 101–2, 105–6; and Peebles Farm, 180; and Spotsylvania Court House, 83–84; and the Wilderness, 68–69, 70, 74–75, 82

Matadequin Creek, 117

morale, level of: and Cold Harbor, 115–17, 118–19, 121–24, 127; and the Crater, 154–55, 162, 167–68; and the First Union Offensive at Petersburg, 135–36, 167; and Globe Tavern, 176; and the Ninth Union Offensive at Petersburg, 195–96, 198; and North Anna, 102, 108–9; and Peebles Farm, 178, 180, 182, 184; during the Petersburg Campaign, 142, 146, 148–51, 172–75, 188–89, 191–94; and Spotsylvania Court House, 84, 91–93, 95–96; and the Wilderness, 66, 68, 70–71, 75, 78, 80

Mule Shoe Salient, 85, 92, 97

new regiments, creation of, 37–38

Old Town Creek, 182
Orange Plank Road, 71, 77, 80, 82
Orange Turnpike, 71, 74
Overland Campaign, nature of the, 2, 6–8, 56, 63, 65, 108, 115, 142
Ox Ford, 105–6, 110, 244n3

Parker's Store: building known as, 71; road to, 74–75
Peebles Farm, 180, 182, 184–85
Pegram House, 180–81, 184–85, 187–88
period views of later arrivals: at Cold Harbor, 125–26; at the Crater, 166; at the Wilderness, 81–82; in the First Union Offensive at Petersburg, 140–41; in the Ninth Union Offensive at

Petersburg, 203; at North Anna, 109–10; at Peebles Farm, 186–87; at Spotsylvania Court House, 96; as a whole, 1–3, 9–16, 31–32, 34–35, 40, 60–61, 207–10

Petersburg Campaign, nature of, 6–8

Poplar Spring Church: building known as, 177; road to, 177–78, 180, 182

Potter, Robert B., leadership of: at the Wilderness, 80

Rapidan River, 66, 68–69, 71, 74

rations: and Cold Harbor, 111–13, 122–23; and the Crater, 154, 162–63; and the First Union Offensive at Petersburg, 131, 133–35; and North Anna, 103, 108; and Peebles Farm, 185, 192–93; and the Petersburg Campaign, 143–45, 151, 154, 174, 192, 193; and Spotsylvania Court House, 91–92; and the Wilderness, 68–69

Second Brigade (of Second Division, Ninth Corps), composition of, 228n5, 241n35, 246n24, 256n1
Shady Grove Road, 119–20
Shand House, 134–35, 141
Six-Mile Station, 176
South Side Railroad, 171, 177, 180, 185
Spotswood House, 69, 74, 238n14
Squirrel Level Road, 180
substitutes, 53–54, 229n9

Totopotomoy Creek, 112
training: of the 17th Vermont and 31st Maine for the field, 51–52; and Cold Harbor, 116–17; and North Anna, 104; and Peebles Farm, 179; and the Petersburg Campaign, 149, 174, 188–89; and Spotsylvania Court House, 86, 93; and the Wilderness, 65, 69, 72, 82
Tucker House, 123

unit history, 5–6
United States Colored Troops, 10–11, 13, 146, 152, 154, 160–61, 175

Vaughan Road, 176
veterans in the 17th Vermont and 31st Maine, 38–39, 50–51, 68, 82–83, 213

weather, impact of: and Cold Harbor, 111–14, 117, 122; and the Crater, 157, 162; and the Eighth Union Offensive at Petersburg, 196; and the First Union Offensive at Petersburg, 131, 133, 135, 139; and Globe Tavern, 176; and the Ninth Union Offensive at Petersburg, 198; and North Anna, 102, 105; and Peebles Farm, 177, 184–85; and the Petersburg Campaign, 142–44, 146, 149–50, 175–77, 191–93; on training, 51–52; throughout the service of the 17th Vermont and 31st Maine, 214; and Spotsylvania Court House, 83–84, 86, 88–90, 92–93; and the Wilderness, 68–69, 72, 77
Weldon Railroad, 171, 176, 179–80, 186
Wilderness Tavern, 74, 83

Yellow Tavern, 176

www.ingramcontent.com/pod-product-compliance
Lightning Source LLC
Chambersburg PA
CBHW030257100426
42812CB00002B/479